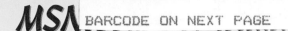

MSN [...] Cheat Sheet

Internet Connection Information

If you don't know what to put in the following blanks, call your Internet service provider for help.

My user ID: ______________________________

My password: DO NOT WRITE IT HERE!!!!

Phone number I dial to access the Internet:

____

Customer service phone number: ______________

My e-mail address: ______________________________

DNS server IP address: _____ . _____ . _____ . _____

SMTP server address: ______________________________

POP3 server address: ______________________________

News server name: ______________________________

My MSN Home Page

Use this space to record the username and street for your free MSN home page.

Username: ______________________________

Street: ______________________________

Home Page address: Your MSN Home Page address is `homepages.msn.com/street/username`. For example, if your street is PlayingFields and your username is Maxwell, your MSN Home Page address would be `homepages.msn.com/PlayingFields/Maxwell`.

Hotmail Accounts

Use this space to record your member name for various MSN services.

Expedia: ______________________________

MoneyCentral: ______________________________

Gaming Zone: ______________________________

Encarta Online: ______________________________

Web Communities: ______________________________

Other MSN Account Information

Use these spaces to record Hotmail member names for you and other family members. Remember: Do not write your passwords down here!

Family member: ______________________________

Hotmail member name: ______________________________

Family member: ______________________________

Hotmail member name: ______________________________

Family member: ______________________________

Hotmail member name: ______________________________

Family member: ______________________________

Hotmail member name: ______________________________

Family member: ______________________________

Hotmail member name: ______________________________

For Dummies®: Bestselling Book Series for Beginners

BESTSELLING BOOK SERIES

MSN.com For Dummies®

Abbreviations and Smileys

Abbreviation or Smiley	What It Means
BTW	By the way
FWIT	For what it's worth
IMHO	In my humble opinion
IOW	In other words
LOL	Laughing out loud
OIC	Oh, I see
BRB	Be right back
AFK	Away from keyboard
PMJI	Pardon me for jumping in
ROFL	Rolling on the floor laughing
TTFN	Ta ta for now (quoting Tigger)
TTYL	Talk to you later
<g>	Grin
<bg>	Big grin
<vbg>	Very big grin
:-)	Just kidding
;-)	Wink
:-(	Bummer

Microsoft Chat Buttons

Button	What It Does
	Send your message to the chat
	Says something privately to another chat member
	Sends your message to the chat as an action

MSN Messenger Service Buttons

Toolbar Button	What It Does
Add	Adds a user to your Contact list
Send	Sends an instant message
Status	Changes your MSN Messenger Service status
Web	Links to useful Web pages

MSN Chat Member Icons

Member Icon	What It Means
	Chat host
	Chat participant
	Chat spectator
	A member who is temporarily away from computer
	A member whom you have ignored

Cheat Sheet $2.95 value. Item 0649-8.

For more information about IDG Books, call 1-800-762-2974.

For Dummies®: Bestselling Book Series for Beginners

™

References for the Rest of Us!®

BESTSELLING BOOK SERIES

Are you intimidated and confused by computers? Do you find that traditional manuals are overloaded with technical details you'll never use? Do your friends and family always call you to fix simple problems on their PCs? Then the *...For Dummies*® computer book series from IDG Books Worldwide is for you.

...For Dummies books are written for those frustrated computer users who know they aren't really dumb but find that PC hardware, software, and indeed the unique vocabulary of computing make them feel helpless. *...For Dummies* books use a lighthearted approach, a down-to-earth style, and even cartoons and humorous icons to dispel computer novices' fears and build their confidence. Lighthearted but not lightweight, these books are a perfect survival guide for anyone forced to use a computer.

"I like my copy so much I told friends; now they bought copies."

— Irene C., Orwell, Ohio

"Quick, concise, nontechnical, and humorous."

— Jay A., Elburn, Illinois

"Thanks, I needed this book. Now I can sleep at night."

— Robin F., British Columbia, Canada

Already, millions of satisfied readers agree. They have made *...For Dummies* books the #1 introductory level computer book series and have written asking for more. So, if you're looking for the most fun and easy way to learn about computers, look to *...For Dummies* books to give you a helping hand.

1/99

MSN.com FOR DUMMIES®

by Doug Lowe

IDG Books Worldwide, Inc.
An International Data Group Company

Foster City, CA ◆ Chicago, IL ◆ Indianapolis, IN ◆ New York, NY

MSN.com For Dummies®

Published by
IDG Books Worldwide, Inc.
An International Data Group Company
919 E. Hillsdale Blvd.
Suite 400
Foster City, CA 94404
www.idgbooks.com (IDG Books Worldwide Web site)
www.dummies.com (Dummies Press Web site)

Library of Congress Catalog Card No.: 99-66420

ISBN: 0-7645-0649-8

Printed in the United States of America

10 9 8 7 6 5 4 3 2 1

1B/QY/QS/QQ/IN

Distributed in the United States by IDG Books Worldwide, Inc.

Distributed by CDG Books Canada Inc. for Canada; by Transworld Publishers Limited in the United Kingdom; by IDG Norge Books for Norway; by IDG Sweden Books for Sweden; by IDG Books Australia Publishing Corporation Pty. Ltd. for Australia and New Zealand; by TransQuest Publishers Pte Ltd. for Singapore, Malaysia, Thailand, Indonesia, and Hong Kong; by Gotop Information Inc. for Taiwan; by ICG Muse, Inc. for Japan; by Intersoft for South Africa; by Eyrolles for France; by International Thomson Publishing for Germany, Austria and Switzerland; by Distribuidora Cuspide for Argentina; by LR International for Brazil; by Galileo Libros for Chile; by Ediciones ZETA S.C.R. Ltda. for Peru; by WS Computer Publishing Corporation, Inc., for the Philippines; by Contemporanea de Ediciones for Venezuela; by Express Computer Distributors for the Caribbean and West Indies; by Micronesia Media Distributor, Inc. for Micronesia; by Chips Computadoras S.A. de C.V. for Mexico; by Editorial Norma de Panama S.A. for Panama; by American Bookshops for Finland.

For general information on IDG Books Worldwide's books in the U.S., please call our Consumer Customer Service department at 800-762-2974. For reseller information, including discounts and premium sales, please call our Reseller Customer Service department at 800-434-3422.

For information on where to purchase IDG Books Worldwide's books outside the U.S., please contact our International Sales department at 317-596-5530 or fax 317-572-4002.

For consumer information on foreign language translations, please contact our Customer Service department at 1-800-434-3422, fax 317-572-4002, or e-mail rights@idgbooks.com.

For information on licensing foreign or domestic rights, please phone +1-650-653-7098.

For sales inquiries and special prices for bulk quantities, please contact our Sales department at 800-762-2974 or write to the address above.

For information on using IDG Books Worldwide's books in the classroom or for ordering examination copies, please contact our Educational Sales department at 800-434-2086 or fax 317-572-4005.

For press review copies, author interviews, or other publicity information, please contact our Public Relations department at 650-653-7000 or fax 650-653-7500.

For authorization to photocopy items for corporate, personal, or educational use, please contact Copyright Clearance Center, 222 Rosewood Drive, Danvers, MA 01923, or fax 978-750-4470.

About the Author

Doug Lowe lives in sunny Fresno, California (where the motto is "At least it's a dry heat") with his wife Debbie, daughters Rebecca, Sarah, and Bethany, and female Golden Retrievers Nutmeg and Ginger. At times he feels a bit outnumbered, but at least Nutmeg and Ginger listen to him sometimes. He toils full-time creating outstanding literary works such as *MSN.com For Dummies* and wonders why he never gets invited to read at the local literary association or had one of his books made into a movie starring Harrison Ford so that he can retire. Doug really thinks that Harrison Ford would be excellent as the Dummies Man and thinks that John Kilcullen's people should call Harrison's people real soon before someone else steals the idea.

In between writing computer books, which leaves about three free hours per month, Doug enjoys golfing and makes it a point to play at least once a decade. Hiking is also a favorite hobby, so much that Doug would really like to write *Backpacking For Dummies* but hasn't had the time to write a proposal yet because these computer books just keep coming up. Maybe someday.

Other titles include: *Internet Explorer 5 For Dummies, PowerPoint 2000 For Dummies* (as well as *PowerPoint 97 For Dummies* and *PowerPoint 95 For Dummies*), *Creating Web Pages For Dummies Quick Reference,* 2nd Edition, *Microsoft Office 2000 For Dummies Quick Reference* (as well as *Microsoft Office 97 For Dummies Quick Reference* and *Microsoft Office 95 For Dummies Quick Reference*), *Networking For Dummies,* 4th Edition, *MORE Word 97 For Dummies* (and *MORE Word 95 For Dummies*), *Client/Server Computing For Dummies,* 3rd Edition, and *The Microsoft Network For Dummies,* 2nd Edition.

ABOUT IDG BOOKS WORLDWIDE

Welcome to the world of IDG Books Worldwide.

IDG Books Worldwide, Inc., is a subsidiary of International Data Group, the world's largest publisher of computer-related information and the leading global provider of information services on information technology. IDG was founded more than 30 years ago by Patrick J. McGovern and now employs more than 9,000 people worldwide. IDG publishes more than 290 computer publications in over 75 countries. More than 90 million people read one or more IDG publications each month.

Launched in 1990, IDG Books Worldwide is today the #1 publisher of best-selling computer books in the United States. We are proud to have received eight awards from the Computer Press Association in recognition of editorial excellence and three from Computer Currents' First Annual Readers' Choice Awards. Our best-selling *...For Dummies®* series has more than 50 million copies in print with translations in 31 languages. IDG Books Worldwide, through a joint venture with IDG's Hi-Tech Beijing, became the first U.S. publisher to publish a computer book in the People's Republic of China. In record time, IDG Books Worldwide has become the first choice for millions of readers around the world who want to learn how to better manage their businesses.

Our mission is simple: Every one of our books is designed to bring extra value and skill-building instructions to the reader. Our books are written by experts who understand and care about our readers. The knowledge base of our editorial staff comes from years of experience in publishing, education, and journalism — experience we use to produce books to carry us into the new millennium. In short, we care about books, so we attract the best people. We devote special attention to details such as audience, interior design, use of icons, and illustrations. And because we use an efficient process of authoring, editing, and desktop publishing our books electronically, we can spend more time ensuring superior content and less time on the technicalities of making books.

You can count on our commitment to deliver high-quality books at competitive prices on topics you want to read about. At IDG Books Worldwide, we continue in the IDG tradition of delivering quality for more than 30 years. You'll find no better book on a subject than one from IDG Books Worldwide.

John Kilcullen
Chairman and CEO
IDG Books Worldwide, Inc.

Steven Berkowitz
President and Publisher
IDG Books Worldwide, Inc.

Eighth Annual Computer Press Awards 1992

Ninth Annual Computer Press Awards 1993

Tenth Annual Computer Press Awards 1994

Eleventh Annual Computer Press Awards 1995

IDG is the world's leading IT media, research and exposition company. Founded in 1964, IDG had 1997 revenues of $2.05 billion and has more than 9,000 employees worldwide. IDG offers the widest range of media options that reach IT buyers in 75 countries representing 95% of worldwide IT spending. IDG's diverse product and services portfolio spans six key areas including print publishing, online publishing, expositions and conferences, market research, education and training, and global marketing services. More than 90 million people read one or more of IDG's 290 magazines and newspapers, including IDG's leading global brands — Computerworld, PC World, Network World, Macworld and the Channel World family of publications. IDG Books Worldwide is one of the fastest-growing computer book publishers in the world, with more than 700 titles in 36 languages. The "...For Dummies®" series alone has more than 50 million copies in print. IDG offers online users the largest network of technology-specific Web sites around the world through IDG.net (http://www.idg.net), which comprises more than 225 targeted Web sites in 55 countries worldwide. International Data Corporation (IDC) is the world's largest provider of information technology data, analysis and consulting, with research centers in over 41 countries and more than 400 research analysts worldwide. IDG World Expo is a leading producer of more than 168 globally branded conferences and expositions in 35 countries including E3 (Electronic Entertainment Expo), Macworld Expo, ComNet, Windows World Expo, ICE (Internet Commerce Expo), Agenda, DEMO, and Spotlight. IDG's training subsidiary, ExecuTrain, is the world's largest computer training company, with more than 230 locations worldwide and 785 training courses. IDG Marketing Services helps industry-leading IT companies build international brand recognition by developing global integrated marketing programs via IDG's print, online and exposition products worldwide. Further information about the company can be found at www.idg.com.

1/24/99

Dedication

To Debbie, Rebecca, Sarah, and Bethany.

Acknowledgments

I'd like to thank project editor Jade Williams who put up with many missed deadlines and countless rewrites due to Microsoft's frequent revamps of MSN.com, yet still managed to whip this book into shape. Thanks also to copy editor James Russell and technical editor Eric Butow for their many excellent tweaks, corrections, and suggestions.

Publisher's Acknowledgments

We're proud of this book; please register your comments through our IDG Books Worldwide Online Registration Form located at http://my2cents.dummies.com.

Some of the people who helped bring this book to market include the following:

Acquisitions, Editorial, and Media Development

Project Editor: Jade L. Williams

Acquisitions Editor: Steven Hayes

Copy Editor: James H. Russell

Technical Editor: Eric Butow

Associate Permissions Editor: Carmen Krikorian

Editorial Manager: Leah Cameron

Media Development Manager: Heather Heath Dismore

Editorial Assistant: Beth Parlon

Production

Project Coordinator: Maridee V. Ennis

Layout and Graphics: Joe Bucki, Barry Offringa, Tracy K. Oliver, Brian Torwelle, Erin Zeltner

Proofreaders: Laura Albert, Corey Bowen, Arielle Mennelle, Marianne Santy, Charles Spencer

Indexer: Johnna VanHoose

Special Help
Amanda Foxworth
Microsoft Corporation

General and Administrative

IDG Books Worldwide, Inc.: John Kilcullen, CEO; Steven Berkowitz, President and Publisher

IDG Books Technology Publishing Group: Richard Swadley, Senior Vice President and Publisher; Walter Bruce III, Vice President and Associate Publisher; Joseph Wikert, Associate Publisher; Mary Bednarek, Branded Product Development Director; Mary Corder, Editorial Director; Barry Pruett, Publishing Manager; Michelle Baxter, Publishing Manager

IDG Books Consumer Publishing Group: Roland Elgey, Senior Vice President and Publisher; Kathleen A. Welton, Vice President and Publisher; Kevin Thornton, Acquisitions Manager; Kristin A. Cocks, Editorial Director

IDG Books Internet Publishing Group: Brenda McLaughlin, Senior Vice President and Publisher; Diane Graves Steele, Vice President and Associate Publisher; Sofia Marchant, Online Marketing Manager

IDG Books Production for Dummies Press: Debbie Stailey, Associate Director of Production; Cindy L. Phipps, Manager of Project Coordination, Production Proofreading, and Indexing; Tony Augsburger, Manager of Prepress, Reprints, and Systems; Laura Carpenter, Production Control Manager; Shelley Lea, Supervisor of Graphics and Design; Debbie J. Gates, Production Systems Specialist; Robert Springer, Supervisor of Proofreading; Kathie Schutte, Production Supervisor

Dummies Packaging and Book Design: Patty Page, Manager, Promotions Marketing

◆

The publisher would like to give special thanks to Patrick J. McGovern, without whom this book would not have been possible.

◆

Contents at a Glance

Cartoons at a Glance

By Rich Tennant

"Their fatal mistake was getting involved with MSN.com's home page building option. It's so easy, it's irresistible. They included a photo of them holding the stolen money next to the get away car, a list of their favorite aliases, banks they'd like to rob again..."

page 263

"Honey—remember that pool party last summer where you showed everyone how to do the limbo in just a sombrero and a dish towel? Well look at what the MSN Daily Video Download is."

page 223

"Did you click 'HELP' on the MSN.com menu bar recently? It's Mr. Gates. He wants to know if everything's alright."

page 309

"This is amazing. You can stop looking for Derek. According to an MSN search I did, he's hiding behind the dryer in the basement."

page 9

"He saw your laptop and wants to know if he can check his Hotmail."

page 151

"I think you're just jealous that I found a community of people on MSN.com that worship the yam as I do, and you haven't."

page 73

Fax: 978-546-7747

E-mail: richtennant@the5thwave.com

World Wide Web: www.the5thwave.com

Table of Contents

Introduction

Your coworkers are doing it. Your neighbors are doing it. Heck, even your dog is probably doing it. These days, everybody is "going online," whatever that means. According to all the latest polls, the whole world is jumping aboard the so-called Information Superhighway, and jumping aboard fast.

Now Microsoft is in on the online revolution. It started a few years back with a modest online service called the Microsoft Network, also known as MSN. The original version of MSN was a bit cumbersome to use and you had to pay hourly connection fees to use it. Nevertheless, people signed up by the hundreds of thousands.

Now Microsoft has thoroughly revamped MSN in an effort to make it the best Web site available anywhere on the Internet. Microsoft wants MSN to be your Internet home — the first Web page you visit every day when you connect to the Internet, and the Web page you use as your home port for your Internet explorations.

To pull this off, Microsoft has loaded MSN with tons of features designed to make you come back again and again. Features such as free e-mail, instant messaging, chat rooms, free home pages, Web communities, online investing, travel services, shopping sites, and more.

The best part about MSN is that it is completely free of charge if you already have access to the Internet. All you have to do is point your Web browser to `www.msn.com`. (If you don't have Internet access, you can sign up with Microsoft's MSN Internet Access or another Internet service provider for a small monthly fee.) What could be easier?

Well, so goes the party line. In reality, there's more to mastering the Internet than pointing your browser to `www.msn.com`. Although Microsoft has done its best to make MSN an inviting place, venturing online is still a daunting experience. If you've never been online before, you have a lot to learn. And even if you're an Internet veteran, MSN is a big place, with its own set of menus to traverse, icons to decipher, nuances to discover, and quirks to work around. Oh bother.

But good news! You've found the right book. Help is here, within these humble pages.

This book is your friendly guide to MSN and the Information Superhighway. It talks about MSN and the Internet in everyday terms. No lofty prose here. The language is friendly — you don't need a graduate degree in computer science or telecommunications to get through it. I have no Pulitzer ambitions for this book (maybe one of these days I'll write a 1,000-page novel about the Civil War, but not today).

Occasionally, I'll take a carefully aimed potshot at the hallowed and sacred institutions of online computerdom, just to spice things up a bit. If that doesn't work, I may even throw in an occasional lawyer joke.

My goal is to bring the lofty precepts of MSN and the Internet down to earth where you can touch them and squeeze them and say, "What's the big deal? I can do that!"

About This Book

This is not the kind of book that you pick up and read from start to finish. Do not take it with you on vacation! If I ever see you reading it at the beach, I'll kick sand in your face. This book is more like a reference, the kind of book that you can pick up, turn to just about any page, and start reading whenever you get the urge to learn something about the MSN or the Internet.

Each chapter is divided into self-contained chunks, all related to the theme of the chapter. For example, the chapter on using electronic-mail (Chapter 6) contains nuggets such as these:

- Sending e-mail
- Receiving e-mail
- Using the address book
- Sending attachments
- Adding a signature

You don't have to memorize anything in this book. It's a "need-to-know" tool: You pick it up when you need to know something, learn what you need to know, and then put it down and get on with your life.

How to Use This Book

This book works like a reference. Start with the topic you want to learn about; look for it in the table of contents or index to get going. The table of contents is detailed enough that you should be able to find most of the topics you'll look for. If not, turn to the index, where you'll find even more detail. After you find your topic in the table of contents or index, turn to the area of interest and read as much or as little as you need or want. Then close the book and get to it.

On occasion, this book directs you to use specific keyboard shortcuts to get things done. When you see something like this:

Ctrl+Z

it means to hold down the Ctrl key while pressing the Z key, and then release both together. Don't type the plus sign.

Sometimes I'll tell you to use a menu command, like this:

File⇨Open

This line means to use the keyboard or mouse to open the File menu and then choose the Open command. (The underlined letters are the keyboard hot keys, which let you use the menus without reaching for your mouse. To use them, first press the Alt key. In the preceding example, you would press and release the Alt key, press and release the F key, and then press and release the O key.)

Whenever I describe a message or information you'll see on-screen, it will be in bold, like this:

```
Are we having fun yet?
```

Anything you are instructed to type appears in bold like in the following sentence:

Type **puns** in the text box.

You type exactly what you see, with or without spaces.

Another little nicety about this book is that when you are directed to click one of those little toolbar buttons that are found scattered about most Windows programs, a picture of the button appears in the margin. This way, you can see what the button looks like to help you find it on-screen.

This book rarely directs you elsewhere for information — just about everything you need to know about using MSN is in here. However, three other books may come in handy from time to time, all published by IDG Books Worldwide, Inc. The first is *Windows 98 For Dummies,* by Andy Rathbone. This book will help when you're not sure how to perform a Windows 98 task, such as copying a file or creating a new folder. Then there's *The Internet For Dummies,* by John R. Levine and Carol Baroudi. This book will help you if you decide to venture into the dark recesses of the Internet. The third book is my own: *Internet Explorer 5 For Dummies*. Although you can use MSN with any Web browser, including Netscape Navigator, MSN is designed to work best with the latest version of Internet Explorer. Turn to *Internet Explorer 5 For Dummies* for complete information about Internet Explorer 5.

What You Don't Need to Read

Much of this book is skippable. I've carefully placed extra-technical information in self-contained sidebars and clearly marked them so that you can give them a wide berth. Don't read this stuff unless you just gotta know and feel really lucky. Don't worry; I won't be offended if you don't read every word.

Foolish Assumptions

I'm going to make only two assumptions about you:

- You use a computer.
- You have or want to get access to the Internet.

Nothing else. I don't assume that you're a computer guru who knows how to change a controller card or configure memory for optimal usage. Such computer chores are best handled by people who like computers. Hopefully, you are on speaking terms with such a person. Do your best to keep it that way.

About Web Browsers

As I've already mentioned, MSN is best viewed using Microsoft's latest Web browser, Internet Explorer 5. If you don't have Internet Explorer 5, you can download it free of charge from Microsoft's Web site at `www.Microsoft.com/ie`.

All the figures in this book show MSN being accessed with Internet Explorer 5. For these figures, I have removed the Standard Buttons toolbar, which normally displays at the top of the Internet Explorer window, so that the graphics show more of the MSN Web page. If you want to remove this toolbar from your Internet Explorer display, just choose the View➪Toolbars➪Standard Buttons command. To reinstate the Standard Buttons toolbar, choose View➪Toolbars➪Standard Buttons again.

If you prefer, you can use Netscape Navigator to access MSN. In this book, I assume that you're using Internet Explorer. Whenever a significant difference comes up for Netscape users, I'll be sure to point it out.

How This Book is Organized

Inside this book, you'll find chapters arranged into six parts. Each chapter is broken down into sections that cover various aspects of the chapter's main subject. There is a logical sequence to the chapters, so it makes sense to read them in order (if you're crazy enough to read this entire book). But you don't have to read them that way. You can flip open the book to any page and start reading. Here's the lowdown on what's in each of the seven parts:

Part I: MSN Basics

In this part, you get the basics of using MSN. It starts with an overview of the features of MSN and information about getting connected to the Internet using Microsoft's MSN Internet Access. Then it shows you how to use basic features of MSN, such as how to navigate through the maze of MSN Web sites, how to use MSN to search the Internet, and how to customize MSN's start page so that the Internet information you need most is at your fingertips.

Part II: Reach Out and Electronically Touch Someone

This part explains how to use MSN's personal communication features, including free e-mail, via Hotmail; MSN's Web Communities, which provide a place where people with common interests can gather to exchange news and information; online chatting; MSN newsgroups; and MSN Messenger Service, which lets you exchange instant messages with other Internet users.

Part III: Learn and Earn on MSN

The chapters in this part describe four of MSN's most useful online services: MSNBC, one of the best online news services available on the Internet; Encarta, an online encyclopedia; Investor, which lets you track your personal finances online; and CarPoint, one of the most comprehensive auto sites on the Internet.

Part IV: The Fun Side of MSN

As they say, "All work and no play makes the Internet a dull place." The chapters in this part show you how use some of MSN's fun features: playing online games, shopping, and planning a vacation.

Part V: Creating Your Own Home Page

MSN does more than let you visit the Internet: It provides a place where you can create and store your own Web pages for others to enjoy. The chapters in this part show you how to create your own MSN home pages.

Part VI: The Part of Tens

This wouldn't be a *For Dummies* book if it didn't include a collection of chapters with lists of interesting snippets: Ten Tips for Using MSN Efficiently, Ten Things That Often Go Wrong, and Ten Safety Tips for Kids on the Net.

Glossary

There's so much technobabble thrown about when discussing online services that I decided to include an extensive glossary of online terms, free of charge.

Icons Used in This Book

As you read all this wonderful prose, you'll occasionally see the following icons. They appear in the margins to draw your attention to important information.

Watch out! Some technical drivel is about to come your way. Cover your eyes if you find technical information offensive.

Danger! Danger! Danger! Stand back, Will Robinson!

Pay special attention to this icon — it lets you know that some particularly useful tidbit is at hand, perhaps a shortcut or a way of using a command that you may not have considered.

Did I tell you about the memory course I took?

Where to Go From Here

Yes, you can get there from here. With this book in hand, you're ready to charge full speed ahead into the strange and wonderful world of MSN. Browse through the table of contents and decide where you want to start. Be bold! Be courageous! Be adventurous! Above all else, have fun!

Part I

MSN Basics

"This is amazing. You can stop looking for Derek. According to an MSN search I did, he's hiding behind the dryer in the basement."

In this part . . .

MSN, Microsoft's new Web portal, is a great place to start your Internet explorations. By tuning in to msn.com, you can gather information from the Internet from one convenient jumping-off point. You can get free e-mail; visit chat rooms; receive personalized news and information; trade stocks; buy airline tickets; and much more.

The chapters in this part give you an overview of what is available on msn.com and how to find your way around the almost dizzying array of MSN pages. You'll discover how to use MSN to search the Internet, and how to personalize your MSN home page to include the information and links you need most. And if you don't already have an Internet account, you'll find out how to use Microsoft's MSN Internet Access to get connected.

Happy surfing!

Chapter 1

MSN: Your Portal to the Online World

In This Chapter

- Discovering MSN
- Exploring what you can do with MSN
- Concluding what MSN is not

I know the story. You just finished the latest issue of *Newsweek* and found out that 35 trillion people signed up to use the Internet this year. Of course, you're the only person left on the planet who isn't yet online, and the average 4-year-old knows more about computers than you do. So now you want to jump aboard the so-called "Information Superhighway" — whatever that is — and become a part of the fabled Information Revolution.

Trouble is, after you get on the Internet, how do you find your way around? After all, the Internet is huge — its vastness defies imagination. As Carl Sagan may have said, the Internet consists of billions and billions of Web pages. How do you sort out the good from the bad and the ugly, and find the best Internet sites? One of the best ways is to turn to MSN.

Getting Acquainted with MSN

MSN is a free Web site sponsored by Microsoft, the company that brings you the software that you love to hate, such as Windows, Word, and Excel. MSN is designed to make the Internet more friendly and accessible by providing the most important Internet features all in one place.

MSN's Web address is, as you might guess, `www.msn.com`. For this reason, MSN is sometimes referred to as *msn.com.* Throughout this book, I use the terms *MSN* and *msn.com* interchangeably.

Figure 1-1 shows MSN's opening page. Look over Figure 1-1 for a moment, you can see some of MSN's most useful features, including:

- A Web search feature that lets you locate Web pages for just about any topic of interest
- Headlines for the day's most interesting news stories
- Links to weather information
- Sites to purchase airline tickets online
- Free e-mail
- Space for creating a free home page
- Local TV listings
- And much, much more!

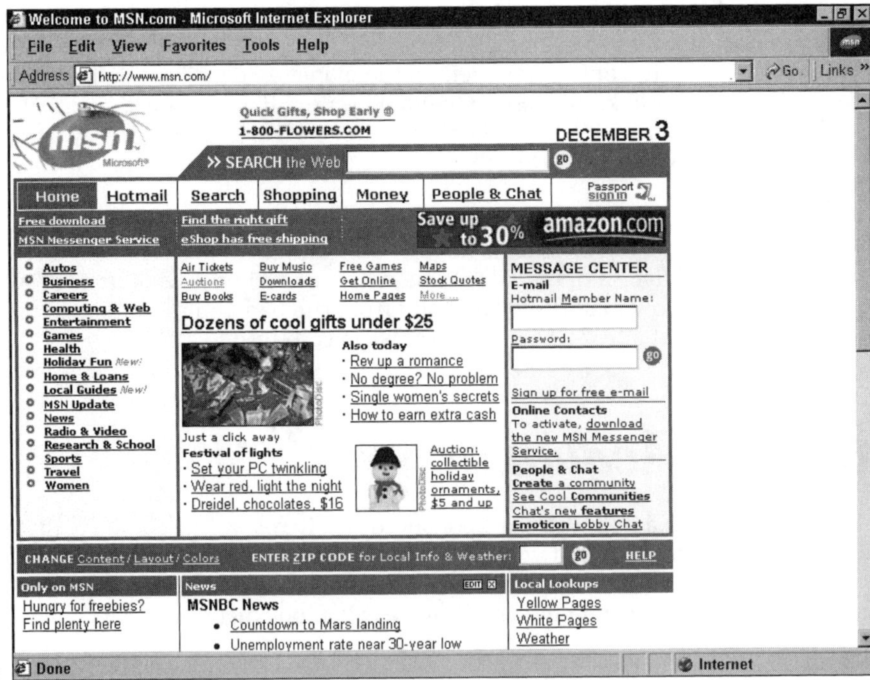

Figure 1-1: MSN's home page: Your portal to the Internet.

Information Superhighway puns

Ever since Vice President Al Gore coined the phrase *Information Superhighway* to refer to the Internet and other online information services, one bad Information Superhighway pun after another began to appear. Needless to say, I grew tired of those jokes long ago. So, when I first learned that I was going to write a book about MSN, I decided right away to bundle all the Information Superhighway puns I could think of in one convenient location near the beginning of the book, and then make a solemn promise not to let them appear anywhere else in the book. So here I go:

- On-ramp: Discloses the means by which one accesses the online world. An on-ramp is an online service, such as America Online, CompuServe, or Prodigy, an Internet Service Provider such as MSN Internet Access, your television cable service, or your telephone company.
- Speed bumps, speed limits, roadblocks, and detours: Hints that the Information Superhighway isn't an easy drive. Traversing the roadways typically requires more computer savvy than the average computer user has, which explains why the Information Superhighway is still largely a gathering place for nerds.
- Road construction: Warns that the Information Superhighway isn't finished. Major portions of it are still under construction.
- Road kill: Symbolizes the victims of the Information Superhighway. These are the poor souls who tried to become a part of the Information Superhighway but bailed before they figured it out.
- Rush hour: This term refers to the sluggishness with which online services respond during peak hours, not to a daily online chat with Rush Limbaugh.
- Toll Road: Informs that access to the Information Superhighway isn't free. Most service providers charge a flat rate of $15–25 per month. If you want a high-speed connection, you'll have to pay more.

Now that I've gotten that out of my system, I promise not to lay any more Information Superhighway puns on you for the rest of the book.

MSN is what Internet gurus like to call a *portal* – a special Web site designed as a stepping-off point for a visitor's excursions onto the Internet. Microsoft hopes that you like MSN so much that you begin all your Internet explorations from the MSN home page. In fact, when you install Microsoft's Internet Explorer Web browser software, MSN is automatically set as your default Web page. That is, the MSN home page displays whenever you connect to the Internet.

MSN is *not* an online service that you pay for — you do not have to subscribe to MSN Internet Access to use MSN. Originally, MSN started as the Microsoft Network, an online service that you did have to pay for. Although this service still exists, it is known now as MSN Internet Access. (If you are not connected to the Internet, you may want to use MSN Internet Access to do so, and Chapter 2 shows you how.) The rest of the original Microsoft Network, namely the Web site and the content on it, has evolved into MSN, access to which is free to anyone who has Internet access.

You do not have to subscribe to MSN Internet Access to use the MSN home page.

Discovering What You Can Do With MSN

So what's the big deal about MSN? What exactly can you *do* at MSN that makes the site worth visiting? Plenty, actually. The following sections describe some of the more useful things that you can do with MSN and directions to the chapters that discuss them.

Customizing MSN

As you can see in Figure 1-1, MSN's home page is a collection of links to useful services, news stories, and other goodies. However, the best part about the MSN home page is that you can customize it so that it displays just the information and links that interest you. For example, if you're a sports nut, you can tell MSN to put the latest baseball scores front and center. If investments are your thing, you can direct MSN to track stock values. For details on how to personalize MSN, see Chapter 5.

Searching the Internet

MSN provides access to some of the best search tools available on the Internet. With MSN's search features, you can:

- Search the Web using MSN's extensive catalog of Web sites.
- Access other search engines, such as Yahoo, Excite, and AltaVista.
- Peruse MSN's Web Directory, which contains links to thousands of Web sites organized into handy categories.

- Search for people using MSN's White Pages, which contains residential listings for the United States, Canada, and parts of Europe.
- Search for businesses using MSN's Yellow Pages, which contains listings for businesses in the United States and businesses that have Web sites.

For information about using MSN's search features, see Chapter 4.

Getting free e-mail service

You probably already have an e-mail account with your Internet Service Provider. But you may want to consider using the MSN free e-mail service, known as Hotmail. Hotmail is Web based, which means that you read your mail using your Web browser rather than an e-mail program. However, if you prefer to use Microsoft's Outlook Express to access your Hotmail accounts, you can.

One of the biggest advantages of Hotmail is that you can use it to create separate e-mail accounts for each member of your family who uses your computer to access the Internet. For more information about using Hotmail, see Chapters 6 and 7.

Chatting with your online friends

MSN includes a feature known as *MSN Messenger Service* that lets you exchange instant messages with your friends who also use the Internet. To use MSN Messenger Service, you first create a list of your online friends who also have MSN Messenger Service. MSN Messenger Service then automatically alerts you whenever any of your friends go online. You can then send and receive messages with your online friends. For more information on using MSN Messenger Service, see Chapter 11.

Visiting Web communities

Web communities are special MSN areas where people who have common interests can gather. Each Web community includes interesting articles, files you can download, chat rooms where people can meet online, and newsgroup forums where you can leave messages that other people can answer later.

In all, there are about 75 MSN communities on topics, such as cars, genealogy, astronomy, photography, and pets. Figure 1-2 shows the opening page for the Pets Web community.

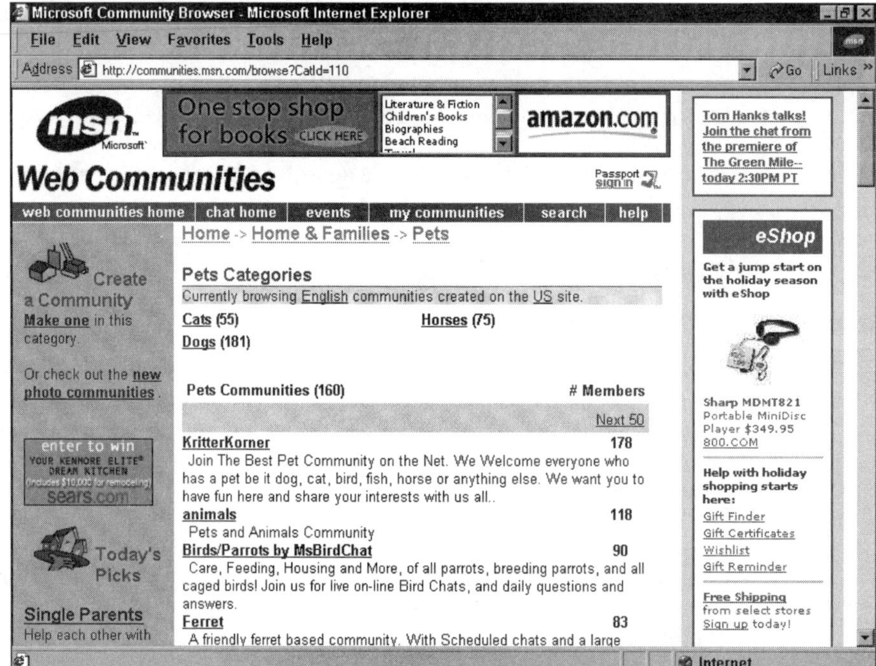

Figure 1-2: A Web Community is a place where people who share a common interest can gather online.

For more information about Web communities, see Chapter 8.

Playing electronic games

For many people, one of the most attractive features of MSN is the Gaming Zone, where you can play games against other Internet users. The Gaming Zone lets you play classic games, such as Checkers, Chess, Backgammon, and Hearts against other Internet users or against computer opponents free of charge. For a fee, you can play premium games, such as *Fighter Ace* or *Hercules and Xena*. You can also use the Gaming Zone to play retail games you have purchased at a computer store, such as *Quake II* or *Star Wars: X-Wing Alliance* against online opponents. For the scoop on the Gaming Zone, check out Chapter 16.

Shopping online

With MSN, you can shop 'til your modem drops. MSN's Shopping section links you to more than 30 online stores, including Barnes & Noble, OfficeMax, and Toys R Us. For more information about online shopping, see Chapter 17.

Planning a vacation

MSN's online travel service, also known as Expedia, lets you plan your next vacation or business trip online. With Expedia, you can plan your complete trip itinerary, shop for airline tickets, reserve a hotel room and rent a car, all with your mouse and keyboard. You find complete information about Expedia in Chapter 18.

Managing your money

MSN includes several features that can help you get ahold of your financial situation. MoneyCentral clues you in to sound strategies for banking, retirement, credit, insurance, and other financial matters. And if you are an investor, check out MSN Investor, an online stockbroker that not only tracks your investments but can help you buy and sell stocks and mutual funds online. For information about using MoneyCentral and Investor, see Chapter 14.

Buying a car

If you're in the market for a new or used car, CarPoint can be an invaluable resource. CarPoint has detailed information about almost every make and model of car, including detailed pricing information, safety and reliability reports, and financing tips. For information about using CarPoint, see Chapter 15.

What MSN Is Not

MSN is not an online service that you have to pay to access — that's MSN Internet Access, which I discuss in Chapter 2. Before continuing, I want to clear up a few other misunderstandings about MSN. Following are some of the things that MSN is not:

- MSN does not require Microsoft's Internet Explorer. You can access MSN from any Web browser, including Internet Explorer's main rival: Netscape Navigator. See the section "Making MSN Your Home Page" later in this chapter to see how.
- You do not have to use MSN just because you use Internet Explorer. In an effort to promote MSN, Microsoft set up Internet Explorer 5 to go to MSN each time you connect to the Internet. But you can easily change that default so that another Web page is displayed when you connect to the Internet. To do so, choose the Tools⇨Options, type in the address of

the page that you want to use as your default start page in the Address field, and then click the OK button.

- MSN is not a sneaky plot that allows Microsoft to creep into your computer and snoop around your hard disk, looking for personal information about you, such as your credit card numbers or what kind of software you use. This fallacy is simply a rumor started by the same people who believe that Microsoft's CEO Bill Gates is actually a clone of the aliens the government has been hiding at Roswell, New Mexico since 1948.
- MSN is not Microsoft's official company Web site. For information about Microsoft's products and other propaganda, visit `www.microsoft.com`.

Making MSN Your Home Page

You can visit MSN at any time with any Web browser by entering `www.msn.com` as the Web address. If you decide that you like the MSN home page enough to make it your default page, follow the steps that apply to your browser as listed in the following sections. After applying these steps, your home page displays whenever you first open your Web browser.

Internet Explorer 5

When you first install Internet Explorer 5, MSN is already set as your default home page. If for some reason you have changed the default home page, you can set it back to MSN by following these steps:

1. **Use the browser to go to `www.msn.com` by typing in the Address and pressing the Enter key.**
2. **Click the Make this your home page hyperlink that appears in the left-hand column on the page.**

   (You may have to scroll down the page to see this hyperlink.) The dialog box, shown in Figure 1-3, appears.

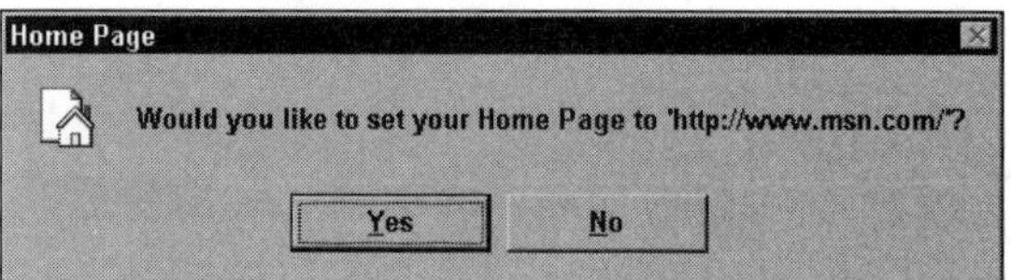

Figure 1-3: MSN asks if you really want to make it your home page.

3. Click the Yes button.

Other Web browsers

If you are using a browser other than Internet Explorer 5, including Netscape Navigator, follow these steps to set MSN as the default home page:

1. **Use your Web browser to go to** `www.msn.com`**.**
2. **Click the Make this your home page hyperlink that appears in the left-hand column on the page.**

   (You may have to scroll down the page to see this hyperlink.) The page, shown in Figure 1-4, appears.
3. **Select the browser that you are using and then follow the instructions that appear.**

When you finish, your Web browser will automatically call up the MSN home page whenever you start the browser.

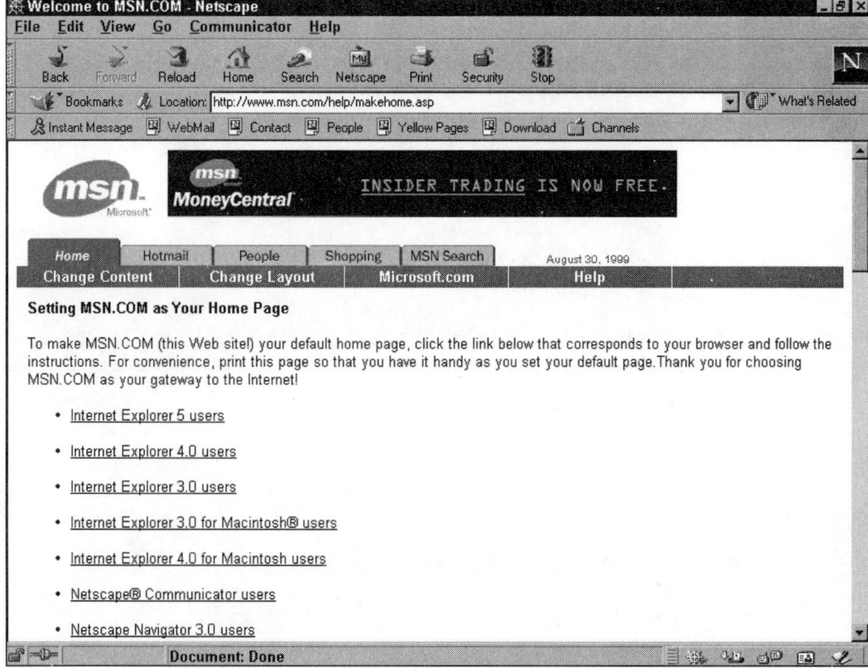

Figure 1-4: Setting MSN as the home page when using Netscape Navigator.

Chapter 2

Using MSN Internet Access

In This Chapter

- Gearing up to use MSN Internet Access
- Signing up for MSN Internet Access
- Connecting to MSN Internet Access after you sign up
- Changing your password, checking your bill, and other menial tasks

Before you can use MSN, you must connect to the Internet. If you don't already have an Internet connection, you can use Microsoft's Internet connection service, known as MSN Internet Access (and sometimes called MSNIA). When you sign up for MSN Internet Access, Microsoft supplies you with a telephone number that your modem uses to connect to the Internet, and a user ID and password which enable you to log on to the Internet. In exchange, you get to give Microsoft your credit card number so they can bill you $21.95 every month.

This chapter shows you how to sign up for and use MSN Internet Access as your Internet service provider (ISP). If you already have an Internet connection, or if you plan to use another ISP, you can skip this chapter.

You don't have to sign up for MSN Internet Access to use the MSN Web site. You can use MSN no matter what Internet Service Provider you use to connect to the Internet.

Collecting the Bare Necessities

Here's a list of what you need before you can use MSN Internet Access:

- **A computer:** The Internet is an online computer system, so naturally you need a computer to access it. You don't have to have the fastest computer in the world, but if your computer is more than three years old, you should consider upgrading to a newer model.

- **A modem:** A device that enables your computer to connect to other computers via a telephone line. The modem may be *internal,* where the modem is physically contained within your computer's case, or *external*, where the modem lives in its own case and connects to your computer via a cable.

  Modems are rated by their speed, using a measurement called baud. Although you can connect to MSN Internet Access with a 28,800-baud (28.8K) modem, your Internet experience is much more satisfying if you use a faster modem, such as a 33.6K or 56K modem. You can purchase a 56K modem for well under $100. (Unfortunately, your phone line might not be able to handle connections faster than 28.8. Even if you upgrade to the fastest modem available, your Internet speed may be limited by the quality of your phone connection.)

  A newer, faster type of modem known as a *cable modem* ties in to the Internet via your cable television service rather than a phone line. However, MSN Internet Access (and most other Internet Service Providers) don't support cable modems. If you want to use a cable modem to access the Internet, contact your local Cable television company to see if Internet access is available in your area.

- **A telephone line:** The modem must connect to a telephone line to work. You don't need a special computer-type telephone line; your standard telephone line that you hold conversations on can work. However, be warned that whenever you connect your computer to MSN Internet Access (or any ISP for that matter), you can't use that telephone line for anytning else. If you try calling home and the phone is busy for hours, don't automatically assume that it's your teenager talking — it could be your spouse using the Internet. (For this reason, many people add a second phone line just for Internet access.)

- **Windows 95/98:** MSN Internet Access is available only to users of Windows 95 or Windows 98. If you have Windows 98, the software you need to sign up for MSN Internet Access is already on your desktop. If you are using Windows 95 and can connect to the Internet, contact Microsoft at `www.microsoft.com`. If you can't get online, contact Microsoft at 1-800-426-9400 and request the MSN Internet Access CD-ROM by mail.

- **A credit or debit card:** Sigh. Cash or checks are not accepted. MSN Internet Access will bill your credit or debit card automatically each month.

Signing Up For MSN Internet Access

Before you can use MSN Internet Access, you must, of course, register and pay for it. Signing up is the electronic equivalent of raising your hand and saying, "Yes, Bill Gates, I would like to use MSN Internet Access! Here is my name, address, phone number, mother's maiden name, credit card number, and deed to my house. Sign me up!"

Microsoft has done everything it can think of to make signing up as easy as possible. The following steps show you how to sign up for MSN Internet Access for Windows 98. If you are using Windows 95 or Windows NT instead, first get the MSN Internet Access CD-ROM from Microsoft, then follow the instructions that come with the CD.

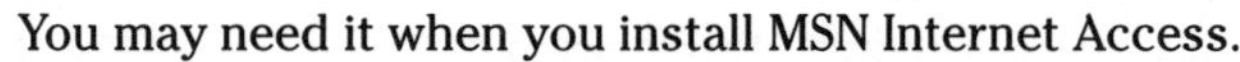

1. **Make sure that you have your Windows 98 CD handy.**

   You may need it when you install MSN Internet Access.

Setup MSN Internet Access

2. **Click the MSN Internet Access desktop icon (shown in the margin).**

   The dialog box, shown in Figure 2-1, appears.

3. **Click the Next button.**

   The dialog box appears and asks you some basic questions about your telephone connection, such as what country you live in, your area code, whether you have to dial a special number to access an outside line, and whether you have touch-tone service.

4. **Answer the questions and then click the Next button.**

   MSN Internet Access uses your modem to make a quick phone call and then displays the dialog box.

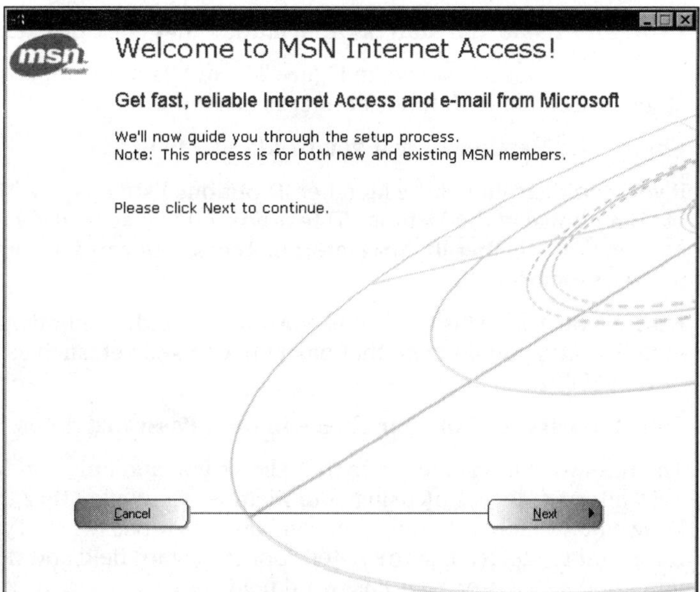

Figure 2-1: Signing up for MSN Internet Access.

5. **Click the Next button.**

   MSN Internet Access now asks for your name and address, as shown in Figure 2-2.

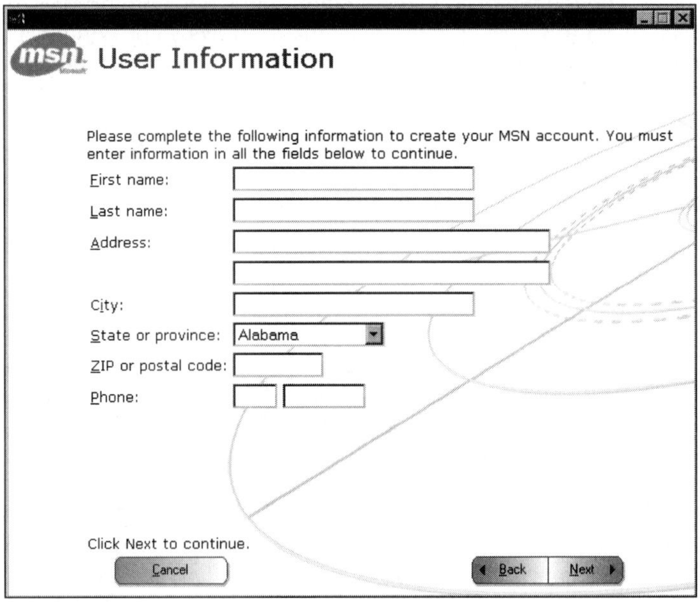

Figure 2-2: MSN Internet Access wants to know your name and address.

6. **Type your name and address information and click the Next button.**

   The screen appears, shown in Figure 2-3, and lists several possible Member IDs that MSN Internet Access has chosen for you.

7. **Choose the Member ID that you would like to use.**

   If you don't like any of the Member ID options listed, type a Member ID of your choice in the Member ID text box. (If someone else has already chosen that Member ID, MSN Internet Access informs you and asks you to choose another ID.)

   Hint: If you want a certain name, you can try adding numbers on to the end of it until you find one that hasn't been used yet, such as ace67098 or barb20061.

8. **Type the password of your choice in both Password fields.**

   The password is a secret code that allows you and only you to access MSN Internet Access by using your Member ID. While other users may know your Member ID, only you can know your password. Type the password twice: once in the Enter Your Password field and then once more in the Re-Enter Your Password field.

msn Member ID & Password

We have selected the following Member ID choices for you.
Please choose one and type a password.

1. Doug_L
2. Doug_99
3. Doug_001
4. Lowe_2
5. Lowe_99
6. Choose your own Member ID:

Please choose a password of at least 8 characters.

Enter your password:

Re-enter your password:

Click Next to continue.

Cancel | Back | Next

Figure 2-3: Member ID and Password options.

Choosing a good password and keeping it a secret is very important. If your password gets out, anyone can log in to MSN Internet Access by using your Member ID and password and pretend to be you. For some sage advice about passwords, see the sidebar "Sage advice about passwords" (clever title, eh?) in this chapter.

9. **Click the Next button.**

   The MSN Internet Access Membership Rules are displayed, as shown in Figure 2-4. The membership rules spell out the terms of your agreement with MSN Internet Access.

10. **Read the License Agreement.**

    Use the scroll bar to scroll through the rules so you can read them all. Unfortunately, these rules appear to have been written by Microsoft's legal department, which means that you can't understand them no matter how many times you read them. For a concise explanation of the rules, see the sidebar, "What the rules really mean."

11. **Click I Accept the MSN Agreement option button and then click the Next button.**

    If you don't accept Microsoft's terms, Microsoft won't accept you for MSN Internet Access. So, if you want to use MSN Internet Access you'd best accept the agreement.

    Figure 2-5 shows the Payment Method dialog box, which is displayed next.

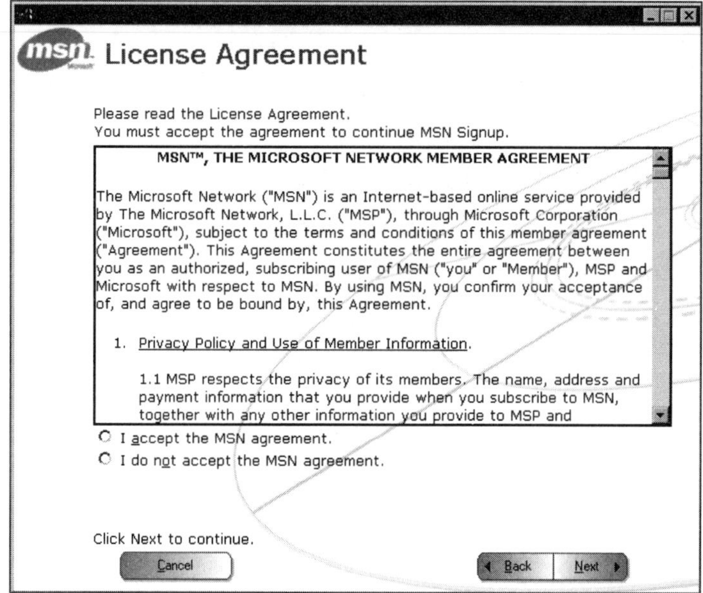

Figure 2-4: The License Agreement rules.

12. **Select the type of credit or debit card that you want to use by clicking one of the four tabs displaying the card's icon, and then type your credit or debit card information in the dialog box fields.**

The sign-up process is the only time that MSN Internet Access will ask you for your credit or debit card number. If anyone claiming to be a MSN Internet Access representative asks you to send your credit card information via electronic mail, contact MSN Member Services immediately so that you can forward them a copy of the offending e-mail. An electronic con artist is swindling you!

13. **Click the Next button.**

    MSN Internet Access displays your account information, including your Member ID, e-mail address, and the phone numbers you dial to connect to the Internet, as shown in Figure 2-6.

14. **Write down this information, keep it in a safe place, and then click the Next button.**

    You need to remember your Member ID, e-mail address, and the Internet Telephone numbers, so write this information down and store it somewhere safe.

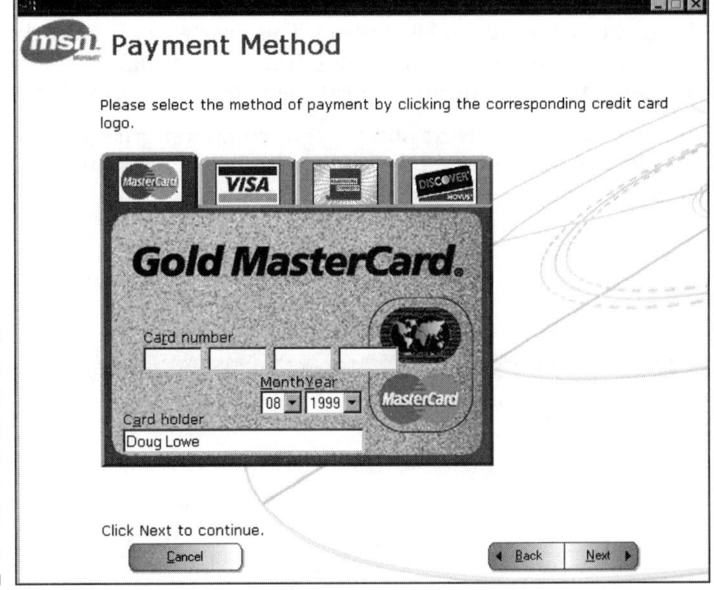

Figure 2-5: MSN Internet Access asks for your credit card information.

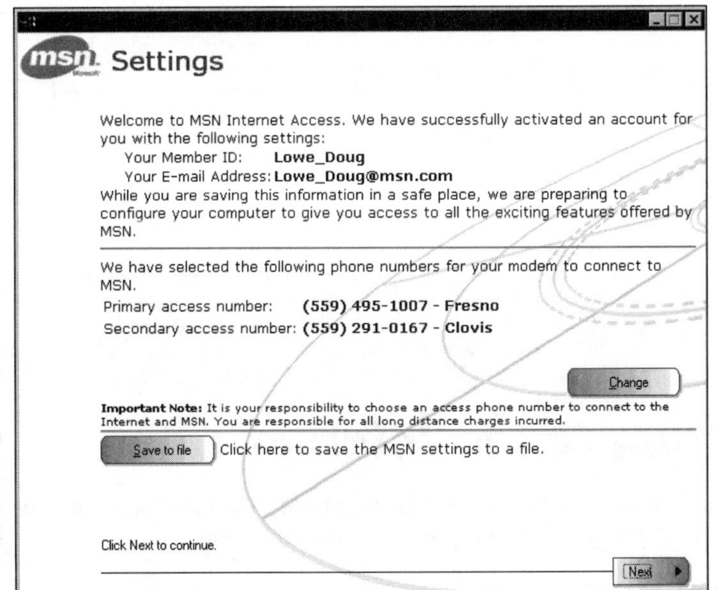

Figure 2-6: Your account information.

You can save your membership information to a file on your computer by clicking the Save to File button. This creates a file named MSN Member Settings.htm on your desktop. Double-click this file at any time to view your MSN Internet Access membership information.

When you click the Next button, your computer grinds and whirs for a moment as MSN Internet Access configures its software. After a minute or so, the screen appears, as shown in Figure 2-7.

15. **Click the Next button.**

    You're done!

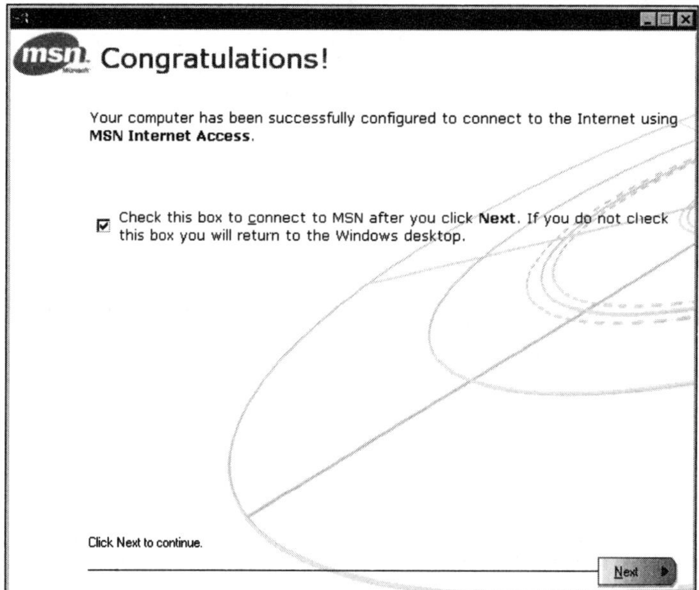

Figure 2-7: Congratulations! You made it.

Connecting to the Internet

Here is the procedure for connecting to MSN Internet Access after you sign up. This procedure should become a familiar one:

MSN Internet Access

1. **Double-click the MSN Internet Access icon on your desktop.**

   The MSN Internet Access sign-in dialog box appears, as shown in Figure 2-8.

Sage advice about passwords

Your password is the only protection you have against unscrupulous users who would access MSN Internet Access by using your member ID. Such access can be embarrassing and expensive for you. Here are some tips for keeping your password secret:

- Don't use obvious passwords like your last name, your kid's name, or your dog's name. Don't pick passwords based on your hobbies, either. I have a friend who is into boating, and he uses the name of his boat as his password. Anyone who knows about his interest in boating could guess his password after a few tries.
- Use unusual words. I like to use words from Chaucer's "Canterbury Tales" because the spelling is so weird. For example, Chaucer's spelling of "Opinion" is "Opynyoun" — perfect for a password.
- A random combination of letters and numbers makes for a good password — as long as you can remember it. For example, no one would guess B49H20C2. (Funny the way the mind works when you get to be my age. My password is a random string of eight letters and digits, which I can recall instantly. But I have trouble remembering to put the trash out on Thursdays and I lose my car keys about three times a week. Sigh.)
- You can write down your password if you need to, but keep it in a secure location. You'll be in a pickle if you forget your password.

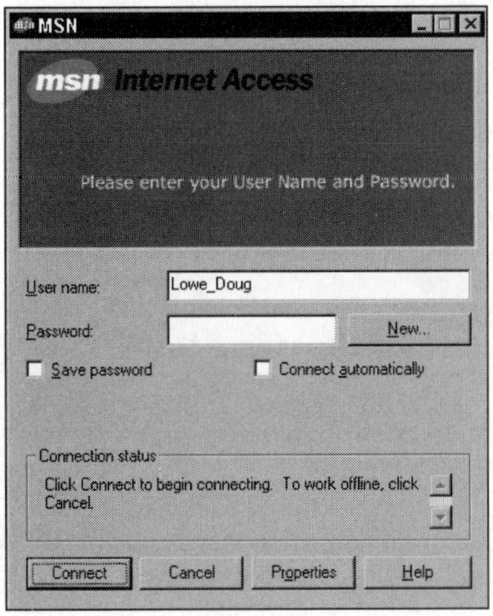

Figure 2-8: The MSN Internet Access sign-in dialog box.

2. **If necessary, type your member ID and password in the User Name and Password fields.**

   Your password doesn't appear on-screen as you type it; instead, an asterisk appears for each character you type. This procedure protects your password from snoopy neighbors.

If you get tired of typing your password every time you sign in, check the Remember My Password check box, and henceforth, MSN automatically provides your password when the Sign In dialog box appears. This feature is convenient (I use it myself), but you may not want to use it if your computer is in an unsecured location where unauthorized users can get to it. While sneaky people can't read your password, they can sign in using your member ID if you've stored your password.

3. **Click the Connect button.**

   MSN Internet Access calls the phone numbers that you saved when you signed up. When the connection is complete, the MSN Internet Access home page (`msnmember.msn.com`) appears, as shown in Figure 2-9.

Note that MSN Internet Access sets your default home page to `msnmember.msn.com` rather than `www.msn.com`. The `msnmember.msn.com` home page is similar to `www.msn.com`, but includes an additional section that is designed for MSN Internet Access users, with links to your e-mail account, MSN's member services pages, and MSN Internet Access news and announcements.

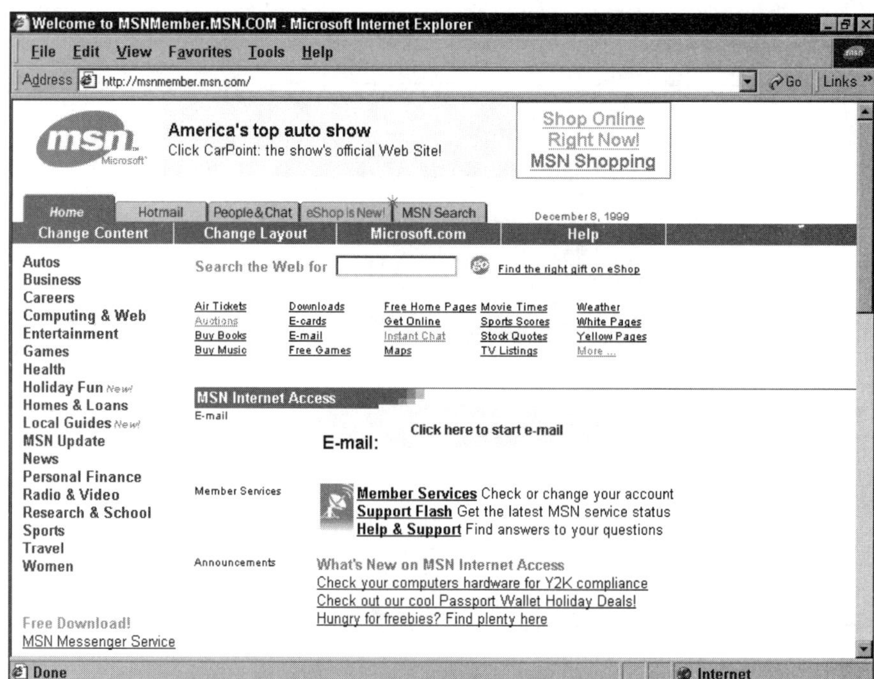

Figure 2-9: MSN.com comes to life.

What the rules really mean

The rules, officially known as the "License Agreement," spell out what you agree to when you sign up for MSN Internet Access. You should probably read the rules carefully, but don't expect to be impressed by lofty prose. After all, lawyers wrote the rules. Basically, the rules say the following:

- You agree to behave yourself.
- You agree to pay your bill.
- Microsoft agrees to nothing.
- You must be 18 years old or older to sign up. Minors can use the network, but only adults can sign up officially. (Of course, Microsoft has no way of verifying that the person signing up really is 18 or over.)

Changing Your Password

Changing your password once in a while is not a bad idea. It helps foil those who would attempt to access MSN Internet Access without paying for it by stealing your member ID and password. To change your password, follow these steps:

1. **Connect to the Internet.**

   Refer to the "Connecting to the Internet" section earlier in this chapter.

2. **Click the MSN Internet Access button that appears in the Windows taskbar, as shown in the margin.**

   A menu appears.

3. **Choose Member Services⇨Member Services Home Page from the menu.**

   The Member Services home page appears, as shown in Figure 2-10.

4. **Click the Your Account link found on the Member Services page.**

   The page, shown in Figure 2-11, appears.

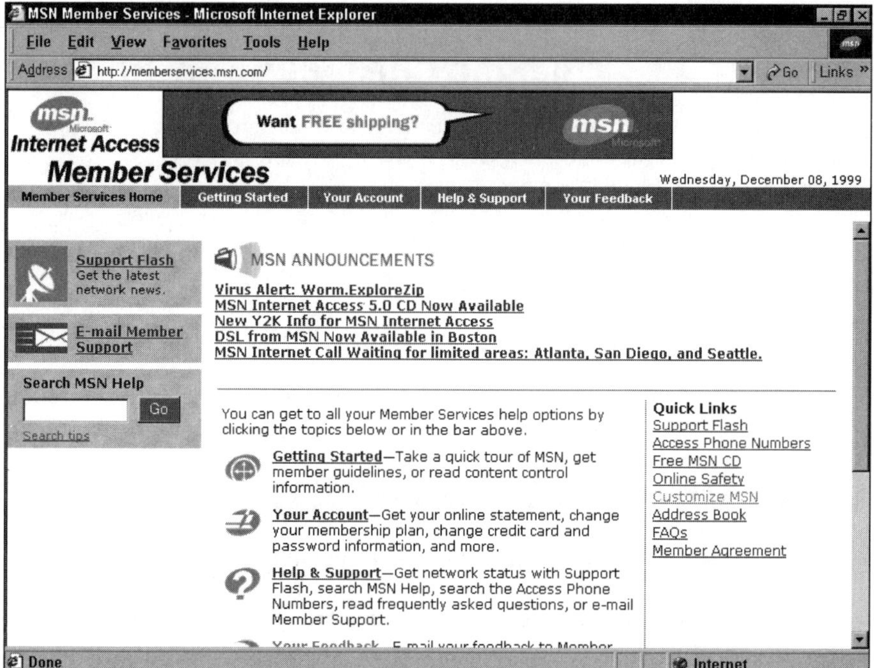

Figure 2-10: The Member Services home page.

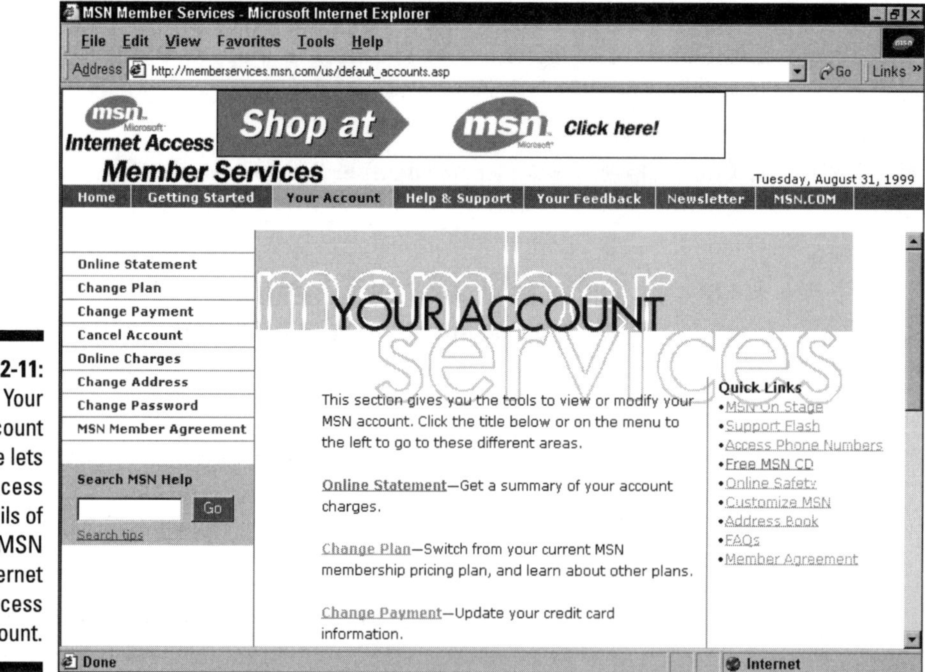

Figure 2-11: The Your Account page lets you access details of your MSN Internet Access account.

5. **Click the Change Password link.**

   This summons the Change Password page, as shown in Figure 2-12. (You'll have to scroll down the Your Account page to find the Change Password link.)

6. **Type your current password, and then type your new password twice in the fields indicated.**

   As a security precaution, the characters in your password display as asterisks as you type them in.

7. **Click the Submit button.**

   The next time you sign in, you must use your new password.

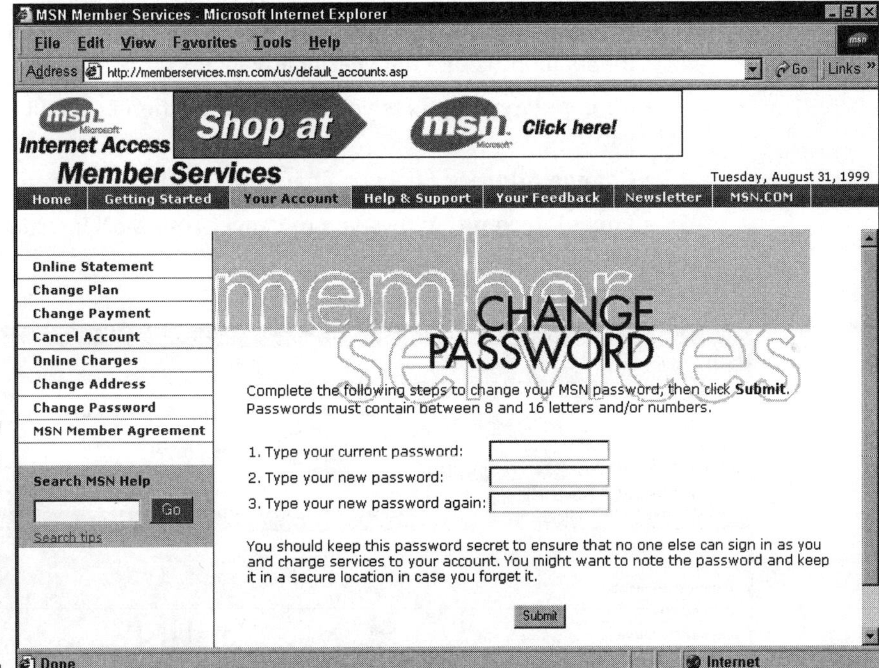

Figure 2-12: The Change Password page lets you change your password.

Checking Your Account Status

If you're curious about your current charges, follow these steps:

1. **Connect to MSN Internet Access.**

2. **Click the MSN Internet Access button in the taskbar (shown in the margin), then choose the Member Services⇨Member Services Home Page command.**

The Member Services home page appears. (Refer to Figure 2-10.)

3. **Click Your Account.**

   This brings up the Your Account page (refer to Figure 2-11).

4. **Click Online Statement.**

   This displays the Online Statement page, as shown in Figure 2-13.

   The Online Statement page presents the status of your account, including any amounts that you owe Microsoft and any premium services you have subscribed to. This page also includes these additional links to let you modify your account:

   - **Change Plan:** Displays your current membership plan and allows you to change plans if you wish. MSN Internet Access has several membership plans you can choose from besides the simple $21.95/month flat rate. For example, you can save money by paying for six months or a full year in advance.
   - **Change Payment:** Lets you change to a different credit or debit card.
   - **Change Address:** Lets you change your address.
   - **Cancel Account:** Allows you to cancel your MSN Internet Access account.

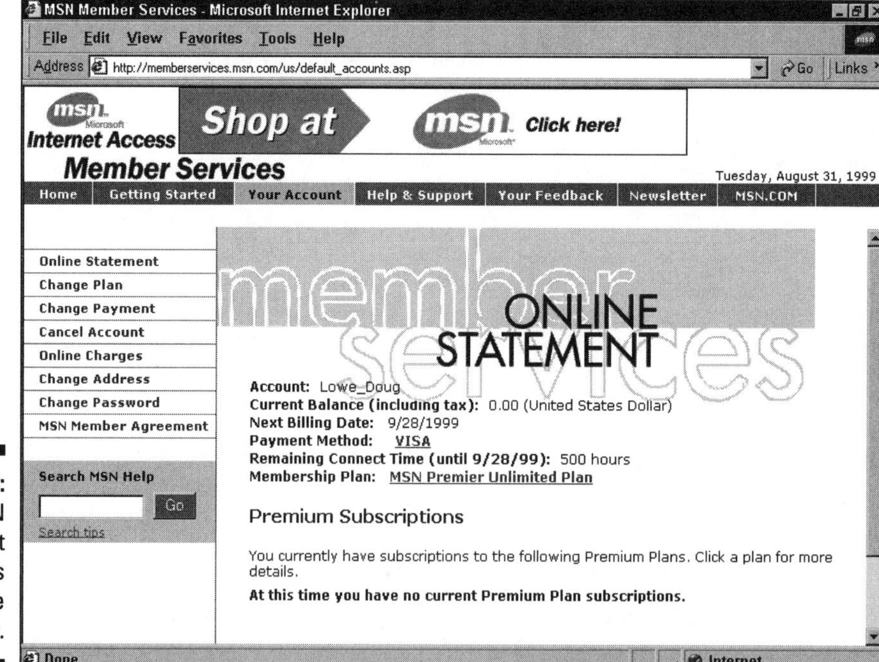

Figure 2-13: An MSN Internet Access Online Statement.

Chapter 3

Getting Around MSN

In This Chapter

- Getting cozy with MSN
- Using Internet Explorer with MSN
- Using the Quick View menu

This chapter is an introduction to finding your way around MSN. The first few times you use MSN, you may have trouble finding your way around. But don't be intimidated. Jump right in. The more you work with MSN, the more familiar with it you become, and the more adept you get at moving around. You'll find your feet in no time.

Don't be afraid to click anywhere you want. The best way to learn how to get around MSN is to start clicking.

Also, keep in mind that Microsoft frequently updates MSN, adding new features, rearranging page layouts, and so on. Don't be surprised if MSN changes just when you finally get it figured out.

Familiarizing Yourself with MSN

Figure 3-1 shows the MSN home page. As you can see, the page is chock-full of useful information and hyperlinks to other areas of the vast MSN Empire, as well as links to other Web sites that aren't a part of MSN. The following sections describe the goodies you can find on the MSN home page.

If you access the Internet by using MSN Internet Access, your default home page sets `msnmember.msn.com` rather than `www.msn.com`. The `msnmember.msn.com` page looks a bit different than the `www.msn.com` page, but contains the same features.

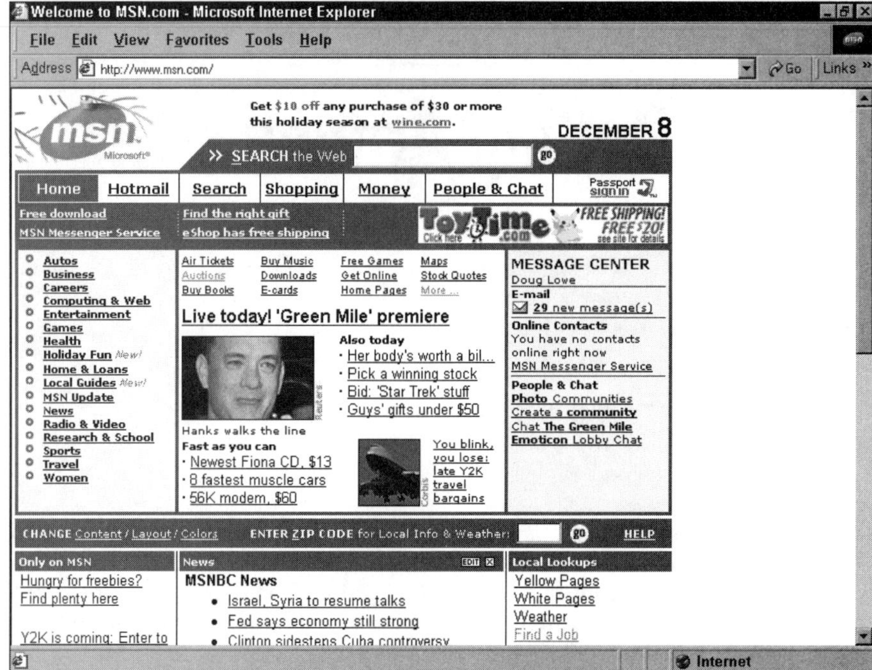

Figure 3-1: The MSN home page.

Presenting MSN: First, a word from our sponsor

Every MSN page is sprinkled with one or more advertisements from MSN sponsors. Like television commercials, these advertisements are annoying but necessary: without them, Microsoft couldn't afford to let you visit MSN free of charge. So take a polite look at the advertisements that appear here. If you are interested in the product or service being advertised, click the advertisement to get more information.

Tabbing your way around MSN

Near the top of the MSN home page is a series of tabs that you can click to go to six of MSN's main sections. The six tabs are:

- **Home:** Click this tab at any time to return you to the MSN home page (see Figure 3-1).
- **Hotmail:** Takes you to the Hotmail page, where you can access your free Hotmail e-mail account, or sign up for a free account if you don't yet have one.

- **Search:** Summons the MSN Search page, where you can perform detailed searches for information available over the Internet.
- **Money:** Takes you to the MSN finance page, known as moneycentral.com, where you can manage your investments, find loans, buy insurance, and attend to other financial needs.
- **Shopping:** Displays MSN's shopping page, with links to dozens of online stores.
- **People & Chat:** Calls up the MSN People & Chat page, making it easy to connect with other people who use the Internet via online chats and Web communities.

Searching for stuff when you just gotta know

At the top of the MSN home page is MSN's quick search tool. Here's the fastest way to search for information on the Web:

1. **Type the word or phrase that you're looking for in the Search the Web For text box.**
2. **Select the search service that you want to use from the Using list box on the right.**

   MSN is the default choice, of course.
3. **Click the Go button to start the search.**

Or, if you prefer, just press Enter. Either way, MSN displays the results of your search on a separate page. For more information about using the search tool and other MSN search features, see Chapter 4.

Connecting with Quick Links

Near the center of the MSN home page is a collection of hyperlinks to a dozen or so of MSN's most useful services, including airline tickets, books, weather, chats, movie times, stock quotes, and more. Table 3-1 gives a brief description of each Quick Link and its free service. Note that MSN periodically changes these links as new services are added and others are removed.

Table 3-1 MSN Quick Links

Hyperlink	*Description*
Air Tickets	Shop for the lowest airfare available through Expedia
Auctions	Online auctions — kind of like a huge garage sale
Buy Books	Purchase books from Barnes & Noble
Buy Music	Buy the latest music from Amazon.com
Downloads	Get software from Computing Central
E-Cards	Send free electronic greeting cards
Free Games	Play games free at the MSN Gaming Zone
Get Online	Connect to MSN Internet Access
Home Pages	Design your own custom Web pages
Maps	Get maps and driving directions for travel
Stock Quotes	Get the latest quotes, research, and news from Money Central on stocks
More	Calls up a page with more than 50 links to additional MSN services

Immediately beneath the list of quick links are links to important news, entertainment, or shopping bargains. These items change on a daily basis, so be sure to look them over each time you access MSN.

Exciting MSN services

Down the left side of the page, you see a list of MSN's various services. Table 3-2 describes each of these hyperlinks. Note that MSN periodically adds or removes hyperlinks in this section as old services are dropped and new services are added. This list also frequently includes seasonal items, such as Back to School in early fall or Summer Fun in the summer months. (I omitted the seasonal links from Table 3-2.)

Table 3-2 MSN Services

Hyperlink	*Description*
Autos	Auto purchasing information from CarPoint
Business	News, advice, and resources from MSN's business page

Hyperlink	*Description*
Careers	Helpful information if you are looking for a job
Computing & Web	Information and help with using your computer and the Internet
Entertainment	Celebrities, movies, music, gossip, and more
Games	Free online games on the MSN Gaming Zone
Health	Health information and services
Home & Loans	Home purchasing information
Local Guides	Information about your favorite city, including weather forecasts and entertainment schedules
News	Local, national, and regional news from MSNBC
Radio and Video	Audio and video events on the Web
Research & School	Reference information and educational material for teachers and students
Sports	News, scores, and analysis from MSNBC
Travel	Flight, hotel, and car reservations from Microsoft Expedia
Women	Helpful information for women

Messaging center

On the right side of the MSN home page is the Message Center. The Message Center lets you access your e-mail via your Hotmail account, use MSN Messenger Service to chat with other Internet users, or visit the People & Chats pages where you can access online Web communities.

Perusing the clips

Clips are the sections of information that appear in the central portion of the MSN home page. Clips contain the information that changes from day to day whenever you call up the MSN home page, such as news headlines, sports scores, and so on. In Figure 3-1, you can see just one clip: News. You can scroll down the page to reveal more clips.

Two clips display on your MSN page by default:

- **News:** Headlines from MSNBC and other news services.
- **Personal Finance:** Follow your favorite companies. By default, MSN shows Dow, Amex, Nasdaq, and S&P 500 industry averages. But you can add your own stocks if you want.

Besides these five clips, you can add additional clips to MSN. For more information, see Chapter 5.

Thrilling Places You'll Go

The main purpose of MSN is to provide a jumping off point for you to explore the Internet. To do so, you need to know how to get around. That is, how to navigate from one Internet location to another, how to get back to MSN after completing your explorations or getting lost, or when you reach a dead end and just want to start over.

The following sections explain how to navigate MSN and the rest of the Internet by using Microsoft's popular Web browser, Internet Explorer 5. The techniques for navigating the Internet with other Web browsers are similar.

Understanding Web addresses

Just as every house in a neighborhood has a street address, every page on the World Wide Web has an Internet address. The Internet address of a Web page is also called a *Uniform Resource Locator* (URL).

URLs are becoming commonplace in our society. Just think about how many times you've seen addresses such as `www.whatever.com` appear at the end of a television advertisement. These days, every company that advertises seems to have a Web page.

To browse the Internet effectively, you need to understand the various parts that make up a typical URL Web address. Typing URLs isn't hard, but it takes some practice.

A URL consists of three parts, written as follows:

```
protocol://host_address/resource_name
```

- For World Wide Web pages, the *protocol* portion of the URL is always `http` (http stands for *HyperText Transfer Protocol,* but you don't need to know that to use URLs).

- The *host address* is the Internet address of the computer on which the Web page resides (for example, `www.msn.com`).
- The final part, the *resource name,* is a name assigned by the host computer to a specific Web page or other file. In many cases, this name contains additional slashes that represent directories on the host system. Most of the time, you can omit the resource name completely if you simply want to display the home page for a company's Web site.

Here are some examples of complete URLs:

```
http://www.microsoft.com
http://www.msn.com
http://carpoint.msn.com/classifieds
http://moneycentral.msn.com/articles/invest/funds/3430.asp
```

Notice that all Internet addresses must be prefixed by `http://`. However, Internet Explorer (and most other Web browsers) cleverly adds the `http://` automatically, so you don't have to type it yourself. Throughout this book, other than the section preceding this one, I leave off the `http://` from any World Wide Web address.

Because you can omit the protocol part (`http://`) and often omit the resource name, the only URL component that you really need to worry about is the host address. Host addresses themselves consist of three components separated from one another by periods, usually called *dots.*

- The first part of the Internet address is usually (but not always) `www`, to indicate that the address is for a page on the World Wide Web.
- The second part of the Internet address is often a company or organization name, sometimes abbreviated if the full name is too long. Sometimes this second part actually consists of two or more parts in itself separated by periods. For example, in the address `www.polis.iupui.edu`, the second part is `polis.iupui`.
- The third and final part of an Internet address is a category that indicates the type of organization the name belongs to. The most common categories are:
    - **.gov:** Government agencies
    - **.com:** Private companies
    - **.edu:** Educational institutions
    - **.org:** Organizations
    - **.net:** Networks

Putting the three address parts together, you get addresses such as `www.msn.com`, `www.nasa.gov`, and `www.ucla.edu`.

MSN uses the first portion of the host name (the part that is usually www) to identify the major areas that make up the complete MSN Web site. For example, the following table lists the addresses for several major MSN areas:

Address	*msn.com area*
`www.msn.com`	MSN home page
`www.hotmail.com`	Hotmail
`carpoint.msn.com`	CarPoint
`communities.msn.com`	MSN Web Communities
`expedia.msn.com`	Expedia
`encarta.msn.com`	Encarta
`homepages.msn.com`	MSN Home Pages
`investor.msn.com`	MSN Investor
`moneycentral.msn.com`	MoneyCentral
`zone.msn.com`	MSN Gaming Zone

Following the links

The most popular method of navigating through the Internet is by following links. A *link* (also known as a hyperlink) is a bit of text or a graphic on one Web page that leads you to another Web page. A link may lead to another page at the same Web site, or it may lead to a page at a different Web site altogether.

In many cases, links are easy to identify on a Web page because they're underlined and displayed in colors different from the rest of the text. For example, the Quick Links on the MSN home page (refer to Figure 3-1) are simple text links.

Not all links are underlined, however. For example, the MSN Services, which appear on the left side of the MSN home page, are also text links, although they are not underlined. Underlined or not, the sure way to spot a link is to watch the mouse cursor when you point to the text. If the mouse cursor changes from an arrow pointer to a pointing hand, you have found a link.

Finding your way back

Exploring the Internet can be like exploring the woods. You see a link that looks promising, so you take it. The page the link leads to has other links that look promising, so you pick one and take it — and so on, until pretty soon you're lost. You should have marked your path with breadcrumbs.

Fortunately, Internet Explorer and other Web browsers let you retrace your steps easily. Two of the buttons on the Standard toolbar exist just for this purpose: Back and Forward. The following table shows these buttons for Internet Explorer and Netscape Navigator and describes their functions:

Internet Explorer	*Navigator*	*What the Button Does*
Back	Back	The Back button moves backward along the path you've taken. Click this button to retrace the links you've followed, only backward. You can click it several times in a row if necessary to retrace your steps through several links.
Forward	Forward	The Forward button moves forward along your path. As long as you keep plowing ahead, this button stays grayed out — meaning you can't use it. However, after you begin to retrace your steps with the Back button, the Forward button becomes active. Clicking the Forward button takes you to the page where you were before you clicked the Back button.

If you prefer to use the keyboard, these buttons have keyboard shortcuts that work in both Internet Explorer and Navigator. The keyboard shortcut for the Back button is Alt+Left Arrow; for the forward button, the shortcut is Alt+Right Arrow.

Both browsers have history features that allow you to visit sites that you have visited previously.

To quickly return to a Web page that you have previously visited in Internet Explorer, click the History button. A list of Web pages that you have visited today and in past weeks appear. To revisit one of the listed sites, simply click the site's address. To make the History list disappear, just click the History button again or click the X in the upper right-hand corner of the History window.

To return to a Web page that you have previously visited in Navigator, select Communicator⇨Tools⇨History to bring up the History window (or just press Ctrl+H). By default, the Last Visited heading appears with an arrow pointing downward, indicating your selection is active. Note that your previously visited sites appear in descending order, starting with the site that you last visited at the top of the list. As you go down the list, the sites get older. You can sort the list of sites by clicking the various column headings in the History window.

For example, click the Title heading to sort by name or the Visit Count to see the number of times that you've visited each site in the list. By clicking the selected heading once, you can change the arrow from pointing down to pointing up (or vice versa), at which point, the list reverses itself into ascending order. For example, by clicking the selected Last Visited column, the site at the top of the list becomes the oldest in the list instead of the most current. Click again to change the arrow back to the downward position (descending order). Click the X in the upper-right corner of the screen to close the History window.

Refreshing a page

The first time you access a page, your Web browser copies the entire page from the Internet to your computer. Depending on the size and complexity of the page and the speed of your connection, this process can take a few seconds or a few minutes.

To avoid repeating this download, the Web browser saves the information for the page in a special area of your hard disk known as the *cache*. The next time you retrieve the same page, the page displays directly from this cache instead of being downloaded again from the Internet. Thus, the page appears more quickly.

However, what happens if the page has changed since the last time you downloaded it? Many Web pages change frequently. Some pages change daily, some change almost hourly. For such pages, you can force Internet Explorer to refresh its view of the page. The page downloads again, so you have to wait for it. But at least you know the information is current.

If you want to reload everything, including images, from scratch (sometimes images load badly and just won't reload properly) hold down Shift as you press Reload and the page will reload ignoring the cache entirely.

To refresh a page, all you have to do is click the aptly named Refresh button (shown in the margin) and then twiddle your thumbs while your Web browser downloads the page again. If you prefer to use the keyboard, press F5 instead.

You can also use the Refresh button to replay an animation or a sound that you want to see or hear again. For example, if you stumble on a page that shows a neat animated space ship flying across the screen, and you want to see the spaceship fly by again, just click the Refresh button.

In Netscape Navigator, the equivalent button (shown in the margin) is called Reload rather than Refresh. The keyboard shortcut for the Reload button in Navigator is Ctrl+R.

Stopping a long download

Every once in a while, you wander into a page you wish you hadn't. The link that led you to the page may have looked interesting, but after you get there, the page isn't what you expected. According to Murphy's Law, that page is filled with complicated graphics and takes forever to download.

Fortunately, you are not forced to sit there and wait while a long graphic that you don't want is downloaded. All you have to do is click the Stop button or press the Esc key and your Web browser cancels the rest of the download. The portion of the page that has already made it to your computer continues to be on display, but anything that hasn't yet arrived does not display. You can then click the Back button to go back to the previous page. The Internet Explorer version of the Stop button is shown in the margin.

Netscape Navigator's version of the Stop button, shown in the margin, is a traffic light.

Playing favorites

MSN has hundreds of interesting destinations. And when you leave the bounds of MSN to venture onto the rest of the Internet, you find literally millions of interesting pages to visit.

How do you zero in on those few pages that you find yourself visiting over and over again? In Internet Explorer, the answer is to use the Favorites feature. Favorites allows you to get to your favorite Web pages — within the MSN site or in the Internet at large — without having to navigate your way through link after link to get to them.

To designate a Web page as one of your Favorites, follow these simple steps:

1. **Browse your way to the page you want to add to your list of favorite pages.**
2. **Choose the Favorites➪Add to Favorites command.**

   The Add Favorite dialog box appears, as shown in Figure 3-2. The Name text box displays the name of the Web site that you want to add to your Favorites menu.
3. **Change the Web site's Name if you want.**

   In many cases, the name proposed by Internet Explorer is acceptable. But if you want to change the name, you can do so by typing a new name in the Name field.

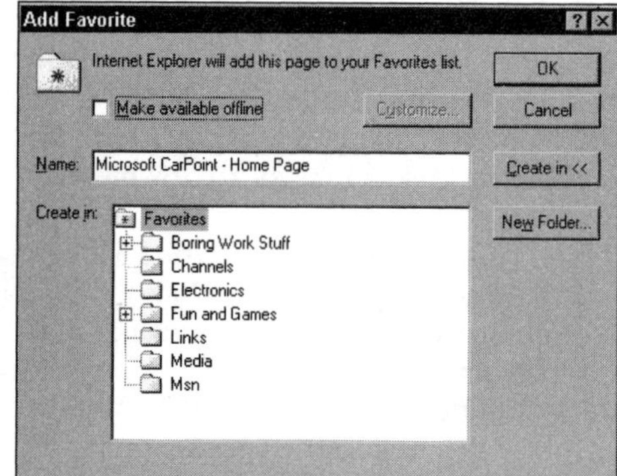

Figure 3-2: The Add Favorite dialog box.

4. **Click the OK button.**

   Internet Explorer adds the Web site to your Favorites menu.

After you add your favorite Web pages to your Favorites menu, you can open the menu to jet away to any of the pages it contains. Here's how:

1. **Choose Favorites from the menu bar.**

   The Favorites menu reveals your list of favorite places.
2. **Select the Web page you want to view, and off you go.**

If you have a lot of Favorites, you can organize them into folders to make the Favorites menu easier to contend with. Each of the folders appears on the Favorites menu as a submenu. To create a favorite in a folder, click the Create In button in the Add Favorite dialog box.

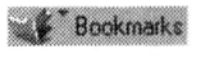

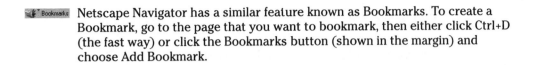

Netscape Navigator has a similar feature known as Bookmarks. To create a Bookmark, go to the page that you want to bookmark, then either click Ctrl+D (the fast way) or click the Bookmarks button (shown in the margin) and choose Add Bookmark.

Using the Quick View Menu (a.k.a. the Hand Icon)

If you are an MSN Internet Access user, you'll find a handy button (shown in the margin) located on the Windows toolbar in the bottom-right corner of the screen. If you click this button, a menu called the Quick View menu appears (see Figure 3-3). The Quick View menu lets you quickly access the most commonly used MSN features.

The Quick View menu has choices that take you directly to the most commonly accessed MSN areas, such as Web Communities, CarPoint, Expedia, and Hotmail. Plus, you can access the MSN Member Services area to check on your account status.

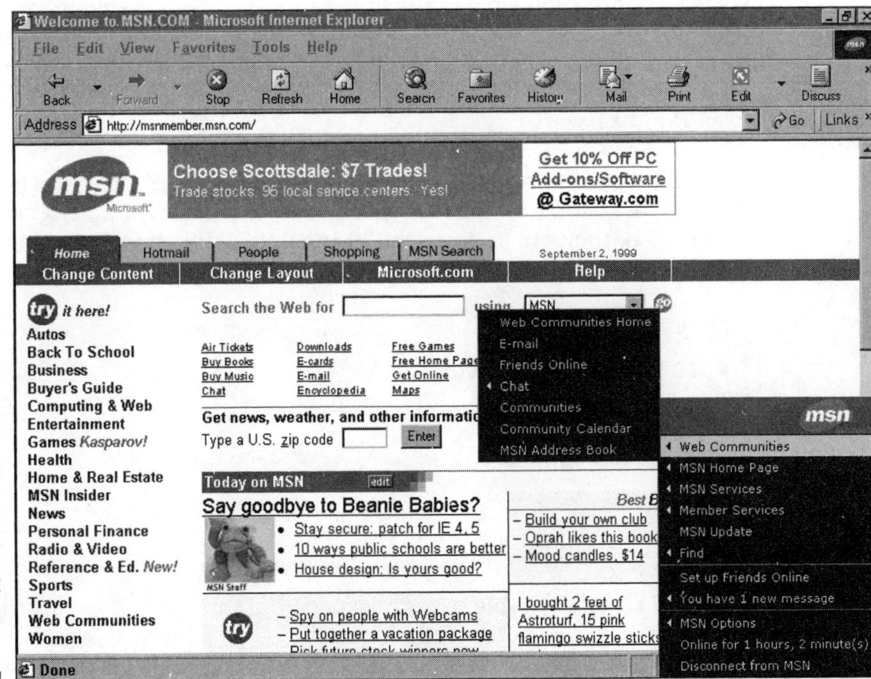

Figure 3-3: The Quick View menu is a handy shortcut for MSN Internet Access subscribers.

Your Passport to the Online World

As you use the Internet, you will discover that many of the sites you visit require you to create an account with a user ID and password. For example, free e-mail services such as Hotmail require that you create an account, as do stock brokerage services such as MoneyCentral and online travel services such as Expedia. It's probable that you'll sign up for a dozen or more accounts with free Internet services.

The problem is, how do you keep track of all the user-ID names and passwords for the services you sign up for? Obviously, you should try to use the same user-ID for each service you sign up for. But that is not always possible: The user-ID you want may be already taken by some other user who got there before you.

One popular way to keep track of your user-IDs and passwords is the sticky-note method: Whenever you sign up for an online service, write the user-ID and password down on a sticky note and stick it on your computer monitor. Unfortunately, your monitor will soon become so cluttered with sticky notes that you won't be able to see the screen.

Thank heavens for Microsoft Passport, a new MSN service that is designed to solve this very problem. Microsoft Passport is a "single sign-in" service that lets you use the same user-ID and password for many different Internet sites. After you sign in to any Web site that uses Passport, you can sign in to any other Passport site with a single mouse click, without having to re-enter your user-ID or password.

In a perfect world, every Web site on the Internet would recognize your Passport account. Unfortunately, the world is still far from perfect: Only a few Web sites participate in Passport. At the time of this book's writing, the following MSN Web sites worked with Passport:

- Hotmail
- MSN Messenger Service
- MoneyCentral
- Web Communities
- Auctions
- Gift Certificates

One MSN service notable by its absence from this list is Expedia, the MSN online travel service. Hopefully, by the time you read this, Expedia will work with Passport, too.

In addition to the MSN Web sites I just listed, about 25 non-Microsoft Web sites work with Passport, and new sites are being added to the list frequently.

The easiest way to create a Passport account is to sign up for a free Hotmail e-mail account. For step-by-step instructions about signing up for Hotmail, see Chapter 6.

In addition to the single sign-on service, Passport also offers a secure way to shop online through its Wallet feature. A Passport Wallet is a list of one or more credit cards and shipping addresses that you can use to purchase goods from online stores that work with Passport. That way, you don't have to type your credit card number and shipping address each time you buy something over the Internet. Instead, the online merchant that you are purchasing from gets your credit card number and shipping address directly from Passport by using a secure connection. For more information about this feature, see Chapter 17.

Chapter 4

Searching the Internet with MSN

In This Chapter

- Using MSN Search to find information on the Internet
- Saving your search results
- Using the Yellow and White pages to find people and businesses on the Internet
- Searching Microsoft's Web site and Internet Newsgroups
- Using Internet Explorer 5's search features

Many people think of the Internet as a vast library of online information, but actually the Net hardly even resembles a library. Unlike a library, the Internet has no librarian to make sure that there is a place for everything and that everything stays in its place. No one person or organization is officially in charge of what goes onto the Internet — anyone can put anything on the Internet, and no one is responsible for making sure that new entries are cataloged in any way, shape, or form.

Fortunately, all is not lost. Several excellent search services are available to help you locate information on the Internet. Although none of these services is truly comprehensive, several of them come pretty close. No matter what you're looking for, these services are likely to turn up a few Internet sites that pertain to your topic.

MSN has its own search service, known as MSN Search, which makes searching the Internet easier than ever. You can perform a simple search using MSN Search directly from the msn.com home page. Or, if you prefer, you can go to the MSN Search page to perform a more advanced search.

In addition to basic keyword searches, MSN Search provides a handful of other valuable search tools, including a White Pages feature that lets you look up your friends and relatives; a Yellow Pages feature that lets you look up businesses; and a Web Directory that lets you browse through a categorized list of Web sites.

Finding Stuff Fast

The easiest way to search the Internet for Web pages on a particular topic is to use the Search field that is included near the top of the msn.com home page. Just follow these steps:

1. **Type the word or phrase that you're looking for in the Search the Web For text box.**

   For example, type the word **arachnid** in the text box, as shown in Figure 4-1.

Figure 4-1: Searching the Internet.

2. **Click the Go button.**

   Your search request is submitted to the search service you selected.

3. **Whistle "Dixie."**

   You should be able to make it through the song at least once before the results of the search appear. Figure 4-2 shows how the MSN Search displays search results.

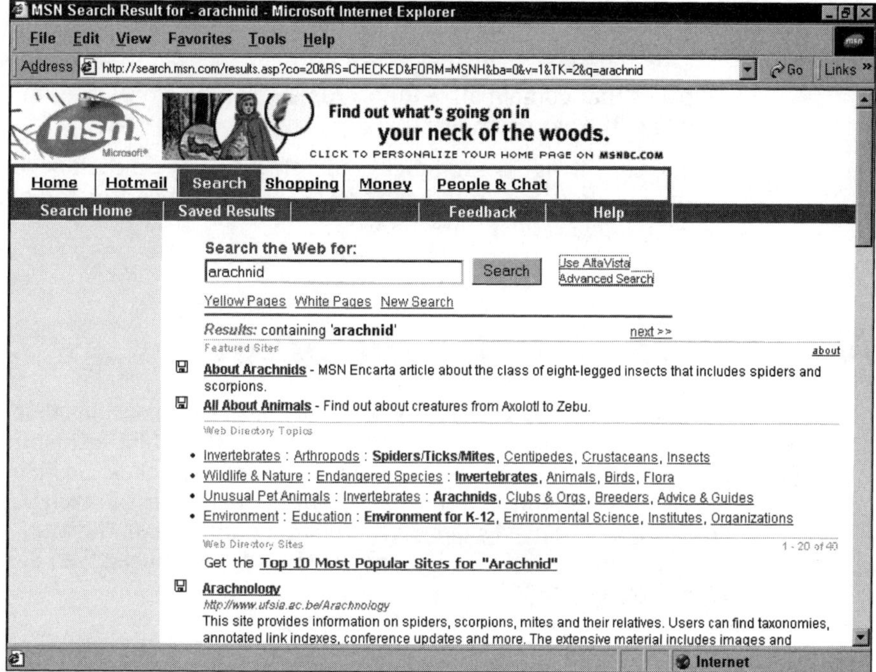

Figure 4-2: Eureka!

4. **If you find something that looks promising, click it.**

   You are taken directly to the Web page you selected (assuming the hyperlink isn't broken, of course, which is all too often the case).

5. **If nothing looks promising, click the hyperlink for the next set of entries.**

   MSN Search displays only 20 *hits* (found Web pages) at a time. If none of the hits shown look promising, scroll to the top or bottom of the page and locate the next >> hyperlink. Clicking this link displays the next set of 20 hits for the search.

Here are some thoughts to keep in mind when searching:

- If the search comes up empty, try again using a different search word or phrase. For example, try *spider* instead of *arachnid.*
- When picking search words, try to think of words that are specific enough that you don't end up with thousands of hits, but make sure they're general enough to encompass the topic you're trying to find.

- MSN Search, like most search services, sorts the results of your search so that the pages that most closely match your search criteria are presented first. In particular, if you search with more than one word, the pages that contain all of the words are listed before pages in which just one of the words appears.
- You can change the number of hits that display on each page by using the Results/Page drop-down box that appears near the top of the MSN Search page (see Figure 4-3.)

Narrowing Down Your Search

MSN Search lets you specify several advanced search options that you can use to narrow down your search in the hopes of pinpointing just the Web sites you're interested in. To use these advanced settings, click the MSN Search tab near the top of the MSN Home page to bring up the MSN Search page. Then, click the use advanced search hyperlink that appears on the MSN Search page near the Search button. This brings up the MSN Advanced Web Search page, as shown in Figure 4-3.

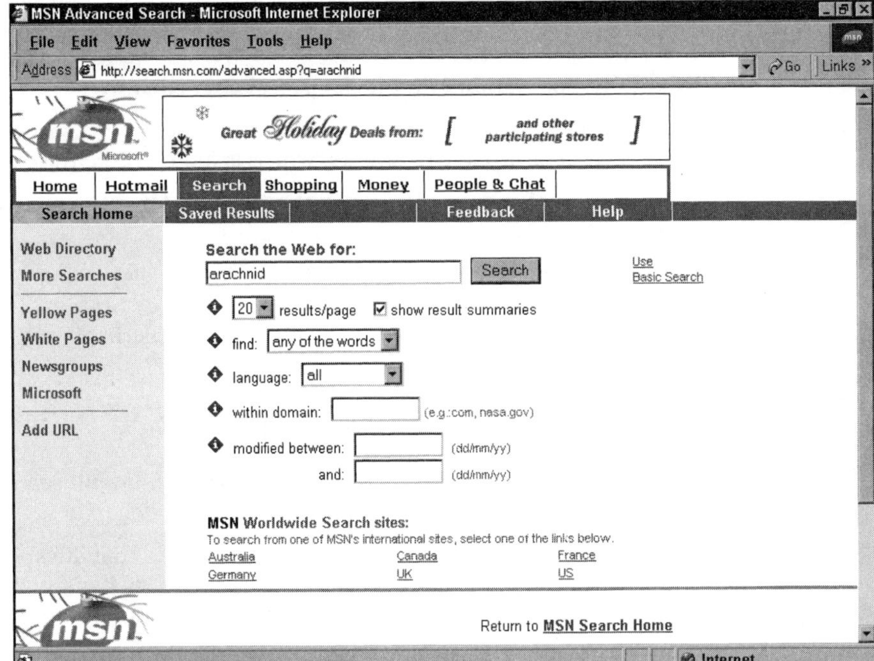

Figure 4-3: The MSN Advanced Web Search page.

The following paragraphs describe each of the search options that are available from the MSN Advanced Web Search page.

- **Results/Page:** Specifies how many hits to include on each results page. The default is 20. The Show Result Summaries check box lets you show or hide a short description of each Web site that matches the search criteria.
- **Find:** Governs how MSN Search uses the word or words you type in the search text field. The options are:
  - **All the words:** Finds pages that include all of the words that you type in the search text. Each page will include at least one occurrence of each word you type in the search text field.
  - **Any of the words:** Finds pages that include any of the words you type in the search text. Each page will include at least one of the words.
  - **Words in title:** Finds pages that include the search words in the Web page title rather than in the body of the Web page.
  - **The exact phrase:** Treats the search text as a phrase rather than as separate words. For example, an exact phrase search for Apollo 13 will find only pages that contain the word "Apollo" followed by "13" with no other words between.

You can also search for an exact phrase by enclosing the phrase in quotation marks. For example, type Apollo 13 (with the quotation marks) to search for the phrase Apollo 13 rather than the separate words "Apollo" and "13."

  - **Boolean phrase:** Lets you use the words AND, OR, and NOT to refine your search. For example, you can search for "planet AND Jupiter" to search for pages that contain both the words planet and Jupiter. To find pages about planets other than Jupiter, you could search for "planet NOT Jupiter."
  - **Links to URL:** Searches for pages that contain hyperlinks to the Internet address you type in the search field. For example, you could search for all sites that contain hyperlinks to `http://www.dummies.com`. You must type the complete URL, including the `http://` prefix, for this to work.
- **Language:** Limits your search to only those Web pages that are written in the language you specify. If your search turns up a bunch of sites written in languages you don't understand, use this option to narrow your search to Web sites you'll be able to read.

- **Within domain:** Limits your Web page search to specific Internet domains. To limit your search to certain types of organizations, use one of the following domains:

`com`	Commercial organizations
`edu`	Educational institutions
`gov`	Government agencies
`net`	Networks
`org`	Organizations (usually non-profit)

  You can also type a more specific domain, such as `microsoft.com`.

- **Modified between:** Searches for recently changed Web pages. The options are: anytime, in the past week, in the past month, or in the past year.

Saving Search Results

MSN Search includes a feature called Saved Results that makes it easier to keep track of promising search results. The Saved Results feature lets you save one or more of the Web sites found by a search so you can go investigate them later. You can then perform other related searches, saving the most promising results from each search. When you are finished, you can go to the Saved Results page to see all the Web sites that you have saved. The Saved Results feature works only with Internet Explorer 5.

To save a search result, just click the floppy disk icon that appears next to the Web site on the results page. To view your saved results, click the Saved Results hyperlink that appears in the navigation bar near the top of any MSN Search page. This takes you to the Saved Results page, as shown in Figure 4-4. The Saved Results page lists the Web sites that you saved for each search.

If you want to delete one or more items on the Saved Results page, first click the check box next to the items you want to delete to select the items. Then, click one of the Delete buttons that appear at the top and bottom of the Saved Results page. The items you selected are deleted.

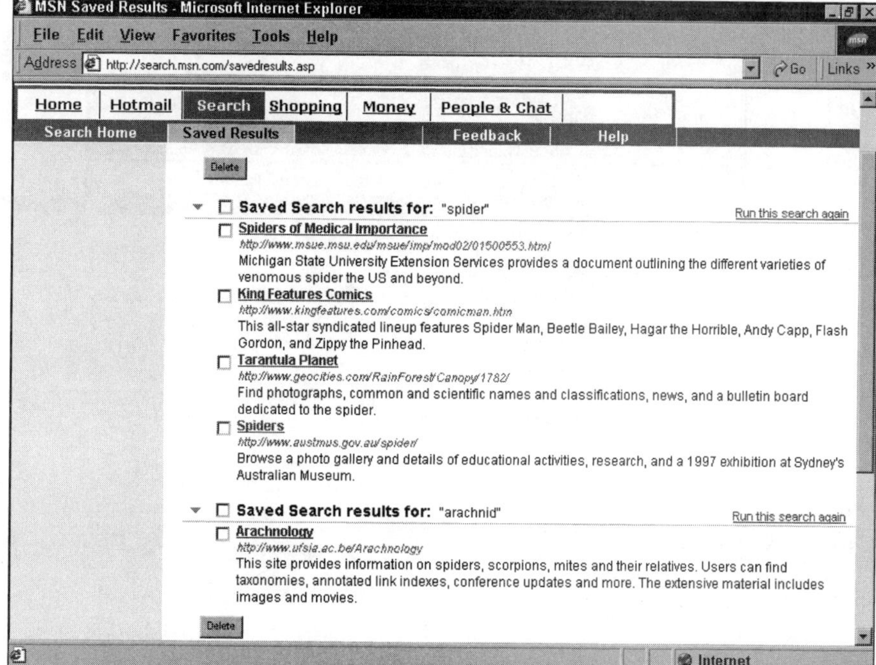

Figure 4-4: Using the Saved Results page.

Using Other Search Services

If MSN Search doesn't help you find the information that you're looking for, you can try one of 22 other search services that MSN is linked to. To use one of these alternative search services, follow these steps:

1. **Click the More Searches option found on the left side of the MSN Search Page.**

   The More Searches page appears, as shown in Figure 4-5.

2. **Choose the search service that you want to use.**

   Four major search services — AltaVista, GoTo, Infoseek, and Lycos — are listed across the top of the More Searches page. Plus, 18 additional services are listed near the bottom of the page.

   The middle portion of the More Searches page shows the search options for the service you have selected. Each time you select a different search service, the middle portion of the More Searches page changes accordingly.

3. **Type the text that you want to search for in the search text field.**

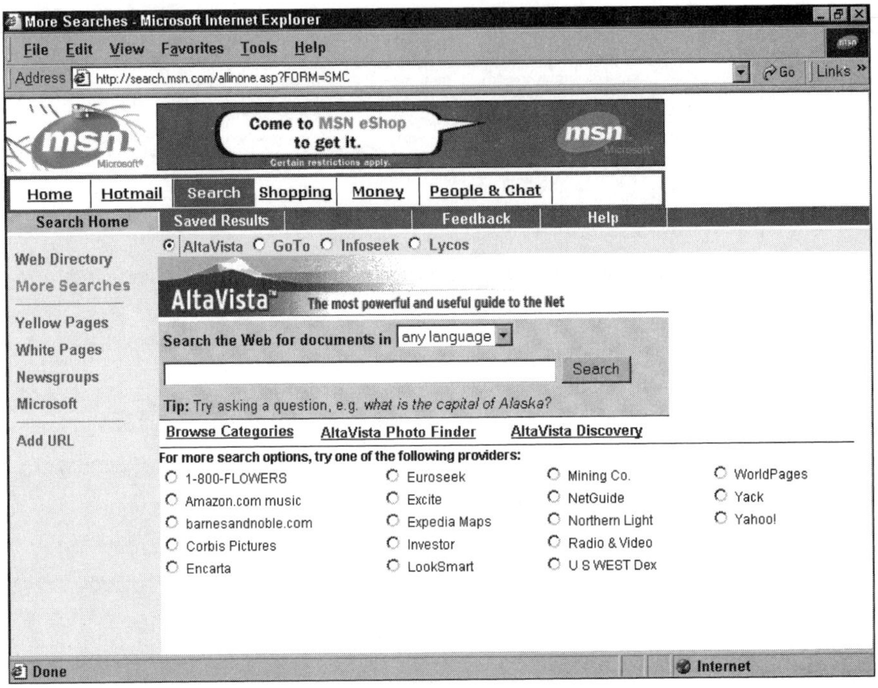

Figure 4-5: The More Searches page.

4. **Click the Search button.**

   For some search services, this button might have a different name. For example, Lycos calls this button *Go Get It!*

5. **Scan the results to find the page that you are looking for.**

   Or, if your search finds too many hits, refine your search by providing an additional keyword or two.

   When the search is complete, a results page displays. The exact appearance of the results page depends on which service you are using.

Finding Businesses with the Yellow Pages

Remember the episode of *M*A*S*H* where Hawkeye, sick of nothing but liver and fish in the mess tent, ordered ribs from his favorite rib house back in Chicago? Much of the episode was spent watching Hawkeye try to remember the name of the restaurant, figuring out how to contact it by phone, and scheming to get a big batch of spare ribs and sauce delivered to Korea. If only Hawkeye had access to MSN's Yellow Pages! He could have just looked up Adam's Ribs online.

MSN's Yellow Pages feature is an index of thousands of businesses in the United States. You can search for businesses by name, category of business, or city. If you only know part of the name, that's okay: Yellow Pages can find the business you're looking for. To search for a business by using MSN's Yellow Pages, follow these steps:

1. **On the MSN Home Page or the MSN Search Page, click the Yellow Pages hyperlink.**

   The Yellow Pages page appears, as shown in Figure 4-6.

2. **Type the name of the business that you are looking for in the text box.**

   If you don't remember the full name, just type as much of it as you can remember. For example, if you don't remember the name of the rib house but you know it has "Ribs" in it, just type **ribs**.

   You can also type a category rather than a business name. For example, **restaurant** or **auto repair**.

3. **Select the location.**

   You can type a city and state, or you can choose one of the other options, including Near You, Online Merchants, or Neighborhood. The more information you provide, the more likely the Yellow Pages can find the business you're looking for.

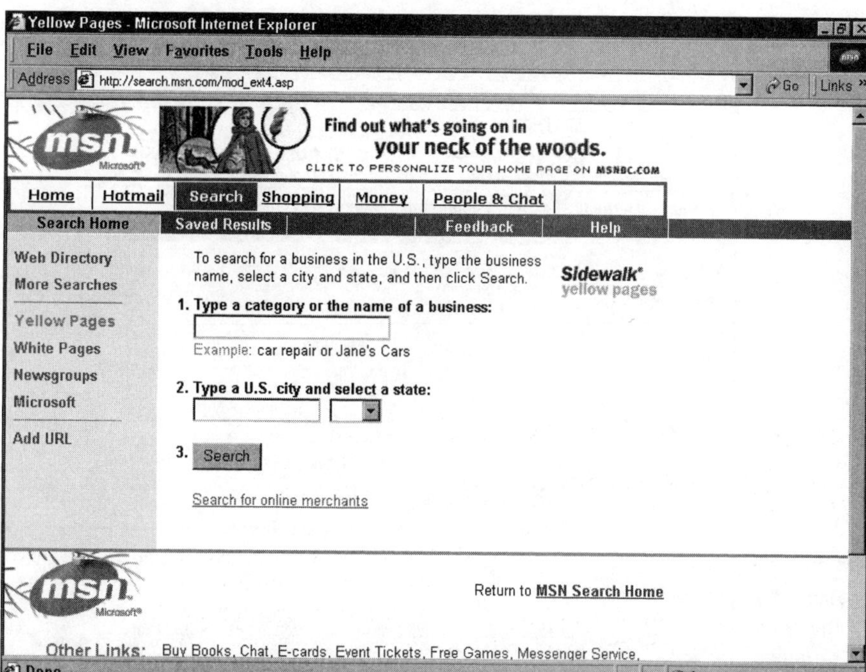

Figure 4-6: The Yellow Pages.

4. **Click the Go button.**

   After thinking for a moment, the Yellow Pages displays the results of your search.

5. **Scan the results page to find the business that you are looking for.**

   If the business you are looking for doesn't appear on the list, try refining your search by using additional or different keywords.

Finding People in the White Pages

MSN's White Pages lets you look up residential addresses, phone numbers, and e-mail addresses for millions of people living in the United States, Canada, and parts of Europe. You can access the White Pages by clicking the White Pages hyperlink on the msn.com home page or on the MSN Search page.

Figure 4-7 shows the MSN White Pages page. To search for someone, type in as much information as you know: first and last name, city, state, and country. Then, click Search. MSN will display a list of matches. If the person you are looking for does not appear on the list, try broadening your search by omitting the city, state, or first name.

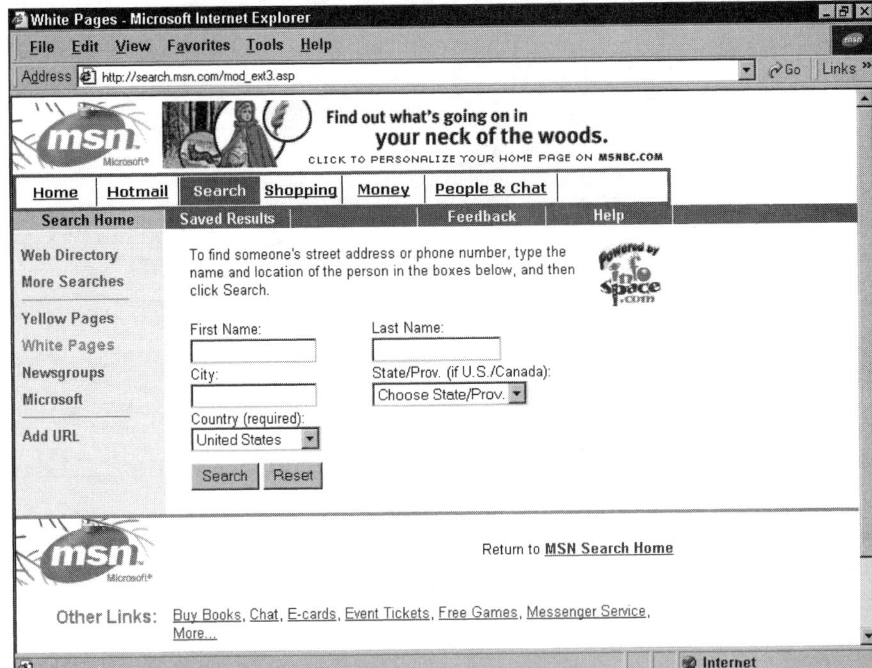

Figure 4-7: The White Pages.

Locating a Newsgroup

The Internet's Usenet newsgroups are great places to gather with other people who share similar interests. However, with about 45,000 newsgroups to choose from, how can you possibly find one that discusses a topic you are interested in? The answer is by searching for newsgroup messages by using MSN Search's link to `Deja.com`, a comprehensive index of newsgroup articles. (Deja.com used to be known as Deja News.)

Follow these steps to search for newsgroup messages:

1. **From the MSN Home page, click the Search tab.**

   This calls up the MSN Search page.

2. **Click the Newsgroups hyperlink at the left on the MSN Search page.**

   The Newsgroups page appears, as shown in Figure 4-8.

3. **Type one or more keywords into the text box and then click Search.**

   If you wish, you can limit your search to specific newsgroups by typing the name of the newsgroup in the Forum text box, or you can search for messages from specific Internet users by typing an e-mail address into the Author field.

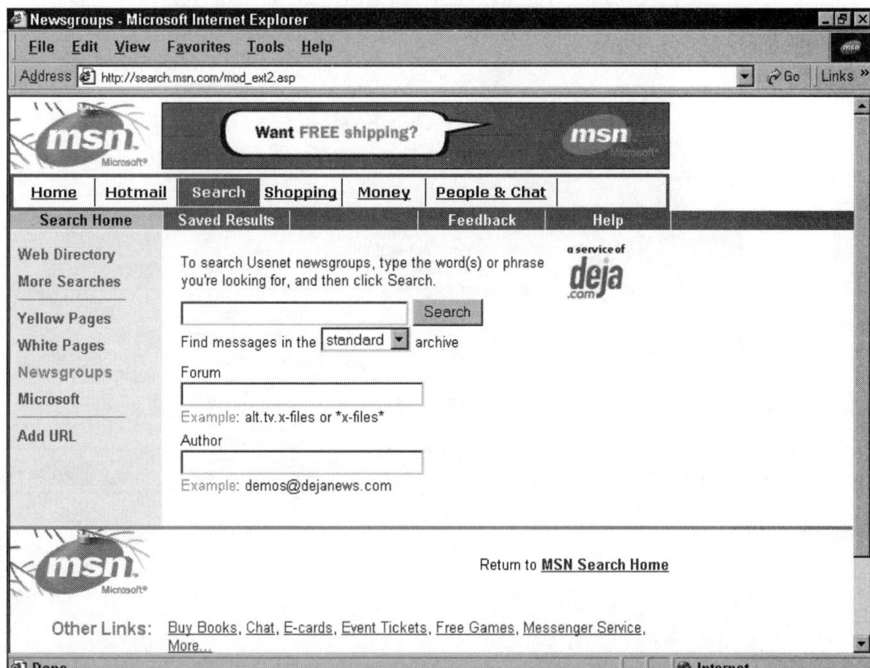

Figure 4-8: Searching for newsgroup messages.

Searching Microsoft

Microsoft's own Web site, www.microsoft.com, is one of the largest Web sites on the Internet. At Microsoft's Web site, you can get up-to-date information about Microsoft products, technical support, free programs, and other goodies you can download. One of the best features of Microsoft's Web site is a huge database of answers to technical questions called the Knowledge Base. If you are having a problem with any Microsoft product, odds are good you can find help in the Knowledge Base.

There is so much information at www.microsoft.com that MSN Search has a special page dedicated to searching it. To access the Microsoft Search page (shown in Figure 4-9), just click the Microsoft hyperlink on the MSN Search page. Then, type one or more keywords that you want to search for, choose a search category (such as Product Information or Support & the Knowledge Base), and click Search.

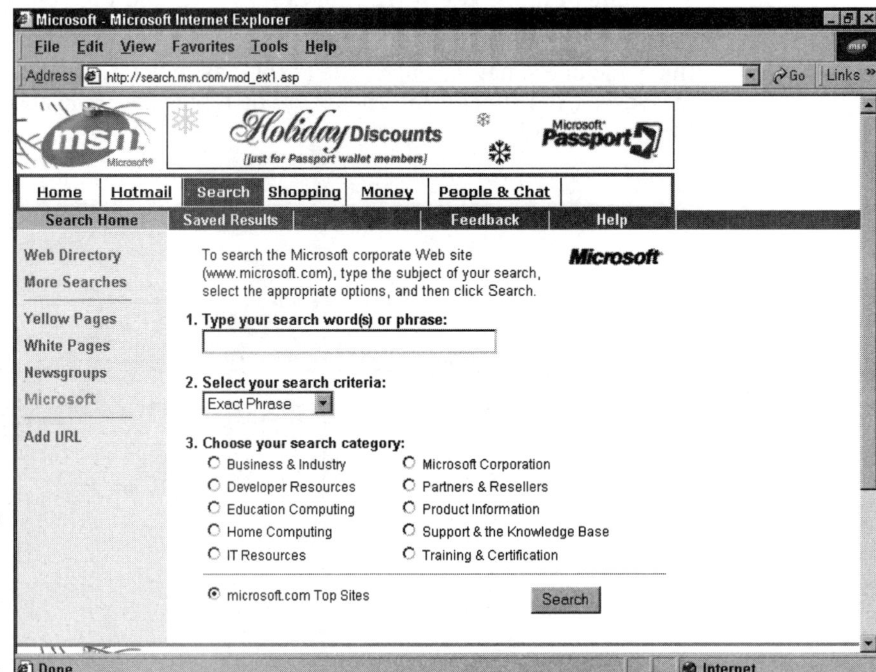

Figure 4-9: Searching Microsoft's Web site.

Exploring the Special Search Features of IE5

Internet Explorer 5 has a few built-in search tricks of its own that you should know about. The most useful of these tricks is the Search bar, a special window pane devoted to searching which appears on the left of the Internet Explorer 5 window. This search bar lets you keep the results of a search visible as you explore the Web sites that were found by the search.

To activate the Search bar, click the Search button on the Internet Explorer 5 Standard toolbar (located just below the menu bar at the top of the window). Type the keyword or words that you want to search for, select the search service you want to use, then click Search. As Figure 4-10 shows, the Search bar lets you display search results and simultaneously view the pages found by the search.

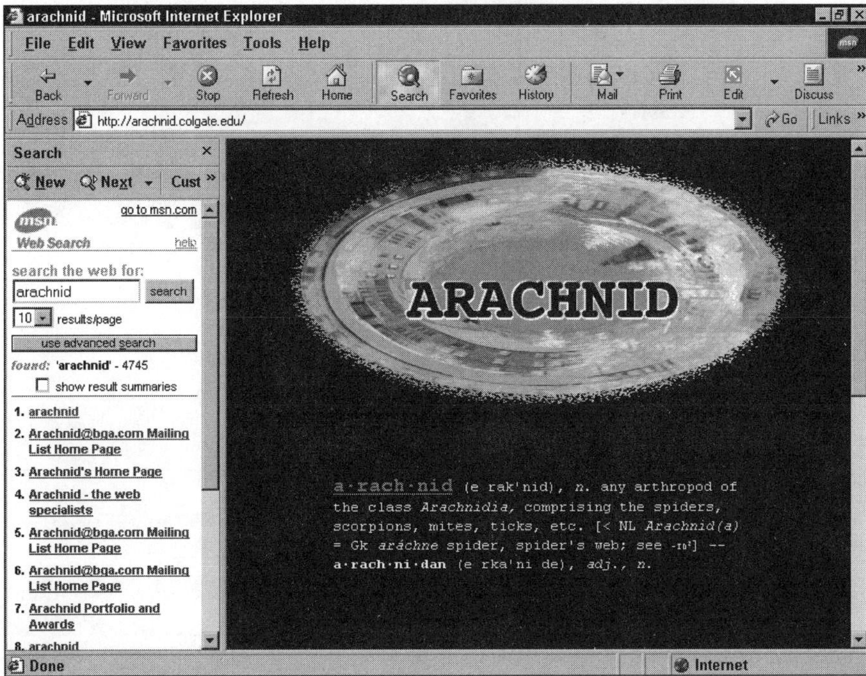

Figure 4-10: Using the Search bar.

Another nifty Internet Explorer 5 feature is called *Autosearch*. Autosearch is a way to quickly search the Internet without even going to a search service. Simply type the word **Find, Go,** or a question mark (**?**) in the Address box, followed by the word or words you want to look up. For example, to search for *arachnid*, type **find arachnid, go arachnid,** or **? arachnid** in the Address box and press the Enter key.

As Figure 4-11 shows, Internet Explorer picks a search service to look up the word or phrase that you typed and displays the results in the Search bar. Then, Autosearch attempts to find a Web address that contains the search text you typed. In this case, Autosearch found a Web site that contains the word *arachnid* in its URL (`www.arachnid.org`).

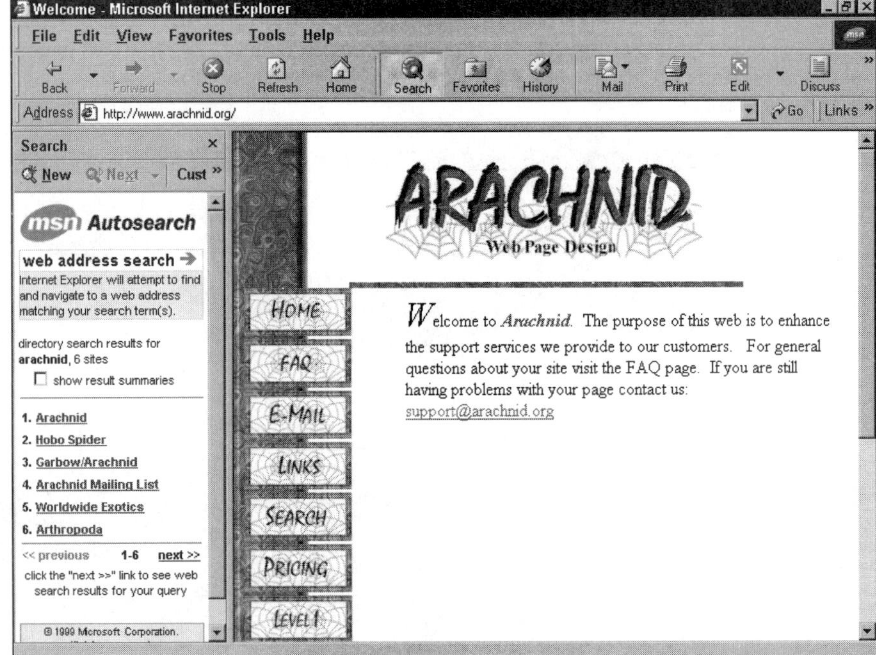

Figure 4-11: Autosearch is a quick way to search for Web sites.

Chapter 5

Personalizing Your MSN Home Page

In This Chapter

- Reviewing options for personalizing your MSN home page
- Troubleshooting when your personalized page doesn't work

One of the great things about the MSN home page is that you can customize it to include information that you're interested in seeing every time you access the Internet. For example, you can add or delete sports scores, daily news, weather reports, and hyperlinks to your favorite Internet locations, as well as other useful information. This chapter shows you how to customize the MSN home page to include just the information you want to see.

Perusing the Clips

Microsoft designed the MSN home page to be the ideal jumping-off point to other information on the Internet. The MSN home page is filled with links to other useful MSN pages such as Hotmail, Web Communities, MoneyCentral, and so on, as well as a search box that lets you find Web pages on any subject imaginable.

However, the MSN home page is more than a search service and a collection of links: MSN also has snippets of useful information such as the major news headlines of the day, updates about new MSN features, and current stock quotes. Microsoft refers to these snippets as *clips*.

Clips are what enable you to create your own customized MSN home page. The generic MSN home page — the one you see by default when you visit MSN — has just two clips on it: News and Personal Finance. However, you can create your own customized version of the MSN home page by adding additional clips of your own choosing.

In all, you have about 90 clips to choose from when creating your own personalized MSN home page. The clips you can choose from are organized in the following categories:

- **Business & Careers:** For the latest business news from the likes of *Forbes* and *The Wall Street Journal.*
- **Computing & Web:** Get the latest technology news from sources such as *Computing Central, Microsoft TechNet, Wired,* and more.
- **Daily Diversions:** Fun things to include on your page, such as a quote of the day and a daily horoscope.
- **Entertainment:** For the latest entertainment news and gossip, you can include MSNBC Entertainment, MTV, and other entertainment features.
- **Games:** For those who enjoy online games, you can include the MSN Gaming Zone.
- **Health:** For health information, include MSNBC Health, the Mayo Clinic, and *Prevention's* Healthy Ideas.
- **Home & Family:** Include information for home and family from sources such as MSN HomeAdvisor, Disney's Family.com, and Parent Soup.
- **Local News & Weather:** If you provide your zip code, your home page can include local information such as a local weather forecast and local news headlines. You can also include the CitySearch City Guide for your favorite city.
- **News:** You can display news headlines from online news services such as MSNBC, CBS, CNN, Fox News, and more.
- **People & Chat:** Display information about upcoming chat events from various MSN Communities and other Web sites.
- **Personal Finance:** Display quotes for specific stocks or stock indexes, as well as financial information from the likes of Charles Schwab, *Forbes,* and Merrill Lynch.
- **Radio & Video:** Listen to the radio or watch TV from your computer using sites such as `broadcast.com` or CBS Events.
- **Reference:** Get the information you need from reference sources such as the Discovery Channel and Merriam-Webster.
- **Shopping:** Keep tabs on daily specials from MSN's online merchants.
- **Sports:** You can get sports news from sources such as MSNBC Sports, CBS Sportsline, and Fox Sports, and include the latest scores for several popular sports (including baseball, football, hockey, and basketball) right on your MSN home page.
- **Travel:** Include travel information from Expedia.
- **Your links:** This section allows you to add up to four hyperlinks of your own to your home page.

Customizing Your Home Page

Now that you know what clips are available, you're ready to create your own customized MSN home page to add the information you're interested in. To do so, follow these steps:

1. **Go to the MSN home page.**
2. **Click Change Content in the navigation bar.**

   The page illustrated in Figure 5-1 appears. You can do your home page customization from this page.

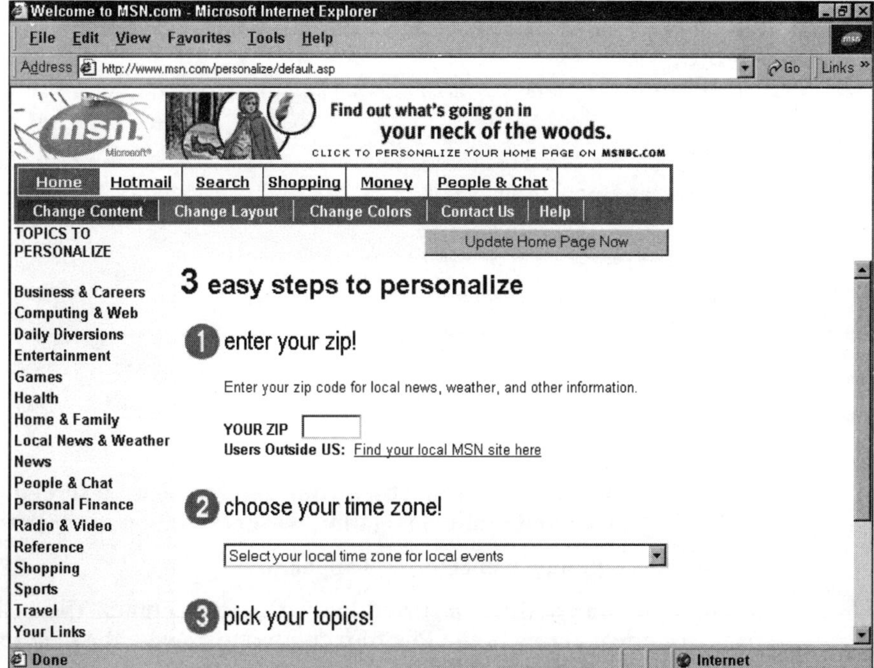

Figure 5-1: Personalizing your home page.

3. **Type your zip code in the Zip Code text box and select your time zone from the drop-down list.**

   This enables MSN to display local information such as movie times and weather forecasts on your home page.

4. **To add a clip to your home page, click one of the categories that appears on the left side of the page; then click the checkbox for the clip that you want to include.**

When you select a category, one or more clip items is displayed. For example, Figure 5-2 shows the clips that are available under the Business & Careers category. To add one or more of these clips to your MSN home page, just click the appropriate checkboxes.

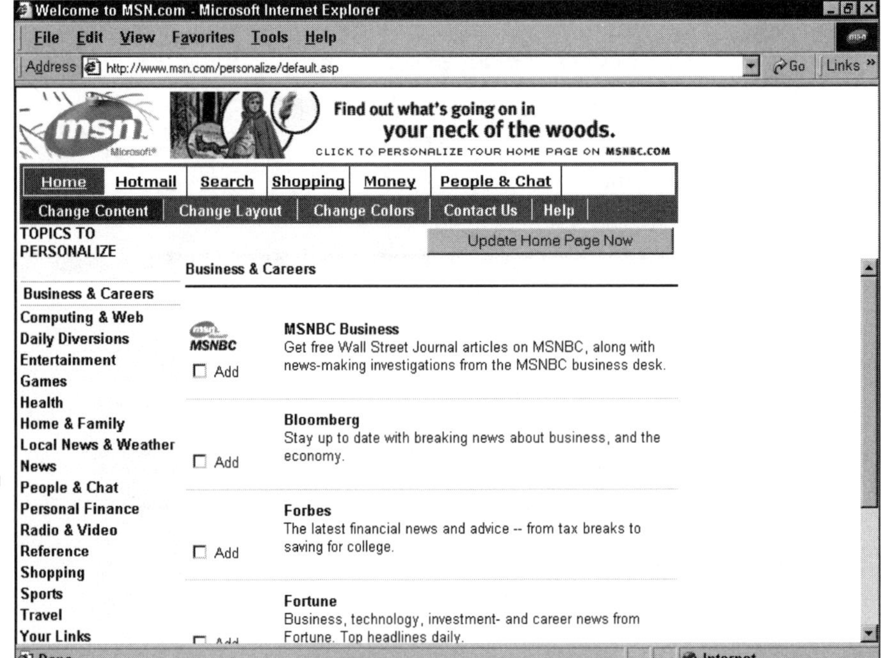

Figure 5-2: Add cool things to your MSN home page.

5. **To change the order in which your items appear on screen, click Change Layout in the navigation bar near the top of the screen.**

   The page shown in Figure 5-3 appears.

6. **Select one of the clips listed in the Content column. Then click the up or down arrow in the Position column to change the position of the clip on your home page.**

7. **When you are finished making changes, click the Update Home Page Now button.**

   Your custom MSN home page is built for you with the features you selected.

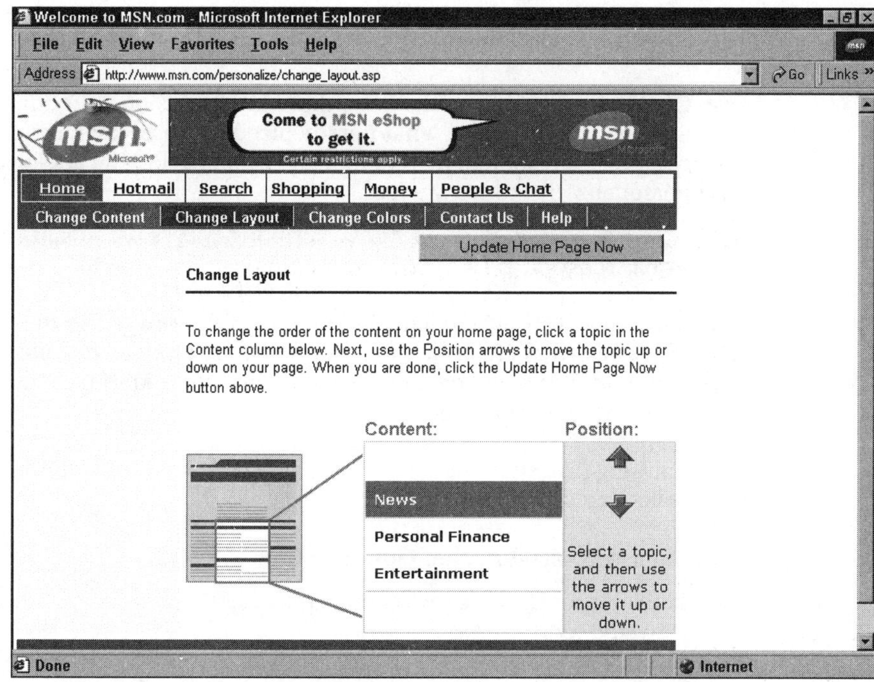

Figure 5-3: Changing the layout of clips on your MSN home page.

Here are a couple of points to ponder while you lay awake at night wondering about customizing your MSN home page:

- When you customize your MSN home page, the clips you select will be displayed only when you view the customized home page from the same computer that you used to customize the page. If you visit the home page from someone else's computer, your personal settings are not in effect.

- Another way to customize the MSN home page is to scroll through it to a section that you want to customize and then click the Edit button that appears in the heading for that section. This takes you directly to the part of the Personalize page that allows you to customize that section.

Help! I Can't Personalize MSN!

Sometimes, the personalization settings you make don't appear when you redisplay your home page. Or, an error message appears when you attempt to display your personalized home page. Arghh!

For personalized settings to work, two settings must be enabled in your Web browser:

- **Cookies.** A cookie is a small file that MSN leaves on your computer to enable it to remember what personalized settings you have chosen. If cookies are disabled, MSN is blocked from leaving the cookie and your personalized settings are lost.
- **Active scripting.** Without Active scripting, MSN's personalization settings won't work.

Normally, these settings are enabled in your Web browser, so the personalized MSN page works fine. But if you or someone else has disabled either of these options, you won't be able to personalize your MSN page until you enable cookies and scripting.

The following procedure describes how to enable cookies and Active scripting in Internet Explorer 5:

1. **Choose Tools⇨Internet Options.**

   The Internet Options dialog box appears.

2. **Click the Security tab.**

   The security options appear, as shown in Figure 5-4.

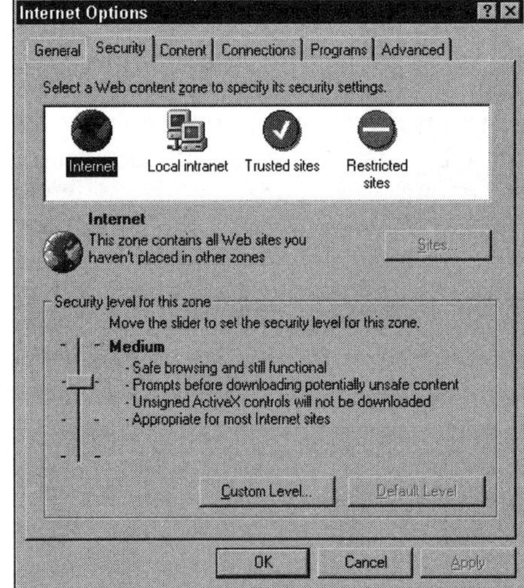

Figure 5-4: The Security tab of the Internet Options dialog box.

3. **Make sure the Internet icon is selected.**

   If the Internet icon is not selected when you bring up the Security tab, click the Internet icon to select it.

4. **Click the Custom Level button.**

   The Security Settings dialog box appears.

5. **Scroll through the Security Settings options until you find the cookies options.**

   Figure 5-5 shows the Cookie options.

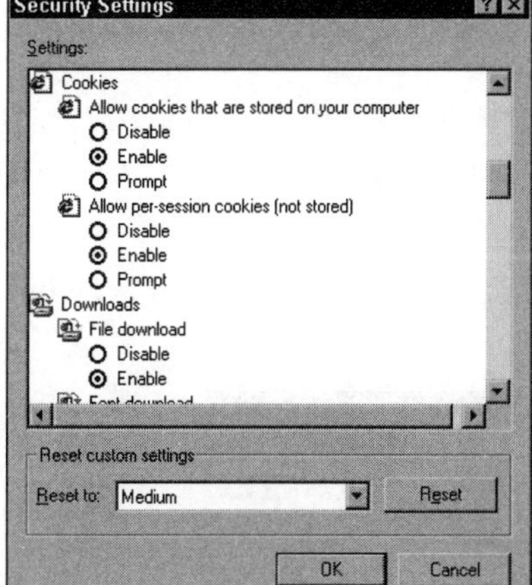

Figure 5-5: The Cookies options in the Security Settings dialog box.

6. **Choose Enable both the Allow Cookies That Are Stored on Your Computer and Allow Per-Session Cookies (not stored) options.**

7. **Scroll down farther to find the Scripting options.**

   Figure 5-6 shows the scripting options.

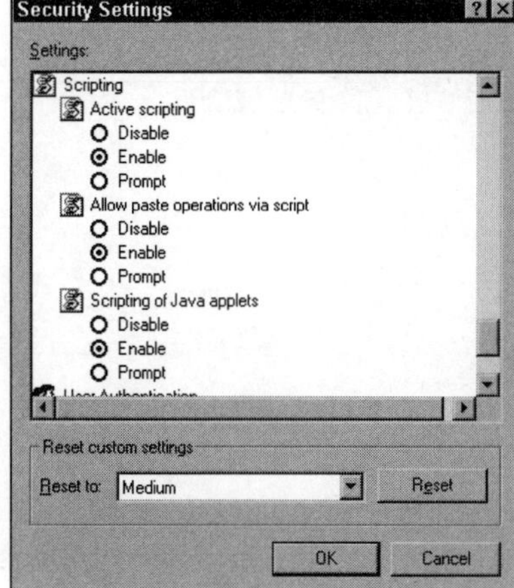

Figure 5-6: The Scripting options in the Security Settings dialog box.

8. **Select Enable for the Active Scripting option.**
9. **Click the OK button.**

   The Scripting Settings dialog box disappears, and the Internet Options dialog box returns.
10. **Click the OK button again.**

    The Internet Options dialog box disappears.

To enable these options in Netscape Navigator, follow these steps:

1. **Choose the Edit⇨Preferences command.**

   This summons the Preferences dialog box.
2. **Click the Advanced tab.**

   This brings up the Advanced preferences, as shown in Figure 5-7.

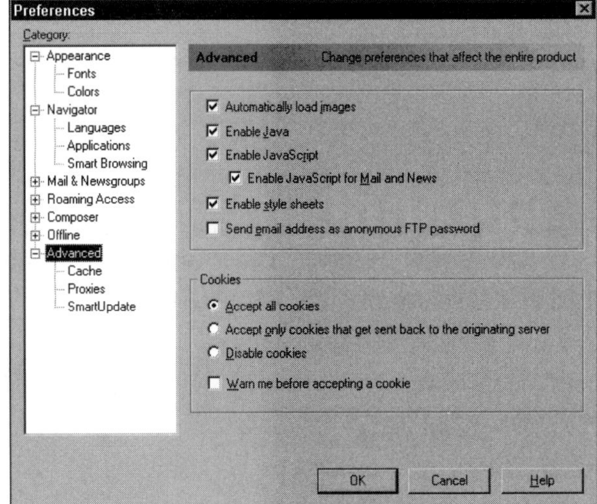

Figure 5-7: Allowing cookies and JavaScript in Netscape Navigator.

3. **Click Accept All Cookies.**
4. **Click Enable JavaScript.**
5. **Click the OK button.**

Once you enable these options, you should be able to personalize your MSN home page.

Part II

Reach Out and Electronically Touch Someone

"I think you're just jealous that I found a community of people on MSN.com that worship the yam as I do, and you haven't."

In this part . . .

Staying in touch is one of the main reasons most people sign up to use the Internet. And MSN makes staying in touch with your online friends easier than ever before. You can get a free e-mail account with Hotmail, visit one of MSN's many online Web communities, chat in MSN's chat rooms, exchange messages on MSN's newsgroups, and even talk to online friends by using MSN's Instant Messenger.

Chapter 6

Hotmail: E-Mail for Free!

In This Chapter

- Signing up for free Hotmail
- Reading your mail
- Sending e-mail messages

One of the most common reasons people dare to venture forth onto the Internet is to use electronic mail — *e-mail,* it's called — which lets you exchange messages with your Internet-connected friends and colleagues. E-mail is much faster than mail delivered by Mr. McFeeley, the bespectacled mailman on *Mr. Rogers' Neighborhood* ("Speedy Delivery!"), and far friendlier than Newman, the obnoxious mailman on *Seinfeld* ("Hello, *Jerry.*").

Sending an e-mail message is much like sending a letter through regular mail. In both cases, you write your message, put an address on it, and send it off through an established mail system. Eventually, the recipient of the message receives your note, reads it, and (if you're lucky) answers by sending a message back.

But e-mail offers certain advantages over regular mail. For example, e-mail arrives at its destination in a matter of seconds or minutes, not days. E-mail can be delivered any day of the week, including Sundays. And, as a special bonus, no way yet exists for your great-aunt to send you a fruitcake through e-mail.

About the only thing that keeps the post office in business anymore (other than transporting fruitcake) is that e-mail only works when both the sender and the receiver have computers that are connected to the Internet. In other words, you can't send e-mail to someone who isn't on the Internet.

This chapter shows you how to send and receive e-mail using Hotmail, MSN's popular e-mail service.

Understanding Hotmail

Most Internet service providers *(ISPs)* — including MSN Internet Access — set up an e-mail account for you when you sign up to use the Internet. Most of these e-mail accounts use version 3 of a standard Internet e-mail feature known as *Post Office Protocol*, or *POP3* for short. To access POP3 mail, you need a specialized e-mail program such as Microsoft Outlook or Outlook Express, Netscape Messenger, or Qualcomm's Eudora.

Some e-mail accounts use an alternative type of Internet e-mail protocol known as *IMAP*, which stands for *Internet Message Access Protocol*. Like POP3 accounts, IMAP accounts require that you use a special e-mail program to access your mail. (Note that most e-mail programs can handle both POP3 and IMAP accounts.)

Hotmail is a free e-mail service that does not require using a special e-mail program to access. Hotmail does not use POP3 or IMAP. Instead, Hotmail works through the World Wide Web, so you can access your Hotmail e-mail account using Web browser.

The best part about Hotmail is that it is free. Microsoft makes money from Hotmail by selling advertising for the Hotmail Web site — not by charging membership fees. Unfortunately, this means you have to put up with sometimes-obnoxious advertisements when you check your mail, but at least you don't have to pay for your Hotmail account.

Of course, you have to have an Internet account to access Hotmail, and most Internet accounts come with an e-mail account. If you already have an e-mail account, why would you bother with Hotmail? There are several reasons:

- Because Hotmail works with your Web browser rather than a special e-mail program, you don't have to worry about the complicated task of configuring an e-mail account. No more cryptic server addresses or port numbers to configure!
- You can access your Hotmail account from any computer that is connected to the Internet, provided the computer has a current version of Internet Explorer or Netscape Navigator. This is a great plus if you need to access your e-mail while travelling.
- With a POP3 or IMAP e-mail account, your e-mail address will change if you decide to switch to a different ISP. In contrast, Hotmail lets you set up a permanent e-mail address that won't change even if you decide to switch to a different ISP.
- If several members of your family use the Internet through a single ISP account, each person can create his or her own Hotmail e-mail account. Although some ISPs let you have more than one e-mail account, many give you only one, requiring all family members to share a common e-mail account.

- If you have an e-mail account at the company where you work, you can use Hotmail to set up a private e-mail account for personal mail. That way, you won't have to worry about your boss snooping through your personal e-mail.

- When you sign up for a Hotmail account, you are automatically registered in a service called *Microsoft Passport*. Microsoft Passport allows you to access a whole gaggle of MSN and other Internet services without having to create a separate user ID and password for each. For more information about Passport, see Chapter 3.

Signing Up for a Hotmail Account

Before you can use Hotmail, you must sign up for a Hotmail account. Fortunately, Hotmail accounts are free and the procedure for setting one up is pretty simple. Just follow these steps:

1. **Connect to the Internet and go to the MSN home page.**
2. **Click the Hotmail tab near the top of the page.**

   This brings up the Hotmail home page, as shown in Figure 6-1.

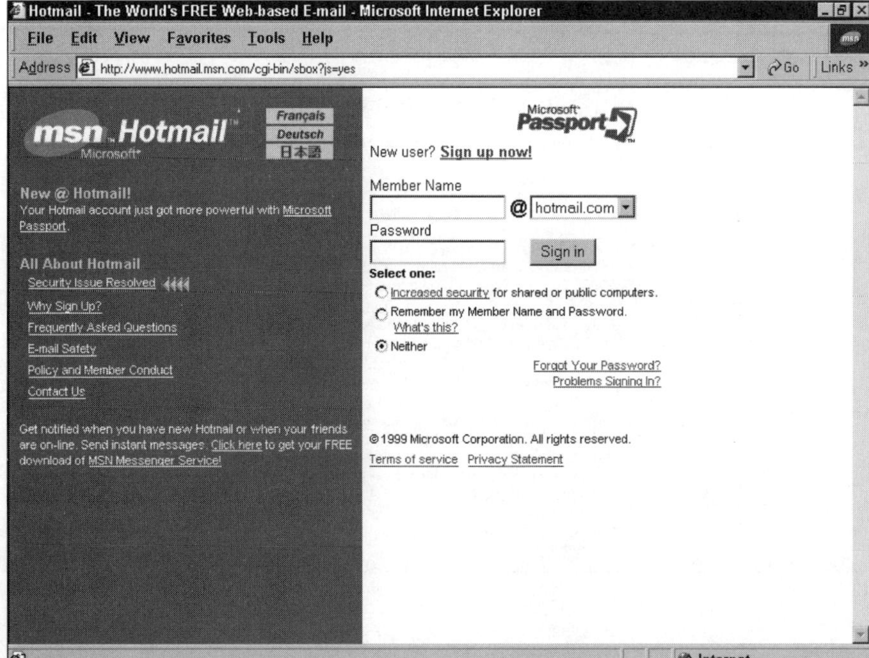

Figure 6-1: Welcome to Hotmail!

3. **Click the Sign up now! hyperlink.**

   This takes you to the MSN Hotmail Terms of Service page (see Figure 6-2), which explains in a mere 2,727 words composed by Microsoft's legal department the rules that you must follow if you want to use Hotmail.

   The rules say that you must behave yourself. For example, you can't send junk mail, chain letters, obscene material, or be otherwise obnoxious to other netizens.

4. **Scroll down to the bottom of the Terms of Service page and click the I Accept button. (Oh yeah, and read it, too!)**

   This takes you to the Hotmail Registration page, as shown in Figure 6-3.

5. **Fill in the identification information requested by the Hotmail Registration Page.**

   Hotmail wants to know your first and last names, the country, state, zip code, and time zone where you live, your gender, and the year you were born.

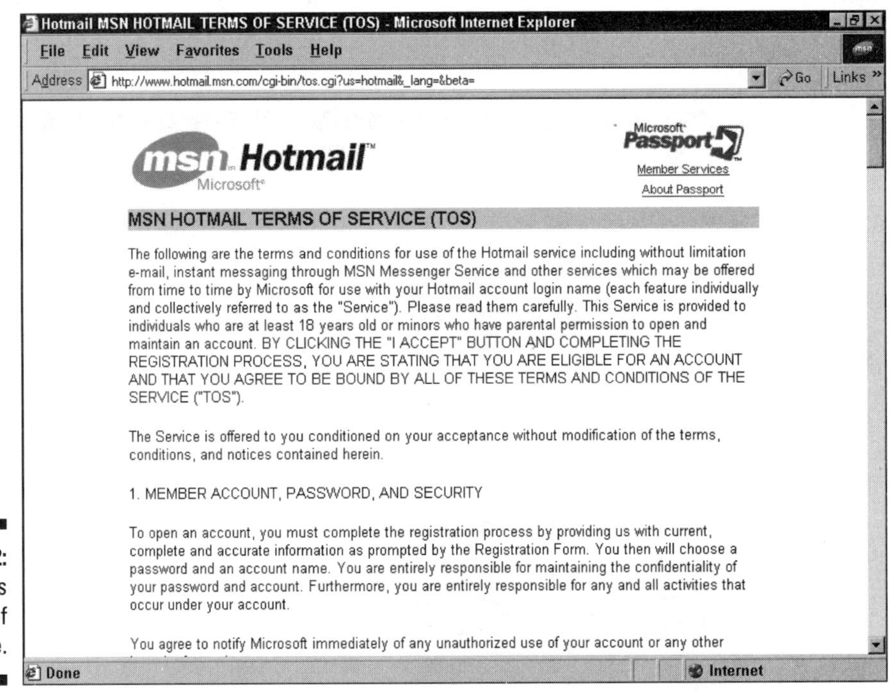

Figure 6-2: Hotmail's Terms of Service.

Figure 6-3: The Hotmail Registration page.

6. **Type the name that you want to use for your e-mail address in the Login name field.**

   Your login name is combined with `@hotmail.com` to form your complete e-mail address. For example, if your login name is George, your e-mail address would be `George@hotmail.com`.

   Don't fret too much over the login name at this point. Because Hotmail already has a few million users, odds are good that the name you want to use has already been taken. You'll see what to do in that case a few steps later in this procedure.

7. **Type the password that you want to use for your e-mail account twice: once in the Password field and again in the Re-enter Password field.**

   For security reasons, your password is not displayed on the screen as you type it. As a result, Hotmail asks you to type the password twice to make sure you didn't type it incorrectly.

8. **Type a secret question and the question's answer in the appropriate fields.**

   The secret question is used to verify your identity in case you forget your password.

Make sure the answer to your question is truly secret. Otherwise, anyone can break into your Hotmail account by answering the question. For example, don't use a question like "Who wrote the Monroe Doctrine?" or "Who's buried in Grant's Tomb?" Questions such as "What is my mother's maiden name?" and "What year did I graduate from High School" are also pretty easy to figure out.

9. **Click the Submit Registration button.**

   Because Hotmail registration is handled over a secure Internet connection, a Security Alert dialog box, shown in Figure 6-4, appears next. This dialog box simply informs you that you are about to engage in a secure connection, kind of like *Get Smart's* Max lowering the Cone of Silence. (Note that this dialog box may not appear if you have checked the In the Future, Do Not Show This Warning check box.)

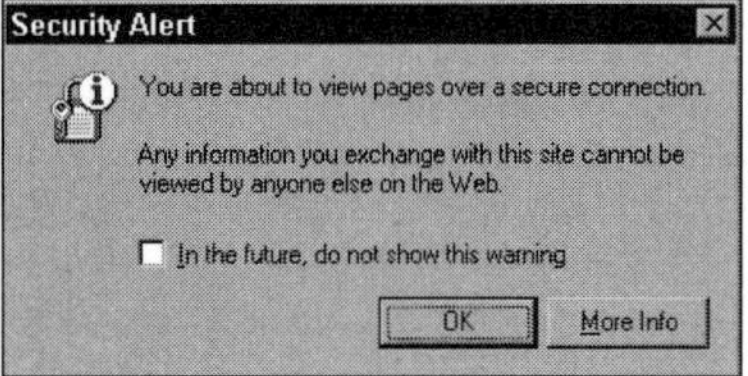

Figure 6-4: You are now entering a secure connection.

10. **Click the OK button.**

    Hotmail processes your registration information. When the information has been safely sent to Hotmail, the dialog box shown in Figure 6-5 appears to inform you that you are leaving the comfort of your secure connection.

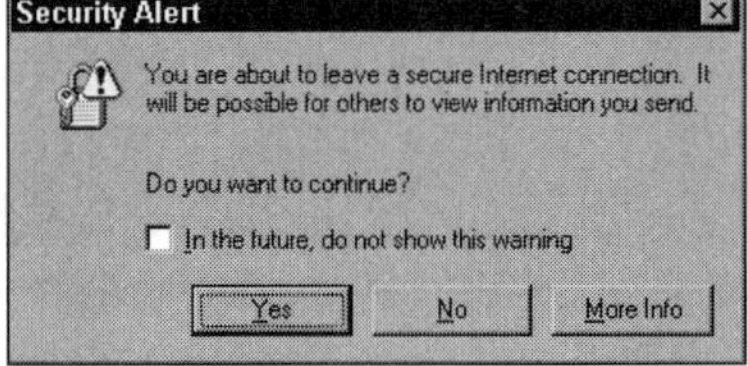

Figure 6-5: Leaving the secure connection.

11. **Click the OK button again.**

    Ninety-nine percent of the time, Hotmail next informs you that the Login name you chose has already been taken. For example, Figure 6-6 shows the screen I saw when I requested "Jetson" as my Login name. As you can see, Hotmail suggests a few alternatives to the name you requested.

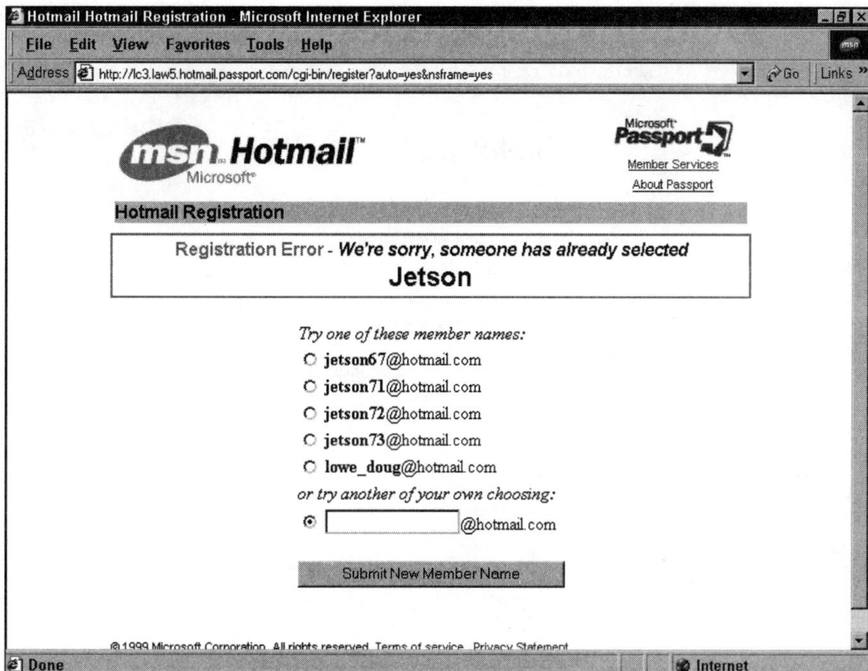

Figure 6-6: That name is already taken.

12. **Pick one of the alternatives suggested by Hotmail, or type a new login name in the text box.**

    If you type a new login name, you may again pick a name that is already in use. In other words, you may have to repeat this step several times before you get a name you like.

    Most of the good names are already taken. You can keep trying to get a cool name such as Mulder, Darth Maul, or Mini-Me. But trust me, the good names are already taken. You may as well just pick one of the alternatives suggested by Hotmail. If you want a cool name, you'll probably have to attach a number to the end of it, such as jetson67 or minime38.

13. **Click Submit New Login Name.**

    The Security Alert dialog box appears again to let you know that you are entering a secure connection.

14. **Click the OK button to continue.**

    If the new name you picked is also one that is already in use, return to Step 12.

    When you finally settle on a unique login name, you'll see a page similar to the one in Figure 6-7.

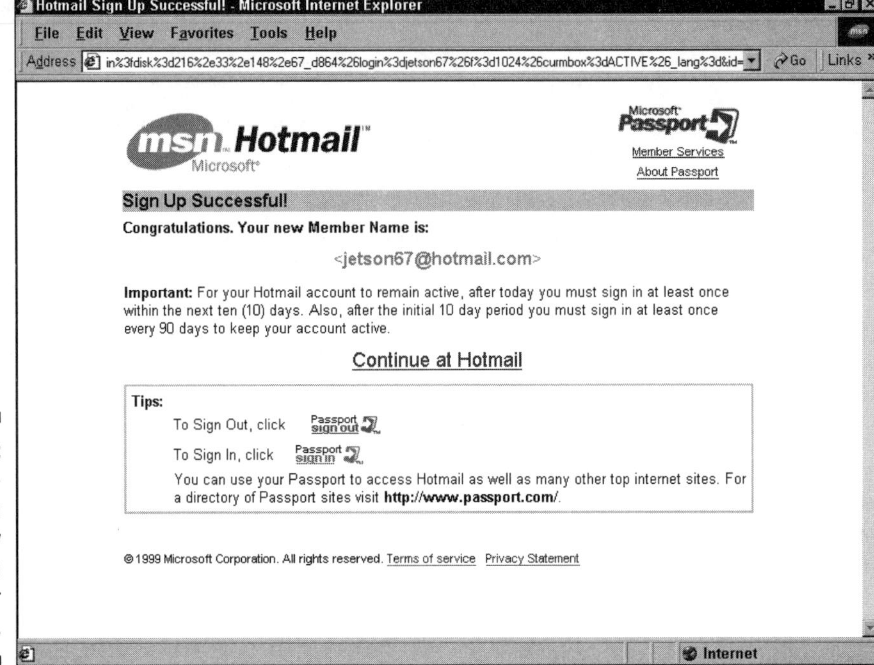

Figure 6-7: Congratulations, you have finally made a name for yourself.

15. **Click the Continue at Hotmail hyperlink to access your Hotmail account.**

    That's all there is to it. You are now an official Hotmail member.

The first time you access Hotmail, you will see a page of services you can subscribe to that automatically send you e-mail about topics you are interested in. Sign up for one or more of these services if any of the topics strike you as interesting.

Using Hotmail

If you created a Hotmail account, you can access it at any time to see if anyone has sent you mail or to compose an e-mail message to send to someone else. To access your Hotmail account, just follow these steps:

1. **From the MSN home page, click the Hotmail tab.**

   This takes you to the Hotmail home page, as shown back in Figure 6-1.

2. **Type your login name and password in the text fields.**
3. **Click the Enter button.**

   You are taken to the Hotmail Mailbox page, as shown in Figure 6-8.

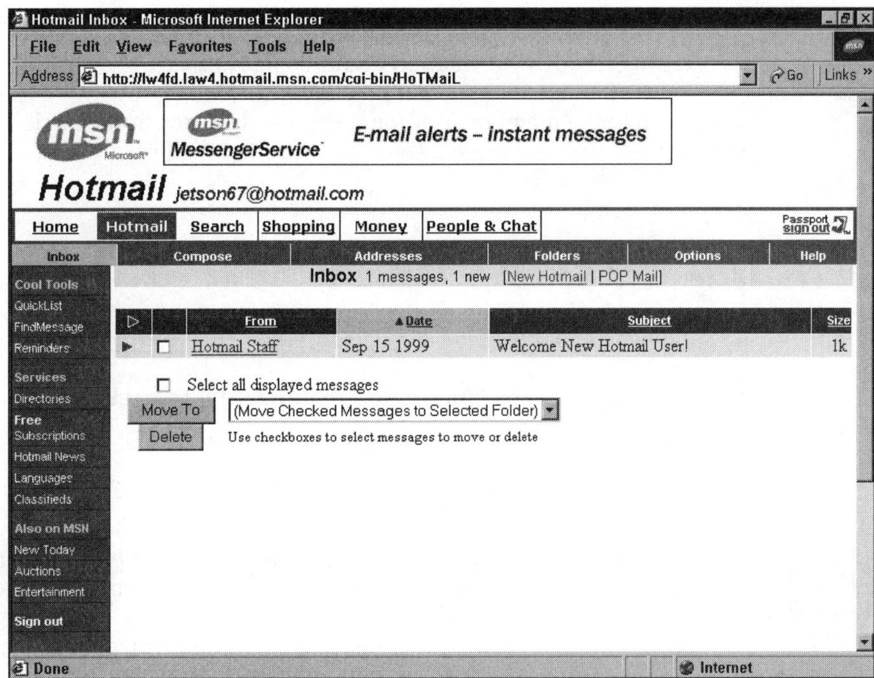

Figure 6-8: The Hotmail Mailbox.

Across the top of the Hotmail page is a horizontal menu that lets you access several basic Hotmail functions:

- **Inbox:** Lets you read mail that has been sent to you. Incoming messages are listed in the middle of the page.

  In Figure 6-8, you can see that I have received one message: a welcome message from the Hotmail staff. You too will receive this friendly welcome when you join Hotmail.

- **Compose:** Lets you create an e-mail message to send to someone else.
- **Addresses:** Lets you keep track of e-mail addresses of the people you frequently send mail to.
- **Folders:** Lets you organize your e-mail by storing messages in folders. Hotmail has several built-in folders:
  - **Inbox:** Holds incoming e-mail messages.
  - **Sent Messages:** Holds messages you have already sent.
  - **Drafts:** Holds drafts of messages until you're ready to send them.
  - **Trash Can:** Holds messages you have deleted.

  You can also create your own folders to help you organize messages you have received. For more information about using folders (including how to create your own folders), see Chapter 7.

- **Options:** Lets you set options that affect how Hotmail works.
- **Help:** Provides information about using Hotmail.

You'll also find a menu of additional Hotmail features down the left side of the page.

Sending E-Mail

To send e-mail, follow these steps:

1. **Click the Compose button in the horizontal menu bar.**

   The Compose page appears, as shown in Figure 6-9.

2. **Type the Internet address of the person to whom you want to send the message in the To: field.**

   You can send mail to more than one recipient by typing more than one name or address in the To: field by typing a semicolon between each name.

   For examples of different kinds of Internet addresses, check out the "Addressing your e-mail" sidebar in this chapter.

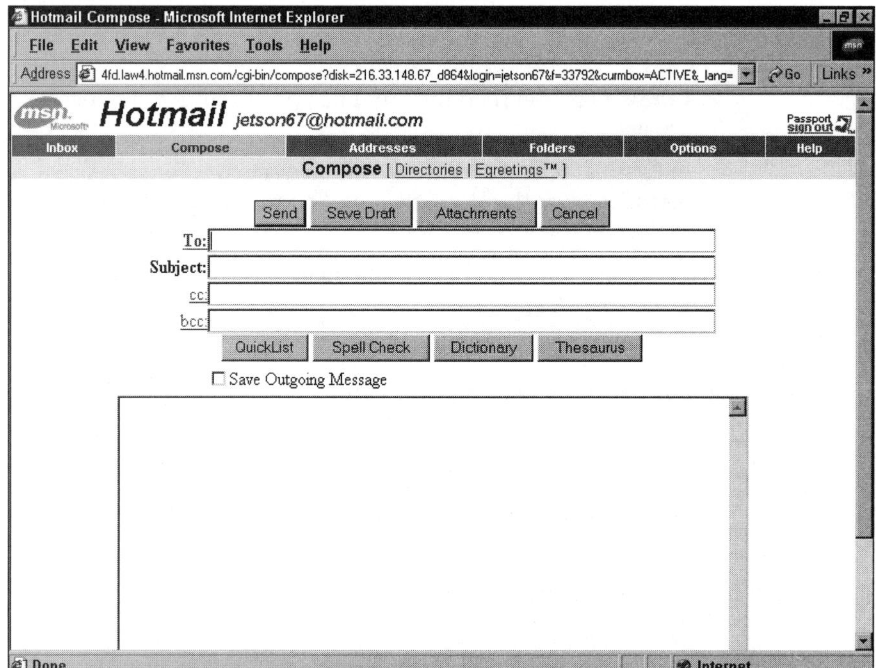

Figure 6-9: A new message.

If you frequently send e-mail to a particular person, you can add that person's e-mail address to your Address Book. Then you can easily retrieve that person's e-mail address from your Address Book whenever you send him or her a message without having to retype the entire address each time. For more information about using the Address Book, see Chapter 7.

3. **Type a succinct but clear title for the message in the Subject field.**

   For example, type **Let's Do Lunch** or **Jetson, You're Fired!**

4. **If you want to send a copy of the message to another user, type that person's address in the cc: field.**

   If you want to send a copy of a message to someone else but you don't want the other recipients to know about it, use the bcc: field instead of the cc: field. A copy of the message is sent to each person listed in the bcc: field, but the people listed in the To: and cc: fields aren't notified of the bcc: recipients. (However, the bcc: recipients *are* notified of who you listed in the To: and cc: fields.)

5. **Type your message in the message area.**

   Figure 6-10 shows what a message looks like with all this information typed in and ready to go.

6. **When you finish typing your message, click the Send button.**

   Hotmail sends your message and displays the page as shown in Figure 6-11.

7. **Click the OK button.**

Addressing your e-mail

Before you send e-mail, you need to know the e-mail address of the person for whom the message is intended (just like that pesky post office expects with paper mail). The easiest way to find out someone's e-mail address is simply to ask for it.

For Hotmail users, the e-mail address is the user's login name followed by `@hotmail.com`. For example, a typical Hotmail address would be `Jetson47@hotmail.com`.

For the major online services, compose the user's e-mail address as follows:

- For America Online users, type the username followed by `@aol.com`. For example, `Lurch@aol.com`.
- For CompuServe users, type the numeric user ID followed by `@compuserve.com`. Be sure to use a period rather than a comma to separate the two parts of the numeric user ID. For example: `12345.6789@compuserve.com`.

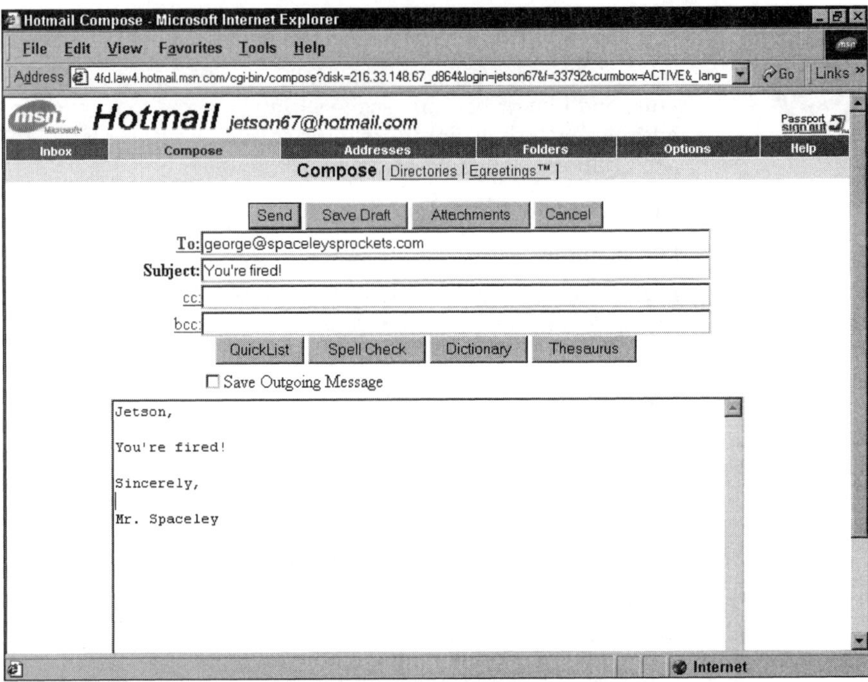

Figure 6-10: A message ready to be sent.

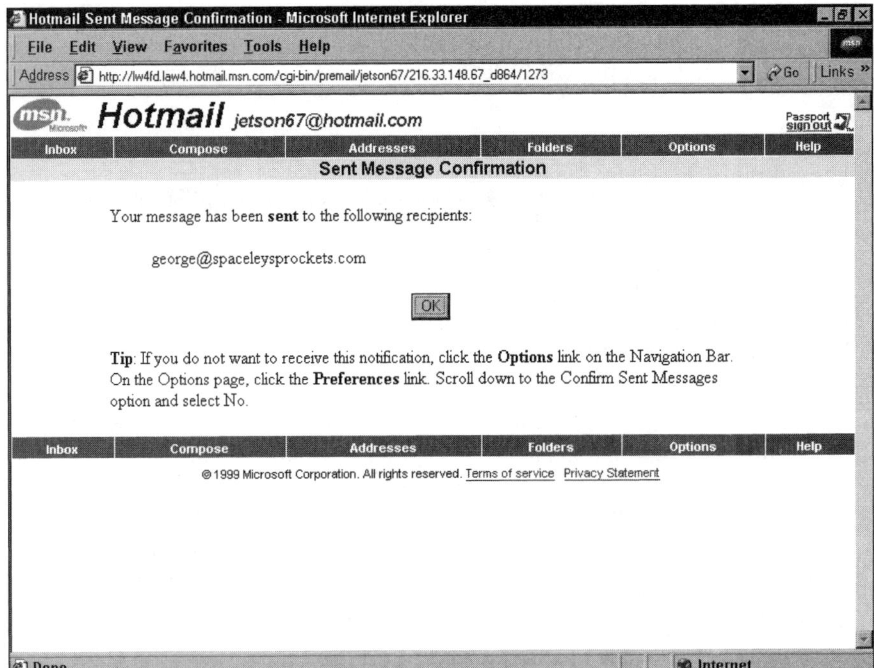

Figure 6-11: Congratulations! Your message has been sent.

If you have started composing an e-mail message but need to leave your computer before you are ready to send the message, click the Save Draft button. This saves a copy of the message in your Drafts folder but doesn't actually send the message. To work on the message later, click Folders in the horizontal menu bar, click Drafts in the folders list and then click the message's link in the list of messages that appears in your Drafts folder. You are returned to your Inbox.

Checking Your Message for Spelling Errors

Hotmail includes a built-in spell checker that is capable of catching those embarrassing spelling errors before they go out to the Internet. The spell checker checks the spelling of every word in your message, looking up the words in its massive dictionary. Any misspelling is brought to your attention, and the spell checker is under strict orders from Bill Gates himself not to giggle or snicker at any of your misspellings, even if you insist on putting an *e* at the end of *potato*. You even have the Add to Dictionary function so you can tell it that you are right and it is wrong — and that it should learn how to spell the way you do.

To spell check a message you are composing, follow these steps:

1. **Click the Check Spelling button after you have finished composing your message.**

   The spell checker comes to life, looking up your words in hopes of finding a mistake.

2. **Try not to be annoyed if the spell checker finds a spelling error.**

   Hey, you're the one who told it to look for spelling mistakes, so don't get mad if it finds some. When the spell checker finds an error, it displays the error along with suggested corrections, as shown in Figure 6-12.

3. **Choose the correct spelling and then click Change, or click Ignore to skip to the next word the spell checker doesn't recognize.**

   If you agree that the word is misspelled, scan the list of suggested corrections and click the one you like. Then click the Change button to change that occurrence of the word. To change all occurrences of the misspelled word in your message, click Change All instead.

   If, on the other hand, you prefer your own spelling, click Ignore. To prevent the spell checker from asking you over and over again about a particular word that it doesn't recognize (such as someone's name), click Ignore All.

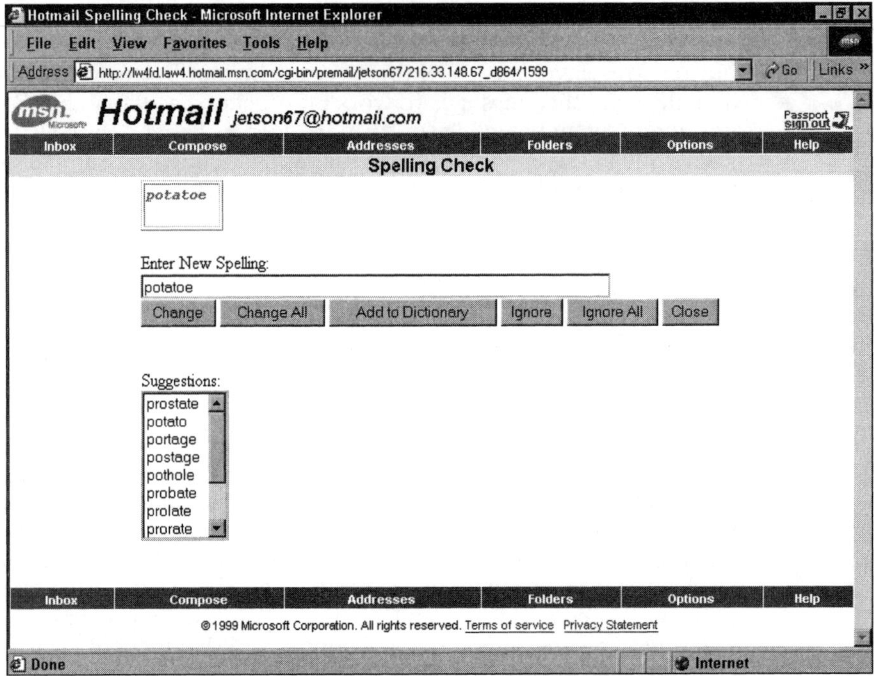

Figure 6-12: The spell checker can be very annoying.

If the word is misspelled but the correct spelling doesn't appear in the list, type the correct spelling in the Enter New Spelling text box, then click Change or Change All.

If the word is spelled correctly and you use it often, click Add to Dictionary to prevent Hotmail from flagging the word as an error in the future.

4. **Repeat Steps 2 and 3 until the spell checker gives up.**

   When the spell check is finished, you are returned to the Compose page. The message `Spelling Check Complete` appears above the message.

Hotmail also provides a dictionary that you can use to look up the definition of common words and a thesaurus you can use to find words that have similar meanings. To use the dictionary or thesaurus, just click the Dictionary or Thesaurus buttons on the Compose page.

Receiving E-Mail

E-mail wouldn't be much good if it worked like a send-only set, sending out messages but not receiving them. (I once had an aunt like that.) Fortunately, you can receive e-mail as well as send it — assuming, of course, that you have friends or family who will write you.

To read e-mail that other users have sent you, follow these steps:

1. **Start Hotmail and go to the Inbox.**

   Refer back to the "Using Hotmail" section near the beginning of this chapter if you're not sure how.

   The Inbox displays a list of messages that you have received. (Refer back to Figure 6-1.)

2. **Click the link for a message that you want to read.**

   The message is opened, as shown in Figure 6-13.

3. **Read the message.**

4. **After you read the message, dispense with it in one of the following ways:**

   - If the message is worthy of reply, click Reply.

     A new compose page appears, allowing you to compose a reply. The To: field is automatically set to the user who sent you the message, the subject is automatically set to `RE: (whatever the original subject was)`, and the complete text of the original message is inserted at the bottom of the new message.

     Compose your reply and then click the Send button.

   - If the message was originally sent to several people, you can click Reply All to send a reply to all of the original recipients.
   - If the message was intended for someone else, or if you think someone else should see it (maybe it contains a juicy bit of gossip or a good joke), click Forward. A new compose page appears, allowing you to select the user or users to whom you want to forward the message. The original message is inserted at the bottom of the new message, with space left at the top for you to type an explanation of why you think the message qualifies for more audience (`Hey Mr. Spacely, get a load of this!`).
   - If the message is unworthy even of filing, click Delete. Poof!

5. **If you have additional messages to read, click the Next or Previous button to continue reading messages.**

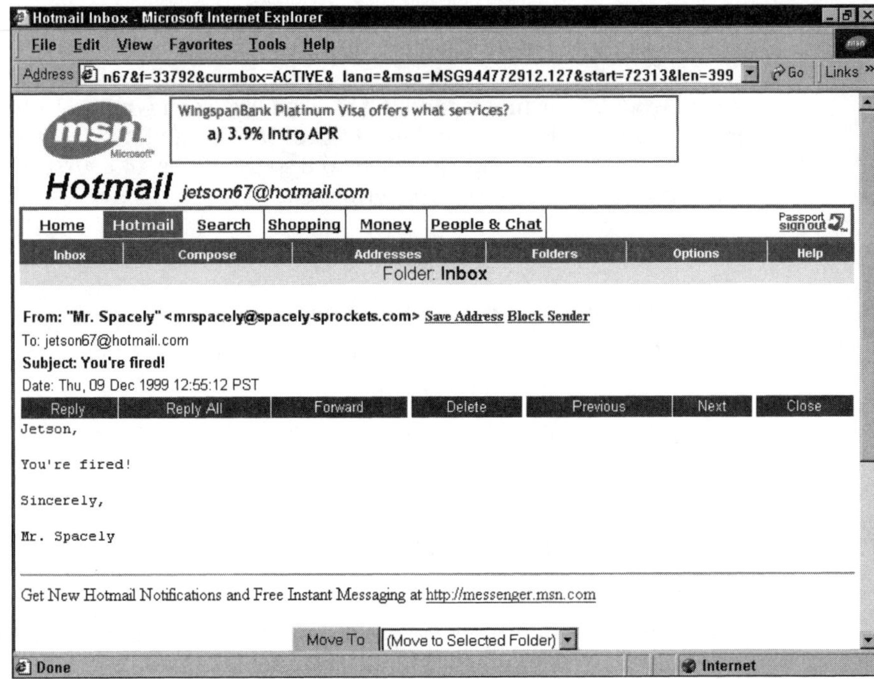

Figure 6-13: Reading a message.

Chapter 7

More Hotmail Tricks You Should Know

In This Chapter

- Using the Hotmail Address Book
- Sending and receiving e-mail attachments
- Working with mail folders
- Attaching stationery
- Customizing your signature
- Filtering mail
- Accessing mail from a POP3 mail account

If you send or receive more than a few e-mail messages each week, you may want to check out the time-saving shortcuts and tricks for Hotmail in this chapter. Here, you find how to save time by creating and using Hotmail's electronic address book. Plus, you can discover how to create folders to store your e-mail messages, filter out e-mail messages that you don't want to read, and other time-saving tricks.

Using the Address Book

Most Internet users have a relatively small number of people with whom they exchange e-mail on a regular basis. Rather than retype their addresses every time you send e-mail to these people, you can store your most commonly used addresses in your Hotmail Address Book. As an added benefit, the address book enables you to refer to your e-mail friends using a nickname (for example, George) rather than by a complete e-mail address (`george@spacelysprockets.com`).

Adding a name to the address book

Before you can use the address book, you must add the names of your e-mail correspondents to it. The best time to add someone to the address book is after you receive e-mail from that person. Here's the procedure:

1. **Open an e-mail from someone that you want to add to the address book.**

   Hotmail displays the message, as shown in Figure 7-1. (For more information about reading e-mail with Hotmail, see Chapter 6.)

2. **Click the Save Address hyperlink.**

   The Create Individual Nickname page displays, as shown in Figure 7-2.

3. **Change the nickname if you wish.**

   Hotmail proposes a nickname, but you might want to change it. For example, you might want to shorten the proposed nickname in Figure 7-2 from `George_Jetson` to simply `George`.

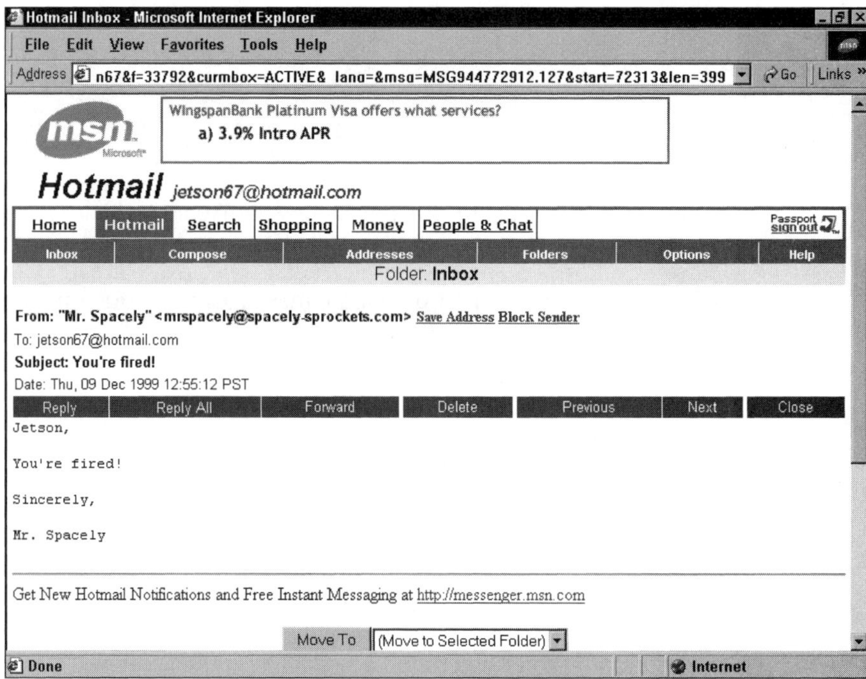

Figure 7-1: An e-mail message in Hotmail.

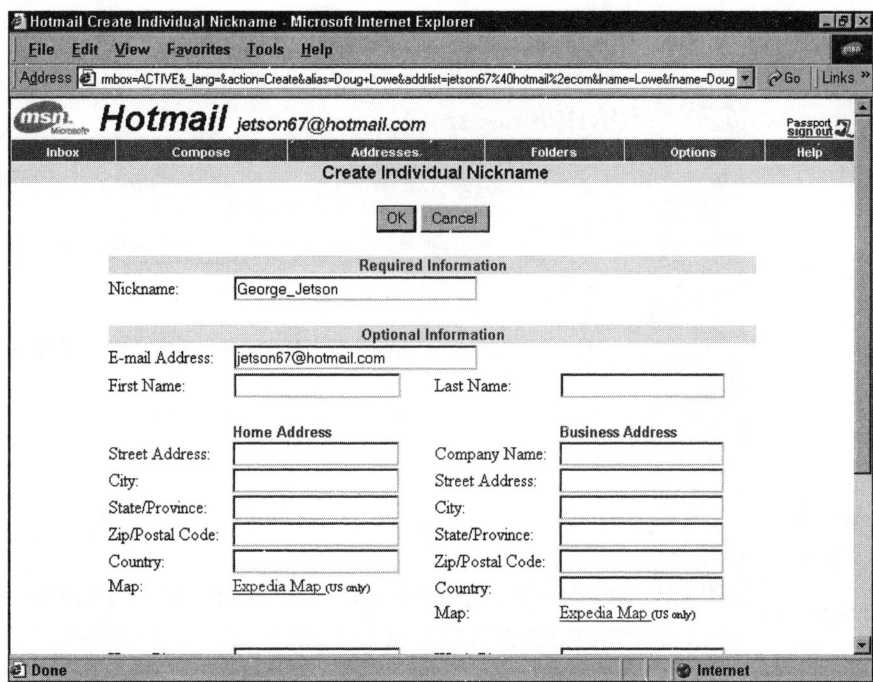

Figure 7-2: Creating a nickname for a friend.

You can use any combination of letters, numbers, dashes, and underscore characters for the nickname.

4. **Enter as much personal information as you want or think you might need.**

   Enter the person's first and last names, plus his or her home and business address and phone numbers, and other information if you know it. Leave out any information that you don't know or don't want to keep.

5. **Click the OK button.**

   The Hotmail Addresses page appears with the address inserted, as shown in Figure 7-3.

Another way to create an address book entry is to go directly to the Hotmail Addresses page by clicking Addresses on the horizontal menu bar and then clicking the Create New hyperlink. This takes you to the Create Individual Nickname page where you can fill in the desired information.

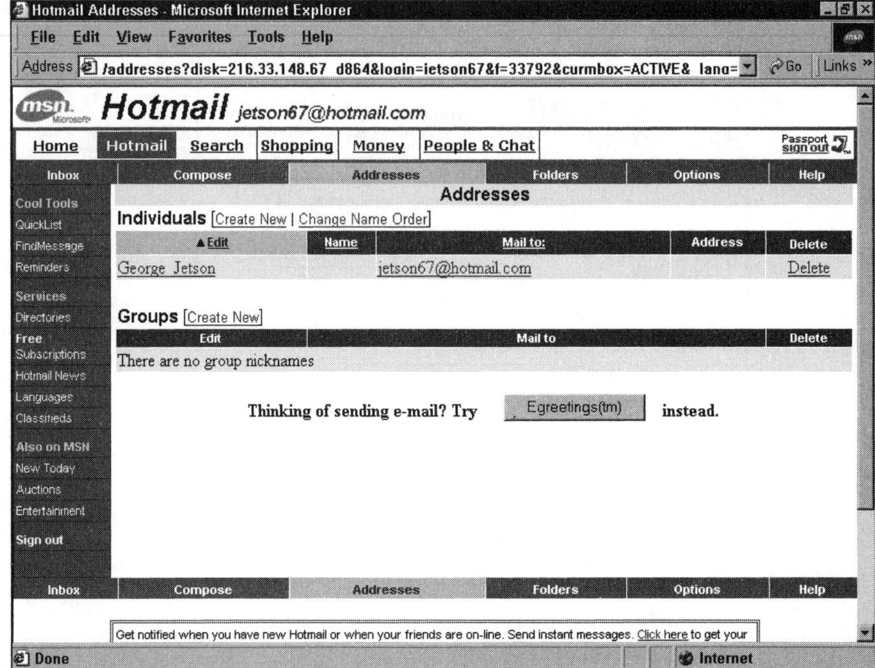

Figure 7-3: A new address has been added.

To remove someone from your Address Book, go to the Hotmail Addresses page and click the Delete hyperlink for the entry you want to delete. To edit an Address Book entry, click the nickname hyperlink. For example, in Figure 7-3 you would click `George` to edit George's address book entry.

Sending a message to someone in the address book

If you want to send a message to someone who is already in your address book, just type that person's nickname in the To: field when you compose your message.

If you can't remember the person's nickname, follow these steps:

1. **In the Compose page, click the To hyperlink.**

   A window similar to the one in Figure 7-4 pops up, listing the names in your address book.

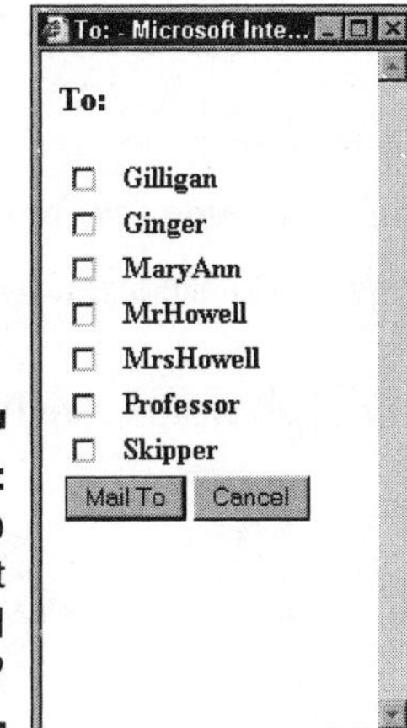

Figure 7-4: Whom do you want to send mail to?

2. **Click the check box next to the name of the person to whom you want to send e-mail.**

   You can send mail to more than one person by checking off more than one name.

3. **After you have selected all the names that you want, click the OK button.**

   Poof! You're back at the Compose page, and the names you selected appear in the To: field.

You can also send mail to someone in your address book directly from the Hotmail Addresses page by clicking the e-mail address of the person that you want to send mail to. This takes you to the Compose page with the To: field already filled in.

Using group nicknames

If you find that you frequently send mail to a particular group of people, you can create a special type of address book entry known as a *group nickname*. A group nickname is simply a list of people selected from your address book. When you send a message to the group nickname, Hotmail automatically sends a copy of the message to each of the people in the group.

To create a group nickname, follow these steps:

1. **Click the Addresses button in the horizontal toolbar.**

   The Hotmail Addresses page appears. (Refer to Figure 7-3.)

2. **Click the Create New hyperlink in the Groups section of the Addresses page.**

   This takes you to the Create Group Nickname page.

3. **Type a nickname for the new group in the Nickname text box.**

   For example, to create a group of your friends who are stranded on a desert isle, type something like **castaways.**

4. **Type the e-mail address of each person that you want to include in the group in the list box.**

   Press the Enter key to type more than one address.

   Figure 7-5 shows how the Create Group Nickname page appears after the nickname and e-mail addresses are filled in.

5. **Click the OK button.**

   Your new group is created.

After you create a group, sending mail to that group is easy. When you are composing a new message, click the To button to summon the list of addresses. Any groups you have created appear in the list along with your individual addresses. All you have to do is click the check box for the group you want to send your e-mail to.

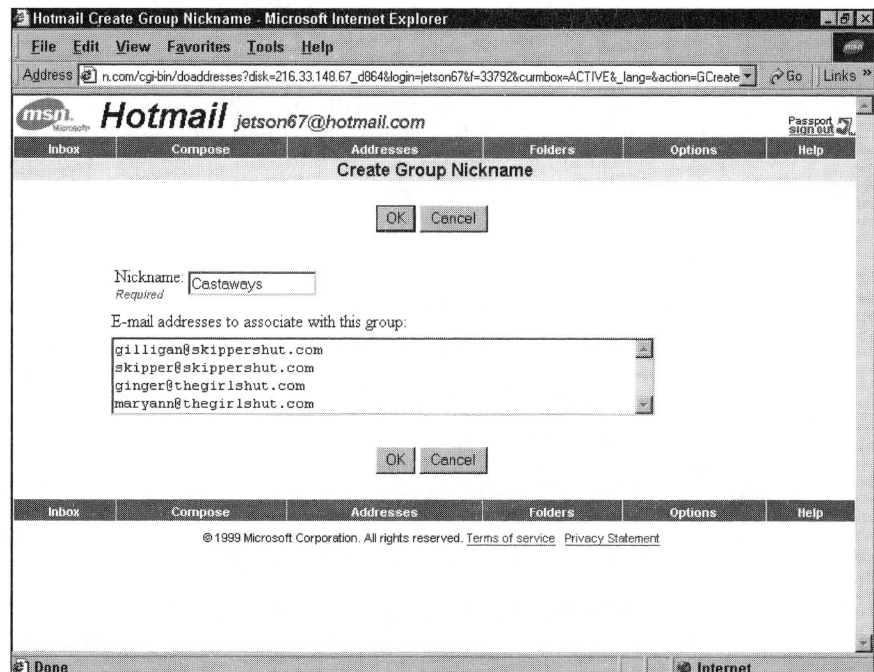

Figure 7-5: Creating a group nickname.

Here are two more points to keep in mind when you work with groups:

- A person's e-mail address can appear in more than one group. This allows you to include Thurston Howell III not only in the Castaways group, but also in another group named Eccentric Millionaires (along with Bill Gates and Ross Perot).
- You can easily add, delete, or change names in an existing group by clicking the group name in the Addresses page. When the Edit Group Nickname page appears, make whatever changes you wish to the group nickname or the list of e-mail addresses.

Dealing with Attachments

An *attachment* is a file that you send along with your e-mail. Sending an attachment is kind of like paper-clipping a separate document to a letter. When you attach a file to a message, the recipient of the message can save the file on his or her disk.

Be aware that sending large attachments can sometimes cause e-mail troubles, especially for attachments that approach a megabyte or more in size. If possible, you should mail several smaller attachments instead of one large one.

The following sections explain how to send and receive messages with attachments.

Sending an attachment

Here is the procedure for adding an attachment to a message you are composing:

1. **Click the Attachments button.**

   The Hotmail Attachments page appears, as shown in Figure 7-6.

2. **Click the Browse button.**

   The Choose File dialog box appears.

3. **Rummage through the folders on your hard drive until you find the file that you want to attach.**

   When you find the file, click the filename to select it.

4. **Click the Open button.**

   This returns you to the Hotmail Attachments page, with the filename that you selected in the Attach File text box.

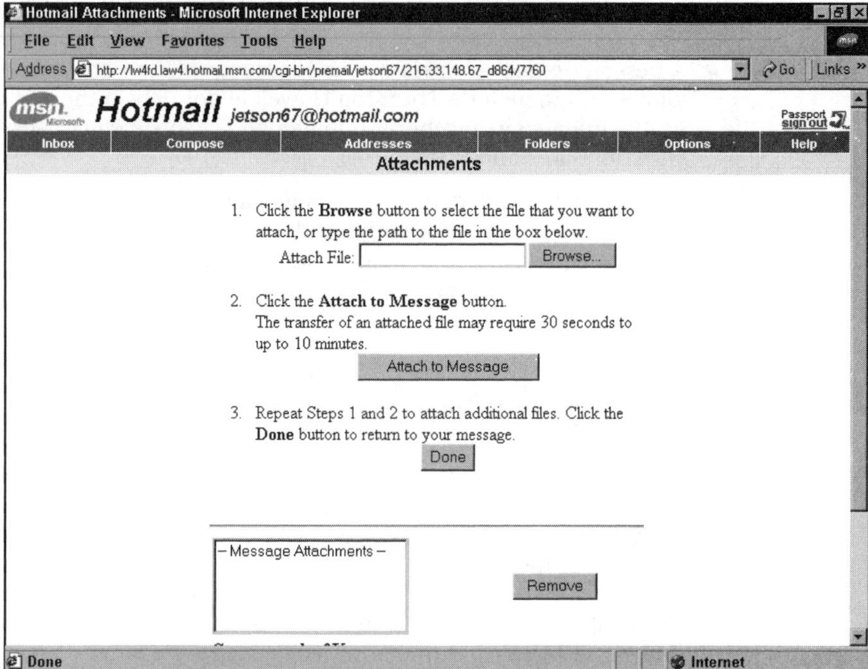

Figure 7-6: The Hotmail Attachments page.

5. **Click the Attach to Message button.**

   When Hotmail finishes uploading the file, the filename appears in the Message Attachment list box at the bottom of the Hotmail Attachments page, as shown in Figure 7-7.

6. **Repeat Steps 2 through 4 for any other files that you want to attach.**

   You can attach more than one file to each message. However, the total size of all the files you attach cannot exceed 1,000K (one megabyte).

7. **When you have finished attaching files, click the Done button.**

   You are returned to the Compose page, where you can finish composing your message.

If you change your mind about an attached file, click the file that you want to unattach and then click the Remove button.

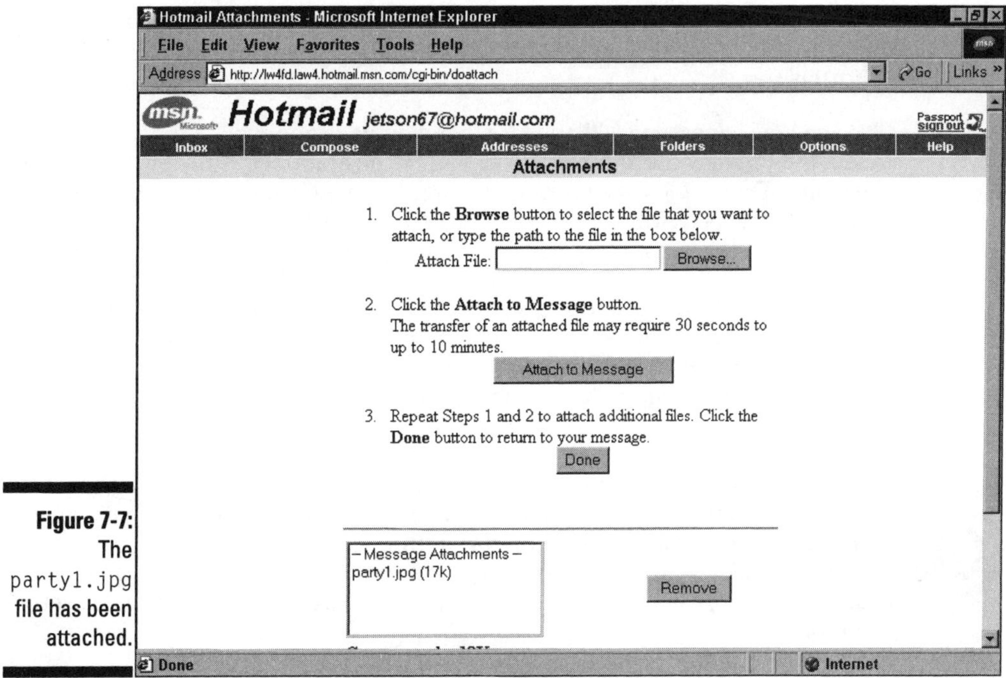

Figure 7-7: The `party1.jpg` file has been attached.

Receiving an attachment

If someone is kind enough to send you a message that includes an attached file, you can easily save the attachment as a separate file. If the attachment is a graphic image, the image will automatically be displayed when you open the message. To save the image as a file, right-click the image and then choose the Save Picture As command from the quick menu that appears.

If the attachment is not an image, two links to download the attachment appear at the bottom of the message. The first link lets you download the attachment without scanning the file for viruses. The second link lets you scan the file for viruses before downloading the file. If the file is anything other than a simple text file, you should opt for the virus scan.

Applying Stationery

Hotmail lets you attractively format your e-mail using what it calls *stationery*. Stationery lets you create fancy messages with colors, pretty fonts, and even background images. To apply stationery to a message, scroll to the bottom of the Compose page to see the Stationery buttons, as shown in Figure 7-8. Then, pick one of the stationery selections from the Use Stationery drop-down list.

To see how a message will appear when you have applied stationery to it, click the Preview button. This takes you to the Stationery Preview page. For example, Figure 7-9 shows how a message appears when formatted with the Mabel stationery. Notice that you can also change the stationery from the Stationery Preview page by using the Change Stationery To drop-down list.

Another way to apply stationery is to click the Stationery Chooser button. This takes you to a page that lets you quickly see all of the stationery choices that are available. However, the Stationery Chooser doesn't show you a preview of your message as it will appear when formatted with the stationery you choose.

The person you send your e-mail to can view the stationery if he or she is using an e-mail program that allows HTML formatting. If the recipient's mail program does not support HTML formatting, he or she will see the text of your message without the stationery. Of course, if you are sending mail to another Hotmail user, the recipient will have no problem viewing your pretty stationery.

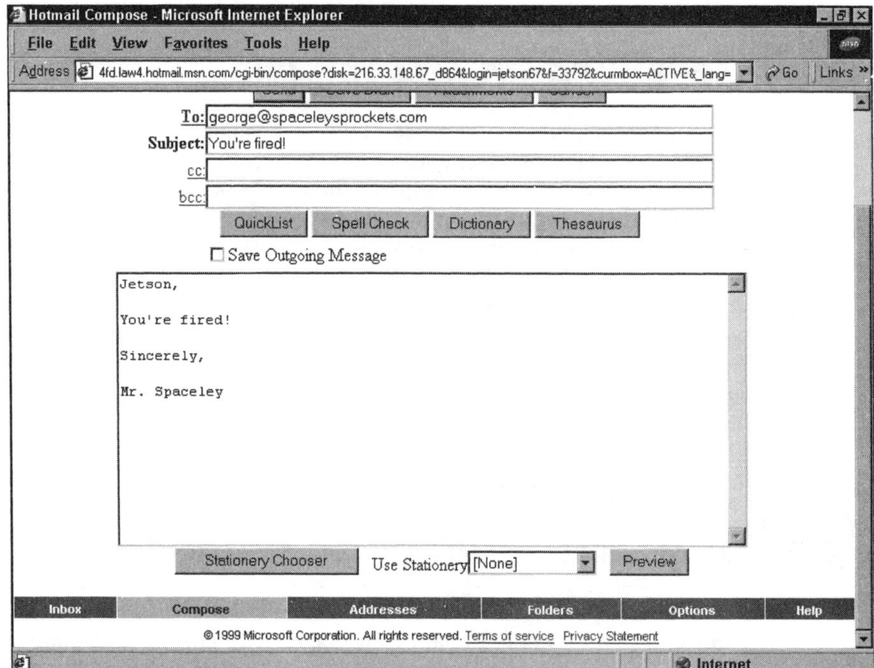

Figure 7-8: The Stationery buttons.

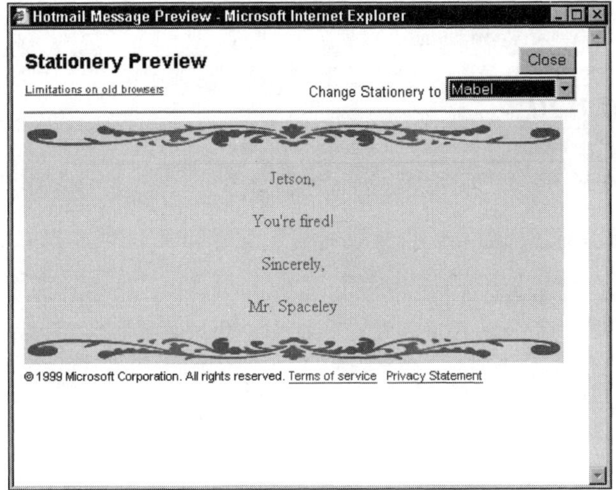

Figure 7-9: Previewing stationery.

Using Signatures

A *signature* is a bit of text that you can easily insert at the end of your messages. Signatures usually include information such as your name, the address of your home page (if you have one), and a witty saying. You can easily configure Hotmail to automatically insert a signature at the end of every message.

To create a signature, follow these steps:

1. **Click the Options button in Hotmail's horizontal menu bar.**

   Doing so summons the Hotmail Options page, as shown in Figure 7-10.

2. **Click the Signature hyperlink.**

   The signature page appears, as shown in Figure 7-11.

3. **Type the text that you want to use for a signature in the signature text box.**

   To create a signature that consists of more than one line, just press the Enter key when you want to start a new line.

4. **Click the OK button.**

Now that you have created a signature, you can add it to your messages by clicking the Add Signature hyperlink on the Compose page after you have composed your message.

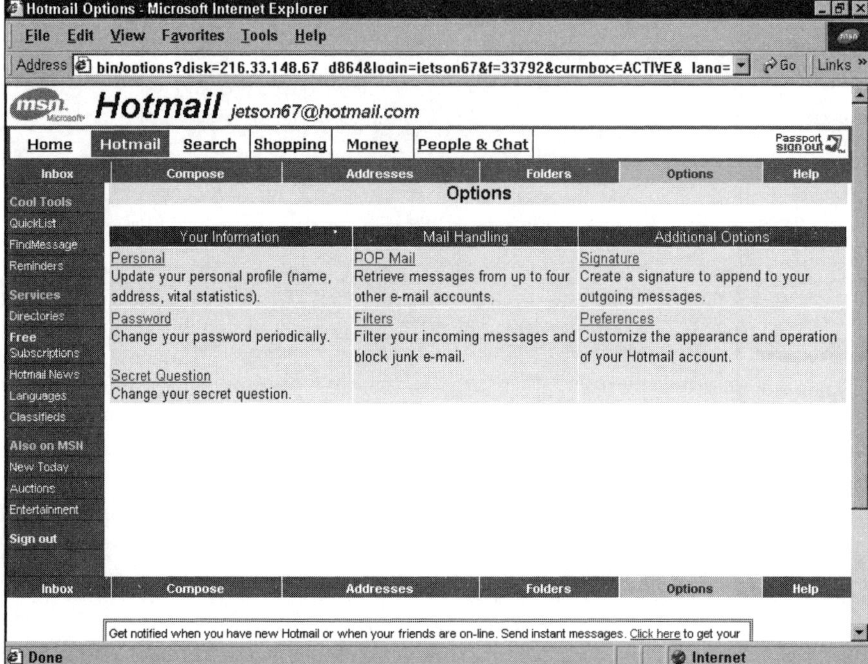

Figure 7-10: The Hotmail Options page.

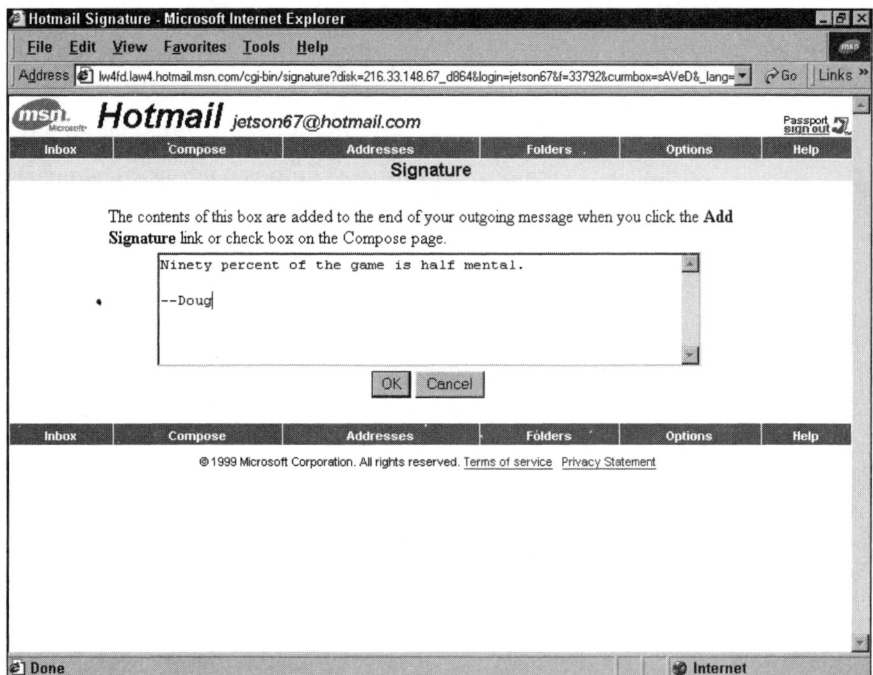

Figure 7-11: Creating a signature.

If you are an HTML guru and have the inclination, you can include HTML codes in your signature. This allows you to apply special HTML formatting to your signature, include a graphic image, a link to your home page, or anything else that might tickle your fancy.

Using Folders

When you sign up for Hotmail, four message folders are set up to hold your messages: Inbox, Sent Messages, Drafts, and Trash Can. Besides these four folders, Hotmail also enables you to create your own message folders. For example, you may want to create separate folders for different categories of messages, such as those that are work-related, those from friends and family, and so on. Or you may want to create date-related folders for storing older messages. For example, you can create a 1999 folder to save all the messages you receive in 1999.

The following sections explain how to work with message folders.

Creating a new folder

Before you start saving important messages, it's wise to create one or more folders in which to save the messages. You can use a single folder with a name such as Important Messages, or you can create several folders to categorize your messages. To create a new folder, follow these steps:

1. **Click the Folders button on the horizontal toolbar.**

   A list of Hotmail folders appear, as shown in Figure 7-12.

2. **Click the Create New hyperlink.**

   This brings up the Create Folder page.

3. **Type a name for your folder in the New Folder Name text box.**

4. **Click the OK button.**

   You return to the Hotmail Folders page, where the new folder appears in the folder listing, as shown in Figure 7-13.

Notice in Figure 7-13 that the new folder has links that enable you to edit the folder (change its name) or delete the folder. The four built-in folders do not have these links because you cannot delete them or change their names.

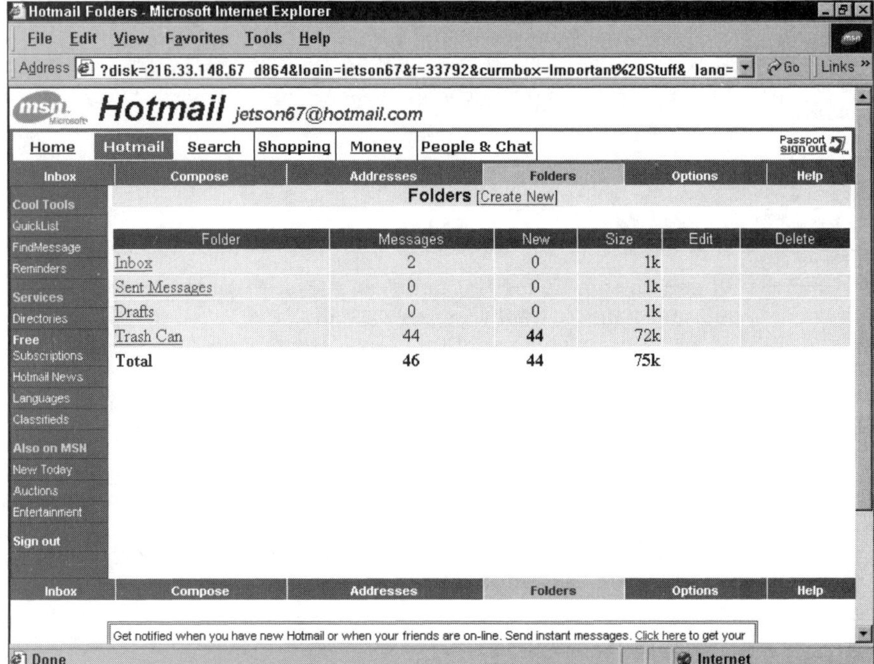

Figure 7-12: Hotmail folders.

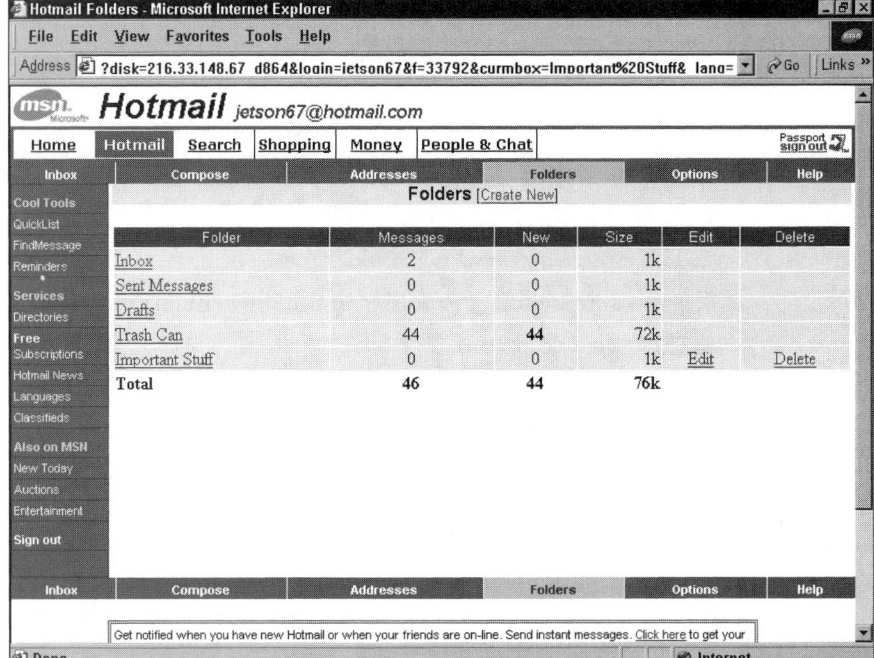

Figure 7-13: A new folder is born.

Moving messages to another folder

After you create a folder for your messages, moving a message to the folder is easy. Just follow these steps:

1. **From the Inbox, click the check box next to each message that you want to move, as shown in Figure 7-14.**
2. **Select the folder that you want to move the messages to in the Move To drop-down list.**
3. **Click the Move To button.**

   The messages are moved to the folder you selected.

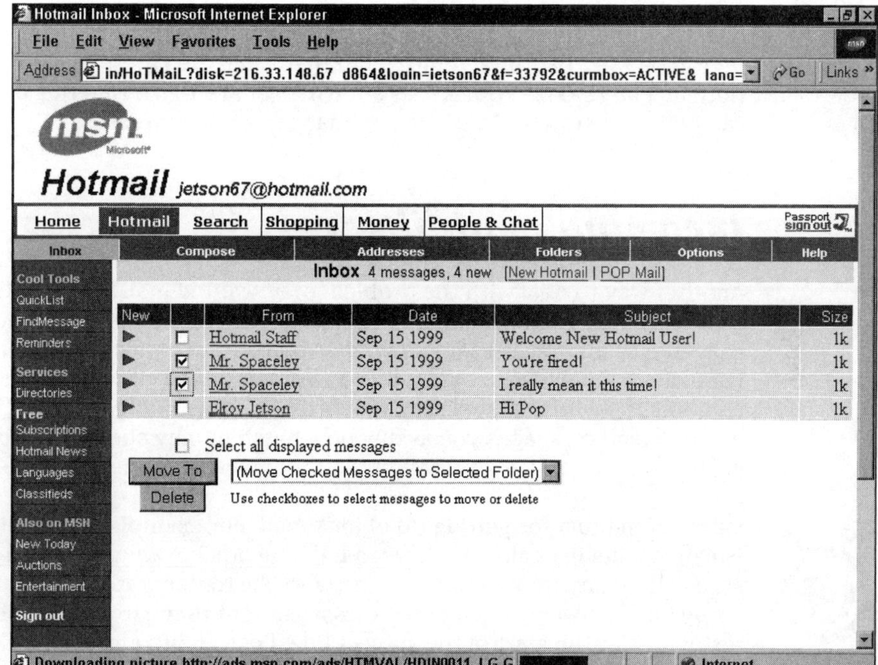

Figure 7-14: Moving messages into folders.

Filtering Your Mail

One of the most common complains of frequent e-mail users is getting too much unsolicited mail. Especially troubling is mail from adult-oriented Web sites or get-rich-quick schemes. Hotmail has two features that let you deal with this problem, as described in the following sections.

Blocking senders

One way to deal with unwanted mail is to create a Block Senders list, which is simply a list of e-mail addresses from which Hotmail refuses to accept mail. If you receive a piece of obnoxious or otherwise unwanted mail (widely called *spam*) from someone, you can quickly add that person to your Blocked Senders list by following these steps:

1. **Open the message.**
2. **Click the Block Senders hyperlink that appears above the message.**
3. **Click the OK button.**

   Future e-mails from that address are automatically moved to your Trash Can folder.

To review the list of e-mail senders you have blocked, click the Options button on the horizontal toolbar and then click the Filters hyperlink. The Hotmail Filters page appears, as shown in Figure 7-15. From this page, you can edit the list to add, remove, or change e-mail addresses.

Incoming mail filters

Another way to deal with the problem of unwanted mail is to create incoming mail filters. Incoming mail filters let you set up Hotmail so that it automatically moves messages to folders based on the message subject or address. For example, you can set up a filter to automatically move any message that contains the word "money" in the subject line to your Trash Can. (Of course, if your friend messages you asking how much money she owes you, that will go, too!)

Filters aren't just for getting rid of junk mail. For example, I subscribe to an e-mail mailing list called Halloween-L that sends me about a dozen or so messages every day from people like me who like to decorate their houses extensively on Halloween. Each of the messages sent to me from this list has the text `HALL:` at the start of the subject line. I use an incoming mail filter to automatically move these messages into a folder named Halloween.

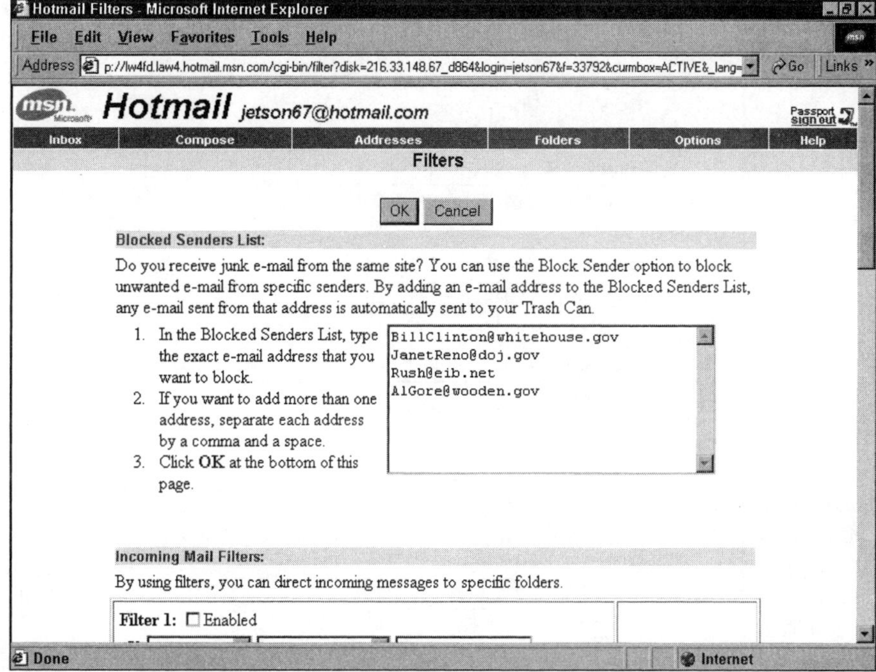

Figure 7-15: Blocking e-mail from someone who sends you unwanted messages.

Hotmail lets you create as many as ten incoming mail filters. To set up a filter, follow these steps:

1. **Click the Options button in the horizontal menu bar.**

   The Hotmail Options page appears.

2. **Click the Filters hyperlink.**

   The Hotmail Filters page appears.

3. **Scroll down the Hotmail Filters page to the filter that you want to set up.**

   There are fields on the Filters page for ten separate filters, as shown in Figure 7-16.

4. **Click the Enabled check box for the filter that you want to create.**

5. **Set the If part of the filter to the condition a message must meet to be processed by the filter and select the folder to move the message to in the Then deliver to list box.**

   For example, to move my `HALL:` messages to the Halloween folder, I set up the If part of the filter so it says `If Subject Contains HALL:` and set the Then Deliver To part of the filter to `Halloween`, as shown in Figure 7-17.

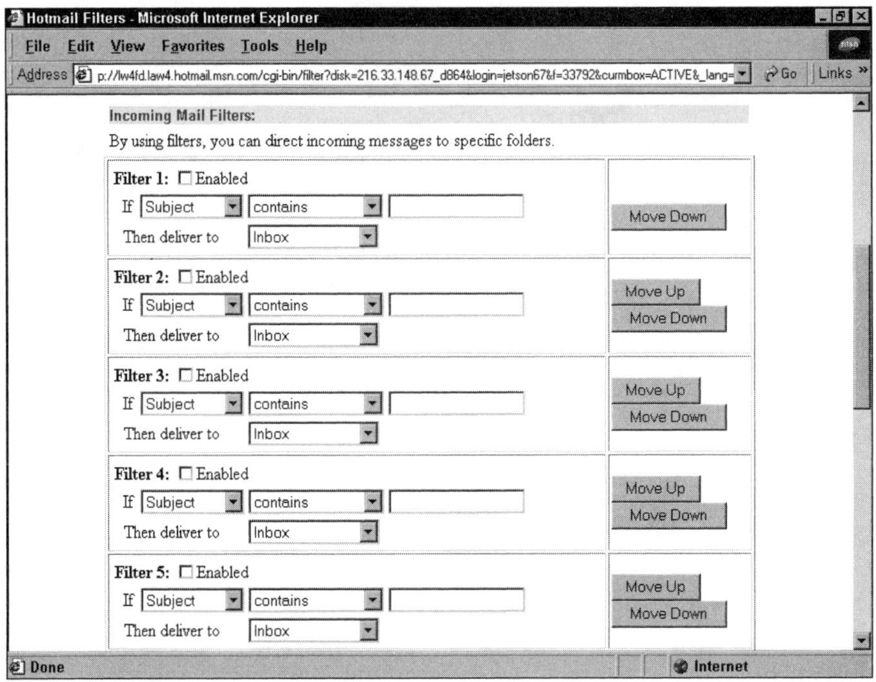

Figure 7-16: Getting ready to set up a filter.

Filter 1: Enabled
If Subject contains HALL:
Then deliver to Halloween

Figure 7-17: A filter all set up and ready to go.

6. **Repeat Steps 3 through 5 for any other filters that you want to set up.**
7. **Click the OK button.**

   The OK button appears at the top and bottom of the page. Either one will do.

If you create more than one incoming mail filter, the filters are applied to your incoming mail in the order in which they are listed in the Filters page. For example, suppose you create a filter to move all messages with "HALL:" in the Subject line to the Halloween folder and then create a second filter to move any messages with "Sarah" in the Subject line to the Sarah's Mail folder. If you get a message with the subject line "HALL: This one is for Sarah," the message is moved to the Halloween folder, not the Sarah's Mail folder.

You can change the order in which filters are listed in the Filters page by using the Move Up and Move Down buttons that appear next to the filters.

To delete a filter, click the Delete button that appears next to the filter.

Accessing a POP3 E-mail Account

If you have a POP3 e-mail account with your Internet Service Provider, you can set up Hotmail so that you can read the e-mail sent to your POP3 account from your Hotmail inbox. All you have to do is tell Hotmail the Internet address of your POP3 mail server, your user ID, and your password. The main reason you would want to do this is so that you can read your POP3 e-mail from any computer.

Before I show you how to set up Hotmail to read a POP3 e-mail account, I want to be sure you understand some of the finer nuances of accessing your POP3 mail from Hotmail:

- Hotmail can receive mail from your POP3 e-mail account, but it cannot send mail using your POP3 account.
- Hotmail does not automatically receive messages from your POP3 account. To download messages from your POP3 mail account to your Hotmail inbox, you must click the POP Mail link on the Hotmail inbox page.
- Hotmail can be configured to delete messages from your POP3 server when you download them to your Hotmail inbox or to leave the messages on the server. If Hotmail is the main way you want to read your POP3 mail, you should configure Hotmail to delete the messages after they are downloaded.

  On the other hand, if you will use another e-mail program (such as Microsoft Outlook Express or Netscape Messenger) to read your mail most of the time and want to use Hotmail only occasionally to access your POP3 mail, configure Hotmail to leave the messages on the server. That way, the next time you access your POP3 mail using your regular e-mail program, those messages will be downloaded into your e-mail program's inbox.
- Hotmail can be configured to access up to four POP3 e-mail accounts.

To configure Hotmail to access your POP3 e-mail account, click Options on the horizontal menu bar, then click the POP Mail link. This brings up the POP Mail page shown in Figure 7-18. Enter the address of your POP3 e-mail account, your user ID, and your password in the appropriate text boxes. If you aren't sure what information to type into these fields, contact your ISP (or, for a company e-mail account, your company's e-mail administrator) to find out. (You may also need to change the Server Timeout and Port Address fields, but the default values for these fields are nearly always adequate.)

If you want Hotmail to leave the messages it downloads on your POP3 server, check the Leave Messages on POP Server option. If you leave this option unchecked, Hotmail will delete any messages it downloads from your POP3 server, so you won't be able to read those messages from your regular e-mail program.

You can also choose from one of seven icons to use as a New Mail indicator for the account. The default choice, a red arrow, is the same icon that Hotmail uses to indicate unread Hotmail messages in your inbox. I suggest you choose one of the other icons to use for the indicator so that you can distinguish your POP3 mail from your Hotmail messages in your Hotmail inbox.

Once you have configured Hotmail for your POP3 e-mail account, you can download messages from your POP3 account at any time by clicking the POP Mail hyperlink on the Hotmail inbox page.

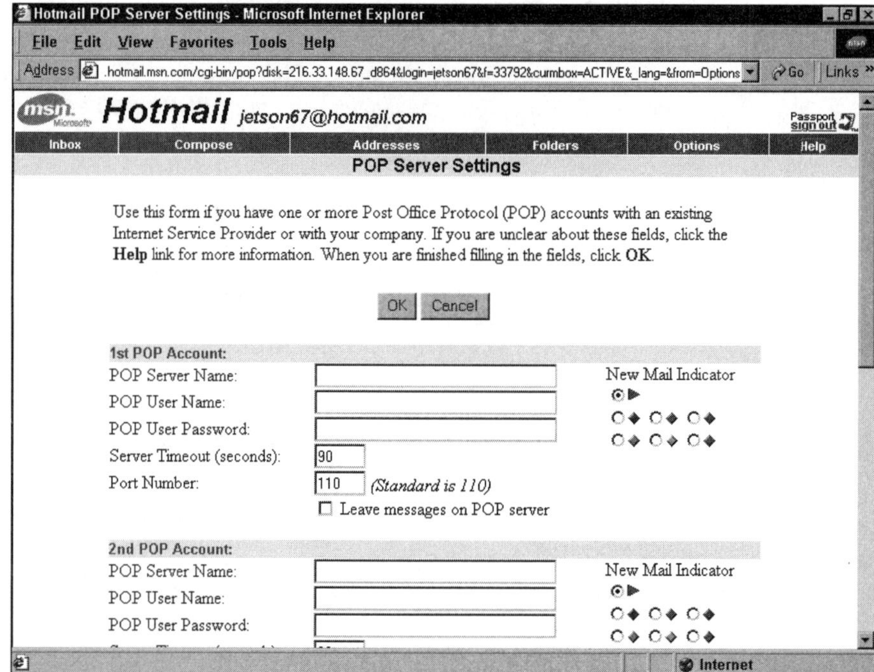

Figure 7-18: Configuring Hotmail to work with a POP3 e-mail account.

Chapter 8

Visiting MSN's Web Communities

In This Chapter

- Exploring the MSN Web Communities
- Finding a Web Community that interests you
- Navigating a Web Community
- Creating your own Web Community

Web Communities are the watering holes of MSN, where people with common interests gather to exchange ideas, swap stories, tell jokes, and generally shoot the breeze. At the time that I wrote this book, a few hundred Web Communities were available on MSN, with topics ranging from Adventure to Web Design. And since MSN lets you create your own Web Communities, new Communities are being added all the time.

This chapter leads you through the basics of using MSN's Web Communities. You discover how to find a Web Community that's interesting to you, how to access it, how to find out about Web Community events, and much more. And I'll show you how to create your own community. I cover two of the most popular Web Community features — Chats and Message Boards — in Chapters 9 and 10.

Discovering Web Communities

A Web Community is a Web site within the overall MSN Web Site that focuses on a particular topic or interest. Although each Web Community has its own unique character, most of them include the following common features:

- A home page that contains general information about the community, highlights interesting features in the community such as new articles or upcoming chat events, and provides links to other community features.
- One or more message boards where people can discuss specific topics that are of interest to the community. For example, the Science Fiction community has message boards on topics such as Books, Movies, TV, Star Trek, Star Wars, and The X-Files.

- A Photo Album, from which you can download pictures related to the Web Community's topic. You can also upload your own pictures to the Photo Album for other people who visit the Community to download.
- One or more chat rooms where you can meet people online for live discussions — some communities schedule chat events with celebrities.

Back when the Microsoft Network was a membership-only online service, Web Communities were called *forums*. When Microsoft decided to make all of MSN's content, including forums, available to the public free of charge, the name *forum* was replaced by *Web Community*. However, you'll occasionally run into MSN old-timers who still refer to Web Communities as forums.

There are two types of MSN Web Communities: public and private. Any Internet user can visit the home page of a public community. However, to access the Message Board, Photo Album, and other community features, you must join the community. Depending on how the public community was set up, membership applications may be subject to review by the Web Community Manager.

Private communities are closed to everyone who is not a member of the community. Membership is by invitation only. Private communities are great for families and small organizations that don't want people popping in and out of their community home pages.

Finding a Community That Interest You

MSN has Web Communities on hundreds of subjects, on topics as diverse as movies, religion, woodworking, and politics. Naturally, you'll want to find the Web Communities that interest you. If you want to talk about World War II, you wouldn't want to do it in the Astronomy Web Community.

Figure 8-1 shows the Web Communities home page, which is the starting point for finding Web Communities on the topics that interest you. To go to the Web Communities Home Page, first click the People & Chat tab on the MSN Home Page. Then, click Web Communities on the navigation bar that appears beneath the MSN tabs.

As you can see, the Web Communities home page has a list of categories such as Business, Computers & Internet, and Entertainment. Clicking one of these categories takes you to a page that lists several subcategories for the category you selected. You can then click one of these subcategories to see a list of the Web Communities in that subcategory. For example, Figure 8-2 shows the Web Communities you can access from Movies, which you'll find under the Entertainment category.

Figure 8-1: The Web Communities home page.

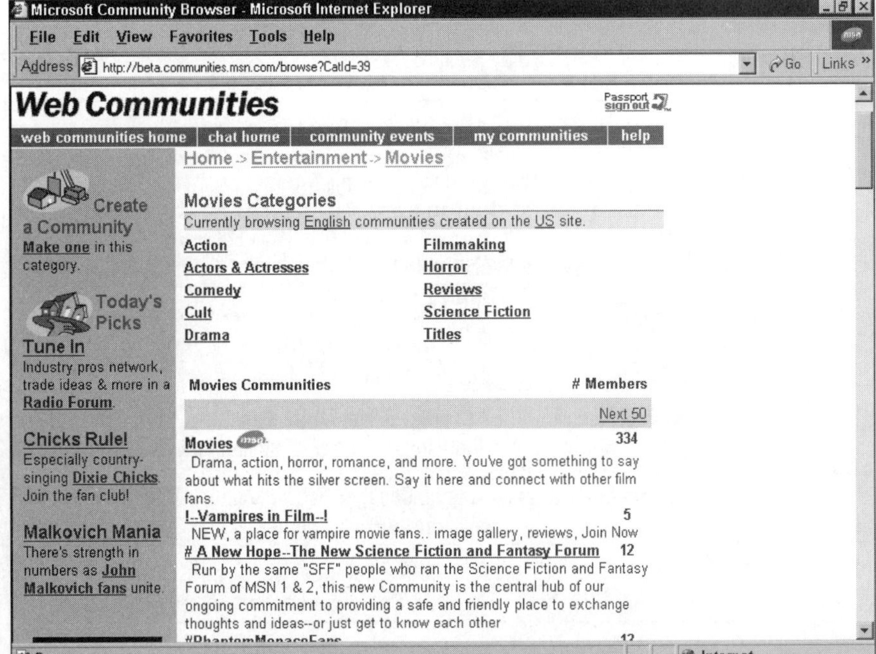

Figure 8-2: The Movies category page lists Web Communities about movies.

To help you find a Web Community on a topic that interests you, I've listed all of the Web Community categories along with their subcategories in Table 8-1.

Table 8-1 Web Community Categories

Category	*Subcategories*
Business	Careers, Companies, Consulting, Home Business, Industry Associations, Professions, Small Business, and Workplace
Computers & Internet	Hardware, Internet, Microsoft Communities, Operating Systems, Programming, Software, and User Groups
Entertainment	Books, Humor, Movies, Performing Arts, Theatre, and TV/Radio
Games	Board Games, Card Games, Multiplayer Internet Games, Other Games, Puzzles & Trivia, Role-Playing Games, Strategy & War Gaming, Toys, and Video Games
Health & Wellness	Health, Medicine, and Support Groups
Home & Families	Families, Genealogy, Home & Garden, Parenting, and Pets
Lifestyles	Food & Dining, Hobbies & Crafts, Men, Shopping, and Women
Money & Investing	Investing, Investment Clubs, Personal Finance, and Real Estate
News & Politics	Government, News, and Politics
Organizations	Abortion, Civil Rights, Consumer, Environment, Ethnic Groups, Men's Movement, Other Organizations, Seniors, and Women's Issues
People	Gay & Lesbian, Artists, Ages, Authors, Celebrities, Personal Communities, Public Figures, Relationships, and Romance
Places & Travel	U.S., Africa, Europe, South America, Asia, Australia & New Zealand, Destinations, Travel Services, Caribbean, Canada, and Mexico & Latin America
Religion & Beliefs	Astrology & New Age, Buddhism, Christianity, Hinduism, Islam, Judaism, Paranormal, Philosophy, and Other Spirituality
Schools & Education	Alumni, Colleges & Universities, Grade Schools (For Teachers & Parents), High Schools, Home Schooling, and Teaching
Science & History	Alternative Science, Biology, History, Mathematics, Physics, Social Sciences, Space, and Weather
Sports & Recreation	Automotive, College Sports, Outdoors, Professional Sports, and Recreational Sports

Maneuvering Around a Community

Although each of MSN's Web Communities has its own unique style, all Web Communities follow a similar format. Figure 8-3 shows the home page for the Movies community, which is pretty typical of how most MSN Web Communities are laid out. In this section, I describe the basics of finding your way around a Web Community, using the Movies community as an example.

Down the left side of the Web Community page is a menu bar with links that take you to the various areas that make up the community. The following paragraphs describe the links you'll find in most MSN communities:

- **Home Page:** The community's home page (shown in Figure 8-3).
- **Message Board:** Takes you to the community message board, where you can post messages to be read by other community members and read their replies. For more information about using the message board, see Chapter 10.
- **Photo Album:** Takes you to a collection of pictures that have been uploaded to the community by other community members. For more information, see the "Using the Photo Album" section later in this chapter.
- **Chat Room:** Takes you to the community chat room. For more information about chatting, see Chapter 9.

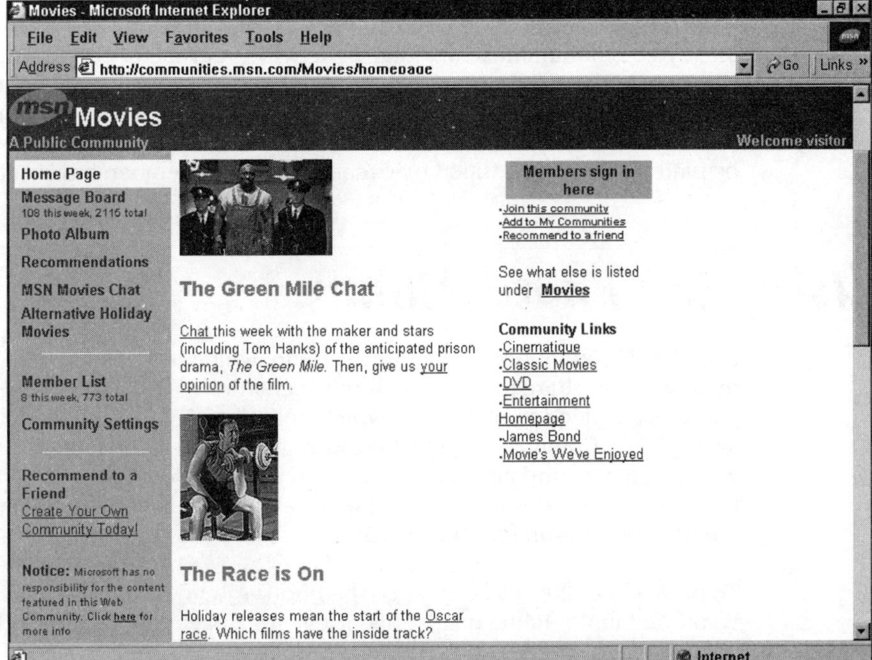

Figure 8-3: The Movies community home page.

- **Member List:** Lists the people who have joined the community.
- **Community Settings:** Displays information about the community.
- **Invite Someone:** Lets you send e-mail to someone whom you think might be interested in the community.

Joining a Community

MSN Web Communities are not exclusive groups. As a non-member you can visit MSN communities, but you can't do much. For example, visitors cannot post messages on the message board. Membership does have its privileges. Here are some of the things you can do when you join a community:

- Post replies to message board discussions and start new discussions.
- View the member list to see who else has joined the community.
- Send e-mail to community members and receive community e-mail.
- View the photo album and upload your own pictures.
- Invite others to join the community.

Joining a community is easy, and it doesn't cost a penny. All you have to do is click the Join This Community link that appears on the community home page. This brings up the Join This Community page, as shown in Figure 8-4. Fill out the information on the page and then click Join Now.

Most Web Communities immediately activate your membership when you join. However, some communities have restricted membership, which means that the Community Manager must review and approve all membership requests. When you join a restricted membership community, it can take a few days, so be patient. You'll be notified by e-mail when your membership is activated.

Using the Photo Album

Every Web Community has a photo album, which is a place where community members can share pictures with other members. The photo album is organized as a collection of albums, which contains pictures related to a particular topic. All Communities start off with an album called Shoebox, which is where you can stuff miscellaneous photos. When you upload a picture, you can place the picture in the Shoebox or another existing album, or you can create a new album for your picture.

To peruse the photo album, click the Photo Album link at the left side of the Web Community home page. This brings up a page that lists the albums that have been created, as shown in Figure 8-5.

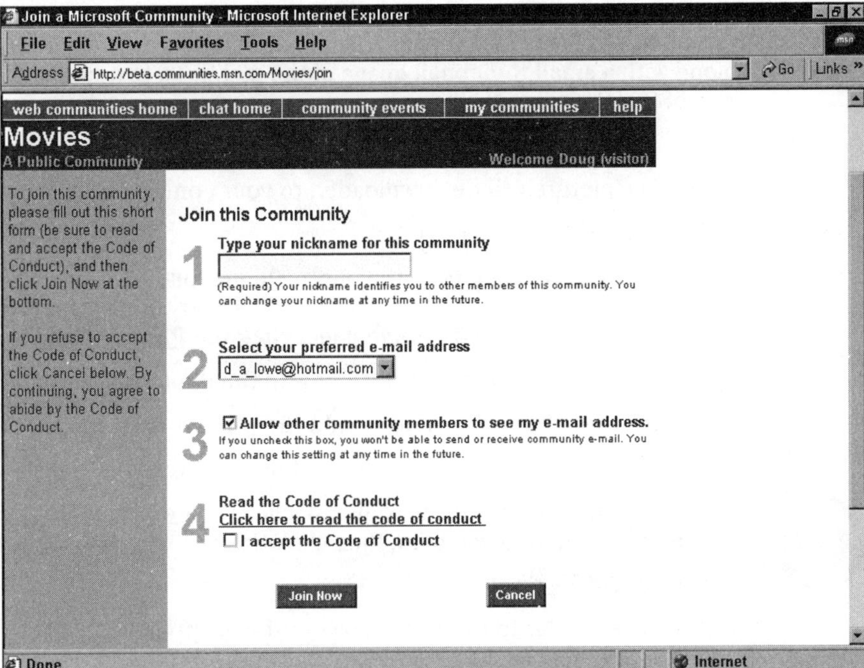

Figure 8-4: Joining a community.

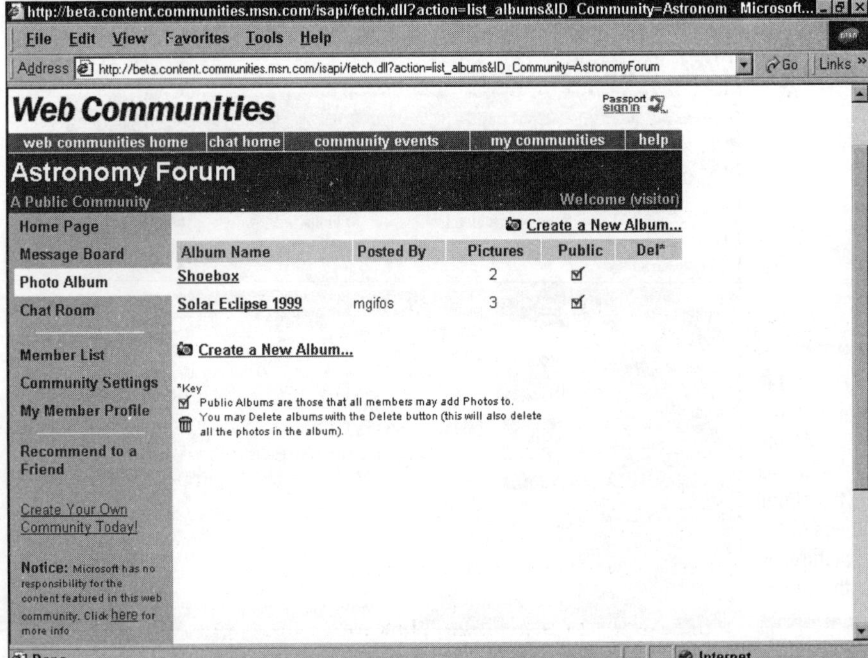

Figure 8-5: The Photo Album page in the Astronomy forum.

To access an album, just click the name of the album. A page similar to the one shown in Figure 8-6 appears, listing each of the pictures in the album along with a small thumbnail image of the picture, a text description, and the size of the picture.

To see a full-size version of the picture, just click the underlined picture name. The picture will be downloaded to your computer and displayed full size.

To upload your own photo to the photo album, follow these steps:

1. **From the Community home page, click the Photo Album link.**

   This takes you to the list of albums in the Photo Album.

2. **Click the album you want to add the picture to.**

   This displays a list of the pictures that are already in the album.

   TIP: If you want to create a new album, click Create a New Album. Type the name for your new album, then click Go.

3. **Click Add a Photo.**

   A page similar to the one in Figure 8-7 will appear.

Figure 8-6: The Photo Album shows a thumbnail image of the pictures in the album.

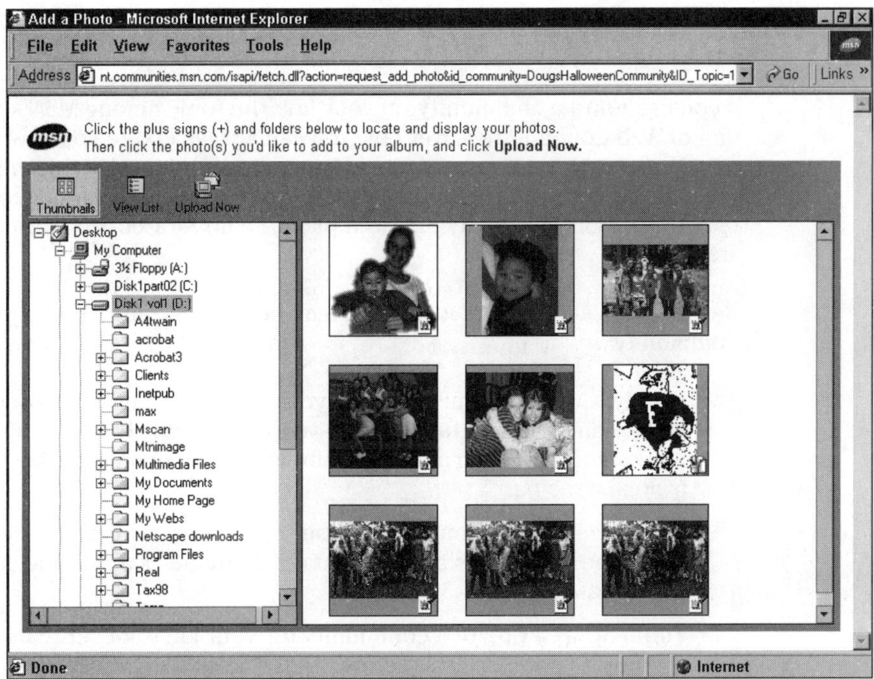

Figure 8-7: Selecting pictures to upload.

4. **Click the pictures you want to upload.**

   You may have to navigate around the drive folder list on the left side of the page to find the drive and folder that contains the picture you want to upload.

   When you click a picture, a check mark appears on the picture to indicate that you have selected it. If you change your mind, click the picture again to remove the check mark.

   When you click the photo, a rotation control appears that allows you to rotate the picture left or right. If the picture is upside down or sideways, click this control to rotate the picture until it is oriented properly.

5. **When you have selected the pictures you want to upload, click Upload Now.**

   The pictures are uploaded to MSN's computers. This will take awhile — several minutes if the pictures are large — so be patient. When the upload completes, the photo album thumbnail page is displayed, this time showing the pictures you have uploaded.

To add a title and description of your photo, click the photo and then click Edit This Photo. This summons a page on which you can enter the title and description.

Creating Your Own Community

If you can't find a community on your favorite topic among MSN's vast collection of Web Communities, fret not. You can always create your own community! You can create a community about any topic you wish, provided you stay within Microsoft's established standards of decency and decorum — remember, MSN is a family-oriented place, so no X-rated Web Communities are allowed.

Here is just a sampling of ideas that may be the basis for a home-grown Web Community:

- **Family:** Create a community for your extended family, so your brother-in-law can post a picture of his 6-year-old scoring the winning goal at last week's soccer match and your aunt Freda can post her prize-winning fruitcake recipe.
- **Work:** Create a community for your coworkers, where you can brag about the company's softball team or share news about the company's Christmas party.
- **Youth Sports:** Create a community for your kid's soccer team, so you can post schedules and pictures of the team's latest exploits.
- **School:** If you are a teacher, create a community for your class and post homework assignments, and information about classroom activities, and pictures from your latest field trip.
- **Hobbies:** If you have a favorite hobby, like model railroading or cross-stitch, create a community where you and like-minded craftspeople can upload photos showcasing your work and discuss your latest projects.

Creating a community is a straightforward process, and it's completely free. To create a community, go to the Web Communities home page and follow these steps:

1. **Click Create a Community.**

   The Create Your Own Community page appears, as shown in Figure 8-8.

2. **Fill out the information on the Create Your Own Community page.**

   Give a name, description, and category for your community.

   Choose a privacy level for your community. You have two choices: Public and Private. Choose Public if you want to allow anyone to join the community. Choose Private if you want to create a members-only community.

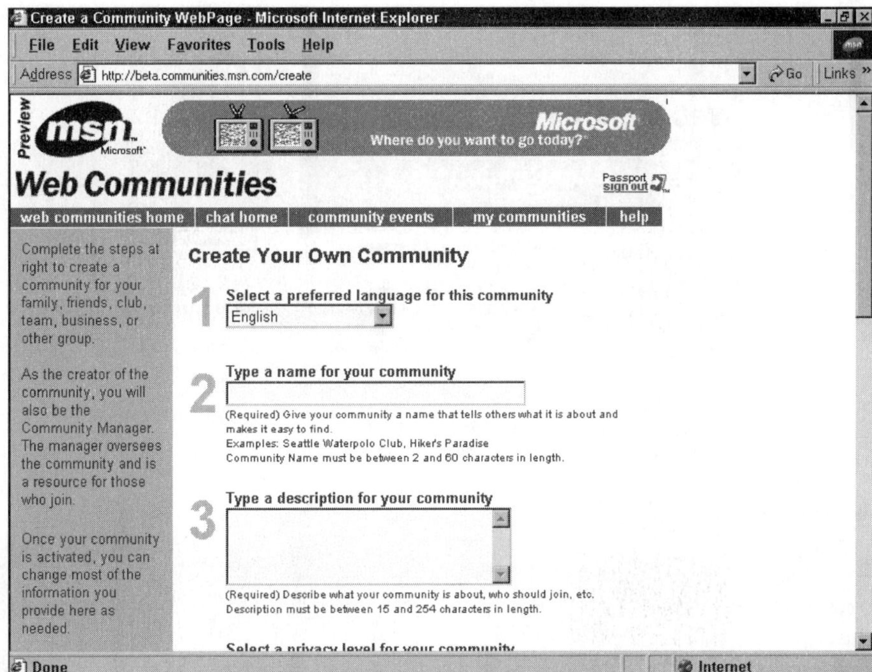

Figure 8-8: Creating your own community.

3. **Click the Go button.**

   A page describing the MSN Code of Conduct appears.

4. **Read through the MSN Code of Conduct and then click Yes, I Agree.**

   You are taken to your new community home page, as shown in Figure 8-9.

5. **Click the Customized Welcome Message link.**

   The page shown in Figure 8-10 appears, allowing you to customize the welcome message for your community.

6. **Type a welcome message for your community and then click Save.**

   If you want, you can use the formatting controls to change the text formatting for your welcome message. You can also insert clip art into your welcome message.

   If you want to insert your own photo into the welcome message, first upload the photo to the community Shoebox in the photo album. Then, select Shoebox from the Select a Category list and double-click the photo.

   You can also include links to other Web pages, such as other Web sites that are related to the topic of your community or your MSN Home Page.

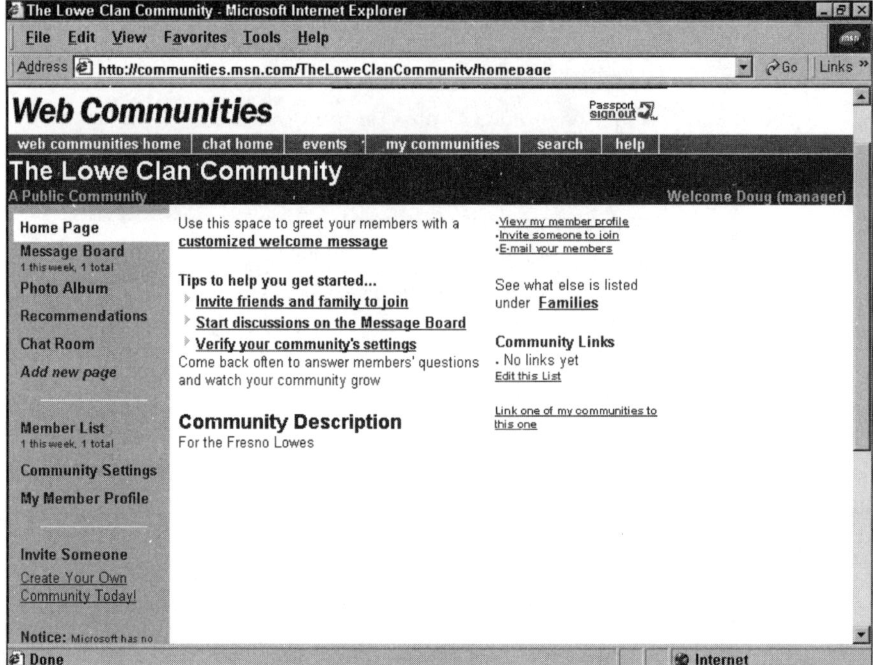

Figure 8-9: A new community home page.

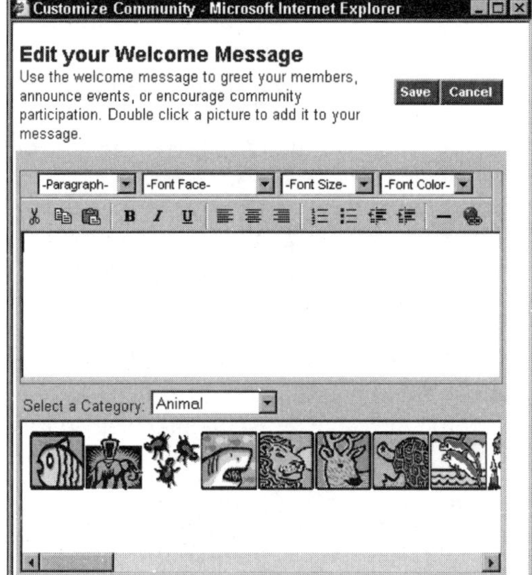

Figure 8-10: Customizing the welcome message for your community.

7. **From the Community home page click Community Settings and then click the Edit These Settings hyperlink that appears next to any community settings that you want to adjust.**

   The following paragraphs list the Community Settings you can change:

   - **General Settings:** The community name and Internet address are fixed and cannot be changed, but you can change the community description at any time.
   - **Access Policy:** You can change the community from public to private, but not the other way around: To protect the privacy of people who join a public group MSN won't let you change a private group to public.
   - **Membership Policy:** You can indicate whether membership requests are automatically approved or whether the manager (that's you) must approve requests.
   - **E-mail Distribution Policy:** Allow only the manager to send e-mail to the entire membership, or allow any member to send e-mail.
   - **Rating Level:** Indicate whether the Community contains content that is suitable for all age levels or adults only.
   - **Directory Settings:** You can change the category and subcategory where your Community is listed in the Web Communities directory.

8. **Check your e-mail.**

   When you set up a new community, MSN Web Communities automatically sends an e-mail message to your e-mail account. Be sure to read this message for important information about your community, such as its Web address, as well as advice about setting up and managing your community.

That's all there is to it. Once you have created your Web Community page, you'll need manage it. To keep your Web Community fresh and interesting, change the welcome message periodically, upload new images to the photo album, and monitor and participate in discussions on the message board.

You can add additional pages to your Web Community by clicking Add New Page. This brings up the page shown in Figure 8-11, which lists the various types of pages you can add. MSN lets you choose from the following page types:

- **A custom Web page:** If you choose this option, you can create a page that contains any combination of text and pictures you wish.
- **A list:** Choose this option to create a page that features a list of items, such as your favorite movies or books, a team roster, a To-Do list, or any other type of list you can think of.

- **A photo album:** This option lets you create additional photo albums to store pictures in your community.
- **A message board topic:** This option lets you create message boards for discussing specific topics in your community. Use this option only if your community is so popular that a single message board is not enough to accommodate all of the community's discussions.

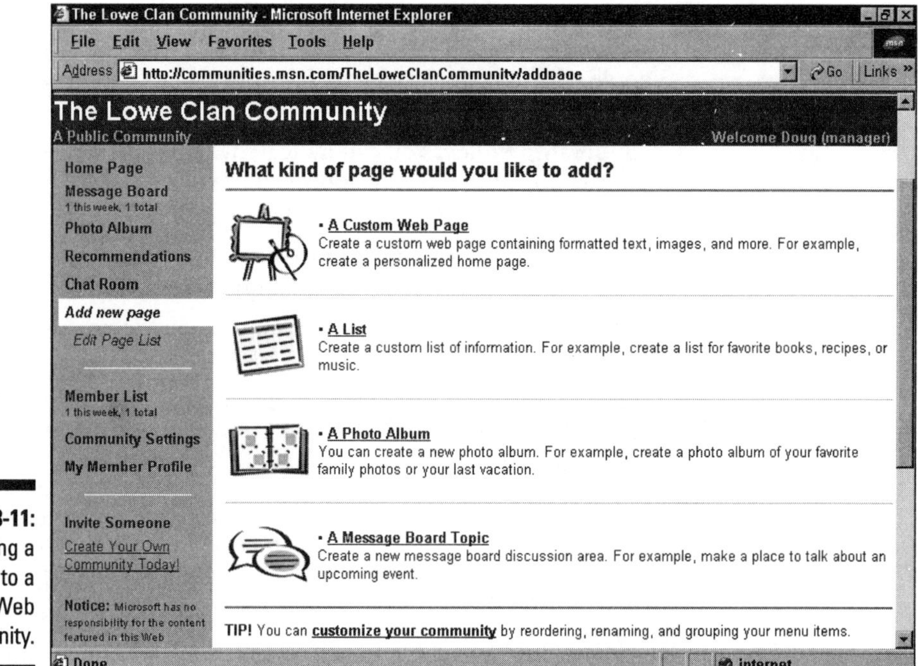

Figure 8-11: Adding a page to a Web Community.

To delete a community, call up the Community Settings page, scroll down to the bottom of the page, and click the Delete Community page. MSN asks if you're sure you want to delete the community; click OK to delete the community or Cancel if you didn't really mean it.

Chapter 9

Chatting on MSN

In This Chapter

- Getting into online chats
- Joining in on the conversation
- Creating your own chat room
- Using Microsoft Chat instead of MSN Chat

E-mail is an effective means of communication because it is convenient yet timely. Still, it may take a day or more for someone to respond to an e-mail. When you absolutely must have instant gratification in your online communications, you need to turn to chat.

A *chat* is an online conversation between two or more Internet users who are signed onto the Internet at the same time. When you chat with another user, your words display almost instantly on the receiver's screen as you type, and vice versa. While e-mail is kind of like sending a postcard or a letter, chat is more like talking on the phone.

MSN uses the standard Internet chatting service, called *Internet Relay Chat* (or *IRC* for short). This means that you can use any Internet chat program to participate in MSN chats. It also means that you do not have to be a paid subscriber to MSN Internet Access to chat at MSN. Any Internet user can join in an MSN Chat.

MSN has a simple Web-based chat interface called MSN Chat. The easiest way to get your feet wet with chatting is by using MSN Chat. However, once you become proficient with MSN Chat, you'll want to consider moving up to Microsoft's more advanced chat program, called Microsoft Chat. Microsoft Chat, which comes free with Internet Explorer 5, offers many advanced chatting features that are not available using MSN Chat.

Another type of online chatting you may wish to indulge in is a program called MSN Messenger Service. MSN Messenger Service allows you to create a list of friends who use the Internet and then informs you when those friends are online and allows you to chat with them. For more information about MSN Messenger Service, see Chapter 11.

Finding a Chat Room

MSN offers hundreds of different *chat rooms* where people gather to discuss whatever is on their minds. Some chat rooms have just a few participants; others may have dozens. In a crowded chat room, messages can fly by faster than you can read them.

To chat in an MSN chat room, call up the MSN home page and then click Chat in the quick links that appear beneath the horizontal menu bar. This will take you to the Web Communities Chat page, as shown in Figure 9-1. This page lists MSN's chat rooms, grouped into categories such as Peers, Entertainment, Lifestyles, and Romance.

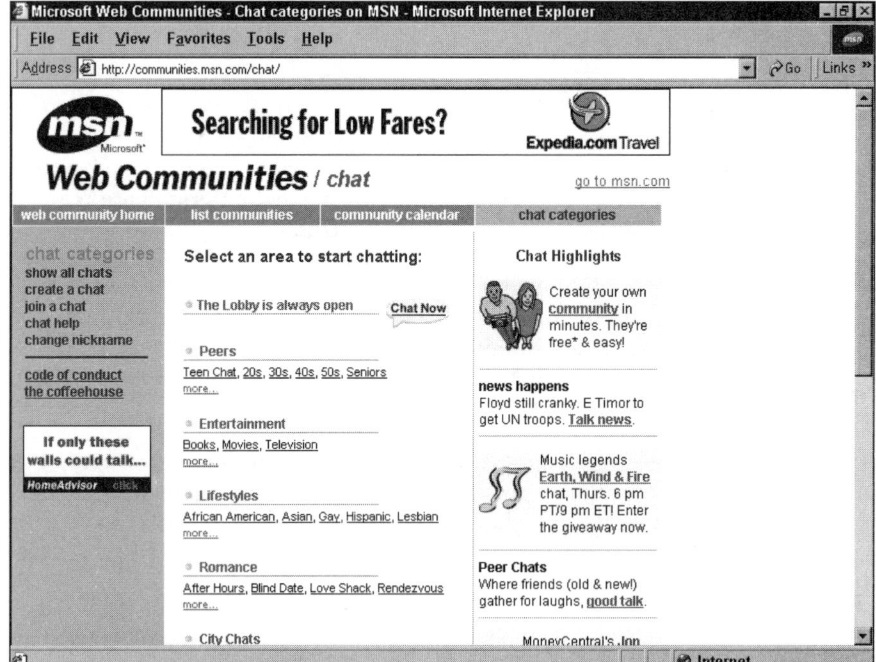

Figure 9-1: The Web Communities Chat page.

There are three ways you can join an MSN chat room. The first — and easiest — is to peruse the categorized list of chats shown in the Chat categories on the MSN page. You'll find links to the most popular chats under each category right on the Web Communities Chat page. To see more chat rooms for a category, click the Category name itself to call up a list of all the chats for that category. When you find a chat that you want to join, click the chat's link. You are teleported instantly into the chat.

For your first chatting experience, I suggest that you choose The Lobby from the Web Communities Chat. The Lobby is a busy chat room where you will find several dozen people to chat with at all hours of the day and night. Plus, The Lobby is always monitored by an MSN host, whom you can ask questions if you get lost.

The second way to join a chat is to click the Show All Chats hyperlink at the left side of the Web Communities Chat page. This takes you to the page shown in Figure 9-2, which lists all the chat rooms that are available on MSN's chat servers. Scroll down this list until you find a chat that you want to join. Click the chat name to join in the fun. (If you can't find a chat that you want to join on the first page of the chat list, click the Next hyperlink to display another page of chats.)

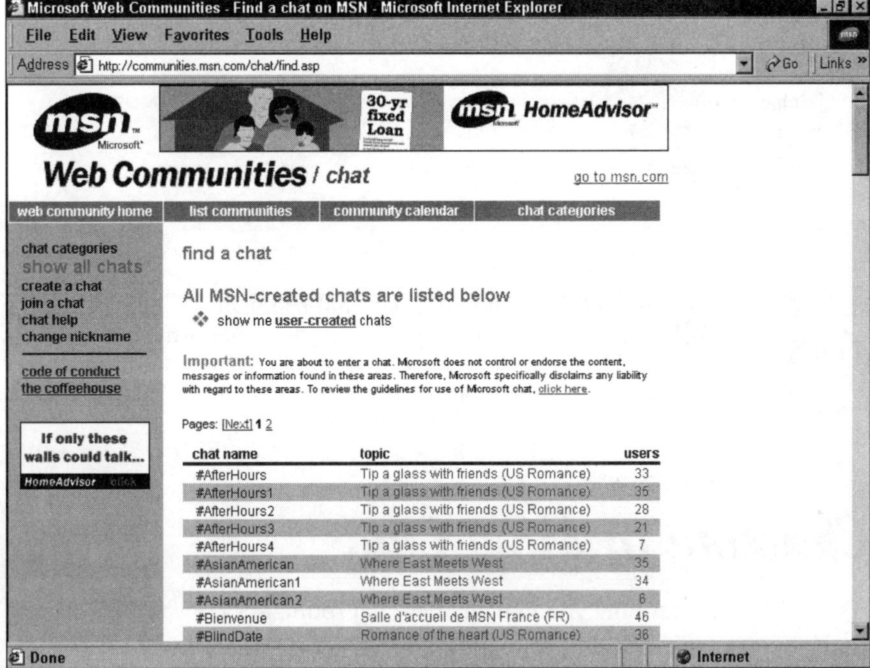

Figure 9-2: You can display a list of all the chat rooms on MSN's chat servers.

The third method of joining a chat is useful if you already know the name of the chat you want to join. In this case, click the Join a Chat hyperlink on the Web Communities Chat page. The page shown in Figure 9-3 appears. On this page, type the name of the chat room that you want to join, type the nickname that you'd like to use in the chat room, and then click the Go button to enter the chat.

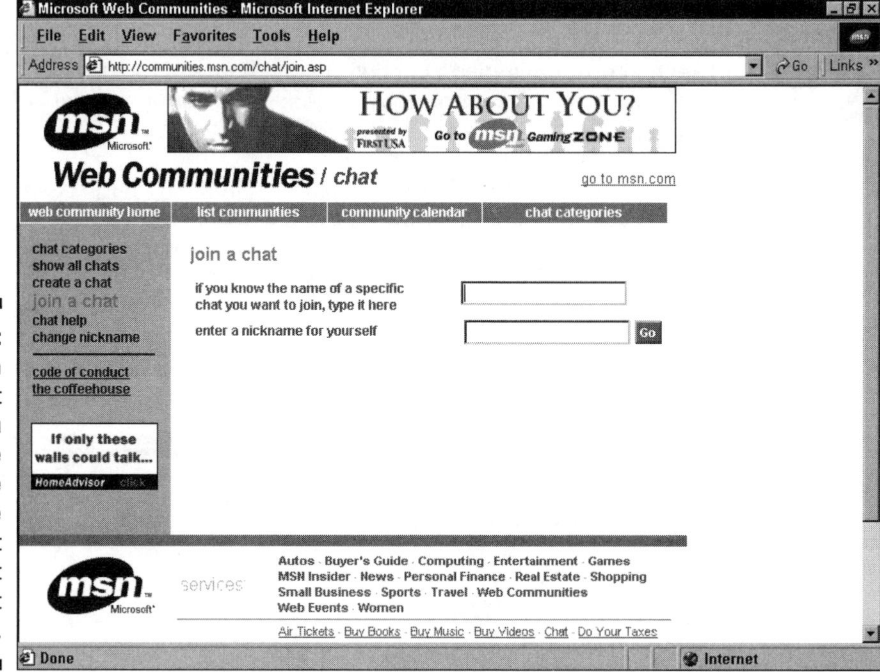

Figure 9-3: Click Join a Chat if you know the name of the chat room that you want to enter.

If you frequently visit a particular chat room, add that chat room to your IE Favorites by choosing the Favorites⇨Add to Favorites command while you are in the chat room. Then, you can return to the chat room at any time by choosing the chat room from your Favorites menu. (In Netscape Navigator, choose Bookmarks⇨Add Bookmark.)

Chatting in MSN Chat

The first time you join an MSN chat room, MSN downloads a small program file that enables MSN Chat to work in Internet Explorer or Netscape Navigator (versions 3.0 and higher). This download takes but a minute or two and happens only the first time, so don't be alarmed. The next time you come to a chat room, you won't have to wait for the software to download.

After the MSN chat software finishes downloading, MSN Chat displays the page shown in Figure 9-4, where you are asked to create a nickname that other chat participants will know you by. Type the nickname you want to use and then click OK to enter the chat room. (If someone else is using the nickname you type, MSN Chat will create a different nickname for you by tacking a number onto the end of the nickname you requested.)

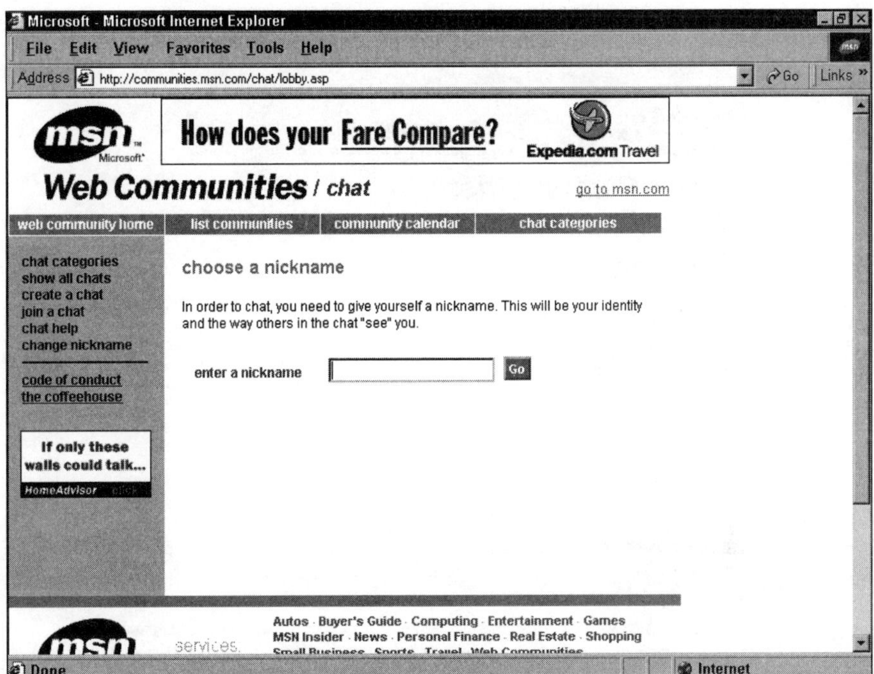

Figure 9-4: Creating a nickname.

After you have selected a chat room, downloaded the software, and created a nickname, MSN Chat connects you to the room and displays a page similar to the one shown in Figure 9-5. This page displays the conversation occurring within the chat room as a never-ending stream of text.

When you first see an MSN Chat, you may be bewildered — especially if you jump into a busy chat room such as The Lobby and messages fly by so fast that you can't read them. After you become familiar with MSN Chat and how chatting works, you won't be so overwhelmed.

The MSN Chat page is divided into three areas:

- The chat itself is in the middle portion of the screen, where you can see messages sent by you and others who are chatting. You can use the scroll bar to scroll up to read messages that fly by so fast that you can't read them.

  When you scroll up to see former messages, you can't see new messages as they are added to the conversation. To return to following the conversation as it occurs, just scroll to the bottom of the chat.

- Down the right edge of the screen is the member list, which lists all the participants who are currently in the chat room. Each participant is identified with one of these five icons:

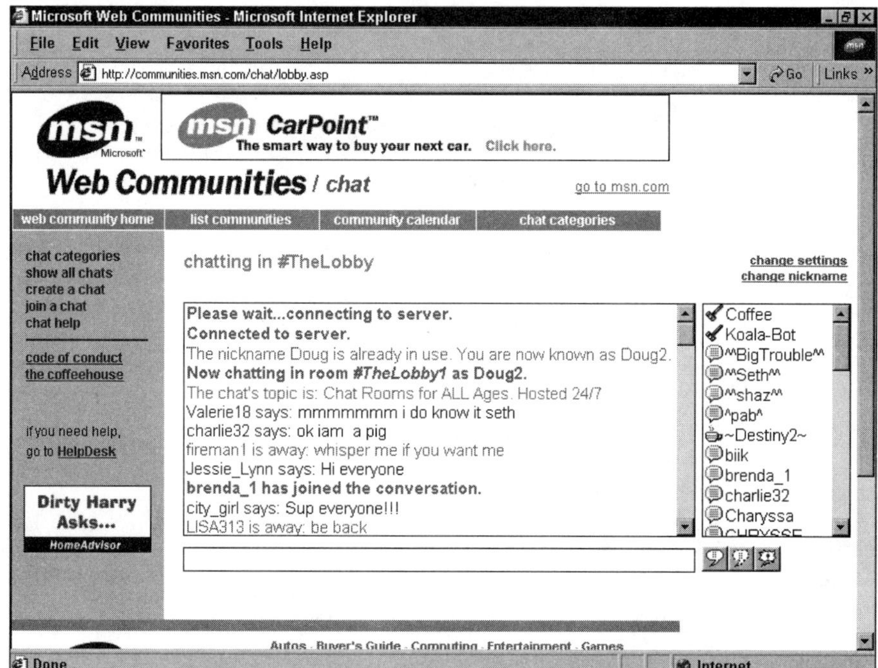

Figure 9-5: Chatting with MSN Chat.

- **Participant:** A regular participant who can listen and speak.
- **Host:** A host moderates the chat. The host tries to keep the conversation on track and makes sure no one crosses the bounds of decorum. If you cross the line, you may find yourself temporarily made a spectator or even get kicked out of the chat room altogether.
- **Away:** Indicates a user who is away — that is, someone who has temporarily left the chat but will be back soon. In the "Signing off from the conversation" section later in this chapter, I'll show you how you can designate yourself as an away participant.
- **Spectator:** Someone who can listen to the conversation but cannot speak.
- **Ignore:** Indicates a participant whom you have decided to ignore, most likely because of his or her repeated obnoxious comments. I'll show you how to ignore someone in the "Ignoring obnoxious chatters" section later in this chapter.

- At the bottom of the page is the *message box,* where you type messages to be sent to the chat.

Sending a message

When you first enter a chat room, your best bet is to eavesdrop for a while to figure out what is happening. When you get up the nerve to contribute your own messages to a chat, follow these simple steps:

1. **Compose a brilliant message in the message box.**

   The message box is at the bottom of the page, beneath the chat itself.

   If you just entered a chat room, it's customary to send a greeting before jumping into the chat. Type **Greetings Earthlings,** or whatever suits your fancy.

   If you're addressing a comment to a specific person, preface your comment with the person's name. For example:

   Hawkeye: Ever heard of the second amendment?

2. **When you're ready to send your message, click one of the Send buttons that appears next to the message box.**

   The three Send buttons determine how your message is conveyed to the group:

    **Say button:** Sends a normal message. MSN Chat prefaces your message with *so-and-so says.* For example, if your nickname is Gilligan, you type **Skipper!!!!** in the message box and click the Say button, the following line will appear in the chat:

   ```
   Gilligan says: Skipper!!!!
   ```

    **Whisper button:** Sends a private message to a single user. First, select the user from the list of chat participants on the right side of the MSN Chat page. Then click the Whisper button.

    **Action button:** Sends a descriptive message, often to suggest body language. For example, *Billy-Bob shrugs and wipes his forehead.*

When you compose an action message, keep in mind that MSN Chat always adds your name before the message. For example, if your name is John and you send the action message "yawns," Microsoft Chat displays the following message:

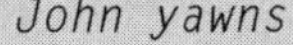

```
John yawns.
```

You can use the following keyboard shortcuts instead of the buttons to send a message to the chat:

Chat button	Keyboard shortcut
Say	Ctrl+S
Whisper	Ctrl+W
Action	Ctrl+A

Ignoring obnoxious chatters

Every once in a while, you get into a chat room with someone who insists on dominating the conversation with a constant stream of obnoxious remarks. Or, you may be pestered by a couple of chat users who go on and on about a topic that's far from interesting to you.

Fortunately, MSN Chat gives you a way to tune these people out. Just follow these steps:

1. **Right-click the nickname of the person that you want to ignore from the member list that appears at the right of the MSN Chat page (refer to Figure 9-5).**
2. **Choose Ignore from the quick menu that appears.**

   Messages from the user that you silenced no longer show up on your computer. The ignored user can still participate in the chat, and other users can see the ignored user's messages as if nothing happened.

To reinstate someone you have ignored, simply repeat the procedure.

The person you tune out has no clue what you did. He or she will keep babbling on, wondering why you never seem to answer. Of course, if no one ever seems to answer you, it could be that *you* are the one who is being ignored!

Understanding Chat Shorthand

Because chatting requires so much typing, chat junkies often use their own cryptic form of shorthand for common words and phrases, like FYI for "For Your Information" and ASAP for "As Soon As Possible." Here are some of the common shorthand abbreviations you are likely to see in a chat:

AFK	Away from keyboard
BRB	Be right back
BTW	By the way
FWIW	For what it's worth
IMO	In my opinion
LOL	Laughing out loud
ROFL	Rolling on the floor laughing
TTYL	Talk to you later

Getting Emotional with Emoticons

Internet chatting lacks the advantage of voice inflections and body language, which can lead to all kinds of misunderstandings. So you have to be careful that people know when you're joking, when you're upset, when you're bored, and so on. Chat junkies have developed a peculiar way to convey tone of voice: They string together symbols on the computer keyboard to create *smileys* (also called *emoticons*). Here are some of the more commonly used (or abused) emoticons:

:)	Your basic smiley
:-)	With a nose
;-)	Wink
:-(	Bummer
:-0	Well, I never!
:-x	My lips are sealed
}:0	Mooo!

Silencing the departure and arrival messages

A busy chat room, where people come and go, can quickly become filled with messages saying that so-and-so has joined the conversation and so-and-so has left the conversation. If these messages become annoying, you can turn them off by following these steps:

1. **Click the change settings hyperlink above the member list.**

   The Change Your Settings dialog box appears, as shown in Figure 9-6.

2. **Uncheck the Show Arrivals and Departures option.**
3. **Click the Go button.**

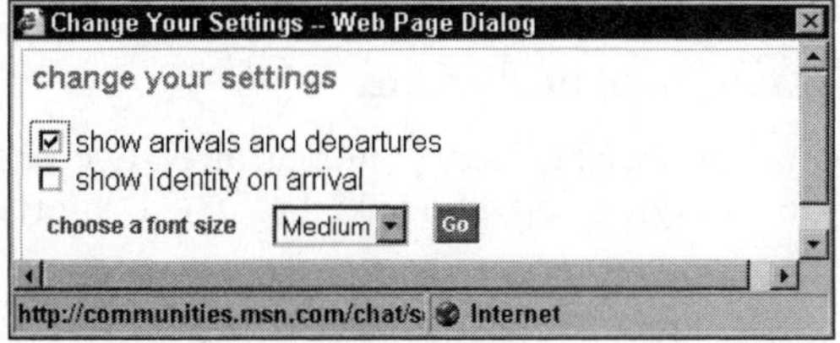

Figure 9-6: Changing your MSN Chat settings.

To reinstate the arrival and departure messages, click the change settings hyperlink again and check the Show Arrivals and Departures option.

Signing off from the conversation

When you're tired of chatting, you can leave an MSN chat room by clicking your browser's Back button. If you've been actively participating in the chat, proper chat etiquette is to say goodbye first. But if you haven't participated in the chat, you can leave without saying goodbye and no one will be offended.

Note that when you leave, a message displays in the chat room indicating that you have left.

Creating Your Own Chat Room

If you don't like the large crowds found in MSN's established chat room, MSN allows you to create your own chat room. This allows you to create a cozy place where you and a few other friends can meet to shoot the breeze without contending with dozens of other chat users who may want to barge in on your conversation.

To create your own chat room, follow these steps:

1. **Click Create a Chat in the left navigation bar on any chat page.**

   The Create a Chat page appears, as shown in Figure 9-7.

2. **Type a nickname for yourself.**

   The last nickname you used appears as the default in the Nickname text box, so you can skip this step unless you want to use a different nickname.

3. **Choose a category from the drop-down list.**

   The categories are Computing and Internet, Entertainment, Family & Kids, Health & Medicine, Interests, Lifestyles, Romance, and Sports & Recreation.

4. **Type a name for your chat in the text box.**

   You can use any name you wish. If someone has already created a chat room with the name you type, you'll be asked to use a different name.

5. **Type in a description of your chat topic in the text box.**

   Describe the topic of your chat room in a few words name, you can restrict your chat room to those friends to whom you tell the chat room name (or any lucky guesses).

6. **Chose the Public or Private option for your chat.**

   If you check Public, other MSN Chat users can find and join your chat. If you check Private, an MSN Chat user must know the exact name of your chat to join. By choosing Private and selecting an obscure chat room

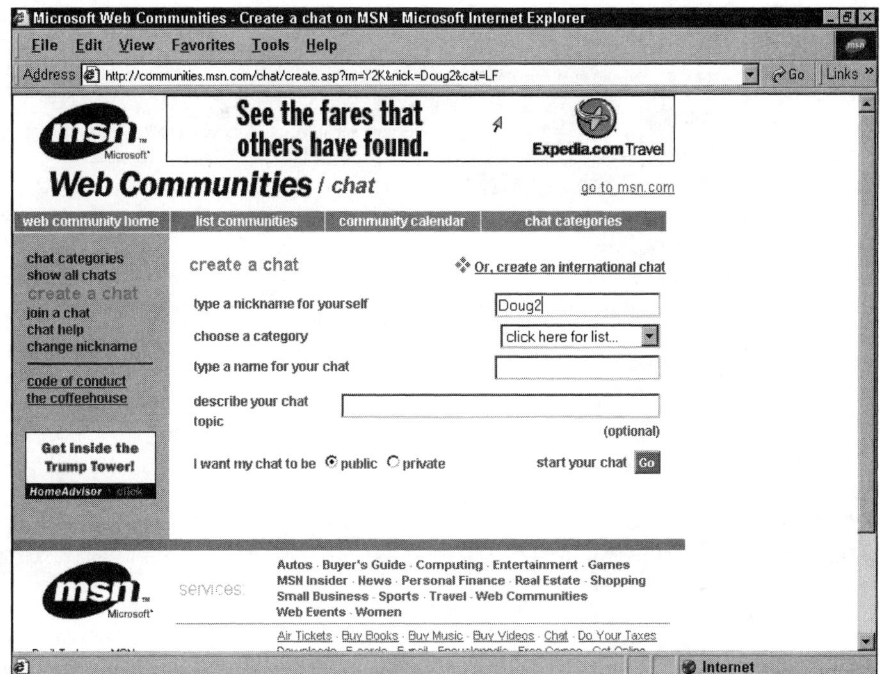

Figure 9-7: Creating a chat room of your own.

7. **Click the Go button to start your chat.**

   You will be taken to the newly created chat room, as shown in Figure 9-8.

User-created chat rooms are not permanent. As soon as the last member leaves a user-created chat room, the chat room is deleted from MSN's chat servers.

Playing host

When you create a chat room, you are designated as the host of the room. What incredible power awaits you! The host has a few additional capabilities that normal chat participants do not. In particular:

- As the host, you can kick someone out of the room if you don't like them. To kick a participant out, right-click the participant in the member list, then choose Kick from the pop-up menu that appears.
- You can elevate any member of the chat to a host by right-clicking that member in the member list and choosing Host from the pop-up menu that appears.
- To demote someone back to a normal member, right-click the member in the member list and choose Speaker from the pop-up menu.

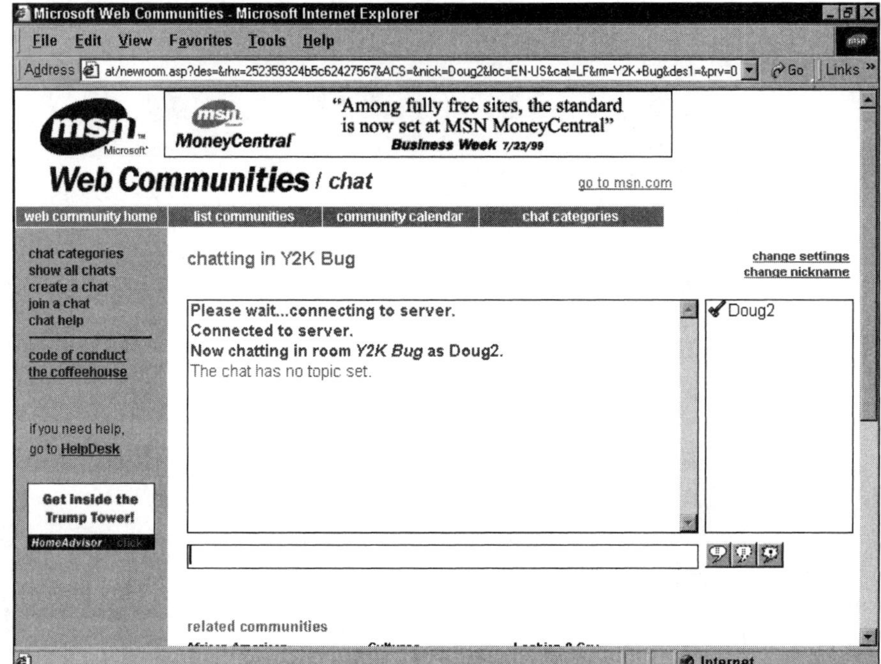

Figure 9-8: A user-created chat room.

Joining some else's chat

You can join a public chat created by an MSN chat user. Just click Show All Chats in the left navigation bar on any chat page, and then click the show me MSN-created chats hyperlink that appears near the top of the list. This will list the user-created chats rather than the MSN-sponsored chats, as shown in Figure 9-9. Don't be surprised to find literally thousands of user-created chats on MSN's chat servers. In Figure 9-9, there are 197 pages of user-created chat rooms listed. Each of these 19 pages lists 250 user-created chat rooms.

To join a private chat, you must know the chat room's exact name. Private chat rooms do not appear in the chat room list. To go to the Join a Chat page, click Join a Chat in the left navigation bar on any chat page. In the dialog box that appears, type the name of the private chat room that you want to join, and click the Go button.

Using Microsoft Chat

Although MSN Chat is a fine chat tool for those who want to chat only occasionally, for more serious chatting turn to Microsoft Chat — Microsoft's full-featured chatting program. Microsoft Chat has many advantages over MSN Chat. Here are just a few:

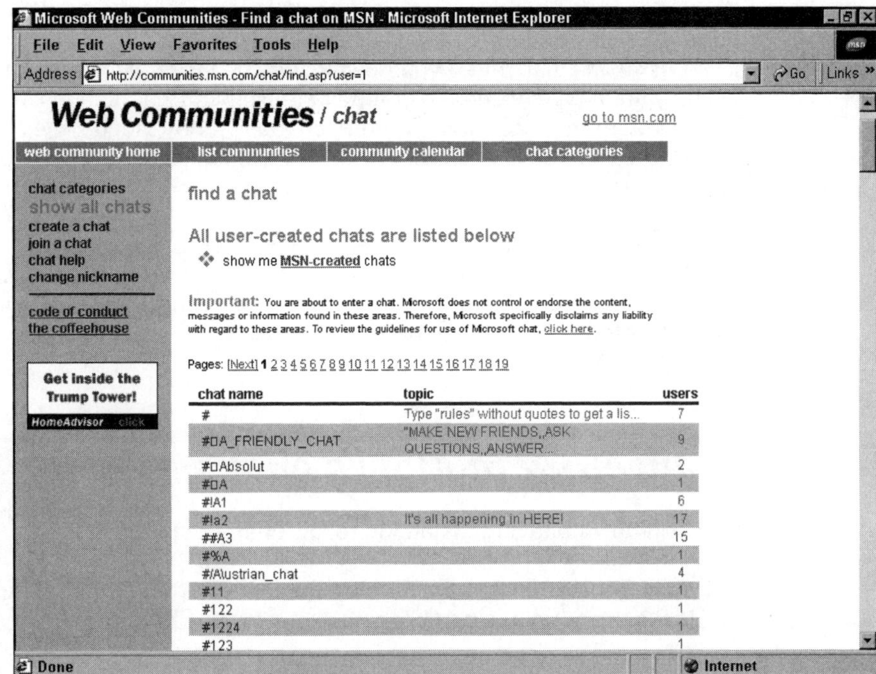

Figure 9-9: My, there are a lot of user-created chats.

- Microsoft Chat lets you chat in more than one chat room at a time and easily move back and forth among chat rooms.
- Microsoft Chat lets you use IRC chat commands. For example, you can use an IRC command to indicate that you have temporarily left the chat but will be back later. You can access IRC commands using Microsoft Chat's menus, or — if you're an IRC junkie and know the commands by heart — you can type them directly in the message box.
- Microsoft Chat lets you create macros, which let you send common messages with a single keystroke.
- Microsoft Chat has more powerful features for the host of a user-created chat room. For example, you can set up an automated greeting that displays whenever anyone enters your chat room. And you can set up Moderated chat rooms, in which members who join are designated as Spectators and not allowed to speak until you promote them to Speakers.
- Microsoft Chat includes a special feature called *comics mode*, which displays chats in a way that resembles a comic book.

Setting up Microsoft Chat

The first step you take to get started using Microsoft Chat is to obtain a copy of the Microsoft Chat program and install it on your computer. If you got Internet Explorer 5 on a CD-ROM or installed on a new computer, you already have Microsoft Chat, and if you downloaded IE 5 from Microsoft's Web site, you may not have chosen the complete download that includes Microsoft Chat. If you didn't, you have to return to the IE 5 download page to download Microsoft Chat. You can access the IE 5 download page via Microsoft's main Web page at `www.microsoft.com`.

After you get to the download page, you can click to the Microsoft Chat link. The Chat program file is about 1750KB in size, so it takes a few minutes to download. After the download finishes, the Microsoft Chat Setup program starts. Just follow the instructions that appear on your screen to install Microsoft Chat.

Connecting to MSN's chat server

After you download and install Microsoft Chat, the fun begins.

1. **Start Microsoft Chat by clicking the Start button on the Windows taskbar and choosing Programs⇨Microsoft Chat.**

   The first time you run Microsoft Chat, a dialog box appears asking you for a nickname that other chat participants will know you by.

2. **Type any nickname that you want and click the OK button.**

   If you downloaded Microsoft Chat with Netscape Navigator (by clicking the link and choosing Save File. . .), locate the downloaded file on your hard drive and double click its icon to start the installation.

   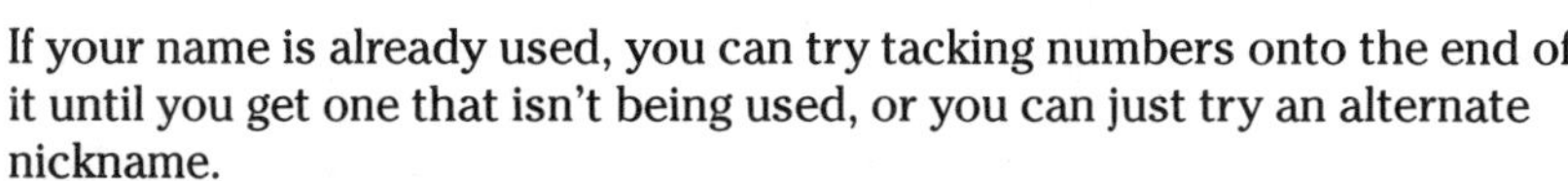

   If your name is already used, you can try tacking numbers onto the end of it until you get one that isn't being used, or you can just try an alternate nickname.

   After your computer grinds and whirls for a moment, the Chat Connection dialog box, shown in Figure 9-10, greets you.

3. **In the Chat Connection dialog box, specify the important information required to initiate a chat with other Internet users.**

   Here's the lowdown on the fields in the Connect dialog box:

   - **Favorites:** As you use Microsoft Chat, you can add the chat rooms you visit most frequently to a list of favorite chat rooms. Initially, though, this list is empty. Microsoft doesn't presume to know what your favorite chat rooms are. (That might come as a shock!)

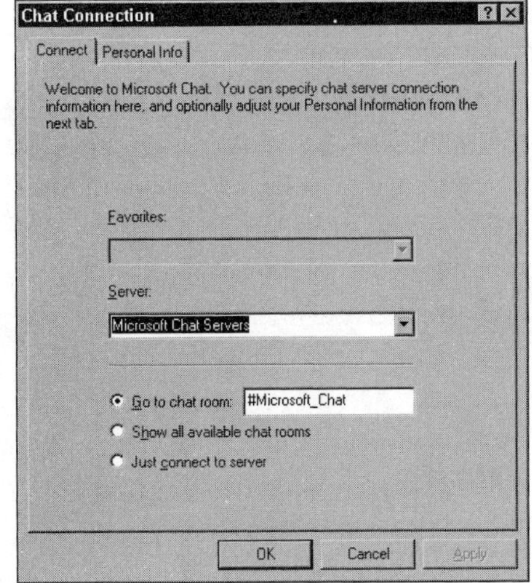

Figure 9-10: The Microsoft Chat Connection dialog box.

- **Server:** This drop-down list lets you choose from several servers to chat on. The default is to use Microsoft's chat servers, but you can choose from several other servers if you prefer.
- **Go to Chat Room:** If you know the name of a chat room that you want to visit, select this option and type the name of the chat room in this field. Otherwise, select the next option.
- **Show All Available Chat Rooms:** Select this option if you don't know the name of the chat room that you want to visit, or if you aren't sure which chat rooms are available on the server to which you can connect.
- **Just Connect to the Server:** Select this option if you want to connect to the server but don't want to enter a chat room.

4. **After you set all the Chat Connection options, click the OK button to connect to the chat server.**

   A Message of the Day dialog box may appear, similar to the one shown in Figure 9-11.

   The Message of the Day provides you with useful information such as the number of other people that are wasting their time on the chat server with you, as well as a disclaimer saying that Microsoft is not responsible for anything that happens to you while you are on their chat server.

   Uncheck the Show This Whenever Connecting option if you don't want to see this message the next time that you connect.

5. **Click the OK button after reading the Message of the Day.**

   The Message of the Day dialog box goes away when you click OK.

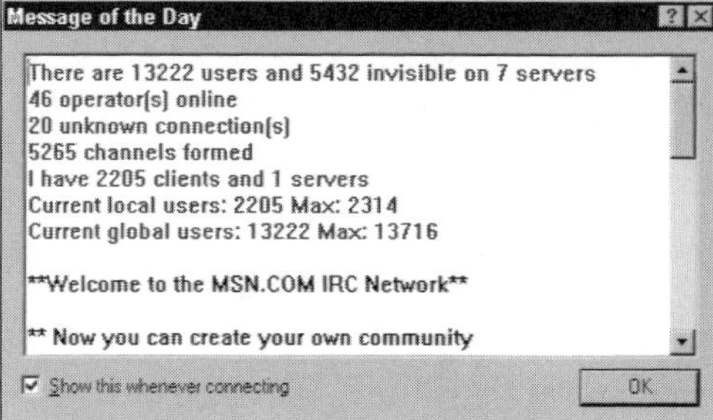

Figure 9-11: The annoying Message of the Day dialog box.

Finding a chat room

If you select the Show All Available Chat Rooms option from the Chat Connection dialog box, you're greeted with a list of all the chat rooms that are available on the server that you connected to, as shown in Figure 9-12. Note that if the Show Only Registered Rooms option is checked, this dialog box lists only the MSN-sponsored chats. If this option is unchecked, all chat rooms on the MSN chat server are listed.

As you can see in Figure 9-12, you can find a wide variety of chat rooms on the Internet. Notice that the descriptions for some of the chat rooms are in languages other than English, illustrating the international flavor of Internet chatting.

Plenty of sleazy chat rooms appear on just about any chat server you may access, including Microsoft's own servers. Beware of such hangouts. You can usually spot the sleazy rooms by their names.

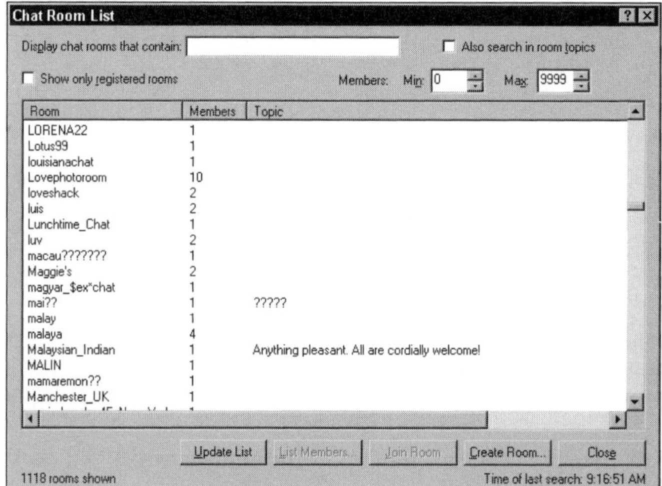

Figure 9-12: The Chat Room list box.

If you find a chat room you like, you can add it to your Favorites by choosing Favorites⇨Add to Favorites after you have entered the room.

Chatting in Microsoft Chat

Microsoft Chat has two basic modes of chatting: text mode and comics mode. You can switch between modes by using the View⇨Comic Strip and View⇨Plain Text commands.

Text view, shown in Figure 9-13, resembles MSN Chat. The chat conversation appears in the middle of the screen; a text box appears at the bottom of the screen for typing messages that you want to send; and a list of chat room members appear on the right of the screen.

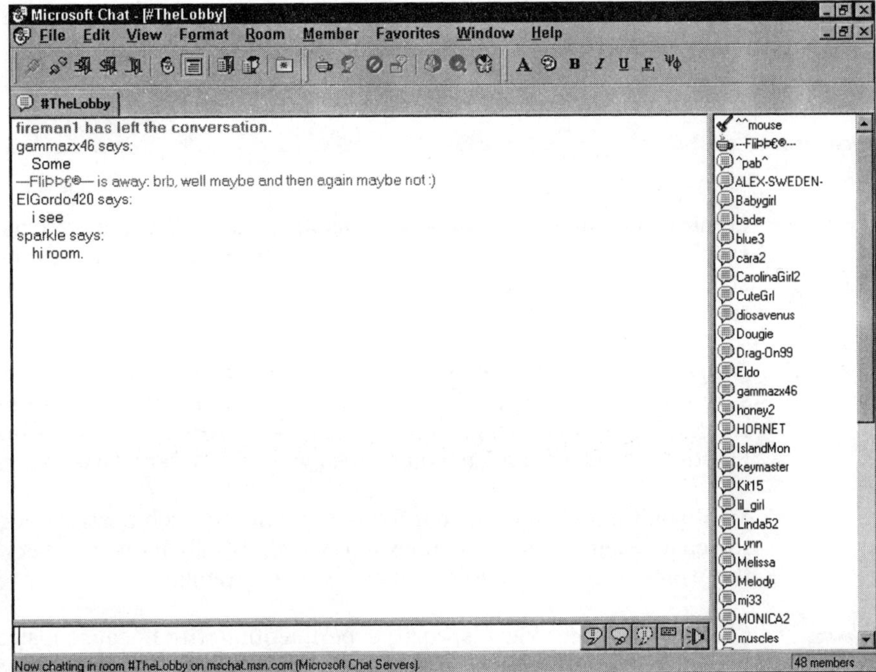

Figure 9-13: Microsoft Chat in text mode.

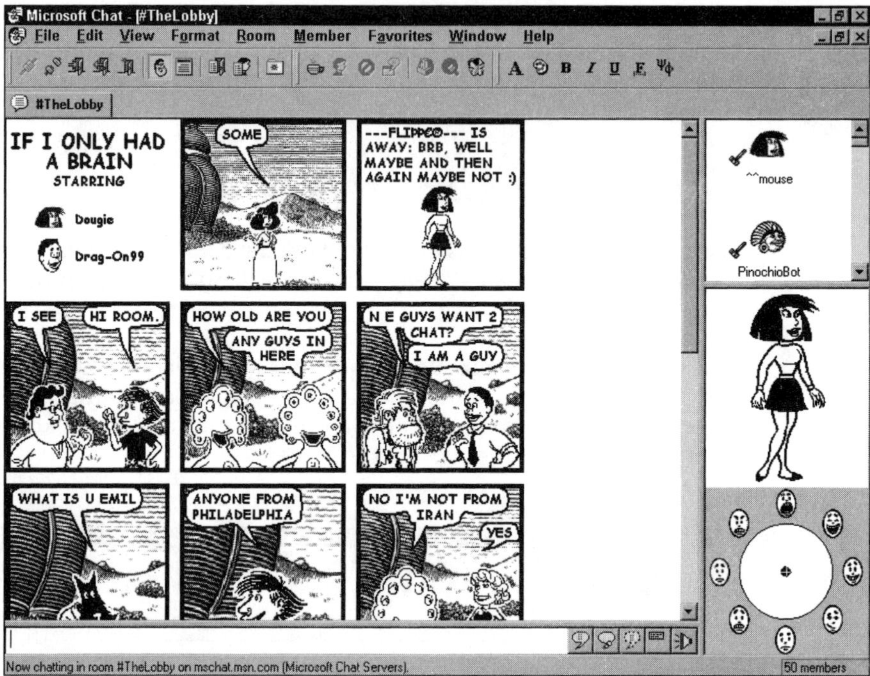

Figure 9-14: Chatting in comics view.

Comics view, shown in Figure 9-14, displays the chat as if it were a comic strip. Each person in the chat room is represented by one of several comic-strip characters that come with Microsoft Chat. You may choose your character of representation, but if you don't choose, a character is chosen for you.

When you switch to comics view, the text-mode view pane is changed to a series of comic strip panels. In addition, a portion of the member list pane is replaced by an image representing your own character and a gizmo called the Emotion Wheel, which lets you control your character's facial expressions.

Microsoft Chat draws the characters in frames as each person contributes to the chat. When a frame becomes full (which usually happens every two or three messages), Microsoft Chat starts a new frame.

Chatting in comics view is worth experimenting with because it's cute, but most users tire of it after awhile. When you grow weary of comics view, choose the View⇨Plain Text command to revert to good ol' text view.

Chapter 10

Using MSN Message Boards

In This Chapter

- Figuring out how MSN message boards work
- Browsing a message board
- Reading and writing messages
- Attaching files to your messages

One of the most important features of MSN Web Communities is its message boards. A *message board* is a place where you can post messages, also known as *articles*, on a particular topic, and read messages on the same topic that others have posted. A message board is a place where people with similar interests gather to share news and information, find out what others are thinking, ask questions and get answers (sometimes), tell jokes, and otherwise shoot the breeze.

Message board articles are similar to e-mail messages, with a few crucial differences:

- E-mail messages are private (or at least, relatively private). Message board articles are public. Anyone who pops into a message board can read any article you or anyone else has posted. (A message board article is sometimes called a *post*, which emphasizes the public nature of message board articles.)
- E-mail messages are addressed to a specific individual. Message board articles are addressed to the message board itself.
- Message board articles remain in the message board until the Web Community manager decides that they have become too old. Depending on how busy and popular the message board, "too old" might mean a week, a month, or a year.

Message boards are similar to Internet newsgroups. However, there are literally tens of thousands of newsgroups on the Internet, whereas there are only a few dozen message boards on MSN. One major difference between an Internet newsgroup and an MSN message board is that you use your e-mail program (such as Outlook Express or Netscape Messenger) to read newsgroups, while you read MSN message boards with your Web browser.

Reading Message Board Discussions

You can access a message board by clicking the Message Board link from the Web Community page. This brings up the Message Board page. For example, Figure 10-1 shows the Message Board for the MSN Movies Web Community.

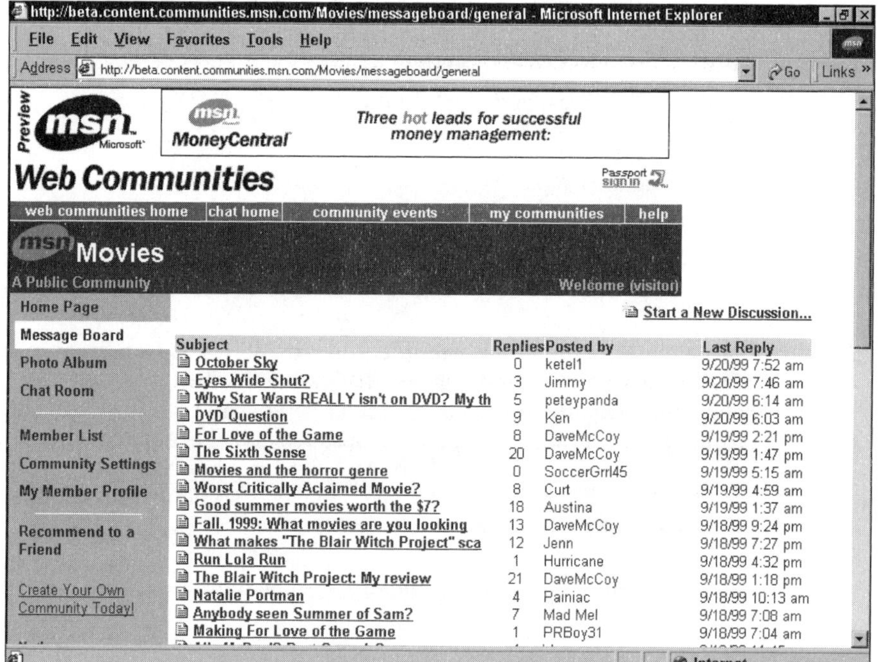

Figure 10-1: A Message Board.

As you can see in Figure 10-1, the main part of the Message Board page displays a list of the messages that are currently available on the message board.

MSN uses the term *discussion* to refer to a message plus any messages that have been posted as replies to the original message, replies to the replies, and so on. The Message Board page lists just one line for each discussion. The Replies column lists the number of replies that are in the discussion. For example, you can see in Figure 10-1 that the message entitled "The Sixth Sense" has 20 replies.

To read a discussion, just click the discussion's subject. The original message, along with all of its replies, appears on a new page, as shown in Figure 10-2. You can scroll down this page to read all of the messages in the discussion.

Figure 10-2: A message on a Message Board.

Replying to a Message

To reply to a message, follow these steps:

1. **Count to ten and then reconsider your reply.**

   Keep in mind that replying to a Message Board is not like replying to e-mail. Only the intended recipient can read an e-mail reply. Anyone on the planet can read your Message Board postings. If you don't really have anything to add to the discussion, why waste your time?

2. **Click the Add a Reply button (shown in the margin) that appears next to the message that you want to reply to.**

   Add a Reply...

   A new message page appears.

3. **Type your reply in the message text box.**

   Figure 10-3 shows how the new message appears after you have typed some text.

   If you wish, you can use the formatting buttons above the message text box to format your message. For more information, refer to the "Formatting Messages" section later in this chapter.

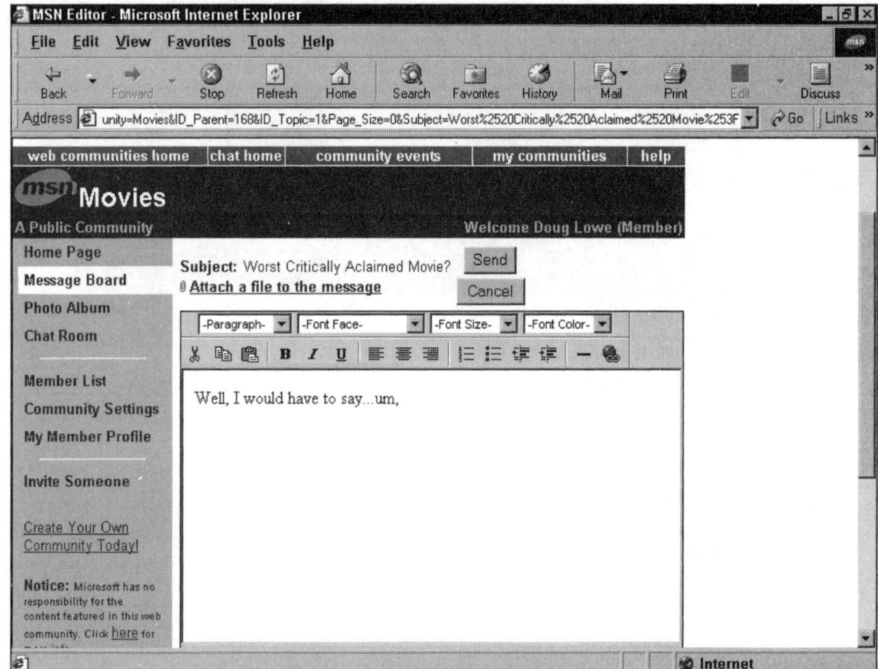

Figure 10-3: Replying to a message.

4. **Click the Send button.**

   Your reply is added to the discussion.

Starting a New Discussion

If you want to start a new discussion in a message board, just follow these steps:

1. **Open the message board in which you want to start a new discussion.**

2. **Click the Start a New Discussion hyperlink.**

   A new message page appears.

3. **Type a subject for the article in the Subject box.**

   Make sure that the subject you type accurately reflects the topic of the discussion.

4. **Type your message in the message area.**

   Figure 10-4 shows how the new message appears after you have typed a subject and some text.

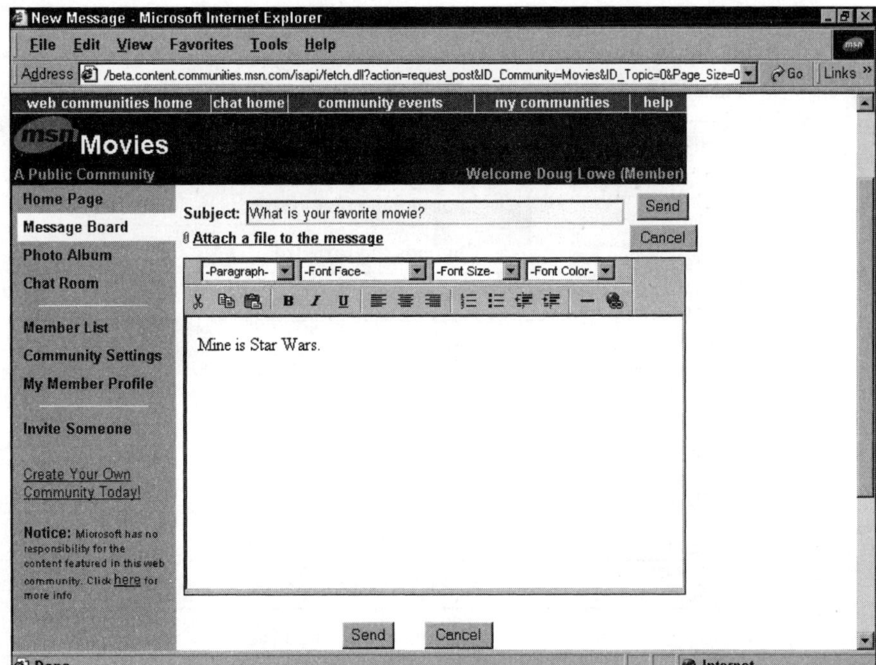

Figure 10-4: Starting a new discussion.

If you want to apply fancy formatting to your message, use the formatting buttons that appear above the message box. For more information, see the following section.

5. **Click the Send button when you're satisfied with your message.**

Your message will be posted to the message board as a new discussion. Be sure to check the message board regularly for the next few days to see any responses your message may generate from other Web Community members.

Formatting Messages

Web Community Message Boards let you apply formatting to your messages by using the formatting controls that appear above the message box. Table 10-1 lists these formatting controls and briefly describes the formatting each of the controls allows you to apply.

Table 10-1: Message Board Formatting Controls

Control	*Explanation*
-Paragraph-	Applies a paragraph format such as Heading 1, Heading 2, Heading 3, and so on
-Font Face-	Changes the text font
-Font Size-	Changes the text size
-Font Color-	Changes the text color
B	Bold
I	Italic
U	Underline
	Left justifies the paragraph
	Centers the paragraph
	Right justifies the paragraph
	Creates a numbered list
	Creates a bulleted list
	Removes indentation
	Adds indentation
	Inserts a horizontal line
	Inserts a hyperlink

Dealing with Attachments

MSN message boards allow you to attach files to your messages. You can attach any type of file you wish to a message, including pictures, sounds, Word documents, program files, and any other type of file you can think of. The only limitation is that the size of the files you attach to a single message cannot exceed 1MB.

To attach a file to a message, follow these steps:

1. **Click the Attach a File to the Message hyperlink on the new message page.**

   This takes you to the Attach File page, as shown in Figure 10-5.

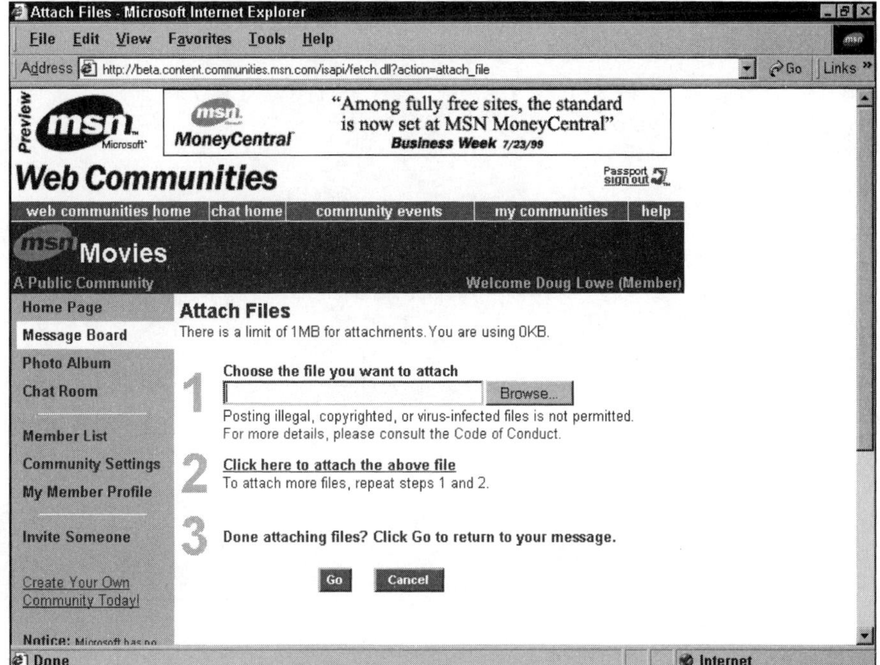

Figure 10-5: Attaching a file to a message.

2. **Click the Browse button.**

   A Choose File dialog box appears.

3. **Rummage around your hard drive until you find the file you want to attach.**

4. **Click Open.**

   The Choose File dialog box closes and you are returned to the Attach Files page. The name of the file you chose appears in the file name text box.

5. **Click the Click here to attach the above file hyperlink.**

   The file is attached to your message.

6. **Repeat steps 2 through 5 if you want to attach additional files to the message.**

   You can attach more than one file to a single message, but keep in mind that the combined size of the files cannot exceed 1MB.

7. **When you have attached all of the files you want, click the Go button.**

   You are returned to the New Message page so you can finish composing your message.

When you view a discussion, any messages that have attachments will list the attachments in the heading area of the message. To download an attachment, just click the attachment's file name in the message heading.

Part III
Learn and Earn on MSN

"He saw your laptop and wants to know if he can check his Hotmail."

In this part . . .

The chapters in this part dive into five of MSN's most useful online services. You'll discover how to stay in touch with friends; stay on top of the news by using Microsoft's premier news site, MSNBC; how to get information about almost any conceivable subject from MSN Encarta; how to manage your finances with Microsoft Investor; and how to get comprehensive information about automobiles by using CarPoint.

This should keep you busy for awhile.

Chapter 11

Staying In Touch with MSN Messenger Service

In This Chapter

- Downloading and installing the MSN Messenger Service
- Building a contact list of online friends
- Sending and receiving instant messages

MSN Messenger Service is a feature of MSN that lets you find out if your friends are currently connected to the Internet and exchange instant messages with them. You must first set up MSN Messenger Service by identifying your friends. In addition, the friends you want to communicate with through MSN Messenger Service must have the service installed on their computers. Once everything is set up, whenever your friends log on to the Internet, you will be alerted. When MSN Messenger Service informs you that one of your friends is online, you can easily send a message, which your friend receives almost immediately. MSN Messenger Service is a great way to stay in touch with your friends over the Internet.

MSN Messenger Service is available to anyone who uses the Internet. You don't have to be an MSN Internet Access subscriber to use MSN Messenger Service, but you do have to sign up for a free Hotmail account.

Installing MSN Messenger Service

Before you can use MSN Messenger Service, you must download and install the program's software. To start the download process, go to the MSN Messenger Service home page, as shown in Figure 11-1. You can find links to the MSN Messenger Service home page on both the MSN home page and the Hotmail home page. Or, if you prefer, you can type **messenger.msn.com** in your Web browser's address field and press the Enter key.

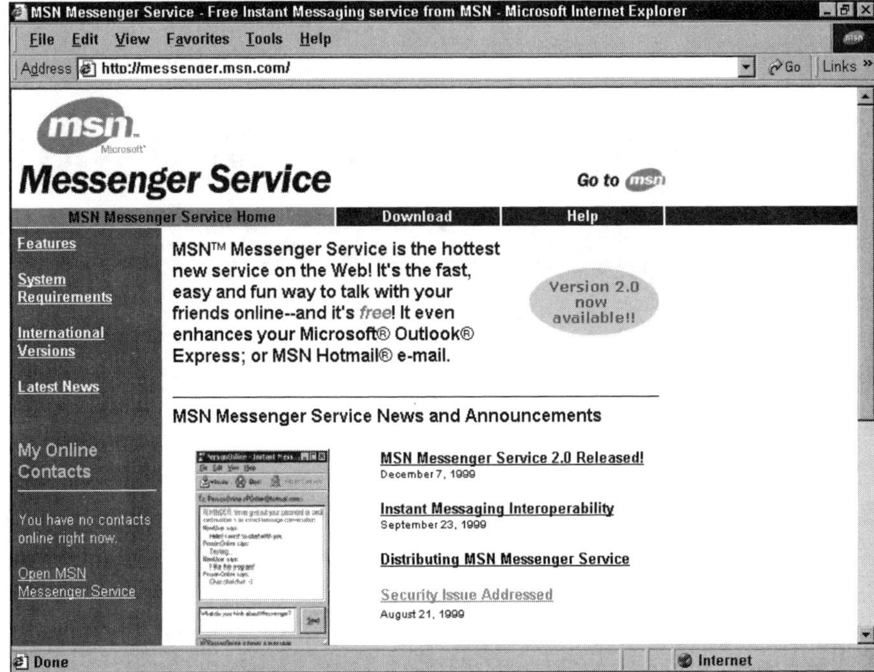

Figure 11-1: The MSN Messenger Service home page.

Once you have arrived at the MSN Messenger Service home page, you can download and install the software by following these steps:

1. **Click Download in the navigation bar near the top of the page.**

   Because you must have a Microsoft Passport account to use MSN Messenger, MSN begins by asking if you have a Passport account, as shown in Figure 11-2.

   MSN Messenger Service requires that you have a Microsoft Passport account. If you have a Hotmail e-mail account, you already have a Passport account so don't worry about registering with Passport to use MSN Messenger. If you do not have a Hotmail or other Passport account, you must create one before you can download and install MSN Messenger.

2. **If you do not have a Passport account, click the click here hyperlink and follow the instructions that appear on the screen to register for your free Passport account.**

   Note that if you have a Hotmail e-mail account, you already have a Passport account so you can skip this step.

   When you click the click here hyperlink, the Passport registration page appears in a separate window. Follow the instructions that appear on the registration page. When you have finished, the registration window closes and returns you back to the page shown in Figure 11-2.

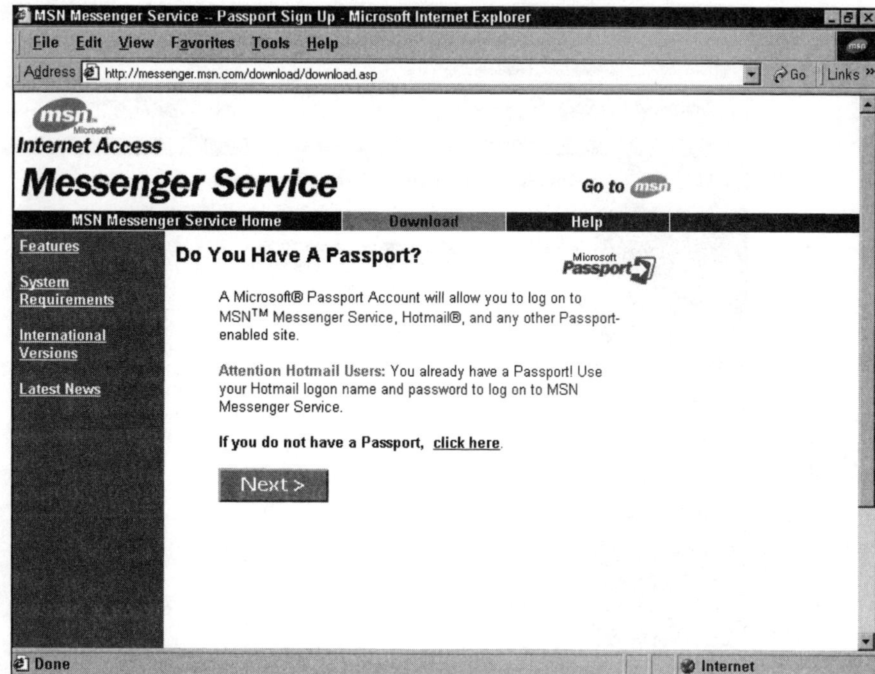

MSN Messenger Service -- Passport Sign Up - Microsoft Internet Explorer
File Edit View Favorites Tools Help
Address http://messenger.msn.com/download/download.asp
Internet Access
Messenger Service
Go to
MSN Messenger Service Home
Download
Help
Features
System Requirements
International Versions
Latest News
Do You Have A Passport?
Microsoft Passport
A Microsoft® Passport Account will allow you to log on to MSN™ Messenger Service, Hotmail®, and any other Passport-enabled site.
Attention Hotmail Users: You already have a Passport! Use your Hotmail logon name and password to log on to MSN Messenger Service.
If you do not have a Passport, click here.
Next >
Done
Internet

Figure 11-2: MSN asks if you have a passport.

3. **Click the Next button.**

   The Start Download page appears, as shown in Figure 11-3.

4. **If you are using a Macintosh computer, click the Change Version hyperlink. When the Change Version page appears, choose the Macintosh version and click OK.**

   The Start Download page reappears.

5. **If you want to change the language setting, click the Change Language hyperlink. When the Change Language page appears, choose the language that you want to use and click OK.**

   The Start Download page reappears.

6. **Click the Start Download button.**

   A File Download dialog box appears, as shown in Figure 11-4.

7. **Select the Run This Program From its Current Location option and click the OK button.**

   The MSN Messenger Service setup file begins downloading. On a 28.8 Kbps Internet connection, the download can take about three or four minutes. A dialog box with a progress bar appears so you can keep track of the download's progress.

   When the download is complete, the Setup program starts by displaying the License Agreement, as shown in Figure 11-5.

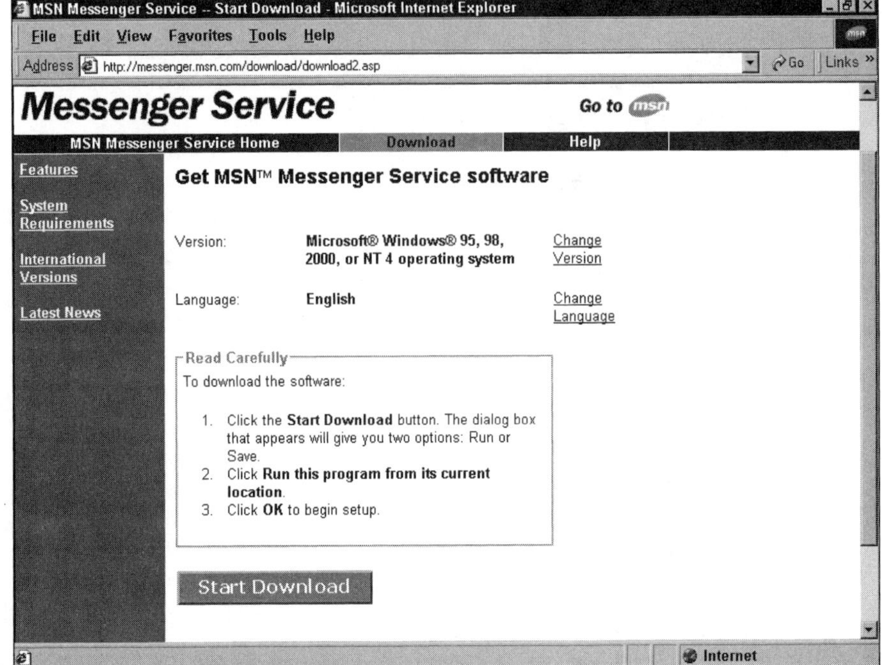

Figure 11-3: Getting ready to download MSN Messenger Service.

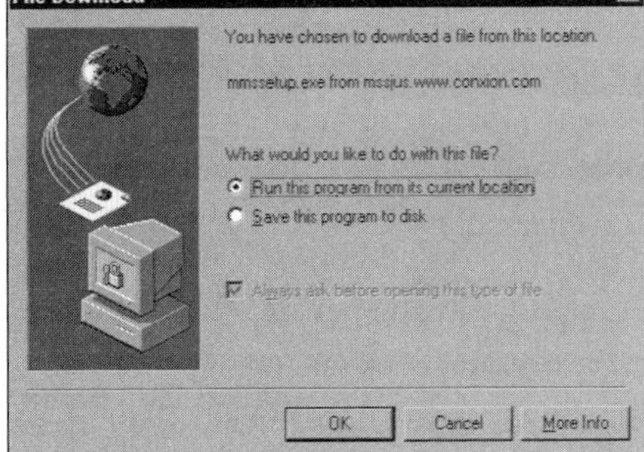

Figure 11-4: The File Download dialog box.

8. **Read the License Agreement if you dare and then click the Yes button.**

   I'm not a lawyer and I don't play one on TV, but I can tell you that the License Agreement for MSN Messenger Service basically says that the software is copyrighted, that you can use the software on your own computer, and that Microsoft is not responsible if you do something stupid like give someone your credit card number while using MSN Messenger Service.

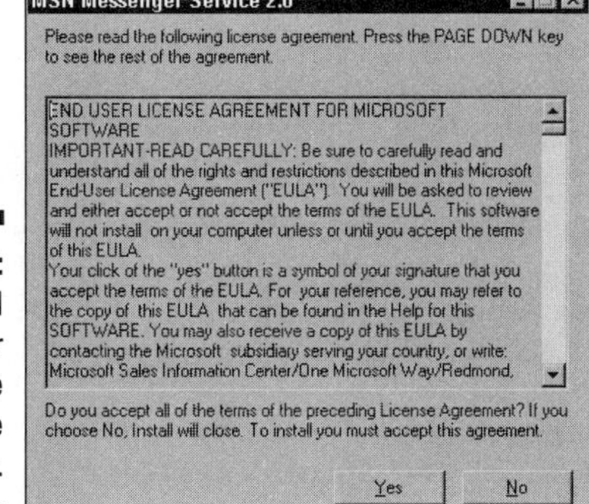

Figure 11-5: The MSN Messenger Service License Agreement.

When you click Yes to accept the License Agreement, the dialog box appears, shown in Figure 11-6, asking which folder you want the MSN Messenger Service software installed in.

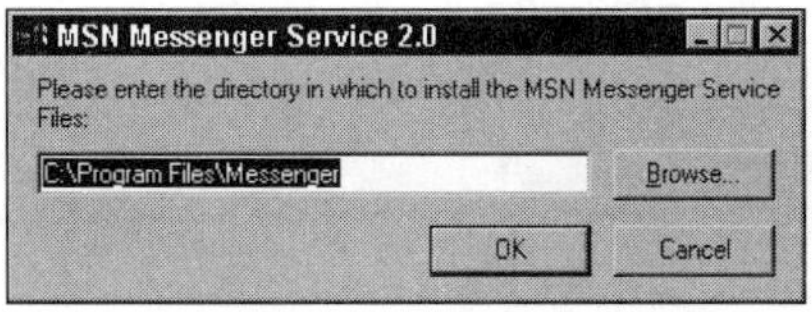

Figure 11-6: Where do you want MSN Messenger Service installed?

MSN Messenger Service 2.0
Please enter the directory in which to install the MSN Messenger Service Files:
C:\Program Files\Messenger
Browse...
OK
Cancel

9. **Change the directory if you wish and then click the OK button.**

   Unless you have some compelling reason to change the directory, I suggest you just click the OK button. The next dialog box you see is the MSN Messenger Service Setup Wizard, as shown in Figure 11-7. This is where the fun starts.

10. **Click the Next button.**

    The Wizard asks if you have a free Passport account, which is required to use MSN Messenger. Since we already took care of getting a free Passport account in Step 2, we'll just plow on ahead here.

11. **Click the Next button.**

    The Wizard asks for your Passport account information, as shown in Figure 11-8.

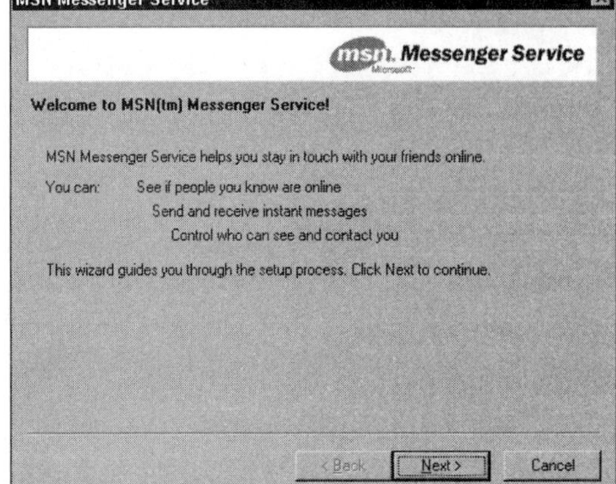

MSN Messenger Service
msn. Messenger Service
Welcome to MSN(tm) Messenger Service!
MSN Messenger Service helps you stay in touch with your friends online.
You can: See if people you know are online
Send and receive instant messages
Control who can see and contact you
This wizard guides you through the setup process. Click Next to continue.
< Back
Next >
Cancel

Figure 11-7: The MSN Messenger Service Setup Wizard.

Figure 11-8: The Wizard wants to know your Passport information.

12. **Type your Passport user ID and password in the appropriate text boxes and click the Next button.**

    If you want MSN Messenger Service to automatically log you on, check the Save This Password... option.

    When you click the Next button, the Wizard displays a message congratulating you for your ingenuity.

13. **Click the Finish button.**

    The Setup Wizard finishes up its business and automatically starts MSN Messenger Service.

What about AOL's Instant Messenger?

Although MSN Messenger Service is a new feature of MSN (introduced in the summer of 1999), some instant message services have been around for years. One of the most successful is America Online's AOL Instant Messenger, also known as AIM. America Online has had some form of instant messaging feature since 1989, but it was limited to America Online subscribers. In 1997, America Online released AIM, which lets anyone who downloads the AIM software exchange instant messages with other AIM users, whether or not they are also America Online subscribers. AIM currently has about 45 million registered users, according to AOL.

When Microsoft decided to get into the instant message game, it realized right off the bat that starting up a new instant message service to compete with AIM would be tough. So Microsoft gave MSN Messenger Service the capability to tap into AIM's vast database of users, allowing MSN Messenger Service users to exchange messages with AIM users, and vice versa.

To instant message users like you and me, allowing MSN Messenger Service users and AIM users to communicate sounds like a great idea. But America Online cried foul, saying that Microsoft illegally hacked into AOL's computer systems to make MSN Messenger Service work alongside AIM. Soon after MSN Messenger Service was released by Microsoft, America Online made a change to AIM's server computers that disabled MSN Messenger Service's ability to access AOL users. Microsoft responded by releasing a new version of MSN Messenger Service a few days later. Of course, a few days after that AOL updated their software to block MSN Messenger Service again, and so on and so on, tit for tat.

Microsoft finally gave up and released a new version of MSN Messenger that does not attempt to work with AIM users. Microsoft and America Online are still trying to work things out, so it is possible that both companies will release versions of their instant messaging software that work together. But until that time, you cannot use MSN Messenger Service to exchange instant messages with AIM users.

However, you can have both services installed on your computer. If you would like to install America Online's Instant Messenger on your computer, go to America Online's home page (`www.aol.com`) and look for the AOL Instant Messenger link. Like MSN Messenger, AIM is a free download.

Getting Familiar with the MSN Messenger Service Window

Once you have installed MSN Messenger Service, the MSN Messenger window, shown in Figure 11-9, displays each time you connect to the Internet. In the center of the MSN Messenger Service window is a list of your online contacts, indicating which contacts are online and which are not. You can send instant messages to any of your contacts who are online. (As you can see, the MSN Messenger Service contact list is empty. For information about adding contacts, see the "Adding Contacts" section later in this chapter.)

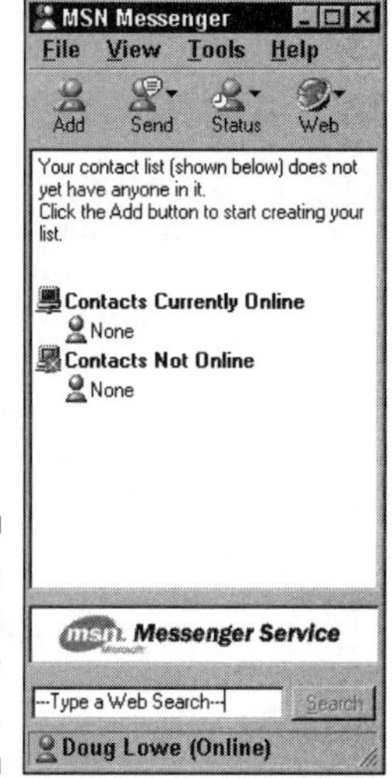

Figure 11-9: The MSN Messenger window.

Below the menu bar at the top of the MSN Messenger window is a toolbar, which contains the following icons:

- **Add:** Adds a person to your contact list.

- **Send:** Sends an instant message to another MSN Messenger Service user.

- **Status:** Changes your MSN Messenger Service status. Use this button to let people know that you are away from your computer, out to lunch, or that you just don't want to be bothered.

- **Web:** Gives you fast access to the MSN home page, the Hotmail home page, or the Hotmail Compose page that lets you send an e-mail message.

At the bottom of the MSN Messenger window is a Search text box, which lets you quickly search the Internet using MSN's search service. To use this feature, type one or more words that you want to search for in the Search text box and then click the Search button. MSN Messenger Service submits your search to MSN's search page and calls up a separate browser window to display the results.

Adding contacts

Before you can use MSN Messenger Service to send instant messages to your online friends, you must first create a list of your online contacts. The trick is that each of your online contacts must also have the MSN Messenger Service software and a Hotmail account. If you try to add someone to your contact list who does not have a Hotmail account and the MSN Messenger Service software, MSN Messenger Service asks for your permission to send that person an e-mail message telling them how to download and install the MSN Messenger Service.

The following procedure shows how to add someone to your contact list if that person has a Passport account and you know his or her Passport sign-in name:

1. **Click the Add button in the MSN Messenger Service toolbar (shown in the margin).**

   The Add a Contact dialog box appears, as shown in Figure 11-10.

2. **Check the By Passport option and click the Next button.**

   This summons the dialog box shown in Figure 11-11.

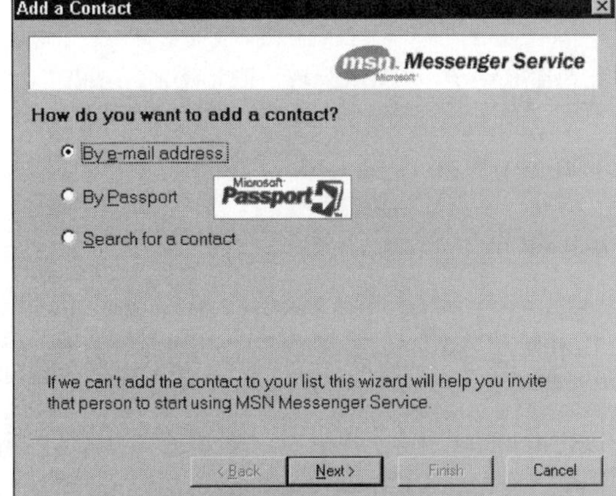

Figure 11-10: The Add a Contact dialog box.

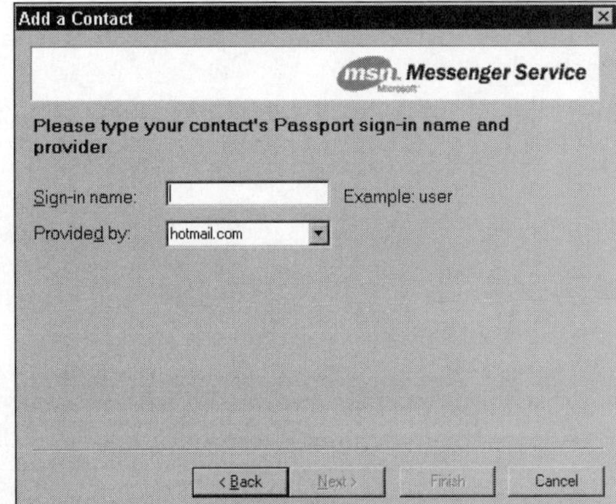

Figure 11-11: MSN Messenger asks for the sign-in name of your contact.

3. **Type your contact's Passport sign-in name in the text box and click the Next button.**

   Note that the Provided By drop-down list lets you choose whether the sign-in name should be accessed via Hotmail or Passport. If your friend has a Passport account but not a Hotmail account, choose passport.com rather than hotmail.com for this setting.

   If the sign-in name is valid, a dialog box similar to the one shown in Figure 11-12 displays after you click Next.

4. **If you want to send an e-mail to your friend instructing them how to download and install MSN Messenger Service, click the Yes option.**

   If you are sure that the person already has MSN Messenger Service installed, click the No button so that the e-mail message is not sent.

You can click the Preview E-Mail button to see a preview of the e-mail message before you send it to your friend.

5. **To add another contact, click the Next button and repeat Steps 2 through 4.**
6. **When you are through adding contacts, click the Finish button.**

   You are returned to the MSN Messenger Service window, where the contact list shows the new contacts you added.

Here are a few points to ponder concerning the contact list:

- If the person you want to add to your contact list does not have a Passport account, use the By E-mail Address option in Step 2 and enter your friend's e-mail address. MSN Messenger sends an e-mail to your friend with information about how to sign up for a free Passport account and download MSN Messenger Service.

- If you don't know the e-mail address of the person you want to add to your contact list, check the Name option instead of the E-mail Address option in Step 2. This summons the dialog box shown in Figure 11-13, which allows you to search Hotmail's database by name, city, state, and country.
- To remove a contact, click the contact to select it and choose the File⇨Delete Contact command or just press the Delete key.

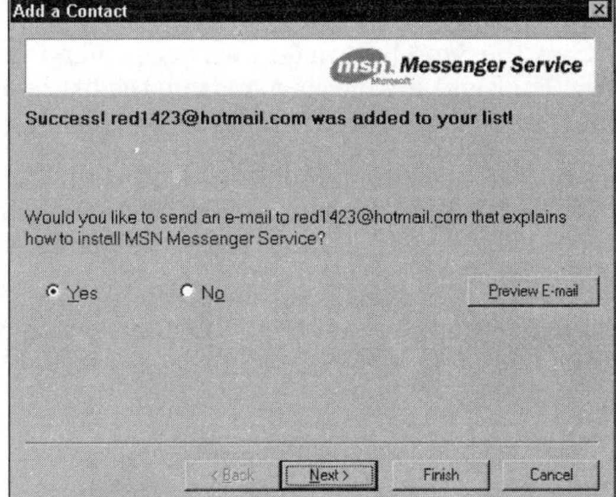

Figure 11-12: Congratulations! You have successfully added your friend to your contact list.

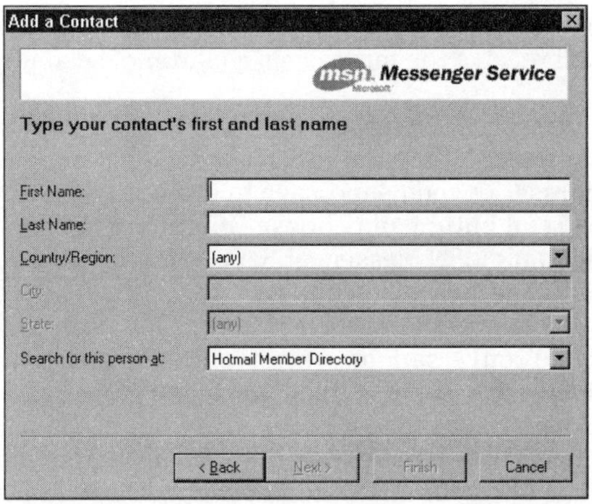

Figure 11-13: Searching for contacts by name, city, state, and country.

Sending an instant message

Suppose you're busy at work playing Solitaire on your computer one day and it suddenly occurs to you that one of your friends is probably playing Solitaire too, and wouldn't it be nice to find out. That's precisely the kind of important communication MSN Messenger Service is designed to enable. Just follow these steps to send your friend an instant message:

1. **Double-click the contact that you want to send a message to.**

   Or, if you prefer, click the Send button (shown in the margin) and choose the person you want to send the message to from the list of online contacts that appears. Either way, an Instant Message dialog box appears.

You can only send instant messages to contacts that appear in the Contacts Currently Online section of the MSN Messenger Service contact list. You cannot send messages to the contacts that appear in the Contacts Not Online section.

2. **Type the message you want to send in the text box at the bottom of the Instant Message dialog box.**

   For example, type "Hey, are you playing Solitaire too?"

3. **Click the Send button.**

   Or, if you prefer, just press the Enter key.

That's all there is to it. Your message is sent over the Internet to your online friend. Your friend will receive the message in a matter of seconds.

You can also send a message to someone who is not on your contact list, provided that person has an MSN Messenger Service account and you know the person's Hotmail address. To send a message to someone who is not on your contact list, click the Send button and choose Other from the menu that appears. Type the person's MSN Messenger Service logon name (their Hotmail address, minus the @hotmail.com, and then click the OK button.

MSN Messenger Service conversations are not limited to just two participants. As many as five people can join in on an instant conversation. To invite someone else to join a conversation, click the Invite button (shown in the margin), choose To Join This Conversation from the menu that appears, and then choose another one of your online contacts from the list that appears.

Receiving an instant message

When someone sends you an instant message, a sound plays on your computer and a flashing window appears in the Windows taskbar. Click the flashing window in the taskbar to open the Instant Message window, as shown in Figure 11-14.

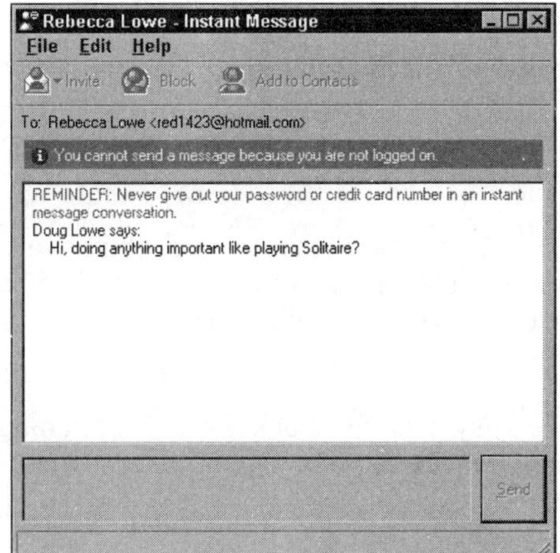

Figure 11-14: Receiving an instant message.

You can reply to the message by composing a message of your own in the text box at the bottom of the Instant Message window and clicking the Send button or pressing Enter.

You and your friend can talk back and forth like this for hours if you want. When you're ready to leave the conversation, choose the File⇨Close command or click the Close button (the X in the upper right-hand corner) of the Instant Message window.

Changing your status

If you are going to leave your computer or be unable to participate in instant message conversations for some other reason, you can let MSN Messenger Service know so that other MSN Messenger Service users will know that you are not available. Actually, there are several different status settings you can choose from:

- **Online:** You are at your computer, able and willing to accept instant messages.
- **Invisible:** You are at your computer, but will appear to be offline to anyone who attempts to contact you via MSN Messenger Service. You can still send messages of your own, however.
- **Busy:** You can't talk now because you're busy doing something else.
- **Be Right Back:** You can't talk now, but you'll be back soon.
- **Away From Computer:** You can't receive messages because you are not at your computer.

- **On The Phone:** You are engaged in a low-tech conversation.
- **Out To Lunch:** Either literally or figuratively.

To change your status, click the Status button (shown in the margin) and choose the status option that you want to use from the menu that appears.

Keep in mind that other MSN Messenger Service users who have added you to their contact list can see your status. The only exception is if you change your status to Invisible. If you do, you will appear to be offline to other MSN Messenger Service users.

If you change your status to Busy, Be Right Back, Away From Computer, On The Phone, or Out To Lunch, be sure to change your status back to Online when you return.

Chapter 12

Surfing the News at MSNBC

In This Chapter

- Getting your news from MSNBC
- Personalizing your front page
- Using News Alert to hear about news as it happens
- Receiving news in to your inbox with E-Mail Extra

MSNBC, the result of a collaboration between Microsoft and media giant NBC, is a Web site that provides online news. The MSNBC Web site provides online coverage of the day's events, updates on breaking stories, and in-depth coverage of major news events.

MSNBC is also the official Web site for two news cable channels — MSNBC Cable and CNBC Cable, as well as all NBC News programs, including "NBC Nightly News with Tom Brokaw," "Dateline," and "Today." So you will find reports filed by NBC correspondents throughout the world, often with audio and video segments.

This chapter gives you an overview of how to use MSNBC. I explain how to read stories in MSNBC, and how to use one of MSNBC's best features: the ability to create your own personalized news page that highlights stories on the topics you are interested in.

In addition, I show you how to use two advanced MSNBC features: News Alert and News Offline. News Alert alerts you to breaking news throughout the day, while News Offline delivers news to your e-mail account so you can read it at your leisure. Both features let you use keywords to select the topics you are interested in.

Reading the News on MSN

MSN lets you quickly access the top headlines from MSNBC via the MSN News home page. To view the MSN News home page, go to msn.com and click the News hyperlink that appears in the list of MSN services on the left side of the page. Figure 12-1 shows the MSN News homepage.

Figure 12-1: The MSN News home page.

The horizontal menu bar near the top of the page has five links:

- **News Home:** The MSN News home page, featuring the top stories of the day.
- **International News:** News stories from throughout the world. This page highlights the top international stories of the day, plus features a list of the top news stories by region (Africa, the Americas, Europe, former Soviet States, the Middle East and North Africa, the Pacific Rim, South and Central Asia, and Southeast Asia).
- **U.S. News:** News stories from the United States.
- **Special Reports:** Reports on topical subjects such as the environment, political issues, technology, and so on.
- **In Today's Newspapers:** Leading news stories of the day from major national newspapers in the United States.

The summary that appears beneath each headline on the MSN News page is actually a link that takes you to the complete story. When you click on a story, MSN grinds and whirs for a moment, and then displays the complete story, as shown in Figure 12-2.

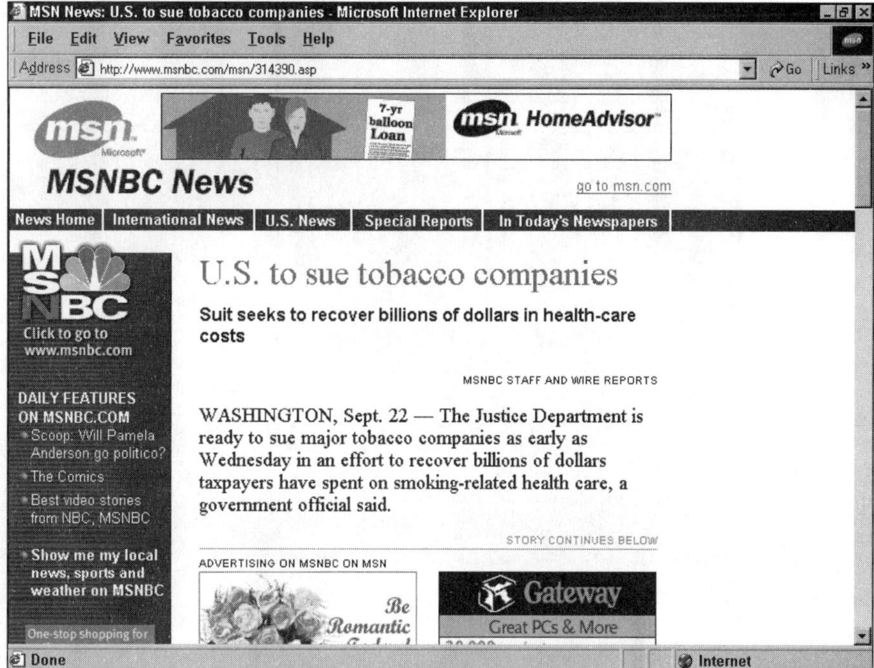

Figure 12-2: A typical MSNBC story.

As Figure 12-2 shows, a typical MSNBC news story shows a headline and a brief summary of the story, followed by some advertisements (MSNBC has to make money somehow). To read the actual text of the story, you'll have to scroll down past the advertisements or click the Story Continues Below hyperlink that appears beneath the summary.

As you read through a news story, you often find links audio or video clips that add to the story or links to related stories on MSNBC. Click these links if you want to dive deeper into the story.

Breaking News Coverage on MSNBC

The MSN News home page is a compilation of the major news stories of the day. If you're serious about your news, you probably want to breeze past the MSN News home page and go to the MSNBC home page, which contains more complete coverage of the day's events. To get to the MSNBC home page, shown in Figure 12-3, click the MSNBC icon that appears near the top of MSN News home page.

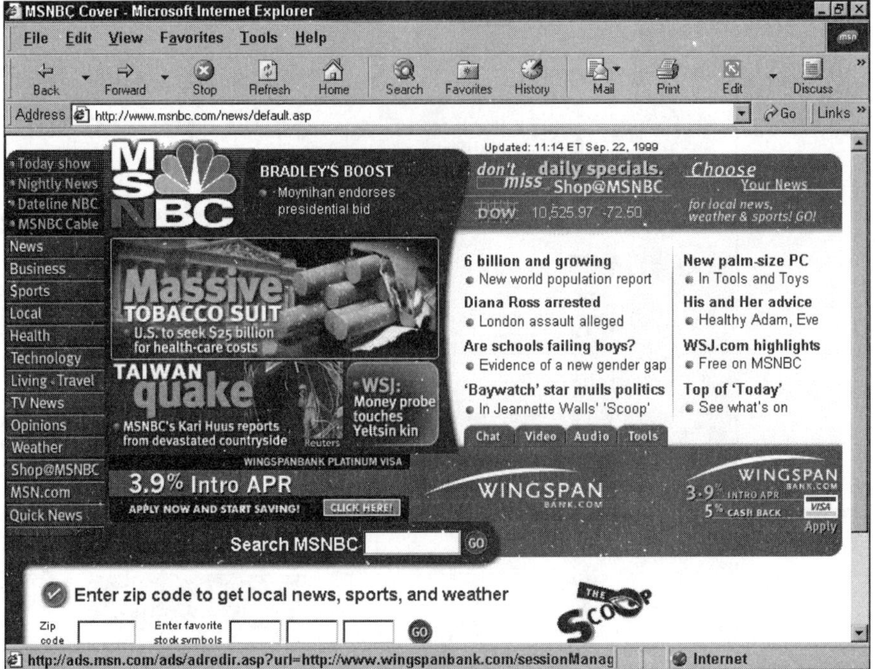

Figure 12-3: The MSNBC home page.

MSNBC is organized much like a daily newspaper and contains the following sections:

- **News:** Includes breaking stories from the United States and around the world — stories about political events, natural disasters, economic news, crime, and so on.
- **Business:** Keeps you up to date on the world of business — economic news, mergers, layoffs, forecasts, and so on.
- **Sports:** Find out who won the big game last night, whether Sammy or Mark hit another home run, and up-to-the-minute scores.
- **Local:** Gives you local news for more than 125 cities in the United States, from Albany, NY to Yuma, AZ. Local news includes stories of local interest, such as local crimes or political news, as well as weather reports.
- **Health:** Follow news from the world of health and medicine, such as stories about breakthroughs in disease treatment, genetics, and health-care management.
- **Technology**: Technology news, such as how the recent earthquake in Taiwan might affect the supply of computer chips and the ubiquitous Y2K story.

- **Living & Travel:** Includes travel news such as hurricanes in the Bahamas and cruise ship mishaps, as well as tabloid stuff like articles about Pamela Anderson and Tom Cruise.
- **TV News:** Ties to feature stories from NBC, CNBC, and MSNBC Cable's news programs, such as "Dateline" and "Today," as well as a complete schedule for news programming on NBC, CNBC, and MSNBC Cable.
- **Opinions:** Check out a variety of online columnists, including Ollie North and Paul Begala, hosts of MSNBC's "Equal Time," Michael Moran's "Brave New World," and others.
- **Weather:** Weather news from around the world, plus local weather forecasts from AccuWeather. The Weather home page features a map of the United States, which allows you to click a city or area to get more detailed weather information and forecasts.
- **Shop@MSNBC:** An online shopping center with links to online stores such as `Amazon.com`, Gap Online, and `Garden.com`.
- **MSN.COM:** A hyperlink to the MSN home page.

The easiest way to find an article in MSNBC is to use the MSNBC News menu that appears on the left side of the MSNBC page. Point to one of the sections in the News menu to reveal a list of stories that are featured in that section. Then click on any story that you want to read.

Each section has its own front page, with lists you can access by clicking the section name in the News menu. Each section's front page lists the stories that appear in that section. For example, Figure 12-4 shows the Sports section's front page.

The first time you use the News Menu, you will be asked to download the small program that makes the News Menu work. To download the News Menu program, click the Yes, download the News Menu now hyperlink. The entire download should take less than a minute.

Here are a few additional tips that can help as you peruse the news on MSNBC:

- Most MSNBC news stories have links to related MSNBC news stories, audio or video clips related to the story, or other Internet sites that pertain to the story. For example, a story on tax cuts might contain links to the IRS Web site, the Clintons' most recent tax return (so you can compare your own finances with the First Family's), and various other tax sites.
- At the bottom of most MSNBC stories is a request for feedback on the story. When you finish reading the story, you can rate the story from 1 to 7 (with 7 being the high score). When you rate an MSNBC story, MSNBC thanks you by displaying a list of the top ten stories as rated by other MSNBC users, as shown in Figure 12-5.

Figure 12-4: The front page of the Sports section.

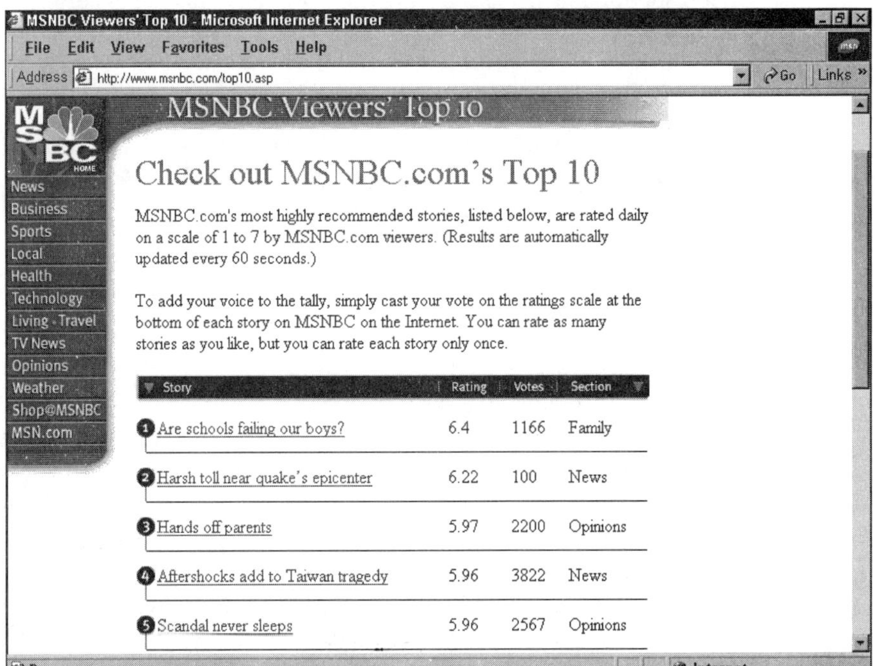

Figure 12-5: MSNBC Viewer's Top Ten stories of the day.

- You can search for MSNBC stories by keyword by clicking Find at the bottom of any MSNBC page. This takes you to a search page, where you can type in a keyword, click a button, and peruse a list of all stories containing the keyword.

Choosing Your News

MSNBC allows you to customize its home page so that it displays local news and information, news stories on subjects that interest you, stock quotes, and other personalized information. For example, if you're interested in UFOs, crop circles, and alien abductions, you can add stories about these subjects to your MSNBC home page.

The following paragraphs list the categories of news information you can add to your personalized MSNBC home page and describes some of the options that are available for each category:

- **News:** You can select international news, U.S. news, or both.
- **Business:** You can include current market quotes for up to 12 stock symbols, market summaries for DOW, S&P 500, NASDAQ, AMEX, and Russell 2000, and business news stories from various sources.
- **Sports:** You can include scores from Major League Baseball, NFL, NHL, NBA, and Major League Soccer — for all teams, or just the scores for specific teams you want to follow. In addition, you can include sports columns from columnists such as Ron Borges and humorist Scott Ostler.
- **Local News:** Here you can choose to include local stories for more than 125 cities, online traffic information for 14 major cities, and state lottery information for the 39 states that run lotteries.
- **Technology:** You can include technology news from three categories: Tech Policy (news about government technology policy), Tools and Toys (news about new products), and Goofs and Glitches (news about technology problems).
- **Living & Travel:** Allows you to include news lifestyle and travel features such as celebrity news, recipes, travel bargains, and home decorating tips.
- **TV News:** Adds links to feature stories from NBC, CNBC, and MSNBC Cable news programs such as "NBC Nightly News with Tom Brokaw," "Today," and "Dateline."
- **Opinions:** You can include your favorite columnists from the MSNBC Opinions page on your customized MSNBC home page.
- **Weather:** Allows you to include your local weather forecast (from AccuWeather) on your customized news page.
- **Topics:** Retrieves current news clips based on keywords you enter.

To personalize your MSNBC news page, follow these steps:

1. **Go to the MSNBC Home Page (`www.msnbc.com`).**
2. **Type your zip code in the Zip Code text box located near the bottom of the page.**
3. **If you want stock quotes, type up to three stock symbols in the Stock Symbol text boxes.**
4. **Click the Go button.**

   MSNBC adds a section called Your News to the MSNBC home page, as shown in Figure 12-6.
5. **Scroll through the Your News section of the MSNBC home page to see what subject categories MSNBC added for you.**

   When you first set up your page, MSNBC automatically adds weather, local news, business news (if you entered stock symbols), and sports news.

Figure 12-6: Part of a personalized MSNBC front page.

6. **To add an additional subject category to the Your News section, select the subject that you want to add from the Add: drop-down list (found near the top of the Your News section) and then click the Go button.**

   This brings up a separate Personalize My News window that shows a page of options for the subject you selected. For example, Figure 12-7 shows the options that appear if you choose Topics from the Add: drop-down list.

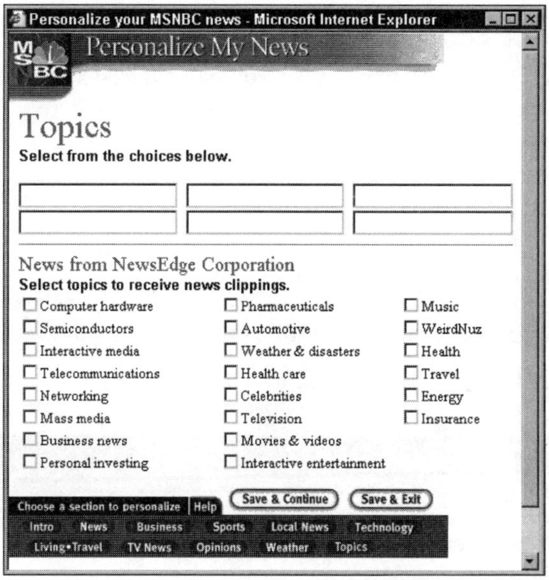

Figure 12-7: Adding information to Your News.

7. **Fill out the options in the Personalize My News window and then click Save & Exit.**

   The options you selected will be added to the Your News section.

8. **Repeat steps 6 and 7 to add other information to Your News.**

After you set up Your News, you can view it at any time by going to the MSNBC Home Page. The Your News section appears beneath the main MSNBC Home Page stories.

To remove an item from the Your News section, click the Remove...From My Page hyperlink that appears next to the item. To change the settings for an item, click the Change... hyperlink that appears next to the item.

Using News Alert

If you're a news junkie, you can set up MSNBC so that it alerts you to breaking news throughout the day. You can select up to five keywords to select the news subjects you're interested in, and specify how often the news alert service should be checked for breaking news — for example, every 10 minutes if you are obsessed with news or every hour if you're just moderately concerned.

Whenever news breaks, a pop-up window will appear displaying the headlines for the stories that interest you. From this window, you can click the headline to display the complete story, or you can click Next to see the next headline. To dismiss the News Alert window, click Close.

Setting up News Alert

To set up News Alert, follow these steps:

1. **Click Cool Tools at the bottom of the MSNBC home page.**

   This brings up the Cool Tools page, as shown in Figure 12-8.

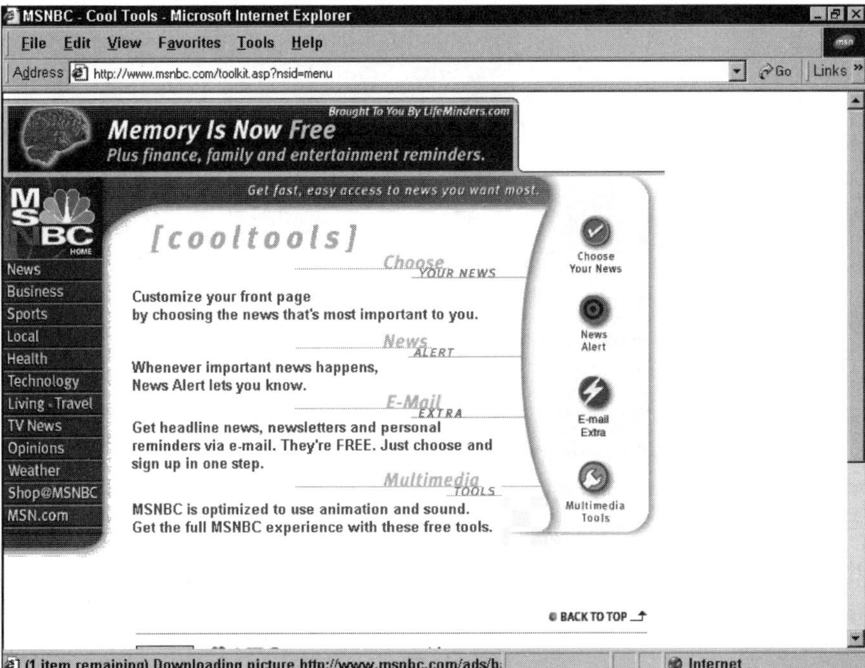

Figure 12-8: The Cool Tools page.

2. **Click the News Alert icon.**

   You are taken to the News Alert page, as shown in Figure 12-9.

3. **Read everything on the News Alert download page.**

   Here you can find out everything there is to know about News Alert.

4. **Find and click the Download tool for Windows 95, 98, or NT hyperlink.**

   This takes you to the News Alert Download page.

   The next few steps of the procedure depend on whether you use Internet Explorer or Netscape Navigator.

5a. **If you're using Internet Explorer, click Download News Alert Now. When the File Download dialog box appears, click the Run This Program From Its Current Location option and then click OK.**

   News Alert downloads itself to your computer. It takes only a minute or so.

   When the download finishes, Internet Explorer may display the security warning dialog box. If you see this dialog box, click Yes to proceed.

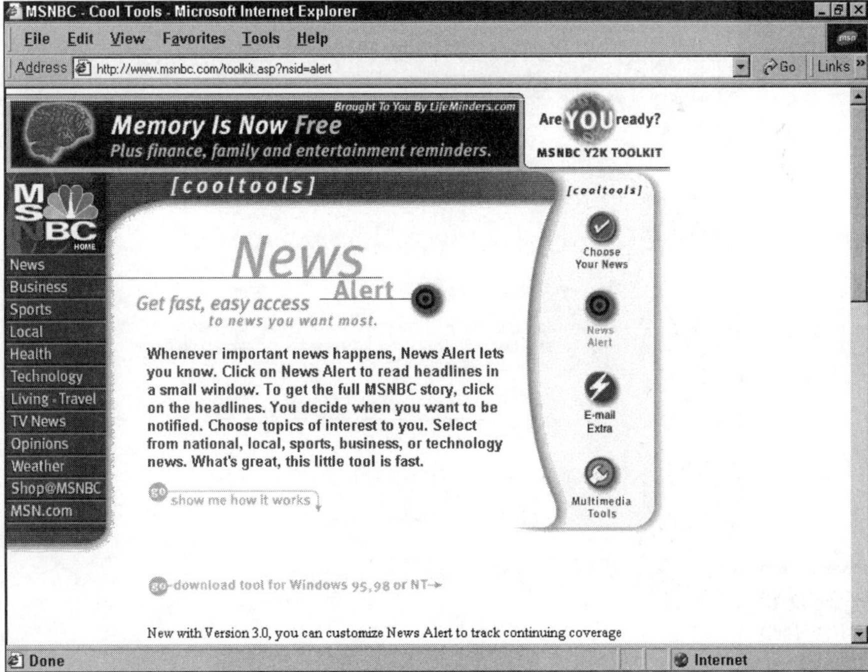

Figure 12-9: The News Alert page.

5b. **If you're using Netscape Navigator, click Download News Alert Now. When the Save As dialog box appears, click the Save button to save the file to your desktop. When the file finishes downloading, close the browser and double-click the nainst.exe icon on your desktop.**

    This starts the News Alert setup program.

6. **Click the OK button.**

   News Alert will install itself, which should take only a moment. When the installation is complete, News Alert displays a Web page listing various News Alert options, as shown in Figure 12-10.

7. **Choose the information you want News Alert to inform you about and then click Save.**

   News Alert congratulates you by displaying a page informing you that you have successfully installed News Alert.

8. **Click Go to MSNBC Cover to return to the MSNBC Home Page.**

You're done! That's all there is to setting up News Alert. The News Alert icon is automatically added to your Windows taskbar. Whenever there is new news, this icon will flash red and you'll hear a sound. You can click on this icon to display the News Alert window.

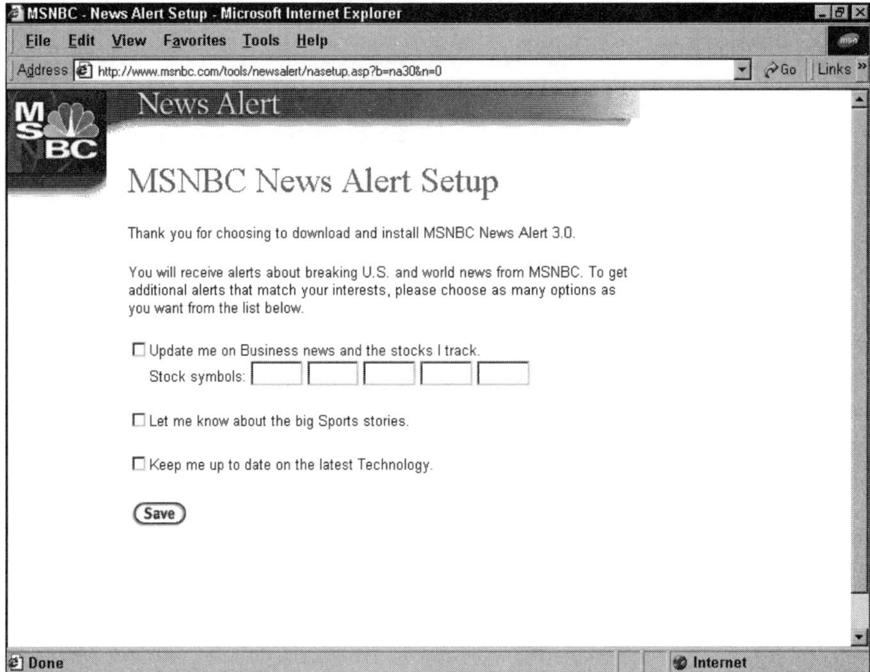

Figure 12-10: The News Alert options page.

Customizing News Alert

Once you have News Alert up and running, you can customize it in several ways. For starters, you can change the news items that News Alert informs you about. To do that, call up the News Alert window, click Customize, and then choose MSNBC News from the menu that appears. This brings up the page shown in Figure 12-11.

From this page, you can select news alerts for subjects such as News, Business, Sports, Health, Local News, and other topics. In addition, you can type in your own keywords to be alerted of stories in special topics that pique your interest.

You can also change how often News Alert checks for breaking stories and how it informs you of new stories by calling up the News Alert window, clicking Customize, and then clicking Delivery Settings from the menu that appears. This brings up the Delivery Settings dialog box, shown in Figure 12-12.

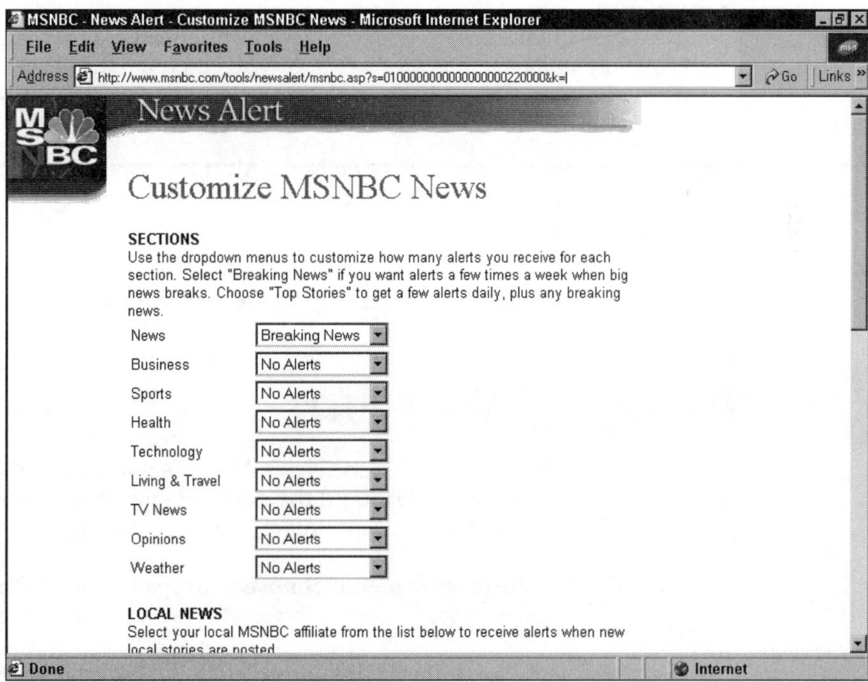

Figure 12-11: Customizing News Alert.

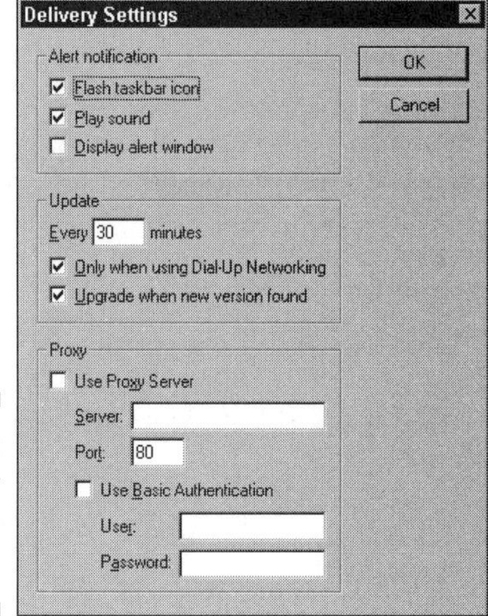

Figure 12-12: The Delivery Settings dialog box.

From this dialog box, you can change the following settings:

- **Alert Notification:** You can have News Alert cause its taskbar icon to flash whenever there is new news, or you can have the News Alert window actually pop up when new news arrives. In addition, you can tell News Alert whether to play a sound when there is news.
- **Update:** This governs how often News Alert lets you know about breaking news. The default is every 30 minutes.
- **Proxy:** Use this option if you connect to the Internet through a proxy server. Be sure to talk to your network administrator or Internet service provider to find out how to configure the proxy settings.

Turning off News Alert

To turn off News Alert, right-click the News Alert taskbar icon and choose Exit. This deactivates News Alert until the next time you restart your computer. To completely deactivate News Alert, follow these steps:

1. **From the Windows Start menu, choose Settings⇨Control Panel.**

   The Control Panel appears.

2. **In the Control Panel dialog box, double-click Add/Remove Programs.**

   The Add/Remove Programs dialog box appears.

3. **In the Install/Uninstall tab, select News Alert, click Add/Remove, and then click OK.**

   MSNBC News Alert is removed.

Using E-Mail Extra: News In Your Inbox

MSNBC has yet another news delivery service — called News Offline — that can deliver customized news stories automatically to you via e-mail every day. You can then read the news articles when you read the rest of your e-mail, without bothering to connect to the MSNBC site.

To activate E-Mail Extra, follow these steps:

1. **From the MSNBC Home Page, click Cool Tools at the bottom of the page.**

   You are whisked away to the Cool Tools page (refer to Figure 12-8).

2. **Click E-Mail Extra.**

   This summons the E-Mail Extra page, as shown in Figure 12-13.

3. **Type your e-mail address in the Enter Your E-mail Address text box.**
4. **Choose the categories for the news you want e-mailed to you each day.**
5. **Click the Subscribe button.**

That's all there is to it. Each day, you'll find e-mail in your inbox with the information you requested.

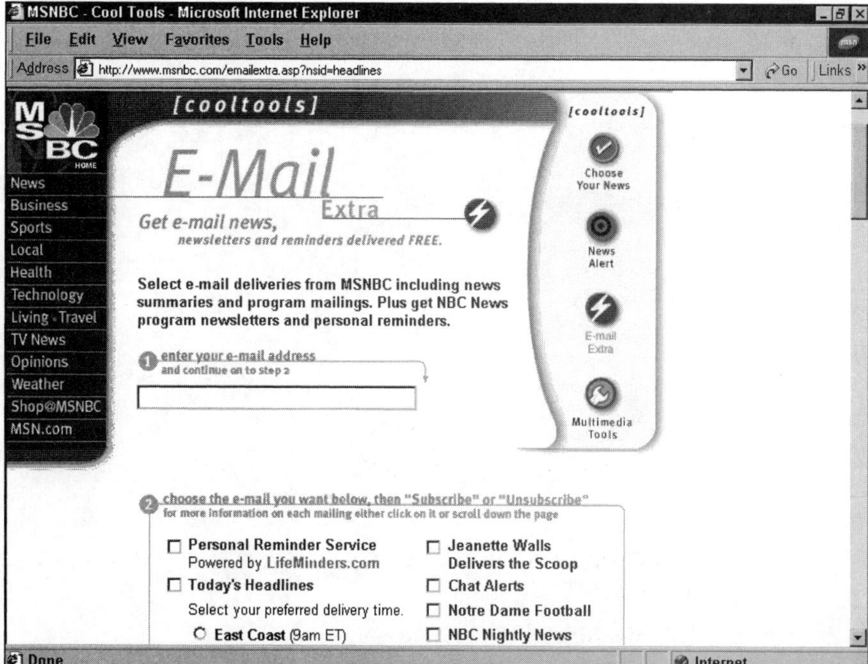

Figure 12-13: The E-Mail Extra page.

If you selected Personal Reminder Service as one of the E-Mail Extra options, you'll be greeted by a series of pages asking for the type of reminders you would like to have sent to your mailbox. LifeMinders can automatically e-mail you messages to remind you about important dates such as birthdays, anniversaries, automobile maintenance, pet immunizations, and so on.

Chapter 13

Encarta: The Online Encyclopedia

In This Chapter

- Using Encarta's free Concise Encyclopedia
- Looking over Encarta's various subscription plans
- Researching with Encarta Online Deluxe

When I was a kid, my parents bought me a set of encyclopedias. I didn't read them much, but they were great for stacking up to make forts for my G.I. Joe figures. Nowadays, you don't have to spend hundreds of dollars on an encyclopedia for your kids: just plug them into the Internet.

Encarta Online Deluxe is an encyclopedia you can access via the Internet. Actually, Encarta Online Deluxe is an Internet version of Encarta, Microsoft's popular CD-ROM encyclopedia program. Both Encarta and Encarta Online Deluxe have tens of thousands of reference articles, photographs, and sound and video clips on topics ranging from Aardvarks to Zygotes. To access Encarta Online Deluxe, just click the Reference & Ed. hyperlink (the Ed. stands for Education) on the MSN home page.

Unfortunately, Encarta Online Deluxe is a subscription service, which costs $6.95 per month to use. Microsoft offers a free seven-day trial so you can check Encarta Online Deluxe out. Microsoft also offers a scaled-back version called Encarta Concise Encyclopedia, which you can use free of charge.

Using Encarta Concise Encyclopedia (It's Free!)

If you have not subscribed to Encarta Online Deluxe, you can still use Encarta Concise Encyclopedia free of charge. The Concise Encyclopedia contains 16,000 short articles that you can search for by keyword.

Although the Encarta Concise Encyclopedia has fewer articles than Encarta Online Deluxe (which has 42,000 articles) and the articles in the concise version of Encarta are not as long as the articles in Encarta Online Deluxe, Encarta Concise Encyclopedia is still useful if you just want to know the basics about a particular topic. (If you want more detailed information, consider subscribing to Encarta Online Deluxe.)

To use Encarta Concise Encyclopedia, click the Research & School hyperlink on the MSN Home Page to bring up the Encarta Learning Zone page. Then click the word Encarta that appears above the search text box near the upper left-hand corner of the page. (If you prefer, you can just type **encarta.msn.com** in the Address bar of your Web browser and press the Enter key.) You are greeted by the Encarta home page, as shown in Figure 13-1.

If you think you'll use Encarta Concise Encyclopedia often, add this page to your Favorites by choosing the Favorites➪Add to Favorites command (Internet Explorer) or bookmark the page by pressing Ctrl+D (Netscape Navigator).

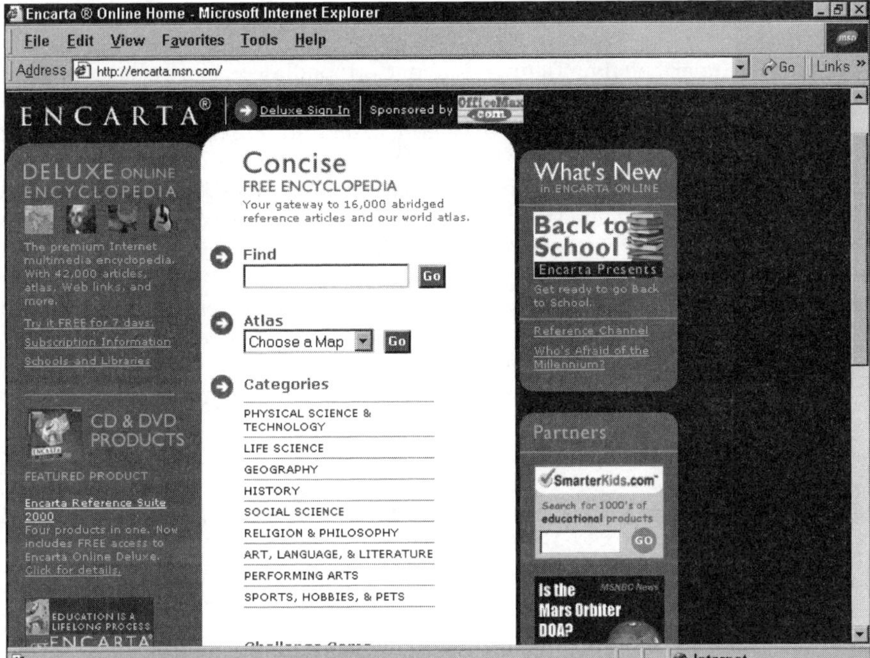

Figure 13-1: Welcome to the Encarta Online Encyclopedia.

Searching for Encarta articles

The easiest way to find an Encarta article is to perform a keyword search, which displays a list of all Encarta articles that contain a particular word or phrase. To find an article by performing a keyword search, follow these steps:

1. **Type the keyword that you want to search for in the Find It text box.**
2. **Press the Enter key or click the Go button.**

   Encarta searches for articles on your subject and displays a results page similar to the one shown in Figure 13-2.
3. **Click the article that you want to read.**

   If Encarta found more than one article on your subject, you may have to scroll down through the page to find the article that you want to read. When you click an article, Encarta retrieves the article and displays it, as shown in Figure 13-3.

If an article is marked with an orange star on the results page, the article is available only to Encarta Online Deluxe subscribers. (Remember, Encarta Online Deluxe has 42,000 articles; the free Encarta Concise Encyclopedia lets you access 16,000 of them free.)

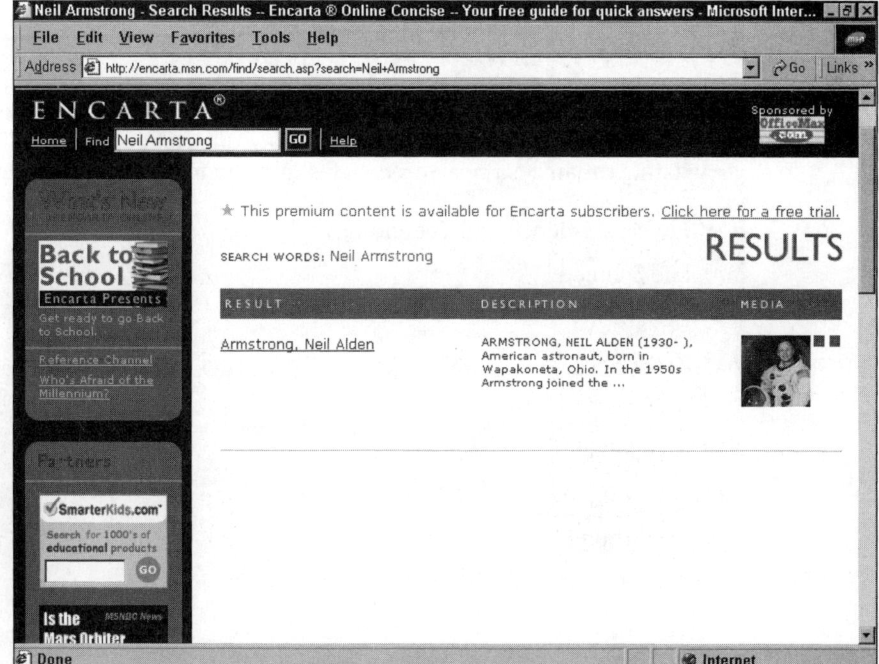

Figure 13-2: Encarta Concise Encyclopedia found this article about Neil Armstrong.

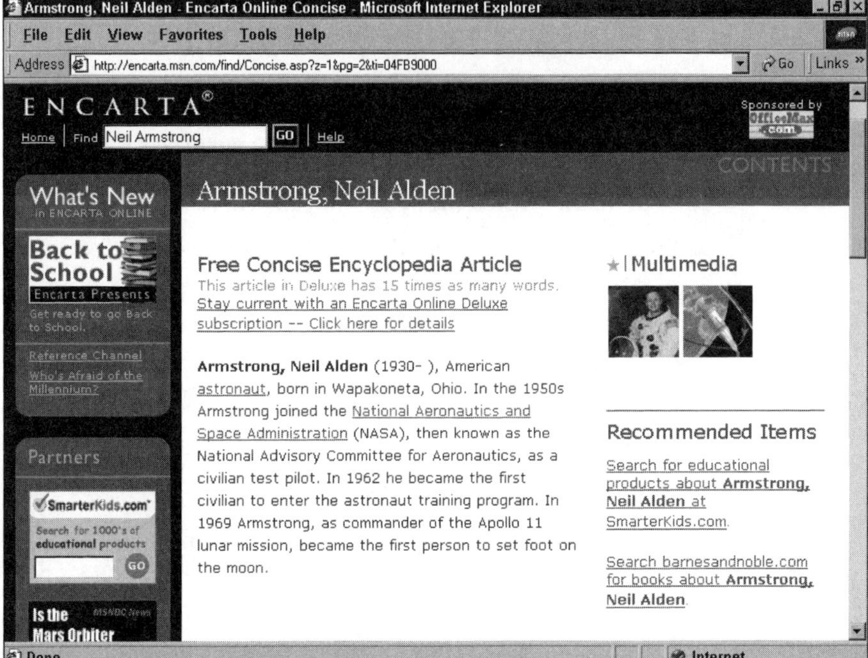

Figure 13-3: An Encarta Concise Encyclopedia article.

Browsing Encarta's categories

In addition to searching for Encarta articles by keyword, you can also browse Encarta's category listings to find an article you are interested in. The category listing organizes Encarta's articles into the following categories:

- Physical Science and Technology
- Life Science
- Geography
- History
- Social Science
- Religion and Philosophy
- Art, Language, and Literature
- Performing Arts
- Sports, Hobbies, and Pets

To browse articles by subject category, just click one of the categories listed in the Categories section of the Encarta home page to bring up the page for that category. For example, Figure 13-4 shows the Physical Science and Technology page.

Each category page lists a number of subcategories that fit within the main category. For example, the Physical Science and Technology page lists subcategories such as Mathematics, Physics, and Chemistry. You can click one of these subcategories to bring up an index of articles that match the subcategory. Then, you can click the article you want to display.

Exploring the World with Encarta's Atlas

If you're into geography or cartography (the study of maps), the Atlas is one of Encarta's more interesting and useful tools. The Atlas lets you view a world map, and then zoom in for more detail by viewing a continent such as Europe or South America. From there you can zoom in to see maps of individual countries.

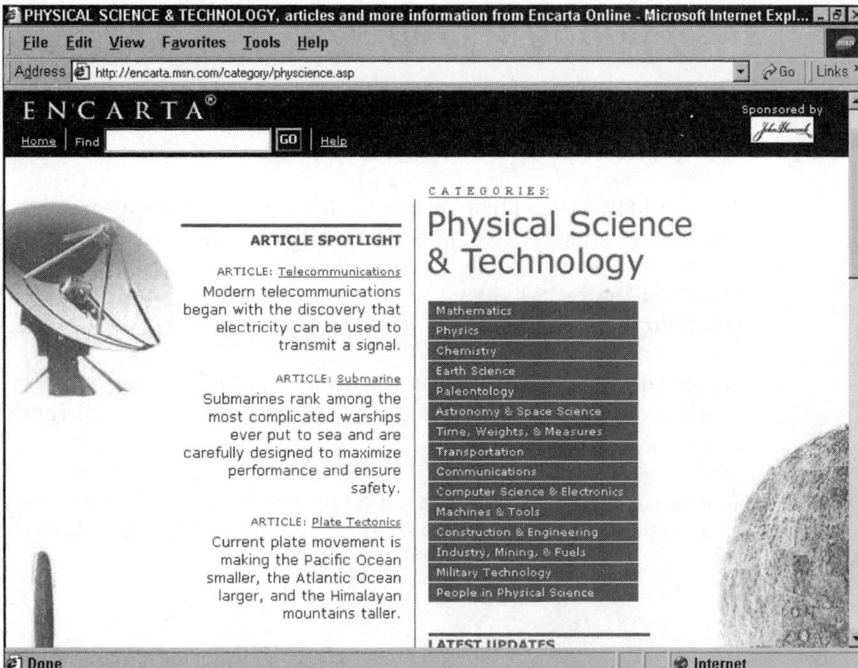

Figure 13-4: The Physical Science & Technology category page.

The Atlas displays five types of maps:

- **Main:** Shows outlines of countries and landforms and the names of major features such as countries and oceans. These maps are designed to download quickly so you can easily navigate from one map to another.
- **Detailed:** Includes more place names, including cities, mountain ranges, lakes, and so on. The Detail maps are relief maps that use color to show elevations.
- **People:** These maps are color coded to show population density.
- **By Day:** Shows what an area looks like from space in daytime. These maps let you see the area's terrain and vegetation.
- **By Night:** Shows what an area looks like from space at night. On these maps, you can see the lights of major cities.

The free Encarta Concise Encyclopedia lets you access the Atlas' Main and Detailed maps. If you subscribe to Encarta Online Deluxe, you get access to the People, By Day, and By Night maps.

Displaying a map

To display a map using the Atlas, choose a country from the Atlas drop down list and click the Go button. If you choose the World map, a map of the entire world appears, as shown in Figure 13-5.

The world map has links for the earth's major land areas and oceans. You can zoom in for a close look at an area by clicking the area of the map that you want to see. For example, if you click the South America hyperlink, the map shown in Figure 13-6 displays. To see an individual country map, click somewhere in the country.

Notice the small world map in the upper-right corner of each Atlas map. This small world map outlines the section of the world that is currently displayed in the main map.

Another way to call up a map for an individual country is to click the link for that country in the Country List that appears on the main World map page.

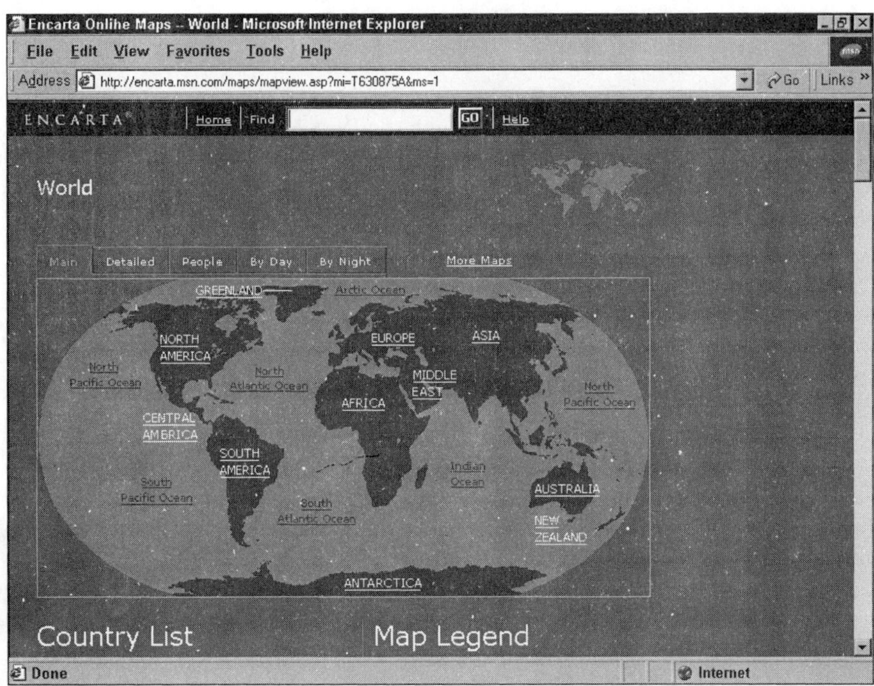

Figure 13-5: Encarta's World Map.

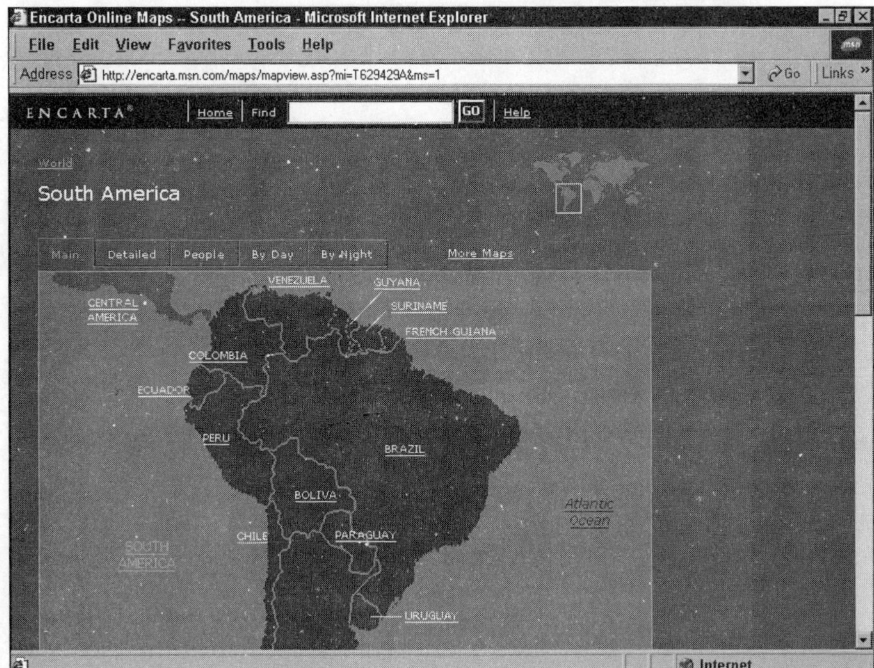

Figure 13-6: South America.

Seeing more detail

Encarta's Main maps show only the outlines of countries and landforms. To see a more detailed map, click the Detailed tab at the top of any map. The detailed maps provide more information, such as major cities, rivers, lakes, mountain ranges, and color-coded elevation information. For example, Figure 13-7 shows the Detail map for Equador.

Scroll down to the bottom of this map to see the Map Legend, which explains the symbols used on the map.

You can go directly from the Atlas to articles about countries and cities that appear on the Detail maps by clicking the country or city name. For example, Figure 13-8 shows the Encarta article about Quito, the capital city of Ecuador. I retrieved this article simply by clicking the city of Quito on the map.

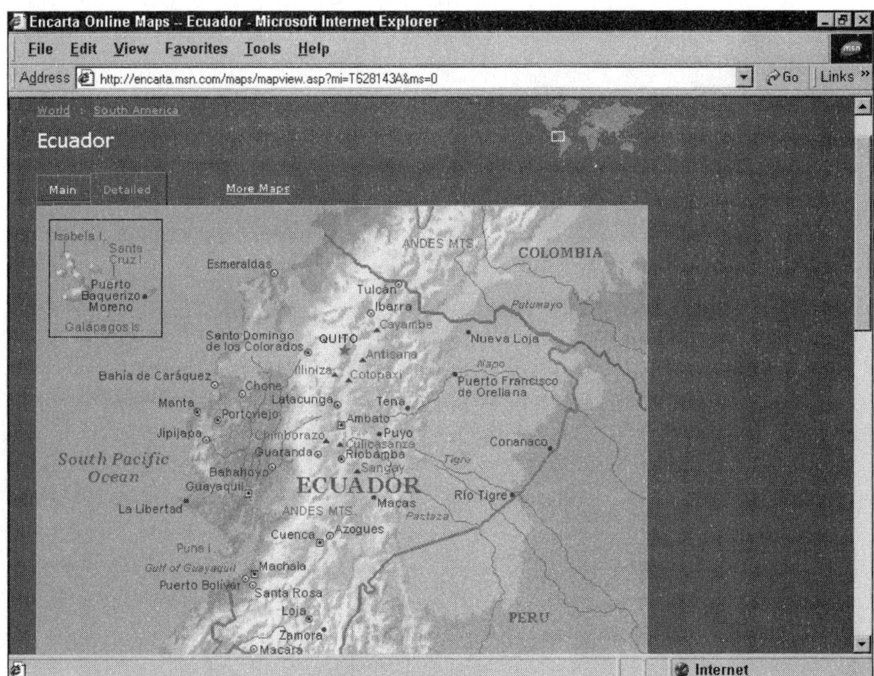

Figure 13-7: A Detail map of Ecuador.

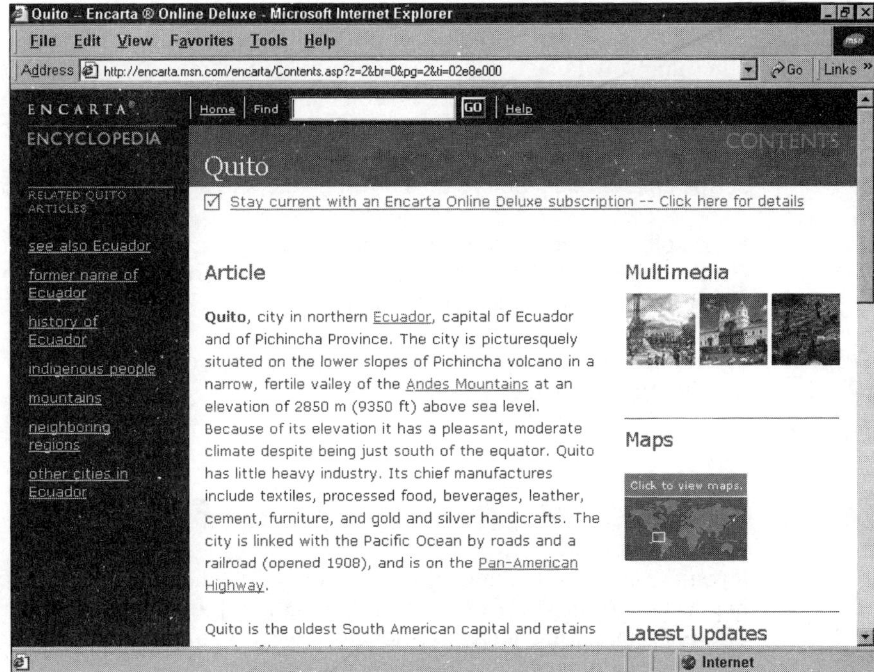

Figure 13-8: You can call up articles about countries and cities on an Atlas map.

Subscribing to Encarta Online Deluxe

Subscribing to Encarta Online Deluxe gives you many benefits over the free Encarta Concise Encyclopedia. In particular, as an Encarta Online Deluxe subscriber, you have access to these additional features:

- Larger and more comprehensive articles. For example, the Encarta Online article about Neil Armstrong is 15 times longer than the brief Encarta Concise article that was shown in Figure 13-3.
- Multimedia features such as pictures, videos, and sounds.
- More information in the online Atlas. In particular, Encarta Online Deluxe lets you view population maps and daytime and nighttime satellite views.
- A Category area where you can browse articles arranged into nine categories: Physical Sciences and Technology; Life Science; Geography; History; Social Science; Religion and Philosophy; Art, Language, & Literature; Performing Arts; and Sports, Hobbies, and Pets.
- Schoolhouse, a special area for teachers and students that contains helpful lesson plans for common subjects and other educational resources.

Encarta Online Deluxe has several subscription plans that you can choose from. You can subscribe on a month-to-month basis for $6.95 per month. If you think you'll use Encarta Online a lot, you may want to consider a longer-term subscription. For example, you can get a one-year subscription for $49.95, which is considerably less than the $83.40 you would pay for a full year of access at the monthly rate. You can also purchase a two-year subscription for $39.95 per year or a three-year subscription for $29.95 per year.

Microsoft also offers a free seven-day trial so you can check out Encarta Online Deluxe to see if you like it. To sign up for the free trial, type your E-mail address in the text box on the Encarta home page and click the Sign Up button.

If you purchase the CD-ROM version of Encarta, you are entitled to free use of Encarta Online Deluxe for one year.

Using Encarta Online Deluxe

If you are an Encarta Online Deluxe subscriber, clicking the Encyclopedia hyperlink on the MSN Research and Education page takes you to the Encarta Online Deluxe home page, as shown in Figure 13-9. From this page, you can access all of Encarta Online Deluxe's features.

Figure 13-9: Encarta Online Deluxe.

As with Encarta Concise Encyclopedia, Encarta Online Deluxe lets you search for articles by keyword or by category. The difference is that your searches will yield more articles, since Encarta Online Deluxe has about two and a half times as many articles as Encarta Concise Encyclopedia. In addition, the articles you find will be more detailed. For example, an article that consisted of just a single paragraph and a photograph in Encarta Concise Encyclopedia may yield several pages of information and a half dozen photographs in Encarta Online Deluxe.

In addition, Encarta Online Deluxe includes several features that simply are not available in Encarta Concise Encyclopedia. For example, Encarta Online Deluxe includes 360-degree panoramic images of interesting places throughout the world. The location of these views changes on a weekly basis, so each week you can see the world from a different vantage point. The panoramic view lets you zoom in and out and change the speed at which the image pans. Figure 13-10 shows a recent panoramic view of downtown Cleveland, OH.

Yet another feature available only to Encarta Online Deluxe subscribers is the Terraserver, a huge collection of satellite images from throughout the world. The Terraserver lets you pinpoint any location on earth and display remarkable satellite images. For example, Figure 13-11 shows a satellite image of the Statue of Liberty. The resolution of this image is one meter per pixel, which means that each dot that makes up this image represents one square meter on the ground.

Figure 13-10: A panoramic view of beautiful downtown Cleveland.

Figure 13-11: A satellite view of the Statue of Liberty.

Chapter 14

Managing Your Money and Investments with MoneyCentral

In This Chapter

- Checking out MoneyCentral's features
- Using Investor to get a stock quote
- Finding a stock when you don't know the symbol
- Tracking your own investments with Portfolio Manager
- Backing up your portfolio

MoneyCentral is the place to go on MSN for help with money matters, up-to-date information about financial and business news, investment and financial planning advice, and the option to pay your bills online.

MoneyCentral also includes Investor, an online investment program that you can use to track your investments, research the market to help you decide which investments to make, and even buy and sell stocks and mutual funds online. Whether you're a large or small investor, Investor is a great way to keep track of your stash.

This chapter assumes that you know a little about personal finances and investing. If terms such as *mutual fund* and *stock index* are foreign to you, I suggest you pick up a copy of *Investing For Dummies* by Eric Tyson (published by IDG Books Worldwide, Inc.).

Getting Into MoneyCentral

To get to MoneyCentral, click the Personal Finance hyperlink in the list of services on the left side of the MSN Home Page. The MoneyCentral Home Page greets you, as shown in Figure 14-1.

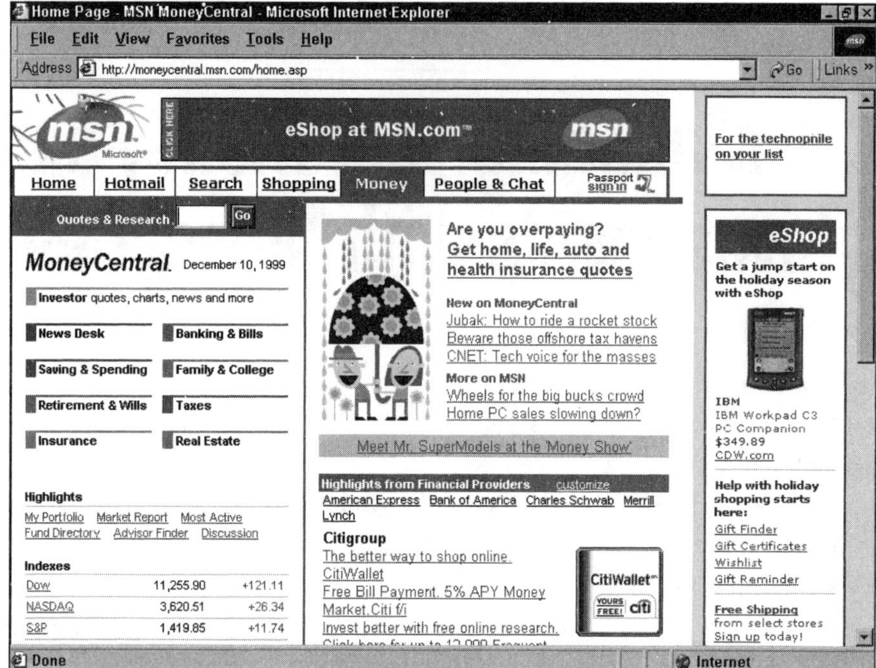

Figure 14-1: Welcome to Money Central.

MoneyCentral consists of the following nine major areas, which you can access by clicking the links on the left side of the MoneyCentral Home Page:

- **Investor:** The heart of MoneyCentral, Investor is an online investment service which lets you buy and sell stocks, bonds, and mutual funds, track your investments, and stay informed about the market.
- **News desk:** The place to go for the latest information and news about personal finance.
- **Saving & Spending:** News and advice about budgeting, managing debts, and finding bargains.
- **Retirement & Wills:** Resources to help you plan for the future.
- **Insurance:** Everything you ever wanted to know (and didn't want to know) about life, health, auto, and disability insurance.
- **Banking & Bills:** With online banking you can pay your bills over the Internet, find the best savings and loan rates, and find out how to deal with banks and creditors.

- **Family & College:** News and ideas about how to save for your family's needs, including college scholarship and financial aid searches.
- **Taxes:** One of the two certain things in life. Here you can find information about tax law changes, tax forms and publications, strategies for paying less tax, a tax estimator, and more.
- **Real Estate:** Online help for buying or selling your home from another MSN Web site known as MSN Home Advisor.

In this chapter, I focus mostly on Investor, because that's where the most interesting and useful of MoneyCentral's features are found.

Getting Started with Investor

Investor is the cornerstone of MSN's MoneyCentral site. To start Investor, click Investor in the list of services that appears on the left side of the MoneyCentral home page. Investor comes to life, as shown in Figure 14-2.

Figure 14-2: Investor's home page.

Some Investor features require that you download some software that enables Investor to work on your computer. The first time you use one of the Investor features that requires this software, Investor displays a page to inform you that the download is necessary. The software takes about five minutes to download. Once you have downloaded the software, you can use all of Investor's features without further delay.

In addition, some Investor features require that you set up a special account known as a Passport account. Passport is tied to Hotmail, so if you already have a Hotmail account, you already have a Passport account. To sign in using your Passport account, follow these steps:

1. **Click the Passport Sign In hyperlink that appears at the top of the Investor Home Page.**

   This summons the Passport sign in page, as shown in Figure 14-3.

2. **Type in your Hotmail Member Name and Password and then click the Enter button to access your account.**

Note that you won't see this sign-in screen until you access an Investor feature that requires a Passport account, such as the Portfolio manager. When you enter your member name and password, Passport validates your membership information and then takes you to the Investor page you were trying to access.

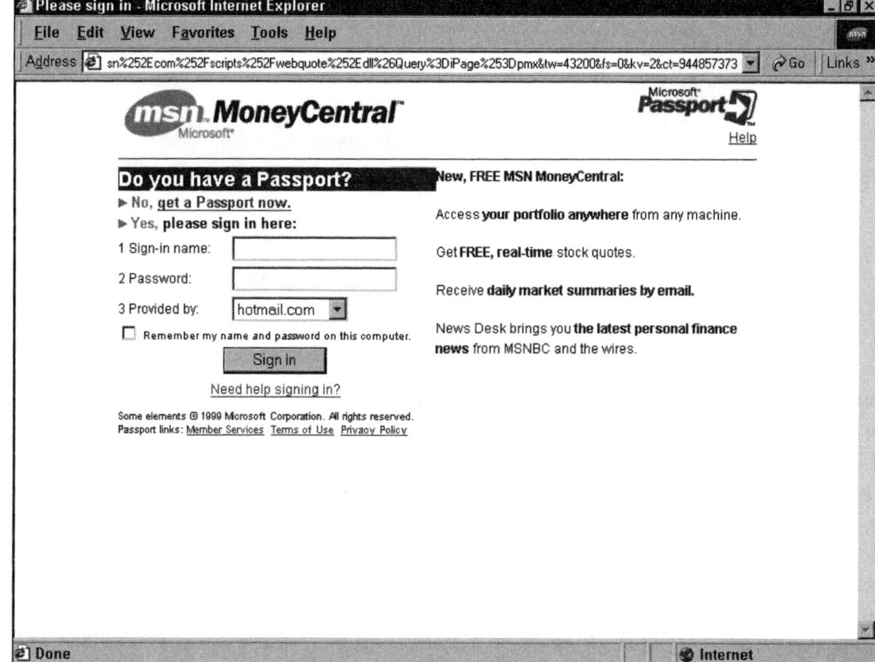

Figure 14-3: The Passport sign in screen.

Obtaining Stock Quotes

One of the most common uses of Investor is to get a current price on a stock or mutual fund. That way, you can keep track of how your investments are doing. You can get stock quotes directly from Investor's Home Page.

The quotes you receive from Investor are on a 15-minute delay. What do you expect from a free service?

Getting quotes when you already know the symbol

Every stock and mutual fund that is traded on the stock exchange has its own symbol. For example, the symbol for Microsoft is MSFT; the symbol for Bank of America Corporation is BAC. If you know the symbol of the stock or fund that you want, you can get a quote by following these steps:

1. **On the Investor home page, type the stock or fund symbol into the Symbol text box.**

   For example, to get a quote on Microsoft, type **msft** in the text box.

2. **Click the Go button.**

   Your stock quotes appear on screen, similar to the Microsoft quote shown in Figure 14-4.

3. **To get another quote, type a different symbol in the Name or Symbol text box and click the Go button.**

Obtaining quotes when you don't know the symbol

If you don't know the symbol for the stock or fund you want, don't panic. Just follow these steps:

1. **Click Stocks in the menu bar that appears at the top of the Investor home page.**

   This takes you to a Stock Research page where you can look up stock quotes.

2. **Click the Find button and then choose Symbols from the menu that appears.**

   The Find Symbol dialog box appears, as shown in Figure 14-5.

Figure 14-4: I should have bought Microsoft at 53 ¾.

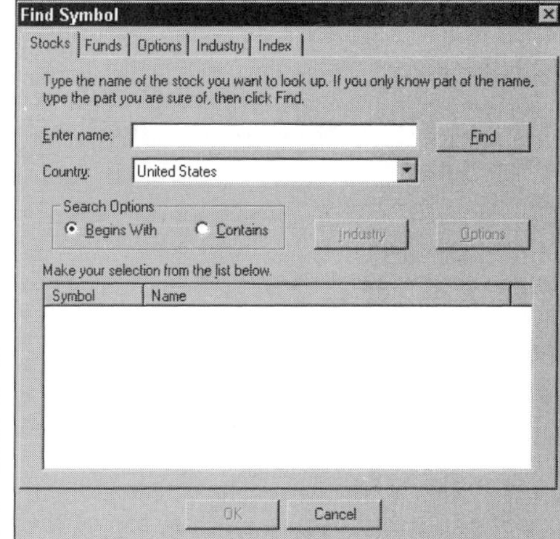

Figure 14-5: The Find Symbol dialog box.

3. **If you are searching for a mutual fund rather than a stock, click the Funds tab.**
4. **Type the name of the stock or fund that you want to search for in the Name text box.**
5. **Choose the stock's or fund's country from the Country drop-down list.**
6. **Click the Find button.**

   After searching for all the companies that match the name that you entered, Investor displays the results, similar to those shown in Figure 14-6. In many cases, more than one company is listed.

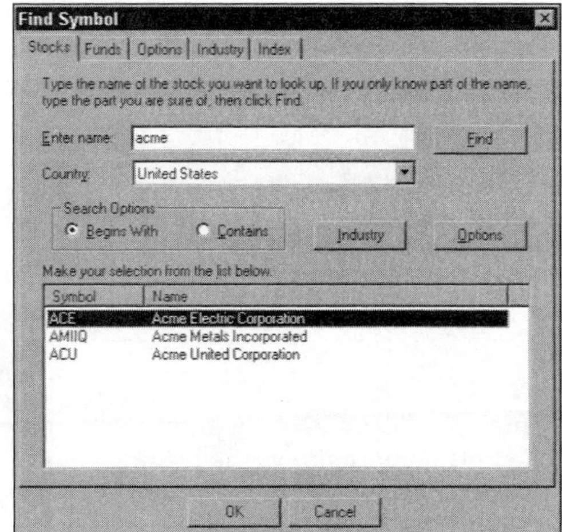

Figure 14-6: There is more than one Acme company.

7. **Click the symbol for the company that you want to look up and then click OK.**

   Investor displays your company's quote.

Charting a stock's performance

You can easily display a chart of a stock's or mutual fund's past performance so you can see if the stock or fund has increased or decreased in value. First, call up the company's or fund's quote. Then, click the Charts hyperlink that appears in the menu on the left side of the Investor page. Investor grinds and churns for a moment and displays a chart similar to the one shown in Figure 14-7.

Figure 14-7: Charting Microsoft's stock.

The top part of the chart in Figure 14-7 shows the movement of the stock's price for the past year. The bottom part shows the trading volume for the same time period.

You can change from a price history chart to a price performance chart or income growth chart by clicking the Chart menu that appears above the chart and selecting the type of chart that you want to display from the drop-down menu. You can also change the time period shown in the chart from one year to a week, a month, a quarter, three years, five years, or ten years just by clicking the Period menu and selecting the time period of your choice from the drop-down menu. (Displaying a 10-year price performance chart for Microsoft will really make you wish you had a few grand to spare back in 1989.)

To plot a graph for two stocks together, type the symbol for the second stock that you want to chart in the Compare with text box on the right and then click Add. This adds a second stock to the chart so you can compare the performance of the two stocks. You can even add additional stocks to the chart in the same manner.

For even more control over the chart, choose Display Options from the Chart menu. This brings up a Price Chart Options dialog box, which allows you to set options such as whether to show dividends and splits, price limit lines, moving averages, and other helpful chart goodies.

Managing Your Portfolio

MoneyCentral's Portfolio Manager is a program that can track your investments for you. To set Portfolio Manager up, you first tell it which stocks or funds you own and in what quantity. Portfolio Manager can then show you the current value of your entire portfolio.

The following sections show you how to perform the basic tasks that you need to track your investments when using Portfolio Manager.

Setting up a Portfolio account

Before you can use Portfolio Manager to track your investments, you must set up a Portfolio account. The account is free, so follow these steps to set one up:

1. **Choose File⇨New Account.**

   The Portfolio Manager New Account Wizard appears, as shown in Figure 14-8.

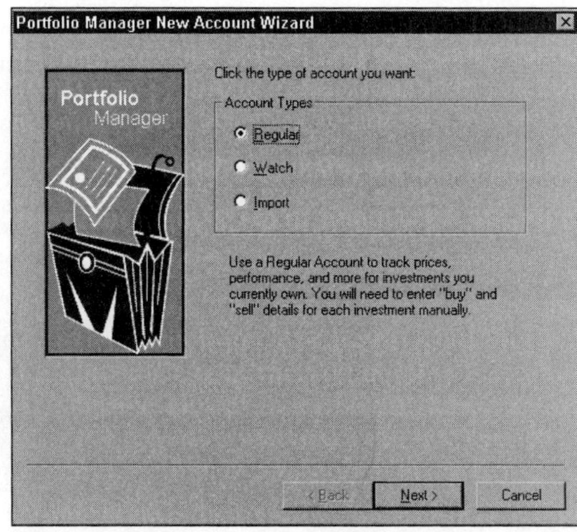

Figure 14-8: The Portfolio Manager New Account Wizard.

2. **Select the type of account that you want to create.**

   Portfolio Manager lets you create two types of accounts: Regular and Watch. A Regular account is for tracking investments you actually own, while a Watch account is for tracking investments you don't own but would like to track. (The third option, Import, lets you copy an account from another program such as Microsoft Money or Quicken.)

3. **Click the Next button.**

   The second dialog box of the Wizard appears, as shown in Figure 14-9.

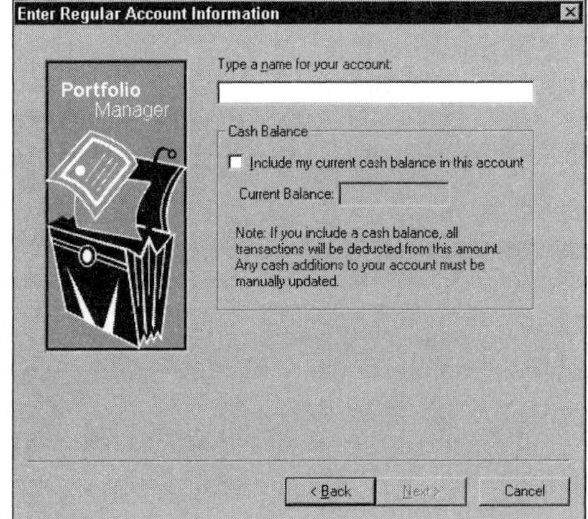

Figure 14-9: Give your account a name.

4. **Type a name for your account in the text box.**

5. **If you want to track a cash amount in this account, check the Include My Cash Balance in This Account option, and type the cash balance in the Current Balance field.**

   Use this option only if you want to track cash that you move through the account. If you just want to track stock values, you can leave out the cash altogether.

6. **Click the Next button.**

   The Wizard brings up a Transaction dialog box so you can start entering transactions for the account.

   If you want to begin entering transactions now, see the "Buying a stock or mutual fund" and "Selling a stock or mutual fund" sections later in this chapter. Otherwise, click the Cancel button to cancel and return to the Portfolio Manager page shown in Figure 14-10.

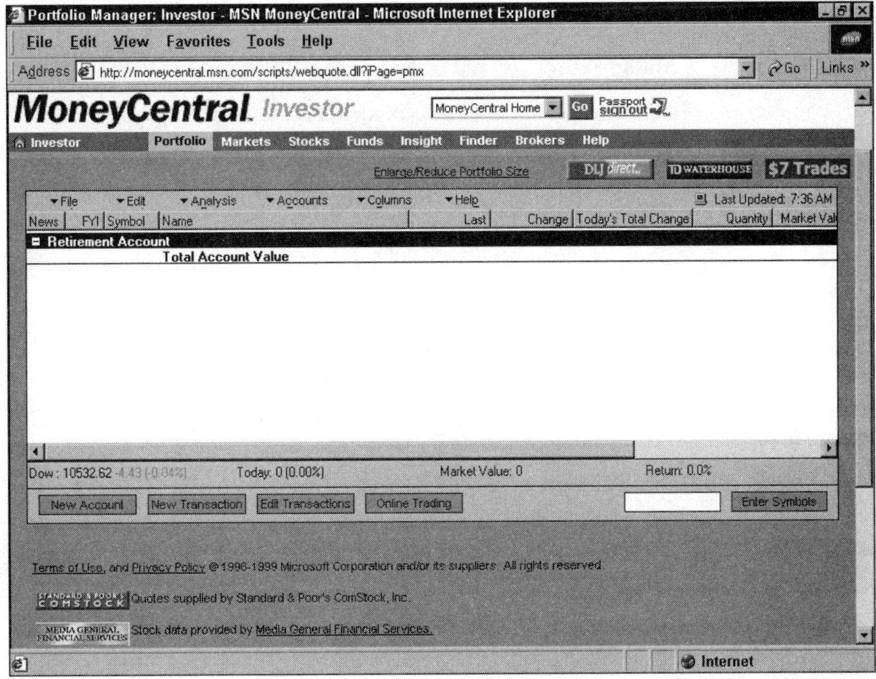

Figure 14-10: A new Portfolio Account, just waiting for investments.

If you want to, you can set up more than one Portfolio account to track separate investments. For example, if you have accounts with more than one stockbroker, you can set up a separate Portfolio account for each one.

Buying a stock or mutual fund

Suppose you get a hot tip on a stock and decide to buy 100 shares of Acme at $31.125 per share (that is, 31 1/8). Whenever you purchase a stock or mutual fund, you should update your Portfolio account to reflect the purchase, so that Portfolio Manager can track the value of your investment.

Portfolio Manager does not actually purchase stocks or mutual funds for you. To actually purchase an investment, you must work with a broker. MSN Investor provides links to several brokerage companies that let you buy and sell stocks online for a modest charge. Once you have purchased a stock or mutual fund through a broker, you can return to MSN Investor's Portfolio Manager to record the purchase.

To record a stock or mutual fund purchase, just follow these steps:

1. **Choose Edit⇨Record a Buy.**

   The Transaction dialog box appears, as shown in Figure 14-11.

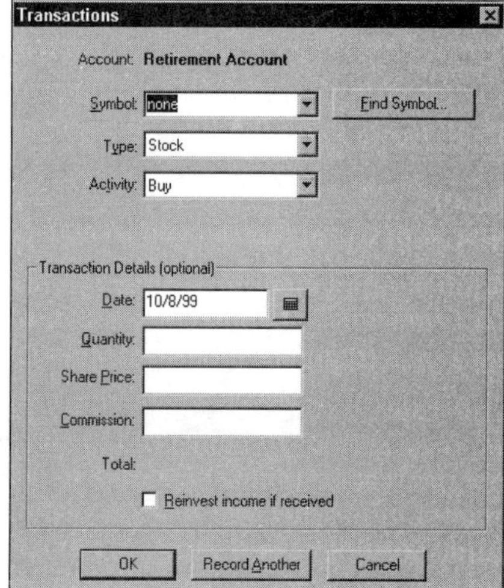

Figure 14-11: Recording a buy.

2. **Type the symbol for the investment in the Symbol text box.**

   For example, type **msft** if you are buying Microsoft.

   If you don't know the stock's symbol, click the Find Symbol button. The Find Symbol dialog box appears (refer to Figure 14-6). Type the name of the company whose symbol you don't know and click the Find Button. A list of companies appears (if the search finds a match, that is). Select the one that you want and click the OK button to return to the Record a Buy dialog box.

3. **Select the investment type from the Type drop-down list.**

   The investment types include: Bond, Certificate of Deposit, Employee Stock Option, Index, Money Market Fund, Mutual Fund, Option, Other, Stock, or Warrant.

   Because you summoned the Transaction dialog box by invoking the Edit⇨Record a Buy command, the Activity drop-down box is already set to "Buy."

4. **Enter the date, the number of shares, the purchase price, and the commission in the appropriate fields.**

5. **Check the Reinvest Income If Received option if you want to reinvest income.**

   If you select this option, any income earned from the investment is reinvested as additional shares. Otherwise, income is accumulated separately as cash.

6. **Click the OK button.**

   The Transaction dialog box disappears and a line is added to the account showing the stock that you just purchased, similar to Figure 14-12.

Hopefully, Acme's stock prices will go through the roof and you'll be able to retire on the small fortune you make.

Selling a stock or mutual fund

Dude! The very day you purchase 100 shares of Acme Robotics at $31.125 per share, the stock begins to skyrocket. By the end of the week the stock is trading at $87.75 per share. Time to sell before everyone realizes how overvalued the stock has become!

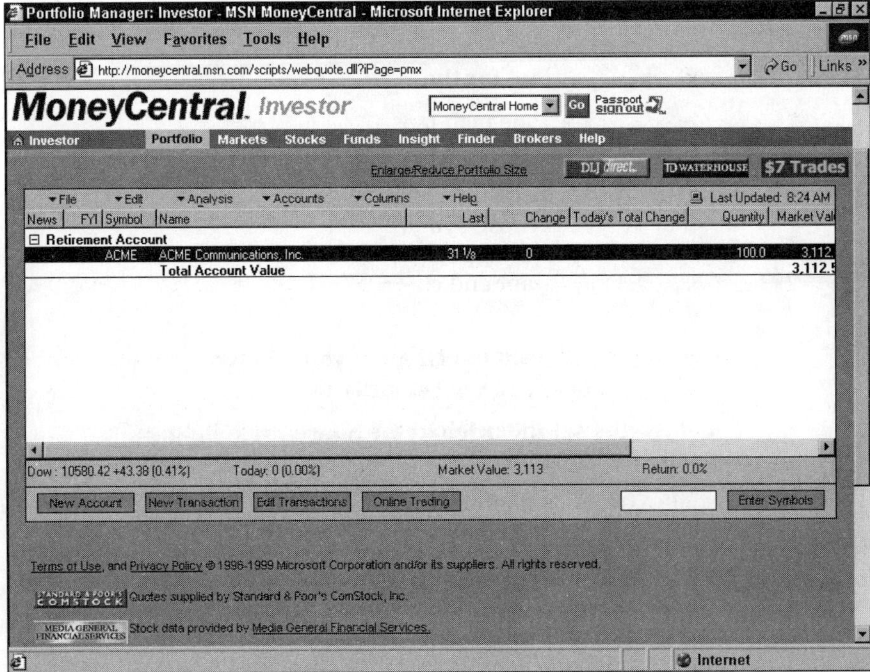

Figure 14-12: The Retirement account after purchasing 100 shares of Acme at $31.125 per share.

MSN Investor does not actually sell stocks or mutual funds for you. For that, you need to use a broker. Once you have sold your investment through your broker, you can come to Portfolio Manager to record the sale so that Portfolio Manager can accurately track your investments.

When you're ready to unload an investment, follow these steps:

1. **Select the investment that you want to sell by clicking the appropriate investment.**
2. **Choose Edit⇨Record a Sell.**

   The Transaction dialog box appears, as shown in Figure 14-13. Notice that most of the information in the dialog box is already filled in: the stock you want to sell, the number of shares, the price, and so on.

Figure 14-13: Recording a sell.

3. **If you don't want to sell all of your shares, type the number that you do want to sell in the Quantity field.**
4. **Type the selling price in the Share Price field.**

   The current price of the stock is filled in for you, but you probably actually sold the stock at a different value. In any event, the amount you sell the stock for is hopefully more than what you paid for it.

5. **Type any commission in the Commission field.**
6. **Click the OK button.**

   Your portfolio is updated to reflect the sold investment.

Charting your account

Whoever said a picture is worth a thousand words must have been an investor. Investors love to look at charts to see how a stock or fund has performed over time. With a good chart, you can tell at a glance whether you're making or losing money.

You can create a chart of your portfolio's performance by choosing Analysis⇨Portfolio Charting. Initially, the chart resembles the one shown in Figure 14-14, but you can change the appearance of the chart in several ways.

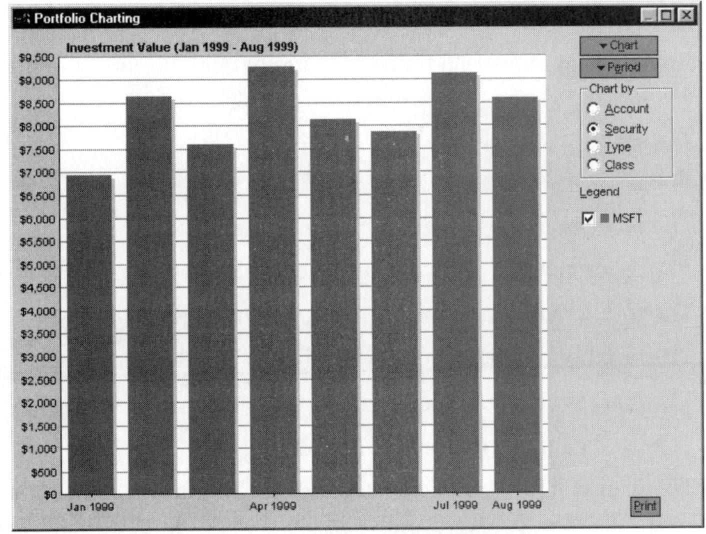

Figure 14-14: Charting your portfolio.

To change the chart type, click the Chart button and then choose from one of three chart types that appears: Investment Performance, Investment Value, or Investment Allocation. The default setting is Investment Value.

To change the period, click the Period button and then choose the time period that you want to show. The default setting is YTD (which stands for year to date). You can also select one of four Chart By options: Account, Security, Type, and Class.

To print the chart, click the Print button. To dismiss the chart so you can return to Portfolio Manager, click the Close button at the upper right corner of the Portfolio Charting window.

Customizing Porftolio Manager's display

Portfolio Manager tracks a great deal of detailed information about your investments — more information than Portfolio Manager can comfortably display on a single Web page. By default, the following information is shown from left to right for each of the securities you buy:

- An icon that appears whenever there is news about the security.
- An icon that appears if there is an important announcement about the security.
- The security's symbol.
- The security's name.
- The most recent trading price.
- The difference between the current price and yesterday's closing price.
- The total change in value for this investment so far today.
- The number of shares you own.
- The market value of your shares.
- The total gain or loss for this investment.
- The gain you have realized from stocks you have sold (as opposed to gain from stocks whose value has increased but which you have not sold).
- The total profit (as a percentage) you would make if you sold all your investments today.

If you are a serious investor, you might want to display some of the additional information that Portfolio Manager tracks for you. For example, Portfolio Manager lets you display the price/earnings ratio for your investments, which many investors consider a key indicator of an investment's performance.

To change the information that Portfolio Manager displays for your investments, choose one of the column options that is available on the Columns menu. Table 14-1 lists the investment information that is displayed by each of these column options.

Table 14-1 Column Options

Column Option	Investment fields displayed
Default	News, Advisor FYI, Symbol, Name, Last, Change, Today's Total Change, Quantity, Market Value, Gain, Realized Gain, ROI All Dates
Asset Allocation	Symbol, Name, Category, Market Value, Equity, Equity Amount, Debt, Debt Amount, Cash, Cash Amount, Other, Other Amount, % of Portfolio
Performance	Symbol, Name, Last, Quantity, Today's Total Change, Market Value, Income, Price Appreciation, Gain, Total Return—All Dates, Total Annualized Return
Return Calculations	Symbol, Name, Market Value, Total Return—1 Week, Total Return—4 Week, Total Return—3 Month, Total Return-YTD, Total Return—1 Year, Total Return—Year, Total Return—All Dates, Total Annualized Return
Valuation	Symbol, Name, Last, Quantity, Cost Basis, Market Value, Income, Price Appreciation, Gain
Quotes	Symbol, Name, Last, Change, % Change, Volume, Size of Last Sale, Bid, Ask, High, Low, 52-Week High, 52-Week Low
Holdings	Symbol, Name, Last Transaction Date, Last, Quantity, Cost Basis, Market Value, Gain, % of Portfolio, Target Price
Fundamental Data	Symbol, Name, Last, EPS, PE Ratio, Dividend Yield, Beta, 52 Week High, 52-Week Low, Shares Outstanding, Market Capitalization

You can also create a display showing any combination of columns by choosing the Columns➪Customize Column Set command. The Customize Column Set dialog box appears, as shown in Figure 14-15.

From this dialog box, you can add an additional column to the Portfolio Manager display by clicking the column that you want to add in the Available Columns list and then clicking the Add button. To remove a column, click the column that you want to remove in the Displayed Columns list and then click Remove.

You can also rearrange the columns' order by clicking the column whose order you want to change in the Displayed Columns list and then clicking the Move Up or Move Down button to move the column up or down in the list.

When the columns are set up the way you want, click the OK button.

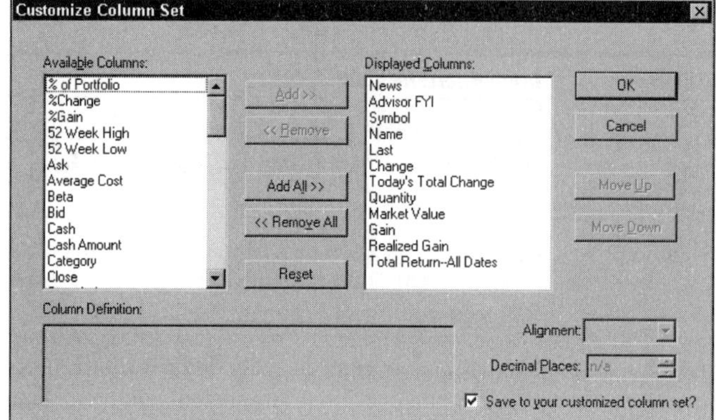

Figure 14-15: The Customize Column Set dialog box.

Backing up your portfolio

If you use Portfolio Manager to track your financial information, you should periodically backup your portfolio just in case you somehow accidentally delete your account, mess up a trade, or nuke your computer. To back up your portfolio, follow these steps:

1. **In Portfolio Manager, choose File⇨Backup.**

   The Save As dialog box appears.

   Make sure you use the File menu that appears on the Portfolio Manager immediately above the account list, not the File menu that appears at the top of the Internet Explorer window.

2. **Type a name in the File name field.**
3. **Choose a location for the backup.**

   If you wish, you can specify a floppy disk for the backup location. That way, your data will be protected if something goes wrong with your computer's hard disk.

4. **Click the Save button.**

   Your backup is saved.

If you accidentally mess up your portfolio and you want to restore from the backup you made, click File and choose the Restore Backup command. When the Open dialog box appears, double-click the backup file you previously created.

When you restore a backup file, any changes you made to your portfolio since the last time you backed up will be lost.

Chapter 15

Car Shopping with CarPoint

In This Chapter

- Researching information about new cars
- Getting secret dealer-invoice information
- Figuring monthly car payments
- Buying a car through CarPoint's online car buying service
- Creating a Personal Auto Page for your car

If you like cars, you'll love CarPoint — it's chock full of information about new and used cars from every manufacturer. If you're in the market for a new car, you can find all the details about the car you're interested in, including a complete listing of dealer invoice prices. You can even buy your next car through CarPoint's network of no-hassle dealers.

But even if you're not in the market for a new car, CarPoint is a lot of fun. You can find out what's hot and what's not, read interesting articles about the auto industry, and catch test drive reviews of the latest cars.

Introducing CarPoint

To start CarPoint, click Autos in the list of MSN services at the left side of the MSN home page. The CarPoint home page appears, as shown in Figure 15-1.

You can access all of CarPoint's features from the CarPoint home page. Throughout CarPoint, a horizontal menu bar appears at the top of each page. This menu contains four buttons:

- **CarPoint Home:** Returns you to the CarPoint home page. Use this button when you're lost deep within the bowels of CarPoint's pages and you want to get back to the top.
- **Table of Contents:** Takes you to a page full of links to the various services available on CarPoint. Use this page to go directly to any CarPoint service.

Figure 15-1: The CarPoint home page.

- **Find:** Allows you to search for a car based on criteria such as the type of car, the car's safety rating, gas mileage, and so on.
- **Help:** Displays information about how to use CarPoint.

Checking Out a New Car

To get information about a particular make and model of car, start by selecting the vehicle category from the list that appears at the left side of the CarPoint home page. CarPoint's new car information is organized into these six categories of vehicles:

- **Passenger Cars:** Passenger vehicles that cost less than $34,000, representing more than 250 models including such favorites as Ford Taurus, Honda Accord, and Toyota Camry.
- **Luxury Cars:** Passenger vehicles that sell for more than $34,000, with about 80 models including cars from BMW, Cadillac, Lexus, and Mercedes.
- **Sports Cars:** Performance-oriented cars targeted at auto enthusiasts, including Ford Mustang, Chevrolet Corvette, Dodge Viper, and Porche 911.

- **Sport Utilities:** Go-anywhere, do-anything vehicles including Ford Explorer, Chevrolet Blazer, and of course the AM General Hummer.
- **Vans & Minivans:** Full-sized vans as well as minivans such as Dodge Caravan and Ram van, Ford Windstar and Econoline, and Honda Odyssey.
- **Pickup Trucks:** Trucks such as the best-selling Ford F-Series, Chevrolet S-10, and Dodge Ram.

Clicking the button for one of these six categories displays general information about the category and a list of vehicle models. For example, Figure 15-2 shows the Sport Utilities page. This page includes news and advice about sport utility vehicles, including a list of 65 sport utility vehicles.

You can display information for a specific model car by selecting the model from the drop-down list that appears at the bottom-left side of the page. For example, Figure 15-3 shows the AM General Hummer page. (Arnold Schwarzenegger supposedly owns *two* of these monsters.) From this page, you can click either the New Model Details or Used Model Details hyperlink to see more details about the vehicle.

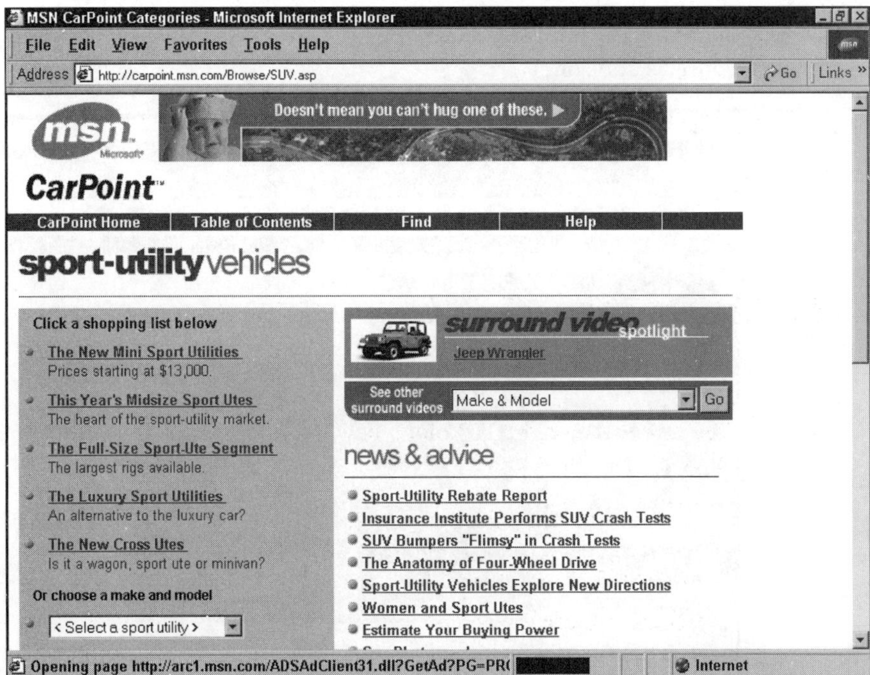

Figure 15-2: Sport Utility vehicles on CarPoint.

In the left margin of each detail page, you find a menu with the following choices:

- **Quick Facts:** A general description and photo of the vehicle. (This is the page that is initially displayed when you call up a Details page.)
- **Compare It:** Comparisons with similar models from other manufacturers.
- **Price It:** Gives you access to detailed retail and dealer invoice price for each model of the vehicle, complete with options.
- **Get a Price Quote:** Allows a dealer in your area to e-mail you a price quote for the vehicle you are interested in.

You can scroll down the page to find links to additional information about the vehicle that you have selected, including details about options and trim packages for the vehicle, safety and crash tests, comfort and convenience features, engine, transmission, fuel economy information, detailed specifications and warranties, and interior and exterior color options. You'll also find expert reviews and a photo gallery showcasing the vehicle.

The pricing information is worth its weight in gold. Armed with this information, you can determine the exact price that the dealer has paid for the car you want to buy, including all options. You can then add whatever amount you think the dealer is entitled to as a profit on the car and then use that figure as your offer.

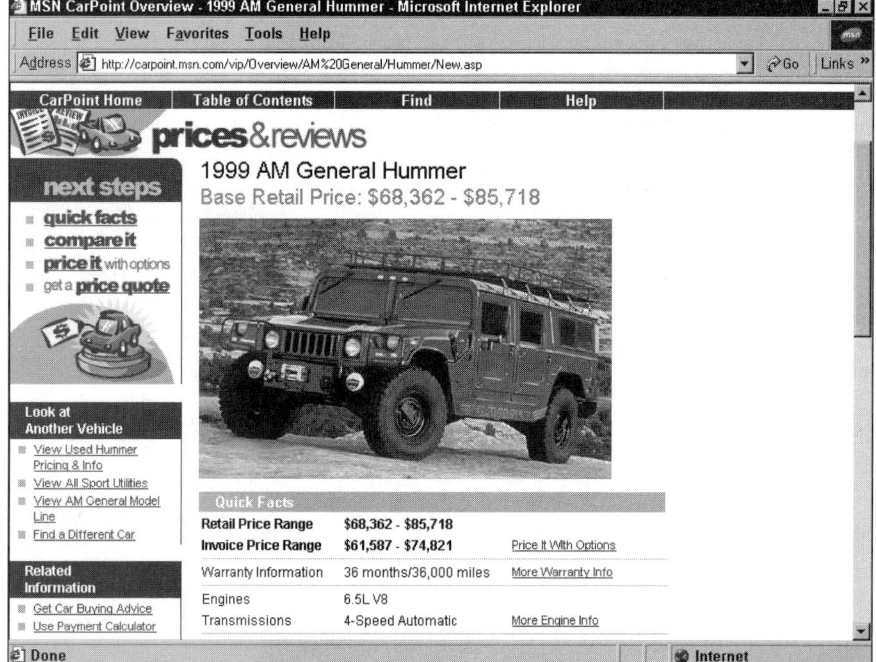

Figure 15-3: The AM General Hummer.

Taking a Look Inside

Many of the vehicles featured in CarPoint include a special Surround Video that lets you view the car's interior in a unique 360-degree presentation. To see if a Surround Video is available for the car, scroll down to the Photo Gallery section of the page. If an icon labeled "Surround Video" appears in the Photo Gallery, click it. The Surround Video only takes a minute or so to download, depending on the speed of your connection to the Internet. (The first time you view a Surround Video, CarPoint may need to download the Surround Video program file. This will also take a few minutes.)

Figure 15-4 shows the Surround Video for the AM Hummer. Once the Surround Video finishes downloading, it automatically starts panning around to show you a complete 360-degree view of the car's interior. You can change the view to a different direction by clicking on the view controls that appear in the lower-right corner of the Surround Video, or you can click and drag the mouse anywhere in the video image to change the panning direction. Don't forget to look up and down!

You can also use the Zoom and Speed slider controls to zoom in for a closer look or to change the video's panning speed. Be careful, though. If you set the speed too high, you'll get dizzy and may need to roll down the window.

Determining How Much Car Can I Afford

CarPoint includes a nifty automobile payment calculator that lets you determine what the monthly payments will be for your car loan. Or, you can use the calculator to determine the maximum amount you can borrow to keep the payments at a certain amount.

To access the payment calculator, click Looking for a Loan? on the CarPoint Home Page. Then, click the Payment Calculator hyperlink. The payment calculator comes to life, as shown in Figure 15-5.

Notice that the payment calculator includes four lines, representing the car's purchase price, the loan's interest rate, the number of months for the loan, and the loan's monthly payment. Initially, the purchase price is set to $20,000, the interest rate is 9.0 percent, the loan term is 48 months, and the monthly payment is a paltry $398.16.

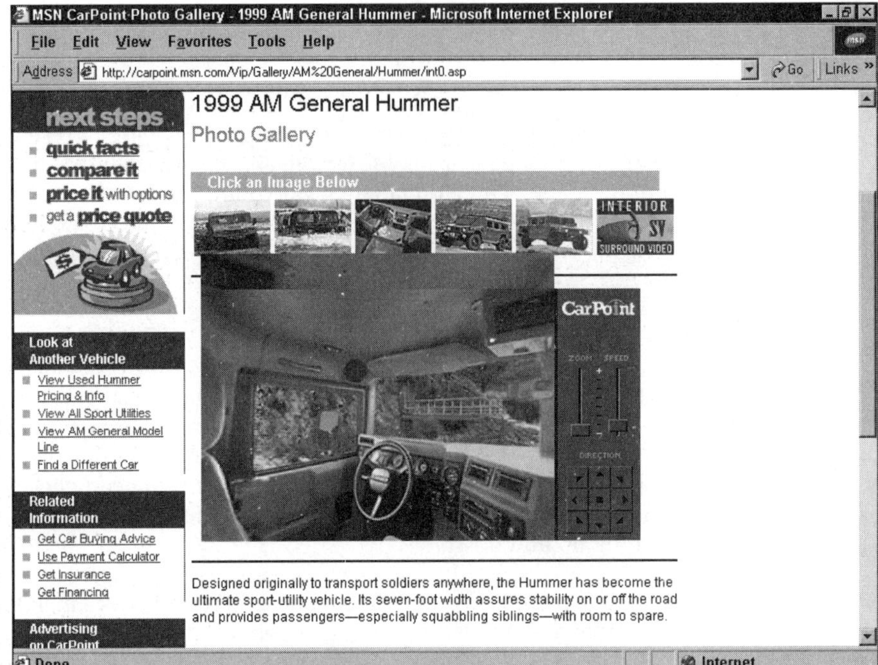

Figure 15-4: A Surround Video view of the Hummer's luxurious interior.

You can change any of these loan variables by dragging the diamond that appears on the line to the left or right. For example, if you want to see what the same car would cost per month if you financed it for 60 months instead of 48, drag the diamond on the loan term line to the right. The monthly payment will change from $398.16 to $332.13. Or, suppose you can get 4.5 percent financing. Drag the loan term diamond back to 48. Then drag the interest rate diamond left until it reads 4.5 percent. The monthly payment changes to $364.85.

Notice also that the payment calculator includes a text box for the down payment amount. You can type the down payment you wish to make, or you can set the down-payment percentage list box (which appears to the left of the Down Payment text box) to 0, 5, 10, 15, or 20 percent and let the payment calculator calculate the down payment amount for you.

The initial setting for the down payment percentage is 20 percent. The down payment is subtracted from the purchase price to set the actual amount of the loan used to calculate the monthly payment. In other words, if the purchase price shows $20,000, the actual loan will be for $16,000 — $20,000 minus the $4,000 down payment.

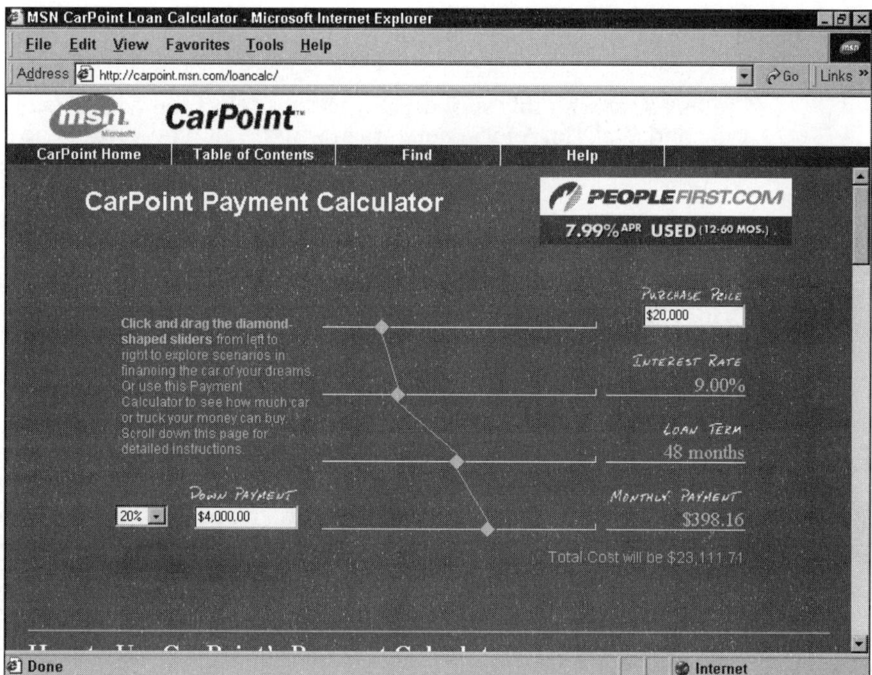

Figure 15-5: CarPoint's payment calculator.

To use the payment calculator to see how much car you can afford for a given monthly payment, drag the interest and loan term diamonds to the best terms you can get for your loan, then drag the monthly payment diamond to the largest monthly payment you can afford. The purchase price diamond will change to reflect the car price you can afford. For example, suppose you can get a 7.0 percent 60-month loan and you can afford $325 in monthly payments. Drag the interest rate diamond to 7.5 percent, the loan term diamond to 60 months, and the monthly payment diamond to $325. The purchase price will jump to $21,834. You won't be able to afford that $60,000 Hummer, but you should be able to get a decently equipped Ford Taurus.

Buying a Car Through CarPoint

If you're actually ready to buy a new car, you may want to try out CarPoint's New Car Buying Service. The buying service consists of a network of dealers who have been screened by CarPoint and have agreed to provide you with their best competitive price on the car you request, with no hassles and no haggling. If you like the price, you can buy the car. If not, you can walk away.

To use the CarPoint Buying Service, go back to CarPoint's home page and then click Ready to Buy? The CarPoint New Car Buying Service page appears.

To buy a car with this service, all you do is select the type of car that interests you and click Go. A form appears in which you type your name and phone number and indicate the make, model, color, and options that you want.

When you have filled out the form, click the Submit button (which appears at the bottom of the form). The form is e-mailed to a CarPoint Sales Consultant in your area who will contact you within 48 hours (except on weekends) with a firm price quote and tell you whether the car is immediately available or if it can be ordered. If you like the price, you can arrange to purchase the vehicle that day. If you don't like the price, you can say "Thanks, but no thanks" and hang up with no further obligation.

CarPoint can help you find a used car — or, to use the more politically correct phrase, a "pre-owned vehicle." From the CarPoint home page, click on the Pre Owned Cars and Trucks icon. This takes you to the Used Car Marketplace, which lets you search for vehicles that have been listed in CarPoint by used-car dealerships. You start by specifying the make, model, and maximum age and mileage of the vehicle you are interested in, and the price range you will consider. CarPoint then displays a list of vehicles that are offered by dealerships in your area.

Setting Up a Personal Auto Page

CarPoint lets you create a Personal Auto Page that is dedicated to your own car. You can use this page to keep track of schedule maintenance and oil changes, and you can find out what your car is currently worth according to the Kelly Blue Book. CarPoint's Personal Auto Page can even send you e-mail to alert you of scheduled maintenance or manufacturer recalls.

To set up a Personal Auto Page, click All About My Car on the CarPoint home page. A registration page appears asking for the make, model, year, and mileage on your car. When you complete the registration page, a Personal Auto Page similar to the one shown in Figure 15-6 appears.

The Personal Auto Page lists the following information for your car:

- The current estimated Kelly Blue Book value
- When your next oil change is due
- When your next scheduled maintenance is due, and an estimate of the cost
- Any recall reports that are pending for the car

- A repair cost calculator that gives you typical repair costs for about 40 common service items
- Seasonal advice, such as preparing your air conditioning for summer
- Links to the CarPoint Web Community where you can discuss your car with other MSN users
- Links to the CarPoint new and used detail reports for your car

You should visit your Personal Auto Page frequently to stay on top of your vehicle's maintenance needs.

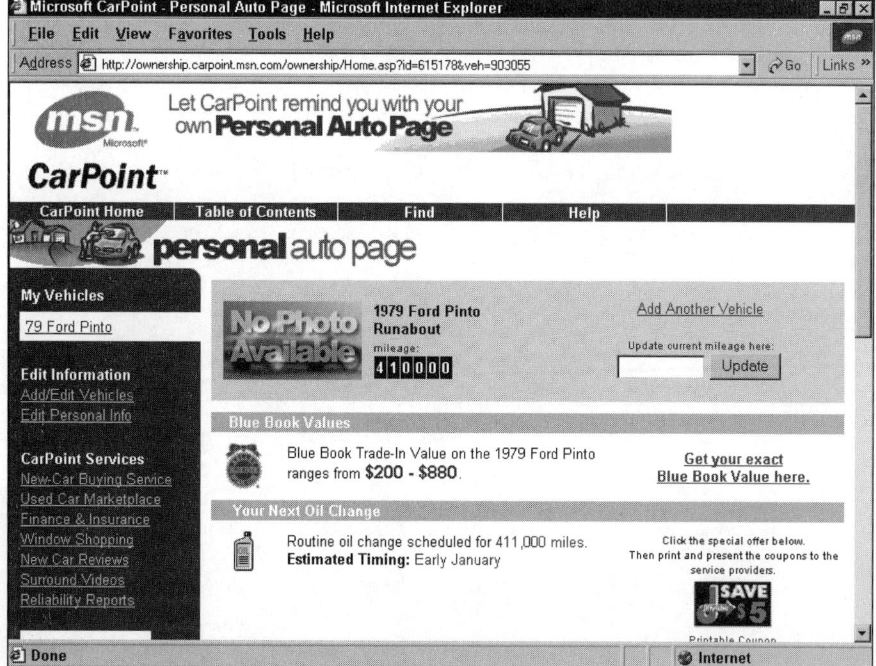

Figure 15-6: A CarPoint Personal Auto Page.

Part IV
The Fun Side of MSN

"Honey—remember that pool party last summer where you showed everyone how to do the limbo in just a sombrero and a dish towel? Well look at what the MSN Daily Video Download is."

In this part . . .

All work and no play makes Jack a dull boy. All work and no play makes Jack a dull boy. All work and no play makes Jack a dull boy. All work and no play makes Jack a dull boy. All work and no play makes Jack a dull boy. All work and no play makes Jack a dull boy. All work and no play makes Jack a dull boy. All work and no play makes Jack a dull boy. All work and no play makes Jack a dull boy. All work and no play makes Jack a dull . . .

Oh, um, sorry.

This part has chapters that show you the fun side of MSN . . . in particular, playing online games, shopping, and planning your next vacation. Have fun!

Chapter 16

Playing Games Online

In This Chapter

- Signing up at the Gaming Zone
- Checking out the games you can play
- Playing a game of Checkers

One of the most popular areas on MSN is the MSN Gaming Zone, where tens of thousands of people gather at any given time to play online games. The Gaming Zone lets you play classic card and board games such as Hearts, Checkers, and Backgammon, as well as adventure and role playing games, puzzles and word games, sports, strategy, and simulation games. Many of the games on Gaming Zone are free, but some are online versions of games you must purchase at a computer software store, such as Hellbender, MechWarrior, and X-Wing vs. TIE Fighter.

In this chapter, you discover how easy it is to sign up at the Gaming Zone and play free games.

Signing Up

Before you can play games on the Gaming Zone, you must first sign up for a free membership account. The free account lets you select a Zone Name that you can use to identify yourself to other people playing games on the Gaming Zone, and a password that only you know so you can sign in to play games.

To sign up for a free Gaming Zone membership, follow these steps:

1. **From the MSN Home Page, click Games in the list of services at the left side of the page.**

   The Gaming Zone Home Page appears, as shown in Figure 16-1.

2. **Click the Free Signup hyperlink that appears near the center of the page.**

   The page shown in Figure 16-2 appears, explaining the ins and outs of the Gaming Zone and offering to help you sign up for a free membership.

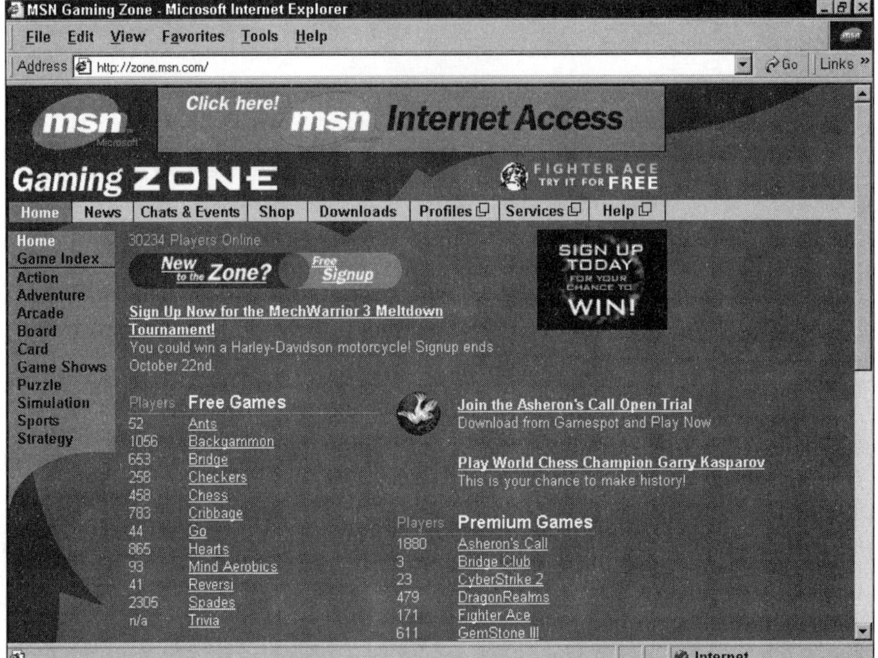

Figure 16-1: Welcome to the Gaming Zone.

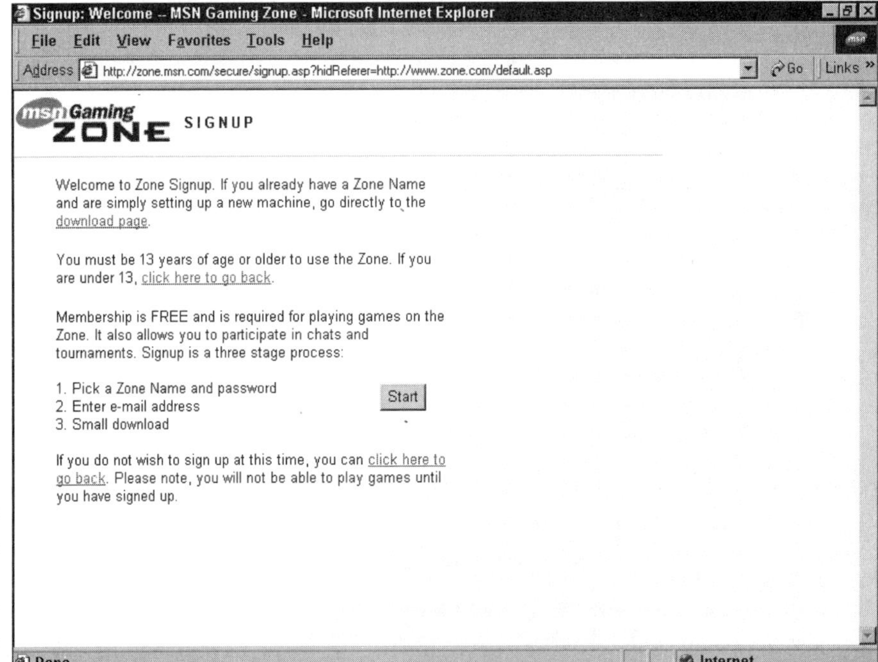

Figure 16-2: Sign up for a free membership.

3. **Click the Start button.**

   The Pick a Zone Name and Password page appears, as shown in Figure 16-3.

4. **Type the name you would like to use for your Zone Name in the Create Zone Name text box.**

   You can use any name you wish, provided the name you choose has not already been taken by another Gaming Zone member.

5. **Type a password in the Password and Confirm Password text boxes.**

   You have to type the password twice so that Gaming Zone can be sure that you typed it correctly.

6. **Click the Continue button.**

   If the Zone Name ID you have chosen is already in use, Gaming Zone asks you to pick another name. Otherwise, the Signup: E-mail page appears, containing a text box in which you can enter your e-mail address.

7. **Type your e-mail address in the text box.**

   Gaming Zone needs to know your e-mail address so that you can be contacted if you win a contest, and so you can receive the Gaming Zone newsletter. (If you'd rather not receive the newsletter, you can uncheck the check box that appears at the bottom of this page.)

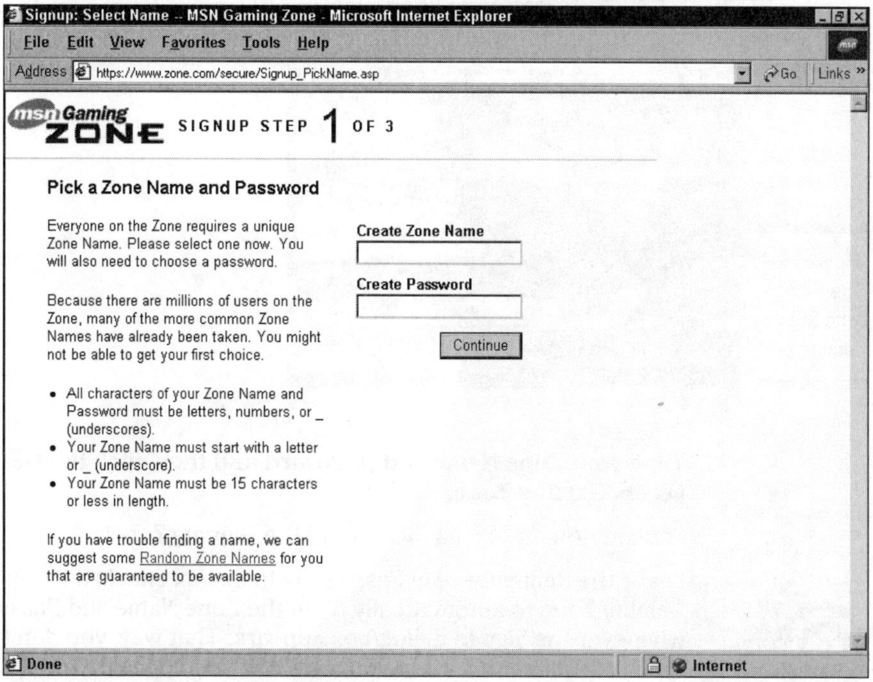

Figure 16-3: The New Player signup page.

8. **Click the Continue button.**

   The third and final Signup page appears, informing you that you need to download some Gaming Zone program files before you can play games. The download should take about 5 minutes on a 28.8K modem.

9. **Click the Start Download button.**

   The Gaming Zone program files will be downloaded to your computer. When the download completes, a picture of a Spade appears on the Signup: Software Installation download page and the Click Here When You See the Spade button appears.

10. **Click the Click Here When You See the Spade button.**

    A confirmation page appears to let you know that you have been signed up for the Gaming Zone.

11. **Click the Logon and take me to the games hyperlink to access Gaming Zone.**

    Gaming Zone now begins to download some additional software required to play games at the Gaming Zone. This download should take no more than a couple of minutes. When asked where you want the software installed (accept the default location unless you have good reasons not to), whether you agree to the Gaming Zone license statement, and whether or not you want to create an icon on your desktop that lets you access the Gaming Zone site directly. Eventually, the Sign In dialog box shown in Figure 16-4 appears.

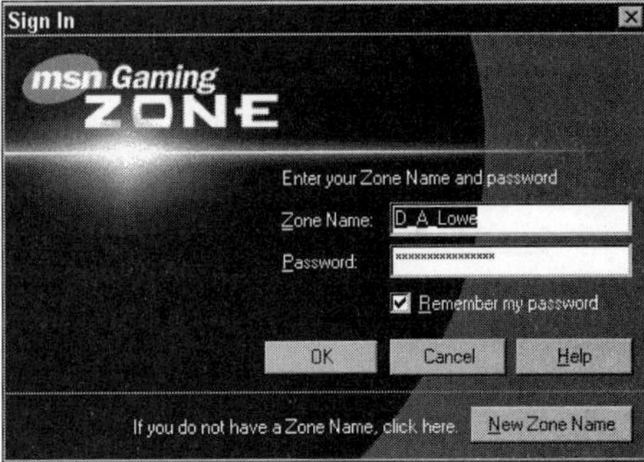

Figure 16-4: The Gaming Zone Sign In dialog box.

12. **Type your Zone Name and password and then click the OK button to access Gaming Zone.**

    You are now an official member of the Gaming Zone!

Leave the Remember My Password check box checked if you want Gaming Zone to automatically fill in the Zone Name and Password fields whenever the Sign In dialog box appears. That way, you don't have to type your password when you sign in. If you uncheck this option, you'll have to type your password each time you sign in to the Gaming Zone.

Many of the Gaming Zone games use software that must be downloaded and installed on your computer before you can play the game. The first time you access a game that requires software on your computer, Gaming Zone will automatically download the software to your computer. However, if you prefer, you can download and install all of the Gaming Zone software at once so you won't have to wait the first time you access a game you haven't previously played. The complete Gaming Zone software is a 9MB download, so you can expect the download to take 15 minutes or more. To download the complete Gaming Zone software, click the Downloads hyperlink on the Gaming Zone Home Page, click the Zone Software hyperlink that appears in the list of links on the left side of the page and then click the Complete Software Install hyperlink.

Perusing the Games

At the time I wrote this book, there were 114 games you could play on Gaming Zone. Gaming Zone periodically adds new games, so by the time you read this even more games may be available.

The Gaming Zone home page has three sections that list popular Gaming Zone games, as described in the following paragraphs:

- **Free Games:** This section lists games that any Gaming Zone member can play free of charge. These games include popular games such as Hearts, Spades, Bridge, Backgammon, Checkers, and Chess.
- **Premium Games:** This section lists games for which Gaming Zone charges a fee to play. These games include a Fighter Ace (aerial combat), Tanarus (tank combat), Hercules & Xena (fantasy role-playing), and others. Most of the premium games cost $9.95 per month, but some of them have other subscription options such as $49.95 for six months or $1.95 for a single day.
- **Retail Games:** This section lists several games which you can purchase at computer software stores and play over the Internet with other Gaming Zone members. At the time I wrote this book, the most popular retail game on the Gaming Zone was Tom Clancy's Rainbow Six, a realistic shoot-em-up combat game. Playing retail games on the Gaming Zone is free, but you must purchase the game before you can play.

You can display an alphabetical list of all the games available on the Gaming Zone by clicking the Game Index hyperlink in the menu that appears at the left of the Gaming Zone home page. This displays a list of Gaming Zone games, as shown in Figure 16-5.

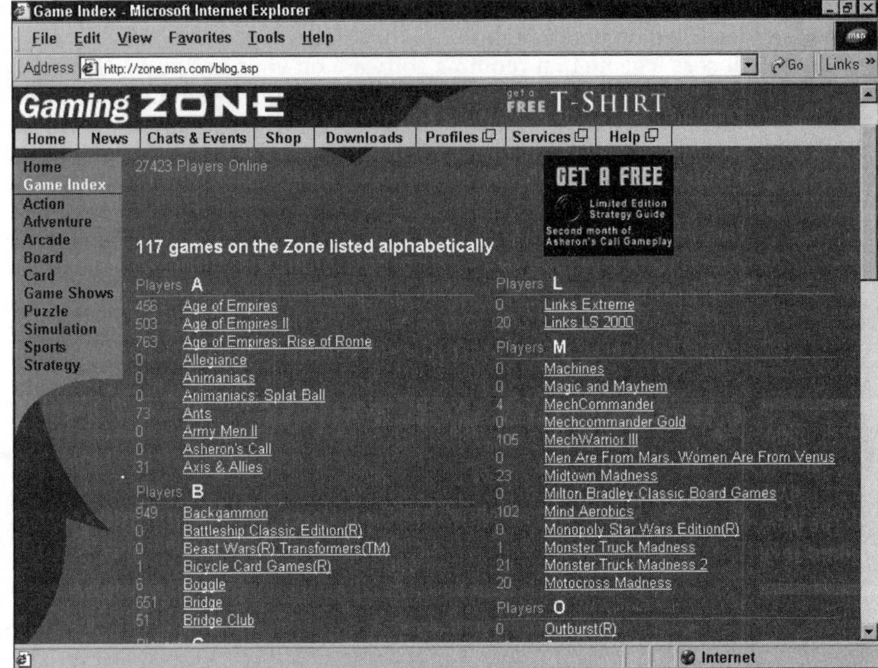

Figure 16-5: An alphabetical list of Gaming Zone games.

If you prefer, you can click one of the following options in the menu that appears at the left side of the Gaming Zone home page to display Gaming Zones games arranged by category. Following is a brief list of just a few of the games in each category:

- **Action:** Fighter Ace, Hellbender, MechWarrior III, Rainbow Six, Star Wars: X-Wing Alliance
- **Adventure:** Asheron's Call, DragonRealms, Hercules & Xena
- **Arcade:** Animaniacs, Frogger, Pinky & the Brain
- **Board:** Backgammon, Checkers, Chess, Risk, SORRY!, Stratego
- **Card:** Bridge, Cribbage, Hearts, Spades
- **Game shows:** Encarta Challenge, Trivia
- **Puzzle:** Crosswords, Trax, Word Search
- **Simulation:** Microsoft Flight Simulator, Monster Truck Madness, Top Gun
- **Sports:** Elite Darts, Fantasy Baseball, Golf 99, Links Extreme
- **Strategy:** Age of Empires, Ants, and more

Playing a Game of Checkers

The easiest way to get your feet wet playing Gaming Zone games is to try a hand at a simple free game such as Checkers. To play checkers, click the Checkers link in the list of free games on the Gaming Zone Home page. This calls up the Checkers home page, as shown in Figure 16-6.

Notice that the Checkers home page lists 11 rooms in which you can play. The rooms are organized into several categories:

- **Social Rooms:** For beginners and casual players. The Social rooms are for people who just want to enjoy a friendly game of Checkers without worrying too much about winning or losing. As you can see, these rooms are where most of the Gaming Zone's Checker players hang out.
- **Competitive Rooms:** For players who take the game seriously and want to play against skilled opponents.
- **Ladder Rooms:** Features an ongoing competition in which players challenge one another to games. The winner of each game moves up the ladder, while the loser moves down the ladder.
- **Rated Rooms:** When you play in one of these rooms, Gaming Zone automatically keeps track of your wins and losses and rates your play. If you are a serious player, you should play in one of the rated rooms so that Gaming Zone can keep track of your wins and losses.
- **Tournament Rooms:** These rooms are where the Gaming Zone conducts tournaments.

Most Gaming Zone games have rooms similar to the Checkers rooms shown in Figure 16-6.

To enter one of the playing rooms to play a game, just click on the room you would like to play in. Your best bet is to click one of the rooms listed under the Social Rooms category. For example, Figure 16-7 shows the Checkers Fireside room.

When you enter a room, you see a collection of tables that have players sitting at them. There are two ways to join a game:

- Click a seat at an empty table. This makes you the host of a new game. You must then wait for another player to join your table.
- Click an empty seat at a table that already has a player sitting at it. This enables you to join a table that has not yet started playing.

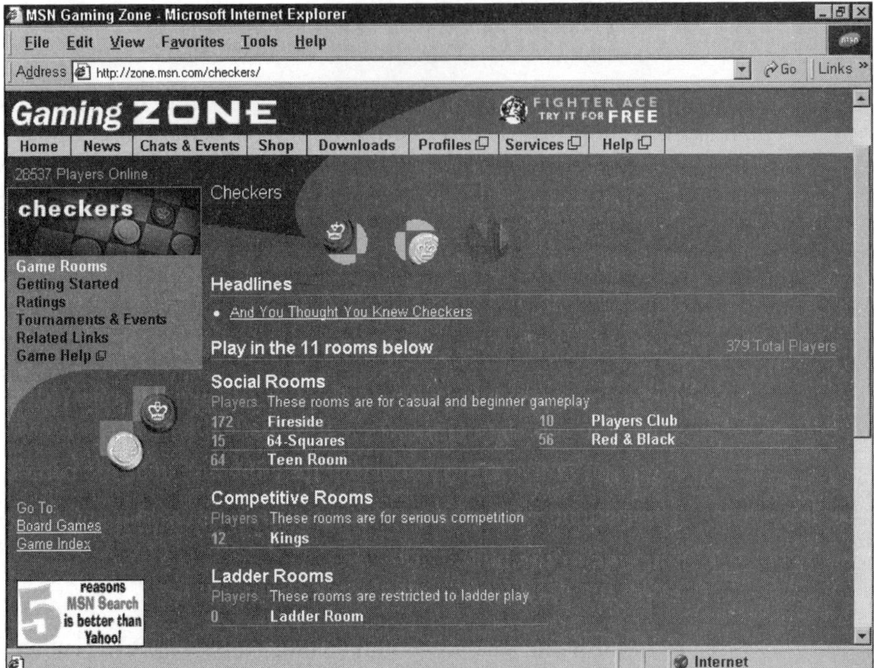

Figure 16-6: Welcome to Checkers.

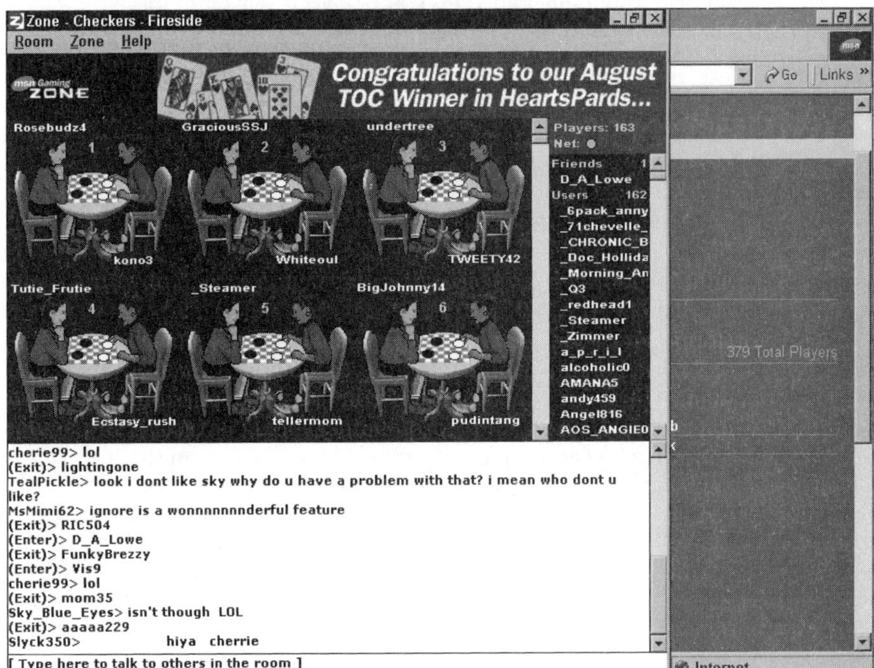

Figure 16-7: A Checkers game room.

When you have sat down at a table, a Start button appears next to the table. Click the Start button to begin playing the game. When you do, the game board will appear in a separate window, as shown in Figure 16-8.

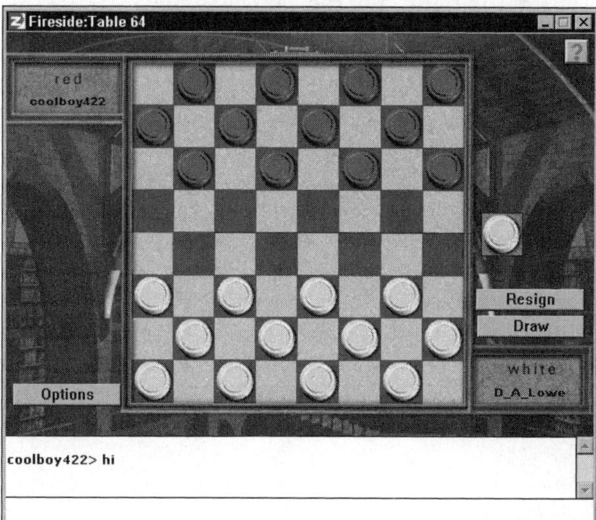

Figure 16-8: Playing a game of Checkers.

Playing the game is simple: when it is your turn, use the mouse to drag one of your pieces to the square you wish to move to. The computer lets you know if you have tried to make an illegal move, such as moving two squares instead of one or not making a jump when a jump is possible.

If you want to resign, click the Resign button. Click the Draw button if you believe the game is a draw; if your opponent agrees, the game will end in a draw.

Here are a few other points to ponder when playing games such as Checkers on the Gaming Zone:

- The number of chairs that appears at each table in a room depends on the number of players that can participate in the game. For two-player games such as Checkers or Chess, only two chairs appear at each table. For four-player games such as Hearts or Spades, four chairs appear at each table.
- Some of the Gaming Zone games, such as Hearts, allow you to play against computer opponents rather than against live opponents. If you click the Start button before human opponents occupy all the chairs at your table, Gaming Zone will fill the empty chairs with computer opponents.

- You can click a player at a table with a game in progress to kibitz — that is, watch in and comment on the game. You'll be able to see the hand of the player you are kibitzing, but not the other players' hands.
- You can chat with the players at your table by typing messages in the chat text box at the bottom of the game window.

That's all there is to playing games on the Gaming Zone. Jump in and have fun!

Chapter 17

Shopping at MSN eShop

In This Chapter

- Finding the best places to shop on MSN
- Buying something over the Internet
- Using MSN's gift reminders
- Creating a Wish List

If you enjoy shopping, MSN eShop is a great place to hang out. MSN eShop is the online equivalent of an outlet mall, with dozens of stores offering name-brand products ranging from chocolates to tools, flowers to computers, and lingerie to linguini.

Remember the famous poet e. e. cummings — the one who didn't like to use capital letters in his poetry? i think he would be proud of the recent fad of preceding internet names with lower-case e's.

Although shopping over the Internet is convenient, it can also be addictive. . . and expensive! Have fun and find bargains, but make sure you don't point-and-click away your life savings.

Taking an MSN Shopping Spree

To get to MSN eShop, simply click the Shopping tab near the top of the MSN Home Page. You are greeted by the MSN eShop home page, as shown in Figure 17-1.

Take a few moments to familiarize yourself with the MSN eShop home page. At the top of the page, beneath the main MSN menu bar, you'll find a smaller menu bar that provides links to eShop's main areas:

- **eShop Home:** The eShop homepage.
- **Find a Gift:** eShop's Gift Center, which helps you buy gifts. You can use a gift guide to help you find the perfect gift, create a wish list of things you'd like to receive as gifts, or send a gift certificate.

- **Find a Deal:** This page spotlights special deals from eShop stores. If you're a bargain hunter, call up this page often to see what's available, as the deals change frequently.
- **Find a Store:** This page lists all of eShop's stores in alphabetical order. This page is the easiest way to find a particular store on eShop.
- **Customer Service:** MSN eShop's Customer Service center, where you'll find information such as the customer service 800 number for each of eShop's merchants and online security tips. Note that Microsoft does not actually provide customer service for the MSN eShop vendors — just a phone number you can call if you have a gripe.

In the center of the MSN eShop home page is a list of store departments such as Books & Magazines, Clothing & Accessories, and Health & Wellness. You can click on any of these departments to display the department's home page. For example, Figure 17-2 shows the Electronics home page. Here, you'll find listings for specific types of products (such as Audio equipment, Camcorders, Cameras, and so on), links to eShop stores, and featured special purchases which change on a daily basis.

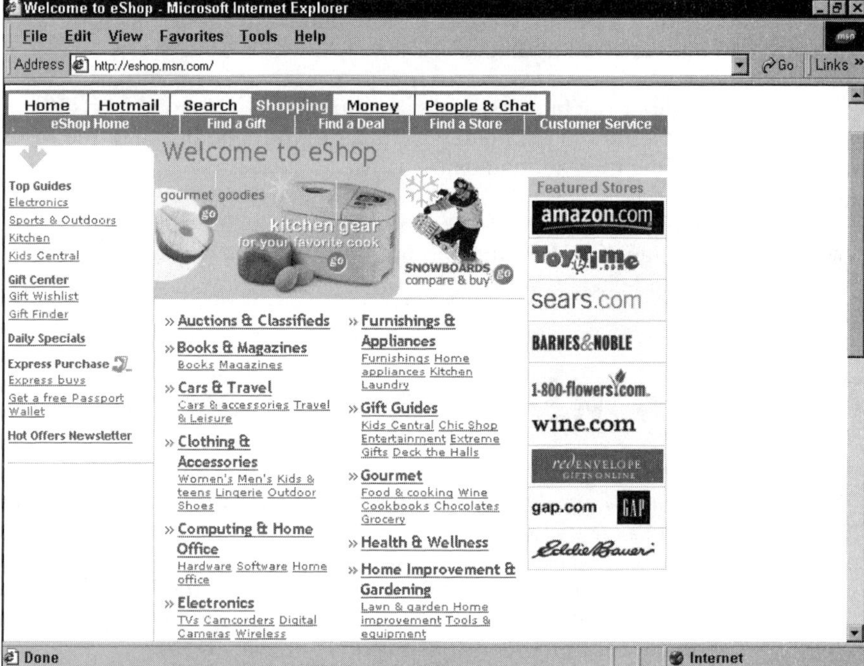

Figure 17-1: Shopping at MSN.

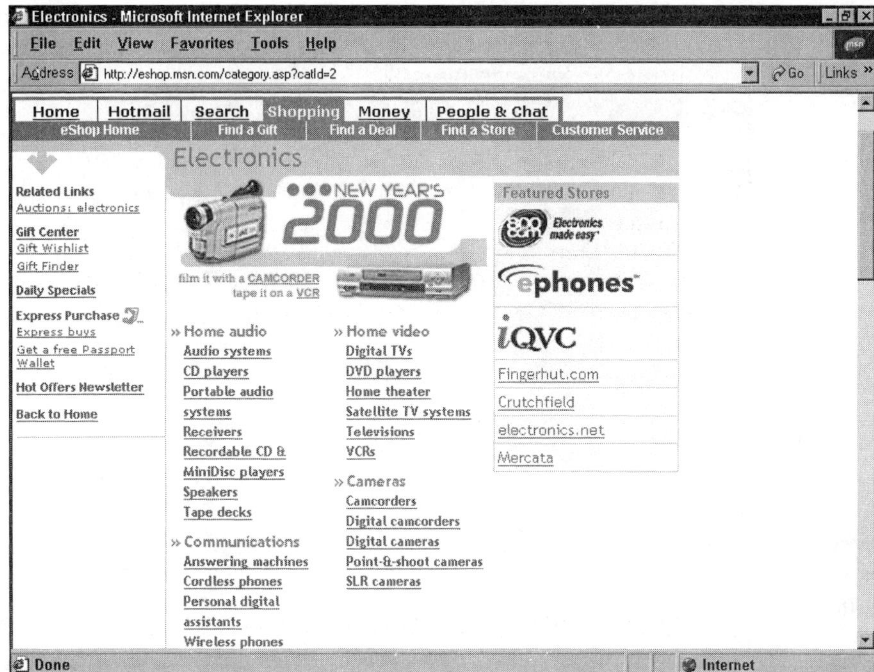

Figure 17-2: eShop's Electronics home page.

The easiest way to go directly to an MSN eShop store is to click Find a Store in the menu bar that appears at the top of all MSN eShop pages. This takes you to the page shown in Figure 17-3, which lists all of MSN eShop's stores in alphabetical order. You can then go directly to the home page for any of the stores listed on this page by clicking the store's hyperlink.

The stores that are represented on the MSN Shopping page are *not* operated or controlled by Microsoft or MSN. Although Microsoft does its best to allow only reputable merchants to hang their shingle on the MSN Shopping page, the merchants themselves operate independently from Microsoft.

Time To Shop!

Although each of the stores on MSN eShop has slightly different procedures for online shopping, all of them take a similar approach. As you browse through the online catalogs or product listings, you can add items to a virtual shopping basket. Then, when you have made all of your selections, you proceed to the checkout where you confirm that you want to purchase the items and provide your credit card number and shipping address. At any time up until checkout, you can change or remove any item from your basket, or you can clear your basket altogether.

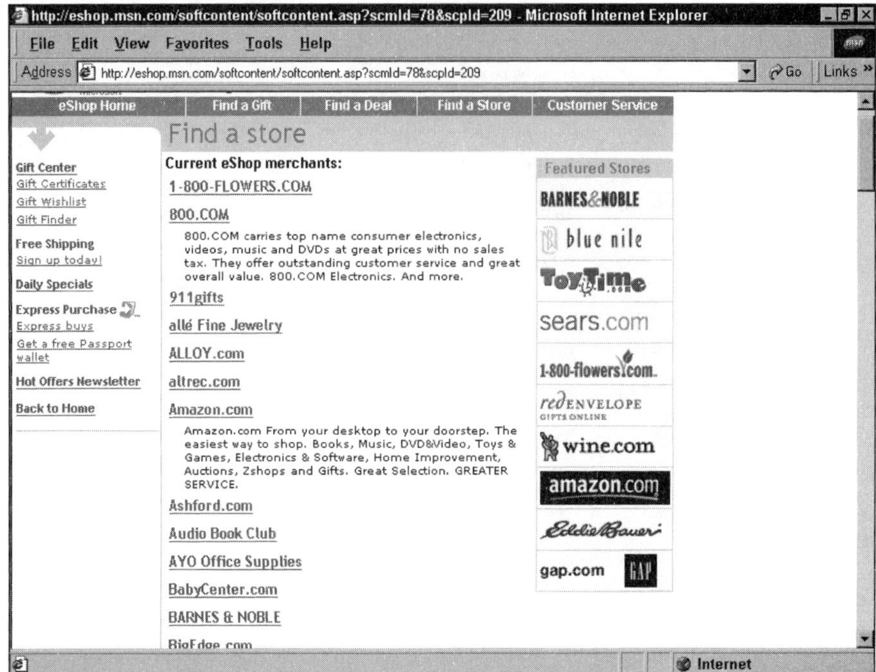

Figure 17-3: The Find a Store page.

To give you an idea of how this online shopping works, the following paragraphs describe the process of purchasing a CD from Amazon.com. To go to Amazon.com, click Find a Store in the menu bar at the top of any MSN eShop page. Then click the Amazon.com hyperlink. The Amazon.com home page appears, as shown in Figure 17-4. Keep in mind that although the other shops vary in the details, they all follow a similar approach.

The best way to shop at Amazon.com is to search its massive database for the selections you're looking for. For example, suppose you want to buy a Spike Jones CD. You'd start by searching the database for all Spike Jones titles. To search the database, choose Popular Music from the Keyword Search drop-down list box, type **spike jones** in the text box and then click the Go button. Amazon.com grinds and whirs for a moment and then displays the results, as shown in Figure 17-5. The top three Spike Jones albums are listed first, followed by the complete results (which shows 21 items).

To inspect an individual album, click the album you're interested in. A page similar to the one in Figure 17-6 displays. You can't see it in the figure, but if you scroll down, the page lists a lot of information about the album, including:

- A list of all the songs on the album
- Samples of songs that you can download and listen to

- Reviews from Amazon.com customers who have purchased the album
- Links to other artists that people who have purchased Spike Jones albums have also purchased.

Most other online stores use a similar method for shopping: you peruse the store's online catalog, adding items you wish to purchase to an online shopping cart. When you have finished making your selections, you proceed to an online checkout, where you can confirm that the items in your online shopping cart are in stock and where you supply your credit card and shipping information.

To add the album to your shopping basket, click the Add to Shopping Cart button. This places the item in your virtual shopping cart, similar to the screen shown in Figure 17-7.

You can then add additional albums to your basket. When you have collected all the albums you want, click Proceed to Checkout. This leads you to a series of checkout pages, where you supply information such as your name and address, credit card information, an optional gift message, and other information needed to fill your order. Once you fill in the correct information and confirm your order, Amazon.com processes your order and sends you the merchandise that you purchased as soon as possible.

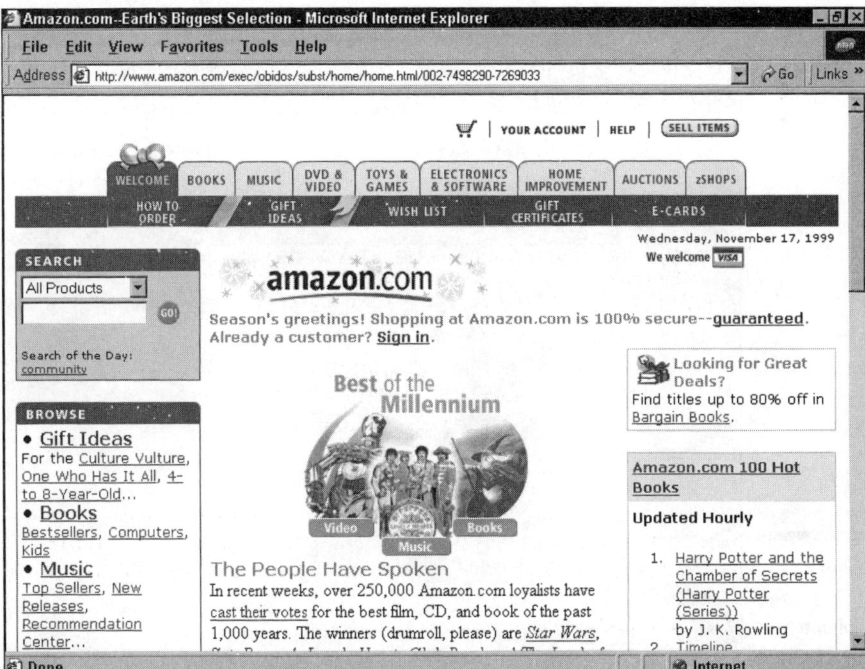

Figure 17-4: Home at Amazon .com.

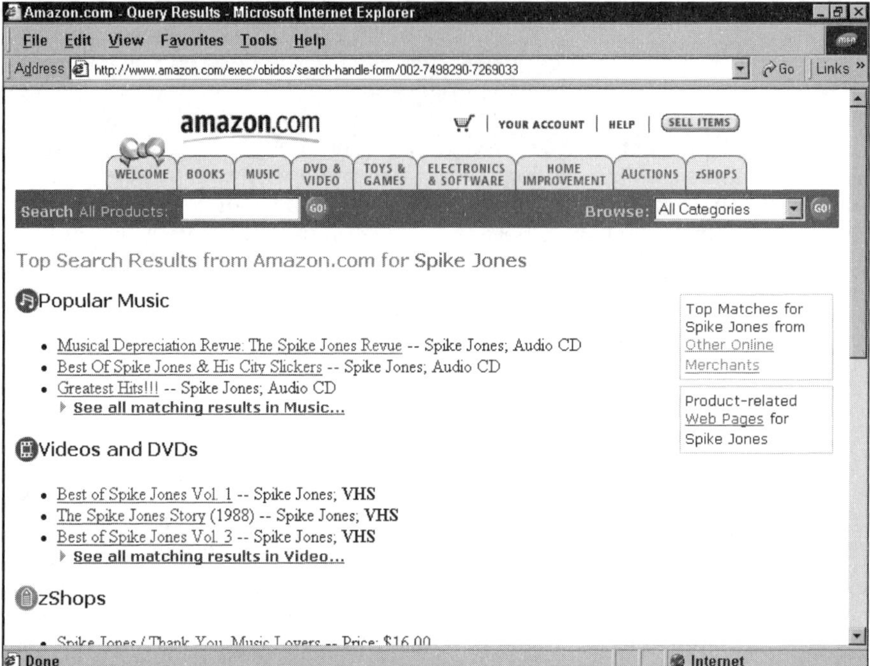

Figure 17-5: Searching for Spike Jones.

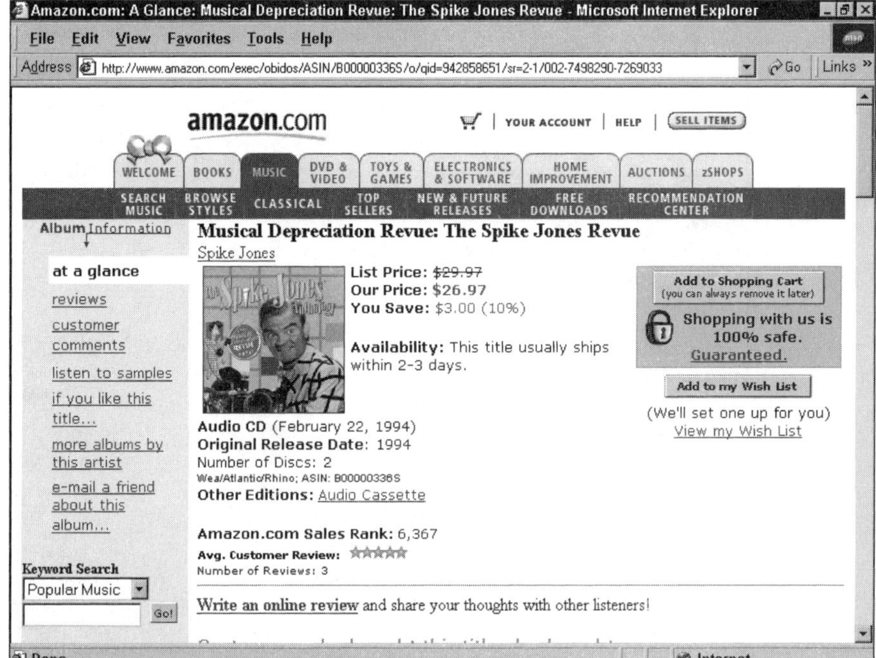

Figure 17-6: This is the album that I need.

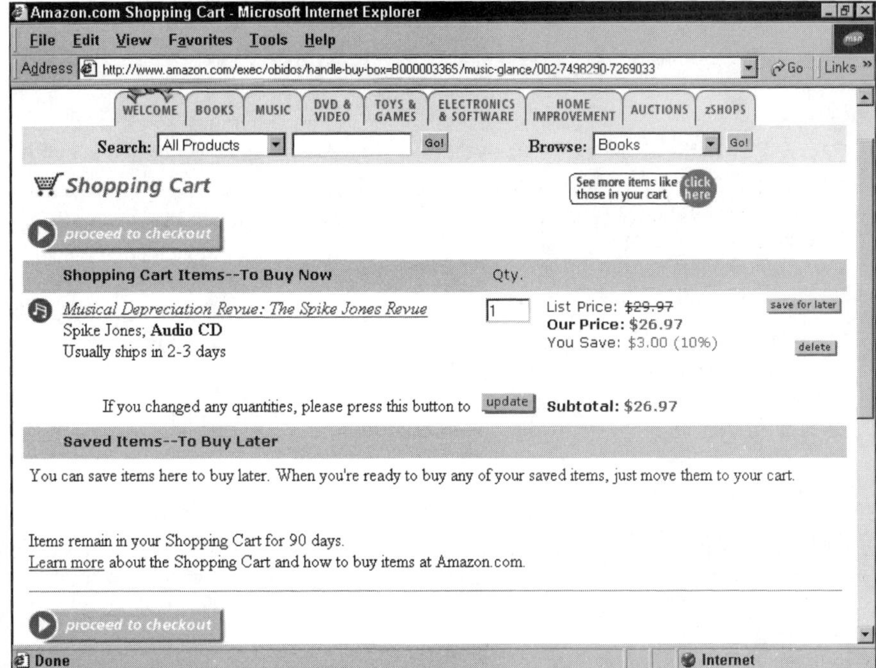

Figure 17-7: Your virtual shopping cart.

Remembering Gifts

It isn't that I have a bad memory — just a strange one. I can remember the mundane details such as the words to the Beverly Hillbillies theme song or the name of the Star Trek episode where Kirk fought the Gorn ("Arena"), but I can't remember my mom's birthday. If your memory is as strange as mine, you'll appreciate MSN's Gift Reminder service. Gift Reminder automatically sends you e-mail to remind you about upcoming special occasions that you need to purchase gifts for.

To access Gift Reminder, go to the MSN eShop Gift Center by clicking the Find a Gift hyperlink in the menu bar near the top of the MSN eShop home page. Then, click the Gift Reminder hyperlink to call up the Gift Reminder home page. Scroll down the page a bit to reveal the input fields shown in Figure 17-8.

To use gift reminder, first register yourself by typing your name, a password, and your e-mail address in the text boxes shown on the Gift Reminder page. Then, type the name of the person you need to get a gift for, the date, and select the occasion from the drop-down list. When you have typed all of the required information, click the Submit button. A confirmation page appears to show that you have set up a Gift Reminder.

Is online shopping safe?

Many online shoppers cancel their order when they realize that they must give their credit card number to the online store, fearing that their number will appear on hacker Web sites throughout the world and that thousands of dollars worth of unauthorized charges will appear on their next credit card bill.

Fortunately, most of these fears are unmerited. All of the online merchants represented on MSN eShop use the latest in security technology to make sure that your credit card number and other information (such as your address and phone number) is kept confidential. In fact, using your credit card over the Internet is probably *more* secure than using it to purchase goods over the phone or in person at a store.

Online stores use a security method known as *Secure Sockets Layer*, or *SSL*, to scramble your credit card number and other information before it sends it over the Internet and to unscramble the information at the other end. The scrambling is done in such a way that other users who might intercept your message cannot unscramble it.

To let you know that a secure SSL connection is being used to transmit confidential information, both Internet Explorer and Netscape Navigator use icons in the status bar to let you know when a secure connection is being used:

Internet Explorer displays this padlock icon in the status bar whenever a secure connection is in use.

Navigator displays a padlock icon in the lower left corner of the Navigator window at all times. The padlock is open when the connection is not secure. When a secure connection is used, the padlock is closed.

Do not type your credit card number or other confidential information on a Web page unless the padlock icon is visible in the status bar of your Web browser.

The confirmation page sports the following buttons that you can use to manage your Gift Reminders:

- **Review Your Reminders:** Displays a list of all your reminders.
- **Add Reminder:** Creates a new gift reminder.
- **Discontinue Reminder:** Service cancels your account.
- **Update Register Information:** Changes your name, password, or e-mail address.

Wishing for the Moon

Want a home entertainment system for Christmas or a diamond ring for your anniversary? MSN eShop's Wish List feature is just what you need! The Wish List feature that lets you peruse items that are available from eShop's online merchants, add the ones you just have to have to your Wish List, and then e-mail your Wish List to your friends so they'll know what to get you for your birthday.

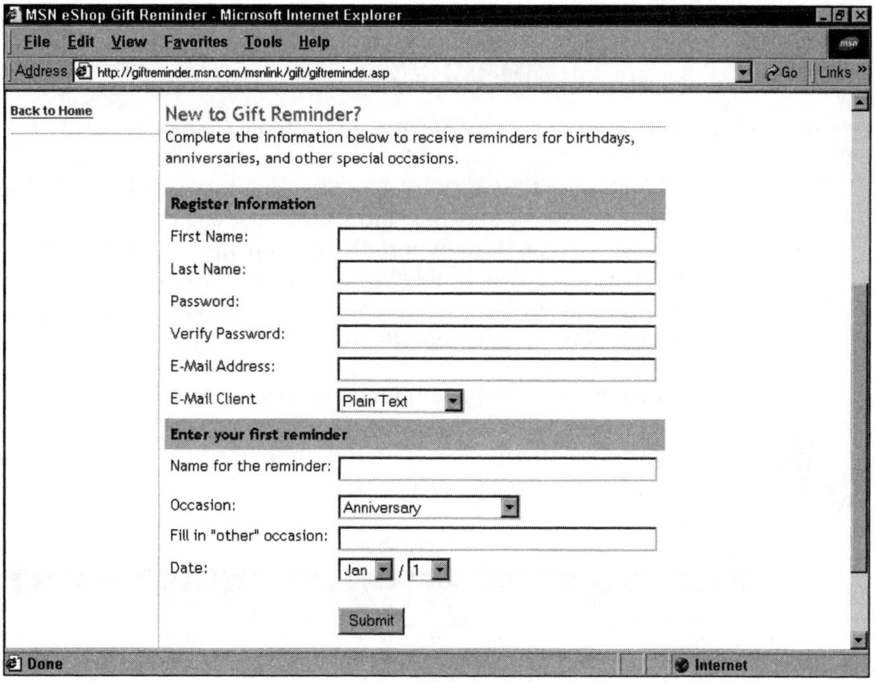

Figure 17-8: Use these fields to register for MSN's Gift Reminder service and to set up your first reminder.

To create a Wish List, follow these simple steps:

1. **From any MSN eShop page, click Find Gift in the menu bar.**

   This takes you to the Gift Center.

2. **Click the Create a Wish List hyperlink.**

   This calls up the Create Your Wishlist page, as shown in Figure 17-9.

3. **Type a name for your Wish List in the text box.**

   The default name, "My Wish List," will work but is pretty uncreative. Something like "Debbie's Ridiculous Birthday Wants" or "Doug's Unequivocal Christmas Demands" would be better.

4. **Click the Save button.**

   This creates a Wish List using the name you typed in Step 3. However, at this point, the list is empty — so you'll need to go shopping.

5. **Go shopping.**

   Peruse the MSN eShop Department pages, looking for items to add to your Wish List.

6. **When you find something you want, click the Add to Wishlist hyperlink.**

   The item adds to your Wish List, as shown in Figure 17-10.

7. **Repeat steps 5 and 6 until you are bored, or done.**

To add something to your Wish List that isn't featured in MSN eShop, go to the Wish List page by clicking Find a Gift, then clicking Create a Wish List. Then, click the Click Here hyperlink that appears under the But I Can't Find It heading. This summons the dialog box and shown in Figure 17-11, where you can type in a description of the item you want. Type a description of the item then click Add to add the item to your Wish List.

When you have finished compiling your Wish List, click the Email My List hyperlink on the Wish List page. This brings up a page in which you can enter your name and other personal information, plus the e-mail address of the friends you want to send the list to. Good luck!

Figure 17-9: Creating a Wish List.

Figure 17-10: Now here's something I really need.

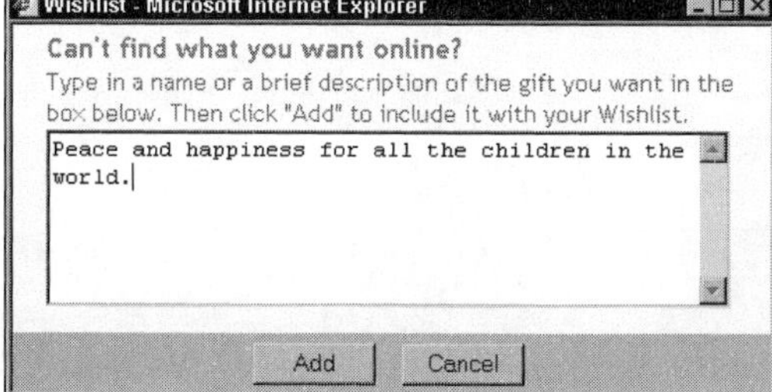

Figure 17-11: You can add anything you want to your Wish List.

Chapter 18

Planning a Vacation with Expedia

In This Chapter

- Signing up for Expedia
- Planning a trip
- Purchasing airplane tickets online
- Reserving a hotel room
- Renting a car
- Surfing for cheap airfares

Microsoft Expedia is an online travel agency that you can use to plan your next vacation or business trip. With Expedia, you can shop for airline tickets to get the lowest price available for the flights you want, set up a travel schedule for your trip, and reserve hotel rooms and rental cars. About the only thing Expedia cannot do for you is pack for your trip!

Signing Up

Before you can use Expedia to plan a trip, you have to sign up. Expedia doesn't cost anything extra, but member ID is required before you can access Expedia's reservation systems. Expedia uses your member ID to keep track of the travel plans you have created.

At the time I wrote this, Expedia was not set up to work with Microsoft's own Passport, the one-in-all Internet sign-in service. However, Microsoft hopes to have Expedia working with Passport soon. By the time you read this, you may be able to access Expedia using your Passport account instead of having to create a separate Expedia account. Refer to Chapter 6 for more information.

To sign up for Expedia, just follow these steps:

1. **Go to Expedia by clicking Travel from the MSN home page.**

   The Expedia home page appears, as shown in Figure 18-1.

2. **Click the Join Now. It's Free! hyperlink that appears on the left side of the page.**

   Because the Expedia home page is a bit cluttered, the Join Now. It's Free! link can be hard to find. Look for it under the Customer Support heading on the left side of the page. You are whisked to the Create an Account page, as shown in Figure 18-2.

3. **Fill out all of the information on the Member Information page.**

   The page is big, so be sure to scroll down to see all of it. Expedia asks for these three tidbits of information:

   - **A member ID.** Write this down — you'll need to remember it. (To keep things simple, I suggest you use the same member ID for all of the online services you sign up for.)

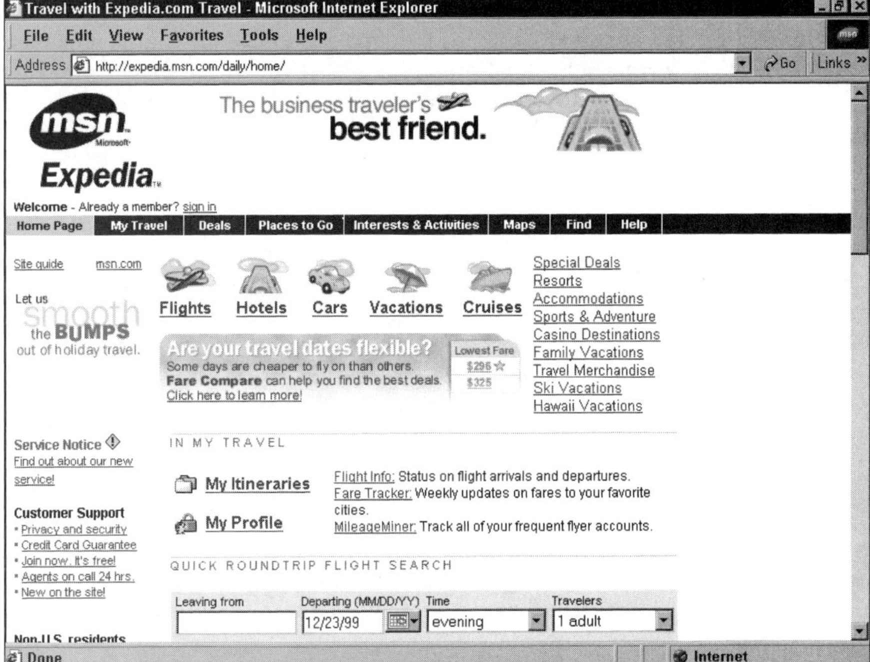

Figure 18-1: Expedia's home page.

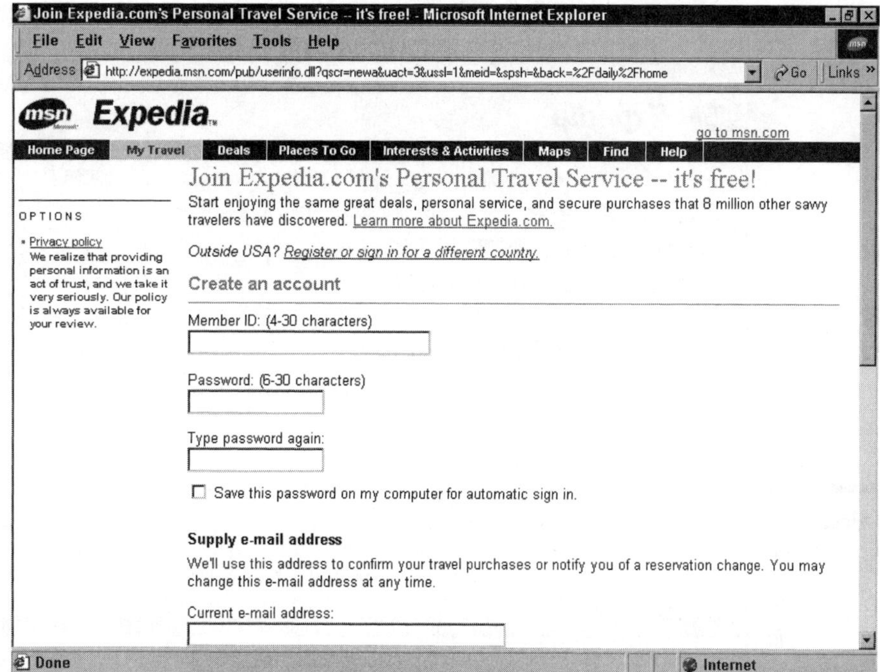

Join Expedia.com's Personal Travel Service -- it's free! - Microsoft Internet Explorer
File Edit View Favorites Tools Help
Address http://expedia.msn.com/pub/userinfo.dll?qscr=newa&uact=3&ussl=1&meid=&spsh=&back=%2Fdaily%2Fhome
Go Links
Expedia
go to msn.com
Home Page My Travel Deals Places To Go Interests & Activities Maps Find Help
Join Expedia.com's Personal Travel Service -- it's free!
Start enjoying the same great deals, personal service, and secure purchases that 8 million other savvy travelers have discovered. Learn more about Expedia.com.
OPTIONS
Privacy policy
We realize that providing personal information is an act of trust, and we take it very seriously. Our policy is always available for your review.
Outside USA? Register or sign in for a different country.
Create an account
Member ID: (4-30 characters)
Password: (6-30 characters)
Type password again:
Save this password on my computer for automatic sign in.
Supply e-mail address
We'll use this address to confirm your travel purchases or notify you of a reservation change. You may change this e-mail address at any time.
Current e-mail address:
Done
Internet

Figure 18-2: Creating an Expedia account.

- **A password.** (Once again, I suggest you use the same password for all your online accounts.) You should also write your password down so you'll remember it. Keep the password in a safe place — not on a sticky note stuck on your monitor.

- **Your e-mail address.** If you want to sign in automatically whenever you access Expedia, check the Save This Password for Automatic Sign In option.

4. **Read the Membership Agreement.**

   The Membership Agreement was written by lawyers, so don't worry if you don't understand a word of it.

5. **Click the Sign up and continue using Expedia.com hyperlink.**

   Your Expedia account is now set up.

When you use Expedia, the Sign In page, shown in Figure 18-3, appears whenever Expedia needs you to sign in. Fill in your member ID and password and then click the Sign In hyperlink. (If you forget your member ID or password, click the Having trouble signing in hyperlink.)

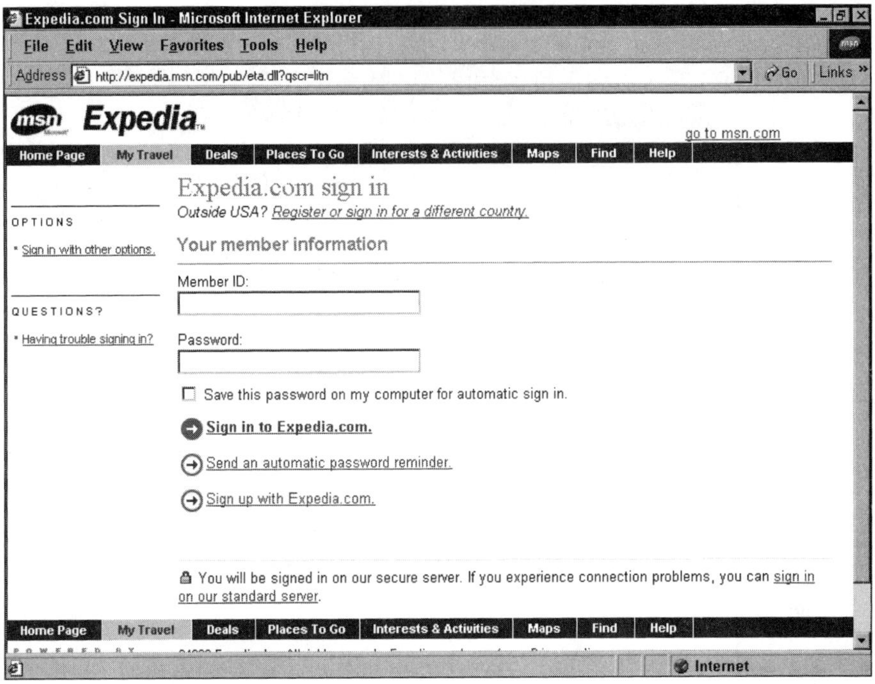

Figure 18-3: Expedia waits for you to sign in.

Planning a Trip with Expedia

In Expedia, each trip you plan is called an *Itinerary*. An itinerary holds all the Expedia information about a particular trip, including: travel dates, flight info, car and hotel reservations, prices, confirmation numbers, fare or rental rules or restrictions, and so on. You can change any item in an itinerary at any time, and you can print out an itinerary or e-mail it to a friend.

(Unfortunately, you can't use Expedia to reserve bus or train tickets. If you want to take the bus or train, you'll have to reserve those tickets yourself.)

Expedia automatically creates an itinerary for you when you save information about a flight, hotel, or car reservation, so you don't have to do anything special to create an itinerary. Expedia lets you keep itineraries for up to ten separate trips, and you can delete old itineraries to make room for new ones.

Each item in an itinerary (for example, each flight or hotel stay) has a status associated with it. The status can be one of the following:

- **Not reserved:** This means (naturally) that you have not yet reserved this item. This happens when you click Save this information in an itinerary after looking up a flight, hotel, or car rental. Because these items are not reserved, they are not guaranteed.
- **Reserved:** This means that you have clicked the Reserve hyperlink for the flight, hotel, or car rental. For hotels and autos, the itinerary will include a confirmation number indicating that the reservation is confirmed. However, for flights the reservation is held only until midnight of the day after you make the reservation. You must purchase the tickets before then to guarantee the rate.
- **Pending:** This status applies only to hotels and cars. A hotel or car reservation is placed in pending status until the hotel or car rental company sends Expedia a confirmation number guaranteeing the reservation.
- **Purchased:** This means that your tickets have been issued. (Purchased status applies only to flights.)

The following sections describe how to create the three most common elements of an itinerary: flight reservations, hotel reservations, and auto reservations.

We Can Fly!

If you are going to travel by airplane, you'll want to begin your itinerary by arranging your flight plans. Just follow the bouncing ball through these steps:

The following procedure assumes that you are reserving tickets for a round-trip flight. Rest assured that the procedures for a one-way trip are similar.

1. **From the Expedia home page, click the Flights hyperlink.**

   The Flight Wizard comes to life, as shown in Figure 18-4.

2. **Click the Roundtrip Search hyperlink.**

   The Roundtrip Search page appears, as shown in Figure 18-5.

3. **Type the city or airport code that you are departing from in the From field.**

   If you know the airport code for the city you are traveling from, type the code in. If you don't know the airport code, just type the city. If the city has more than one airport, Expedia displays a list of airports for that city from which you can choose.

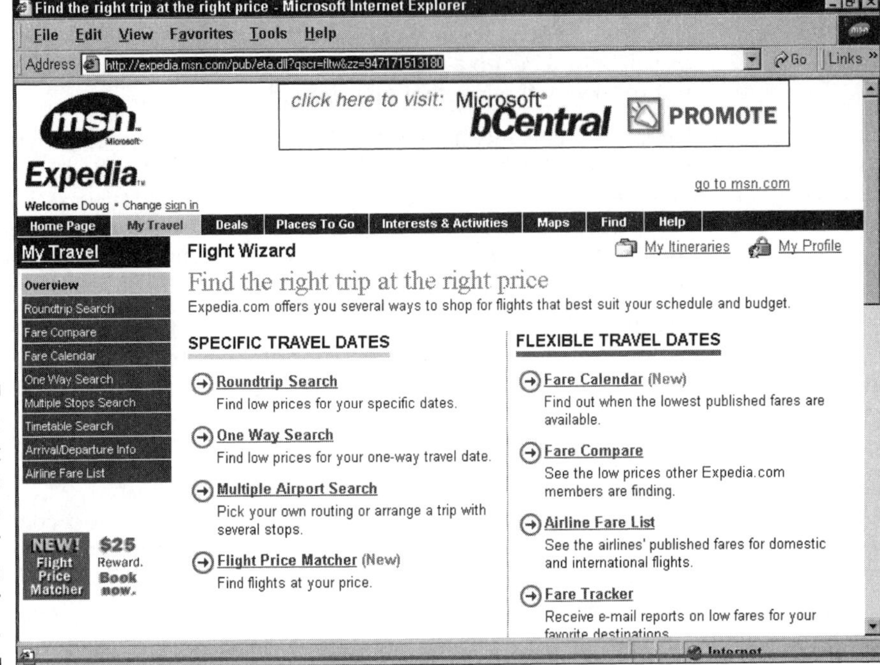

Figure 18-4: The Flight Wizard is ready to gather information about your flights.

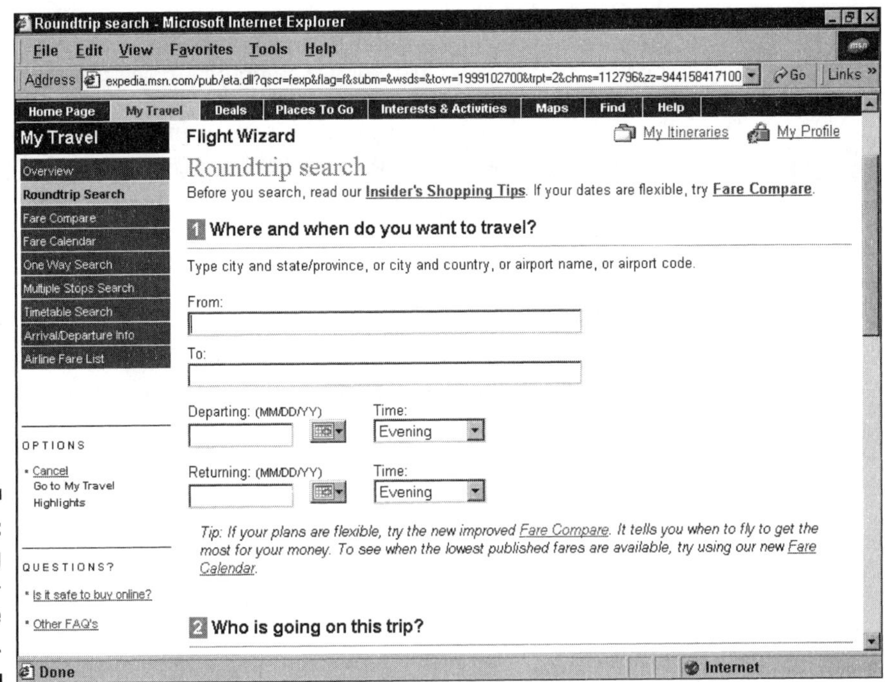

Figure 18-5: Searching for round-trip airplane tickets.

4. **Type the city or airport code you are traveling to in the To field.**

   Again, it's best to type the airport code if you know it. If you don't, just type in the city. You can choose the airport from a list of airports for that city later.

5. **Type the departure date into the Departing field, then select your preferred departure time from the Time drop-down list.**

6. **For the return date, type your departing date into the Returning field and select preferred departing time from the Time drop-down list.**

7. **Scroll down the page and fill out the rest of the information required by the Flight Wizard.**

   In addition to the cities and departure and return dates, the Flight Wizard needs the following information:

   - The number of passengers, and how many are adults, children, infants, and seniors.
   - The ticket class you prefer (coach, first class, or business class).
   - Search options, which let you limit your search to direct flights, flights with no change penalties, or flights with no advance purchase restrictions.
   - Your airline preference (any airline or a specific airline).

8. **When you've filled out all the information, click the Search for best available fares hyperlink.**

   Expedia searches through its massive database of flight information and displays the flights that best match your request, similar to the results shown in Figure 18-6.

9. **Scroll through the list of flights until you find one that you like and then click the Review details and purchase options hyperlink for that flight.**

   A page that lists the details of the flight that you selected appears, similar to the one shown in Figure 18-7.

10. **Carefully read over the details of the flight that you have selected.**

    Pay special attention to the flight restrictions. Make sure you understand whether the ticket is refundable, whether there are fees if you change or cancel the flight, and other restrictions.

11. **Click the appropriate link at the bottom of the page.**

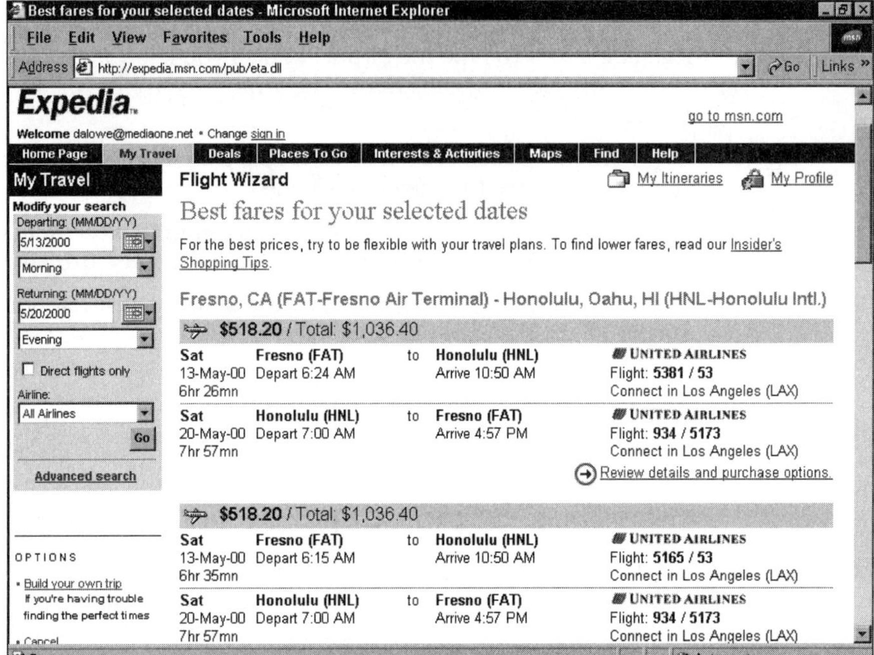

Figure 18-6: Expedia displays a bunch of flights.

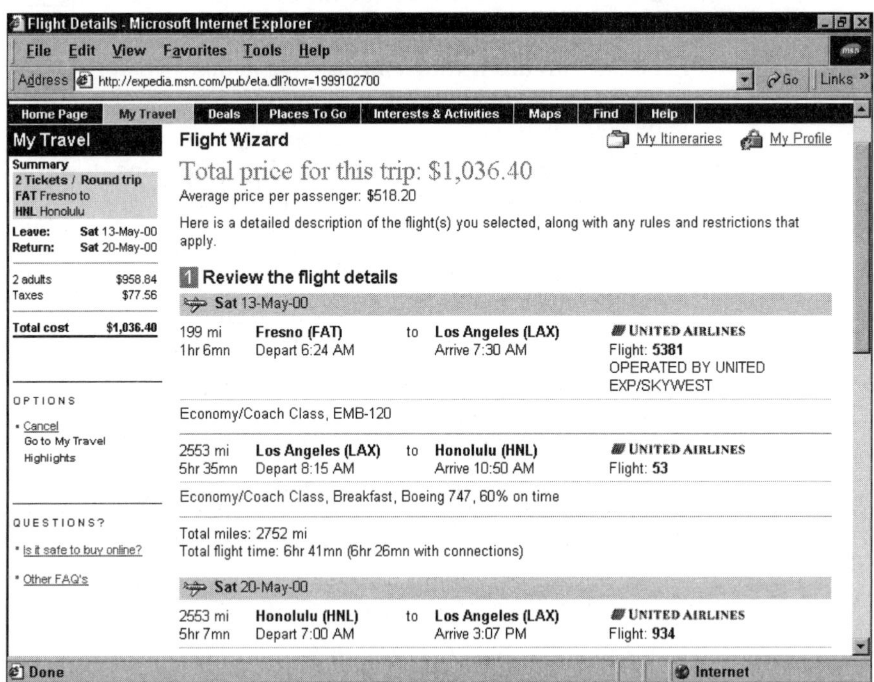

Figure 18-7: Details for a flight.

If you click the Reserve... hyperlink, a page appears giving you the option of reserving the ticket for 24 hours or actually purchasing the ticket. You'll have to supply your credit card information at this point. (Because of flight restrictions, not all flights offer a Reserve... hyperlink.)

If you click the Purchase... hyperlink, you'll be asked for your credit card number and the tickets will be issued. Note that for some flights, the tickets may be nonrefundable, so make sure you really want the tickets before you purchase them.

If you click the Save this information in an itinerary hyperlink, the flight will be added to your itinerary but no ticket will be reserved or purchased. This is a good way to plan a tentative trip without actually purchasing tickets, but keep in mind that by the time you get around to purchasing the tickets, the flight might by full. See the "Reviewing Your Itineraries" section later in this chapter.

Booking a Room

Unless you plan on rooming with friends or relatives or sleeping on a park bench, you may want to book a hotel reservation as a part of your itinerary. Here are the steps:

1. **From the itinerary page, click the Add hotel reservation hyperlink, then click the Hotel Wizard hyperlink.**

   This fires up the Hotel Wizard, as shown in Figure 18-8.

2. **Fill in all the information requested by the Hotel Wizard.**

   The Hotel Wizard needs the following information:

   - **The location.** You can indicate that you want a hotel in a city, near an airport, or near a major attraction such as Disneyland or Yellowstone. If you have added a flight to your itinerary, the city will automatically be set to your destination city, but you can change the selection to any city you want.
   - **A hotel chain.** If you have a preference.
   - **Amenities.** Examples of these are nonsmoking, wheelchair accessible, meeting room, restaurant, exercise room, and swimming pool.

3. **When all the information is filled in, click the Search for all hotels or Search only for hotels that can be reserved online hyperlinks.**

   After a moment of deep thought, Expedia displays a list of hotels that meet your criteria, as shown in Figure 18-9.

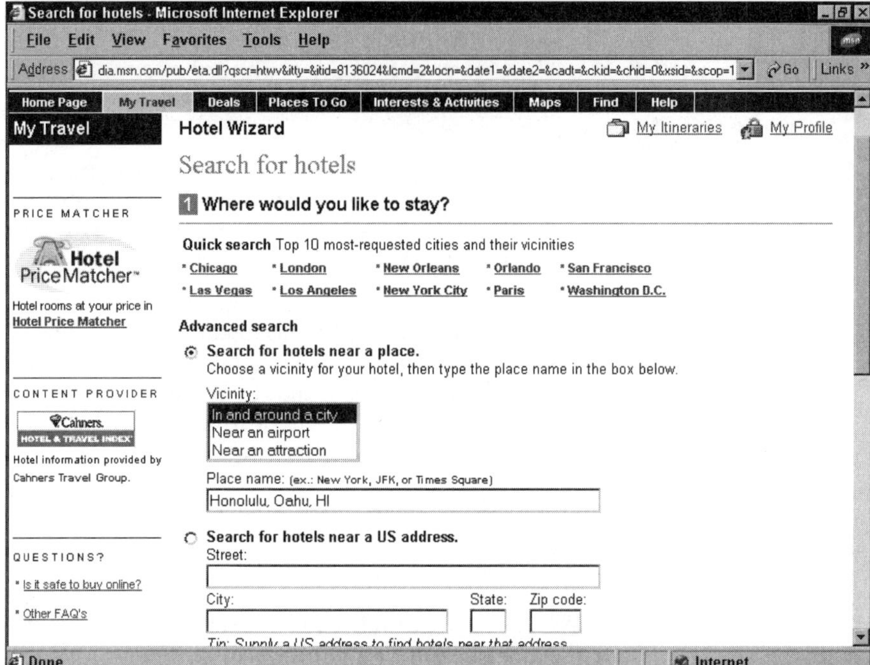

Figure 18-8: The Hotel Wizard.

4. **Click the hotel you're interested in to display additional information about the hotel.**

   A page similar to the one listed in Figure 18-10 appears, showing valuable information such as the types of accommodations, amenities available at the hotel, important telephone numbers, and so on.

5. **Click the Go button in the Room Availability portion of the page to see what rooms are available.**

   The Room Availability controls are located at the top left of the page. You can change the check-in and check-out dates before you click Go. Expedia displays a list of the rooms that are available for the dates you selected, as shown in Figure 18-11.

6. **Click the room you're interested in.**

   A page of detailed information about the room displays.

7. **To reserve the room, click the Reserve... hyperlink, or click the Save this information in an itinerary link to add the room to your itinerary but not actually reserve it.**

   If you elect to reserve the room, you must supply your credit card information again. Whether you reserve the room or just add it to your itinerary, this page defaults back to the Itinerary page. This time, the room appears on the itinerary.

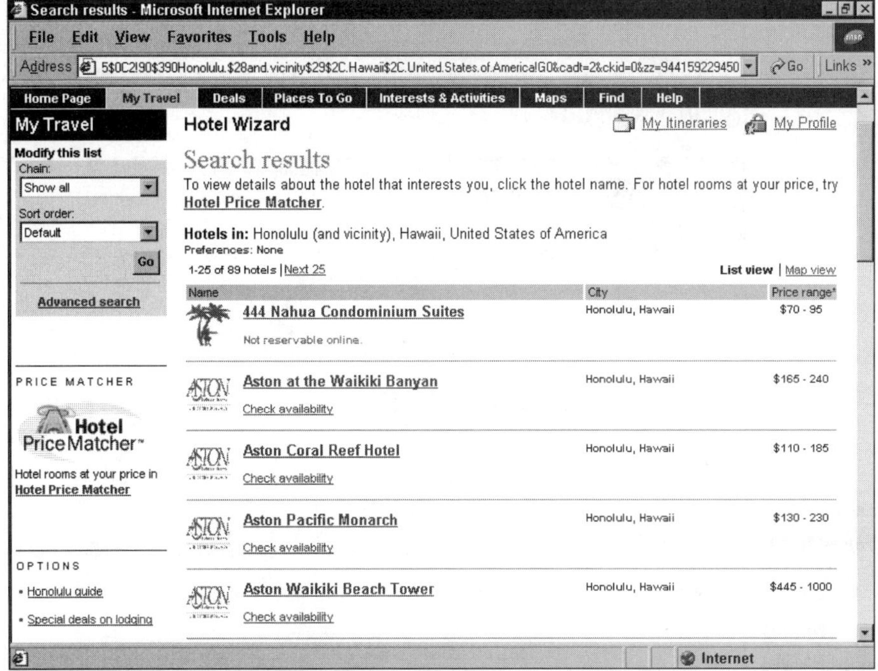

Figure 18-9: Expedia suggests these fine establishments.

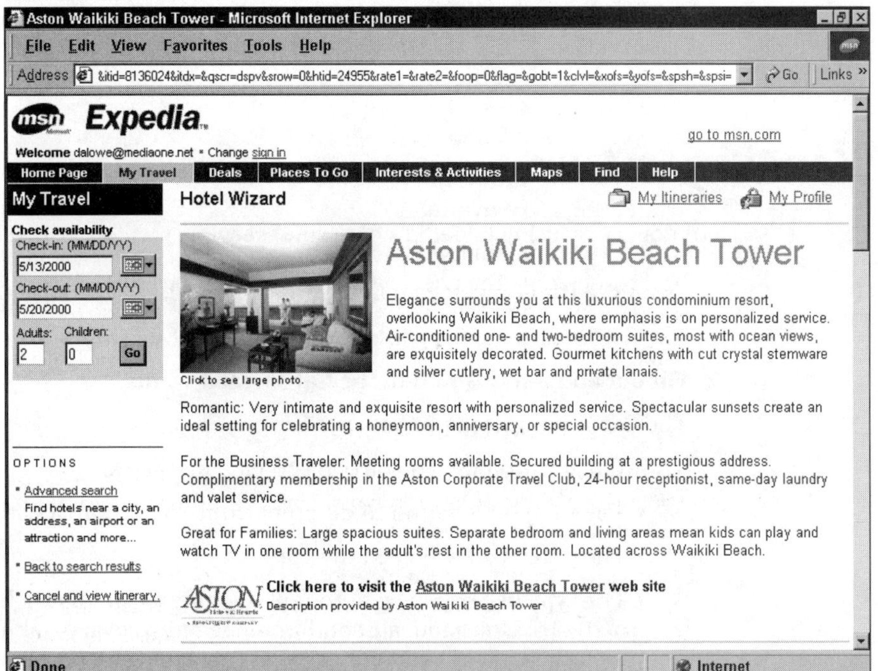

Figure 18-10: Hotel details.

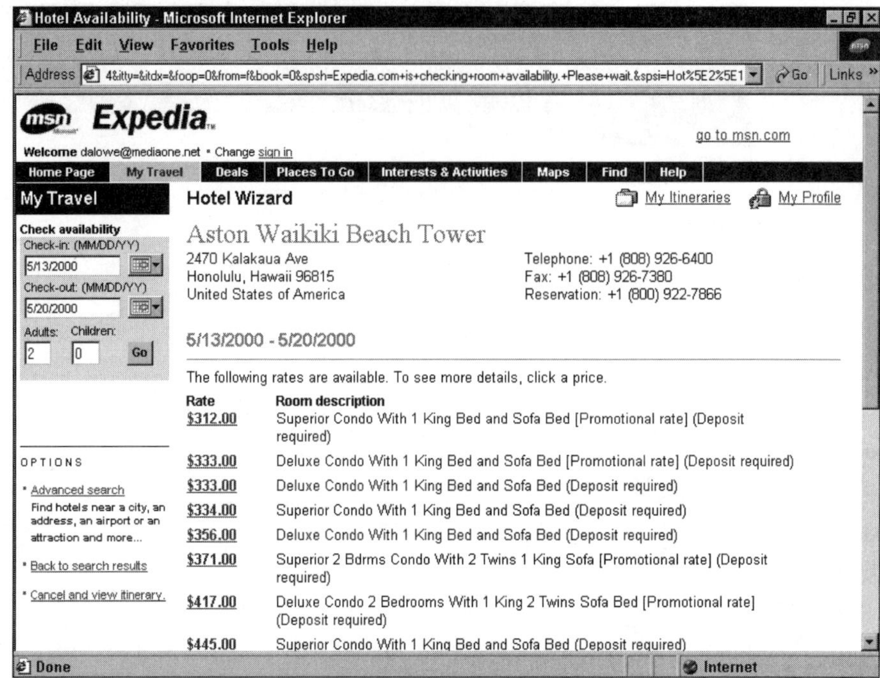

Figure 18-11: Checking for available rooms.

You're done! From the Itinerary page, you can easily change or cancel your hotel reservation, and you can add additional hotel reservations if you wish.

Renting a Car

To rent a car by using Expedia's car rental service, just follow these steps:

1. **From the Itinerary page, click <u>Add car rental</u>.**

   The Car Wizard appears, as shown in Figure 18-12.

2. **Fill out all the information the Car Wizard wants.**

   The Car Wizard needs to know:

   - The location where you want to pick up the car.
   - The drop-off location (if different from the pick up location).
   - The dates you will need the car.
   - The type of car you want to rent, including options such as automatic transmission, air conditioning, and special equipment such as bicycle racks or infant car seats.

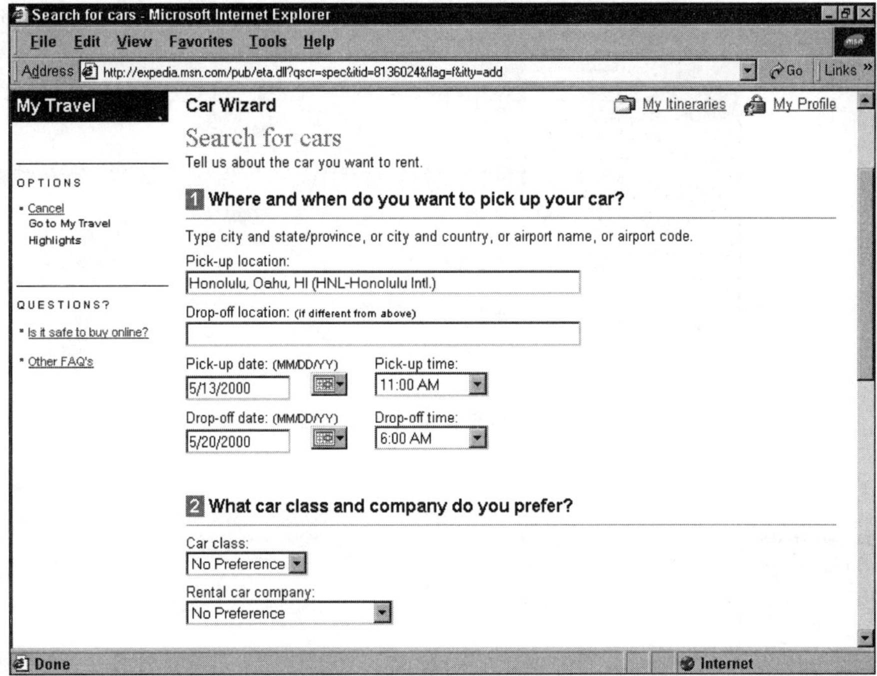

Figure 18-12: The Car Wizard.

- The rental company you prefer, if you care (otherwise, you can let Expedia pick the rental company).

3. **Click the Search for cars hyperlink.**

   A list of possible rentals appears, as shown in Figure 18-13.

4. **Click the Verify rate and continue hyperlink that appears next to the car you want to rent.**

   Expedia asks for a bit of information, such as your name, frequent flyer membership information, and whether you will be using the car for business or pleasure.

5. **Fill in the rental information and then click Continue to car details.**

   The Car Details page displays, as shown in Figure 18-14.

6. **To reserve the car click the Reserve... hyperlink, or click the Save this information in an itinerary hyperlink to add the car to your itinerary without actually reserving it.**

   If you choose to rent the car, you get to type in your name, credit card number, and all that good stuff. (Oh boy!) Then, follow the steps that appear on the screen when you click the Reserve... hyperlink.

   If you click Save this information in an itinerary, you'll be returned to the itinerary page with — you guessed it — your car rental information added.

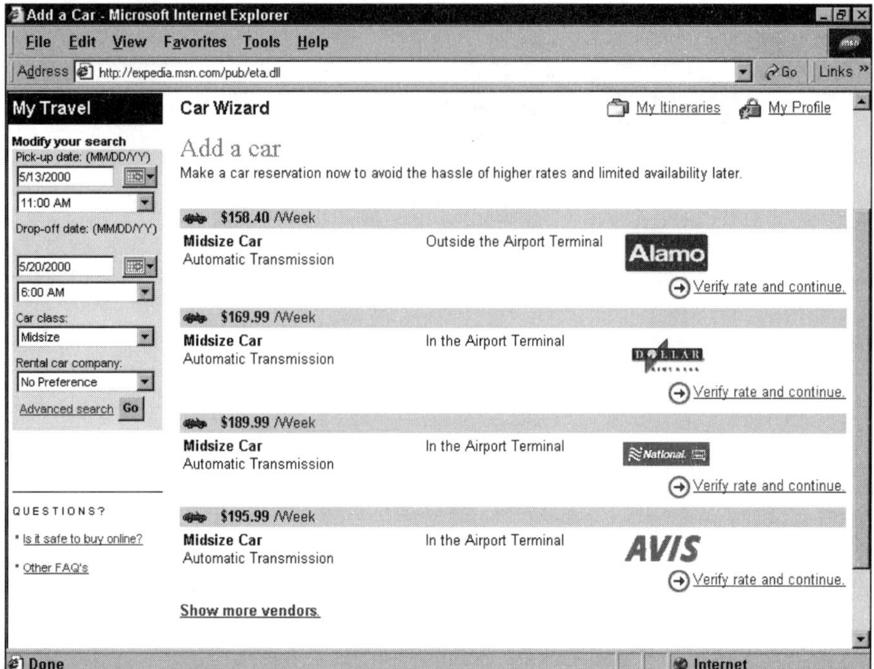

Figure 18-13: Cars you can rent.

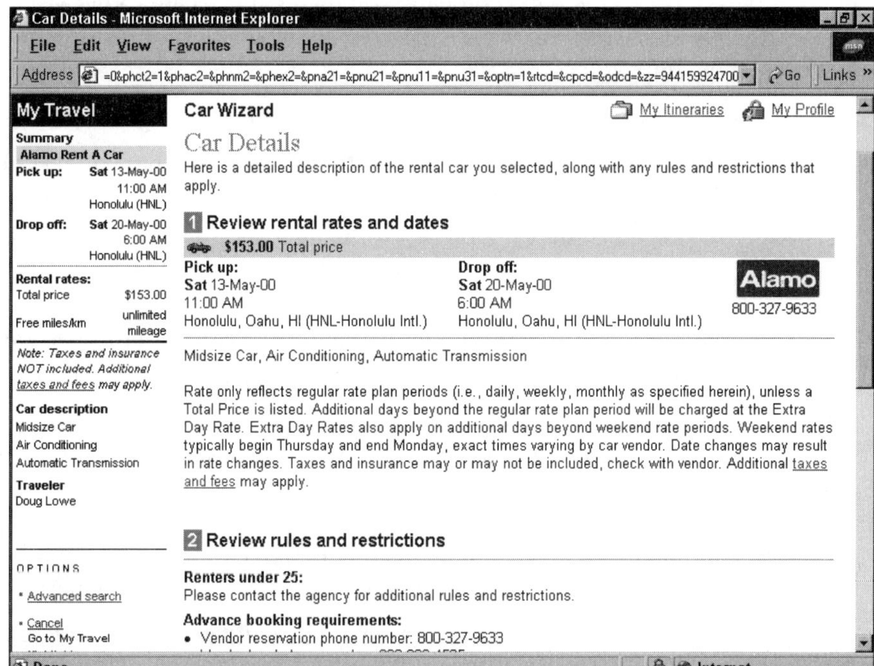

Figure 18-14: Details about a car you might want to rent.

Reviewing Your Itineraries

Expedia lets you store itineraries for up to ten separate trips. To review your itineraries, click the My Itineraries hyperlink which appears near the top of most Expedia pages. This brings up the My Itineraries page.

You can view any of the itineraries you have created by simply clicking the name of the itinerary you want to open. For example, Figure 18-15 shows the itinerary for a trip to Honolulu.

You can display an itinerary in one of three views, from which you can select by clicking the view buttons near the top left of the Itinerary page. The views are:

- **Standard view:** Shows most of the information you need to plan your trip: travel dates, prices, airline flight information, hotel names, confirmation numbers, and so on.
- **Detailed view:** Includes more detailed information than is shown in Standard view. For example, Detailed view lists flight restrictions and auto rental rules.
- **Summary view:** Lists only basic information.

Figure 18-15: An itinerary for a trip to Honolulu.

The left side of the Itinerary page also includes hyperlinks that allow you to add an additional flight, car, or hotel reservations, e-mail the itinerary to a friend, change the name of the itinerary, or delete the itinerary.

Using Fare Tracker

If your in-laws are always bugging you to come visit, or if you're the type who can't turn down a cheap trip to Vegas, you might be interested in an Expedia's Fare Tracker feature. Fare Tracker can keep you informed of the lowest available prices on airfares for up to three destinations by e-mailing you a fare update every week.

To use Fare Tracker, follow these steps:

1. **Click the Fare Tracker hyperlink on the Expedia home page.**

   The Fare Tracker page appears.

2. **Fill in the information for the flights you are interested in tracking.**

   Fare Tracker asks for the names of the cities that you want to depart from and travel to.

3. **Scroll to the bottom of the page and click the Yes, send me email... hyperlink.**

   That's it! Now you just have to watch your Inbox for a weekly update on the lowest airfares for the destinations you selected.

Part V

Creating Your Own Web Page

"Their fatal mistake was getting involved with MSN.com's home page building option. It's so easy, it's irresistible. They included a photo of them holding the stolen money next to the get away car, a list of their favorite aliases, banks they'd like to rob again..."

In this part . . .

One of the hottest new features of MSN is the ability to create your own Web site, free of charge. The first chapter in this part is an introduction to MSN Web pages, where you'll learn how to create a simple Web page and how to access Web pages created by others. Then, in Chapter 20, you'll discover how to use some of MSN's more advanced tools for creating Web pages. Finally, Chapter 21 shows you how to use MSN to keep your Web site up to date.

Chapter 19

Welcome to MSN Home Pages

In This Chapter

- Introducing MSN Home Pages
- Viewing other people's home pages
- Creating your own basic home page

One of the best features of MSN is that it lets you create your own home page, which can be viewed by other Internet users. Your home page can be as simple as a single page that gives basic information about you and your family, such as the names and ages of your kids, your job, hobbies, how you spend your summer vacation, or why dogs are better than cats. Or, it can be an entire Web site consisting of several pages with complicated formatting including frames, scripts, and other HTML niceties. The only limits are your imagination, your patience (it takes time to cobble together an extensive Web site), and the 12MB of disk space MSN allots each user.

This chapter is a gentle introduction to MSN Home Pages. Here, you discover how to visit Web pages created by other MSN users, and how to create a simple Web page of your own from a variety of templates that MSN provides for you. See Chapter 20 for the hardcore tools that you use to create an entire Web site.

Getting the Lowdown on MSN Home Pages

MSN allows any Internet user to create free pages on the MSN Home Pages Web site. All you have to do is sign up by providing your name and a valid e-mail address. You don't have to be a paid subscriber to MSN Internet Access to create your home page.

Figure 19-1 shows a typical example of an MSN home page. An MSN home page can be about any subject you want. I created my MSN home page as a place to show off pictures from my hiking and backpacking trips. (Yes, that really is me out there looking over the edge of Half Dome in Yosemite National Park. I make the trek to Half Dome every couple of years. The trail seems to get a little steeper every year.)

MSN doesn't charge you anything to create a home page. But as they say, there's no such thing as a free lunch. MSN makes its money by selling advertising that will appear on your Web pages. These advertisements show up in a separate window that appears whenever a user views your Web page. Figure 19-2 shows what these ad windows look like. You can close the ad window by clicking on its close button (the "X" in the upper-right-hand corner of the window), but the ad reappears whenever you display the page.

When an Internet user visits your page, the files that make up your page are retrieved from MSN's computers, not yours. As a result, your computer doesn't have to be turned on and connected to the Internet for someone else to view your MSN home page. And, in case you're worried about security problems, there's no way anyone can use your MSN home page to gain access to your home computer.

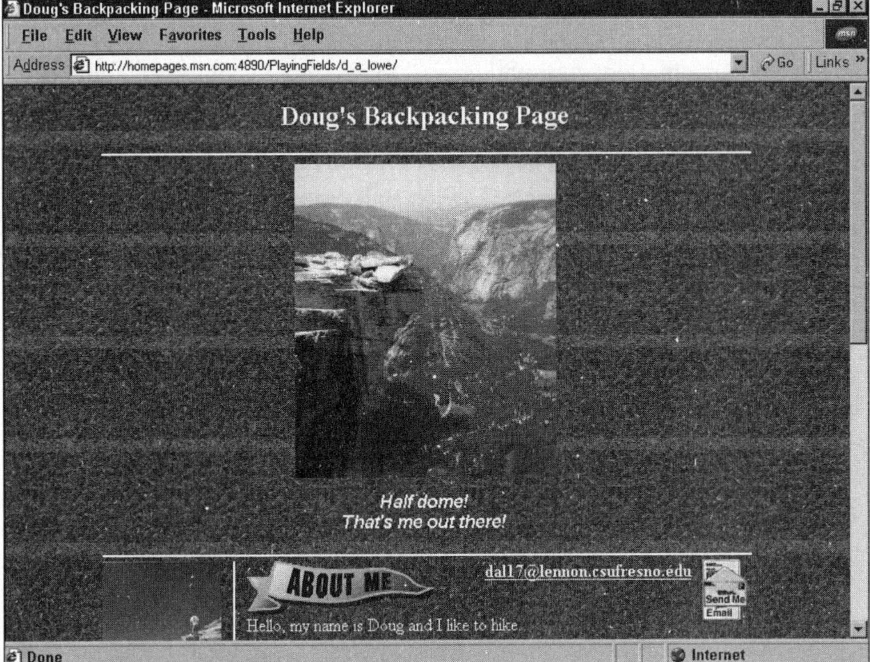

Figure 19-1: My MSN home page.

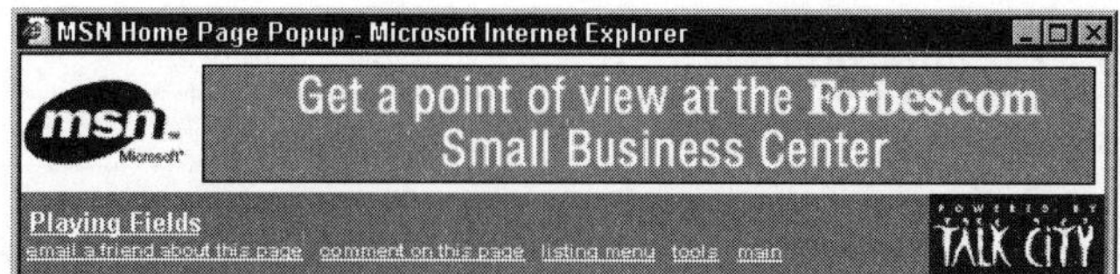

Figure 19-2: A view of an ad window.

MSN gives you 12MB of disk space to store your home page. By today's standards, 12MB may not seem like a lot of disk space, but what do you expect for free? In any event, 12MB is certainly enough space to create a Web page with several pictures. In fact, 12MB should be enough to create a small Web site — that is, several pages linked together.

Discovering the MSN Home Pages neighborhood

The MSN Home Pages Web site consists of thousands of home pages created by Internet users much like you. To keep things organized, MSN organizes the home pages into categories. Within each category are one or more streets, and each home page has an address on one of those streets.

Table 19-1 lists the categories and streets on MSN Home Pages. When you create your own Web page, you'll be asked to set up your page on one of these streets. You can choose any street you want for your home page, but Internet users will be able to find your page easier if you place your page on one of the streets in the category that most closely matches the content of your page. (There isn't really any distinction among the street names within a category, so just pick whichever street suits your fancy.)

Table 19-1 Categories and Streets for MSN Home Pages

Category	*Streets*
Business	Commercial Street, Corporate Way
Computers & Internet	Redmond Ave, Windows Way
Entertainment	Stage Street, Times Square
Games	Arcade, MSN Gaming Zone, Twitch Trail
Health & Wellness	Right Way, Support Street
Home & Families	Pets Place, Picnic Place
Lifestyles	Cooking Court, Hobby Court

(continued)

Table 19-1 *(continued)*

Category	*Streets*
Money & Investing	Bond Street, Treasury Drive
News & Politics	Capitol Drive, Reporter's Alley
Organizations	Non Profit Boulevard, Volunteer Street
People	Flirtation Walk, Twenties Circle
Places & Travel	Passport Place, Resort Road
Religion & Beliefs	Dharma Drive, Spirit Street
Schools & Education	Library Lawn, Student Union
Science & History	LaGrange Lane, Terminus
Sports & Recreation	Playing Fields, Yosemite Drive

Understanding MSN home page addresses

One thing you do *not* get when you create a free home page on MSN is your own custom Web address, such as `www.mypage.com`. Instead, your MSN home page is a part of the vast MSN Home Pages Web site, whose address is `homepages.msn.com`. Therefore, being part of this massive Web site, your address begins with `homepages.msn.com` and includes the name of the street that you place your Web page on, and the User Name that you create when you sign up for a free MSN home page. For example, if you place your home page on Yosemite Drive and your User Name is JohnMuir, your home page address is:

```
http://homepages.msn.com/YosemiteDr/JohnMuir
```

Unfortunately, MSN home page addresses are not easy to remember. To help people find your home page, you can list one or more keywords when you create the page. Internet users can search MSN Home Pages by keyword to find pages they are interested in.

Visiting Existing Home Pages

Before you create your own home page, you should first visit a few home pages that others have created. This not only gives you an idea of what types of pages other people have created, but it also gives you a glimpse of how your page will appear when people visit it.

To view an existing MSN home page, start by clicking the Home Pages hyperlink in the list of services that appears near the top of the msn.com home page. If you can't find this link, just type `homepages.msn.com` in your browser's Address bar and press the Enter key. Either method calls up the MSN Home Pages page, shown in Figure 19-3.

The best way to find an MSN home page is to search for it based on one or more keywords. That way, you can quickly find MSN home pages that contain information that interests you. To search for an MSN home page by keyword, follow these steps:

1. **Type one or more keywords in the Search by Keyword text box located on the left side of the page.**

   For example, if you want to see MSN home pages that have jokes, type **jokes** in the Search by Keyword text box.

2. **Click the Go button found next to the Search by Keyword text box.**

   MSN searches its index of all MSN home pages and displays a list of keywords that match your search, similar to the results list shown in Figure 19-4.

3. **Scroll through the Search Results page until you find a page that looks promising.**

   The search results list of MSN home pages includes the title of each page as well as a brief description provided by the page's creator.

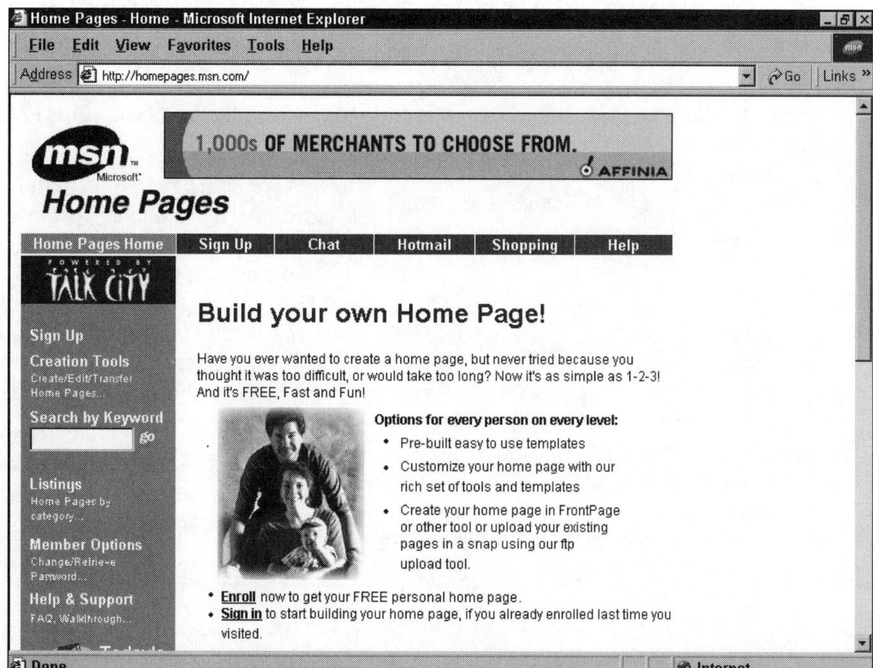

Figure 19-3: Welcome to MSN Home Pages.

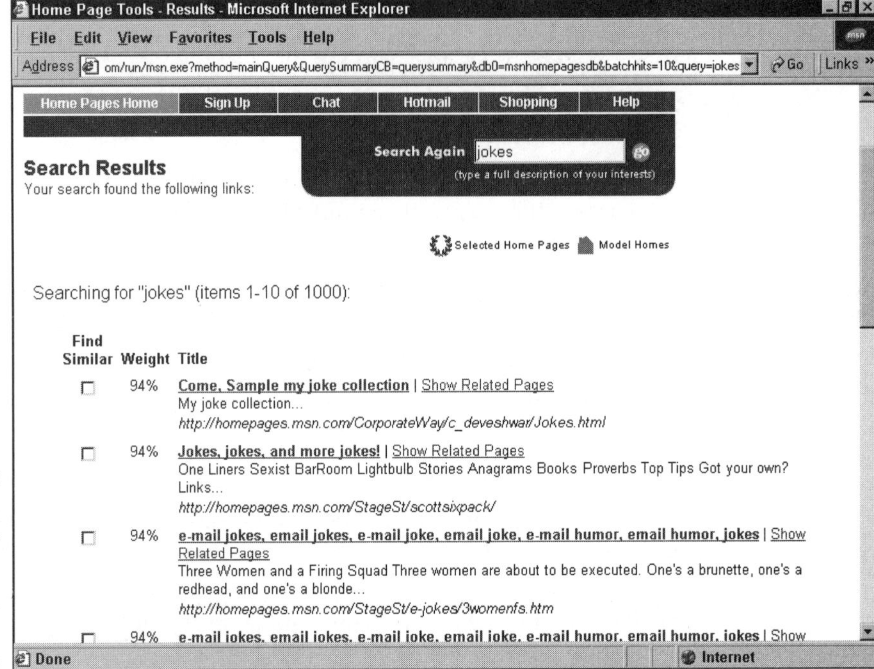

Figure 19-4: Many of MSN's home pages are jokes.

Wandering aimlessly through MSN's home page neighborhoods

Another way to find MSN Home Pages is to browse a directory of pages on the various MSN Home Page streets. To do that, click Listings on the main MSN Home Pages page, then click Category/Street Listing and select the street you would like to peruse.

Unfortunately, the street directories are nothing more than alphabetical lists of the hundreds of users who have built pages on the street. These lists give you absolutely no clue about what type of content you may expect to find on someone's page, so you must actually view each page to find out what is on the page. If each street contained a few pages, that wouldn't be so bad. But with hundreds of pages taking up residence on each street, browsing them all is next to impossible.

To make matters worse, many of the pages listed in the street directory are actually aborted or incomplete attempts at creating home pages. In other words, someone signed up for a home page, selected a street, chose a template for the home page, and then saved the page without modifying the template at all. Many streets are filled with pages that contain nothing at all. Sigh.

That's why it's far more productive to use the search feature as described in the "Visiting Existing Home Pages" section rather than browsing the street directory.

If you don't find a page that interests you, click the Next button at the bottom of the results page to display more search results. Or, type a different keyword and start again.

4. **Click the hyperlink of the page that you want to view (assuming you find one, that is).**

   The MSN home page of your choice appears.

Signing Up for an MSN Home Page

Before you can create your own MSN home page, you must first sign up for an account. Unfortunately MSN Home Pages doesn't use Passport to automatically sign you up for a home page, so you must sign up for an MSN home page even if you have already registered with Passport.

MSN Home Pages are free, so go ahead and sign up by following these simple steps:

1. **From the MSN Home Pages page, click Sign Up.**

   The Sign Up page appears, as shown in Figure 19-5.

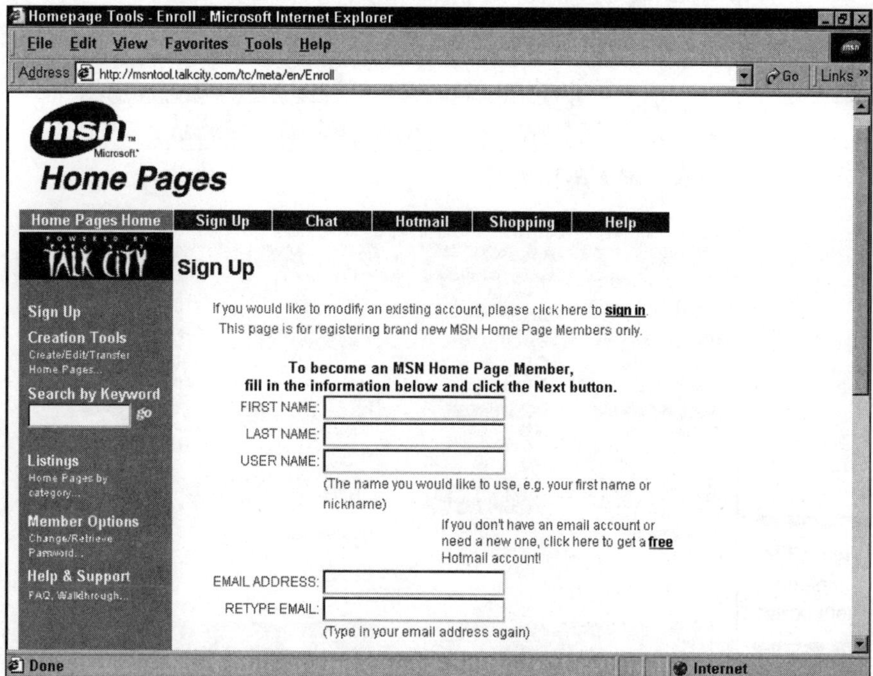

Figure 19-5: Signing up for an MSN home page.

2. **Type the information requested on the Sign Up page.**

   To create an account, MSN requires that you enter your first and last name, a user name you would like to use, a password, your e-mail address, a password hint, and your gender.

3. **Click Next to continue.**

   The address questionnaire appears.

4. **Type your address, city, state, and zip.**

   You don't have to give your address if you don't want to, but Microsoft promises it uses the information only for demographic purposes. Rest assured that Bill Gates won't send a hit squad to your home if you say something nasty about Microsoft on your home page.

5. **If you want to volunteer your time to help police in one of the MSN home page categories, click the Yes, Please Send Me More Information hyperlink. If not, click the No, Leave Me Alone And Don't Ever Bother Me Again hyperlink.**

6. **Click the Done button.**

   An account is created for you. The Homepage Tools page appears, as shown in Figure 19-6.

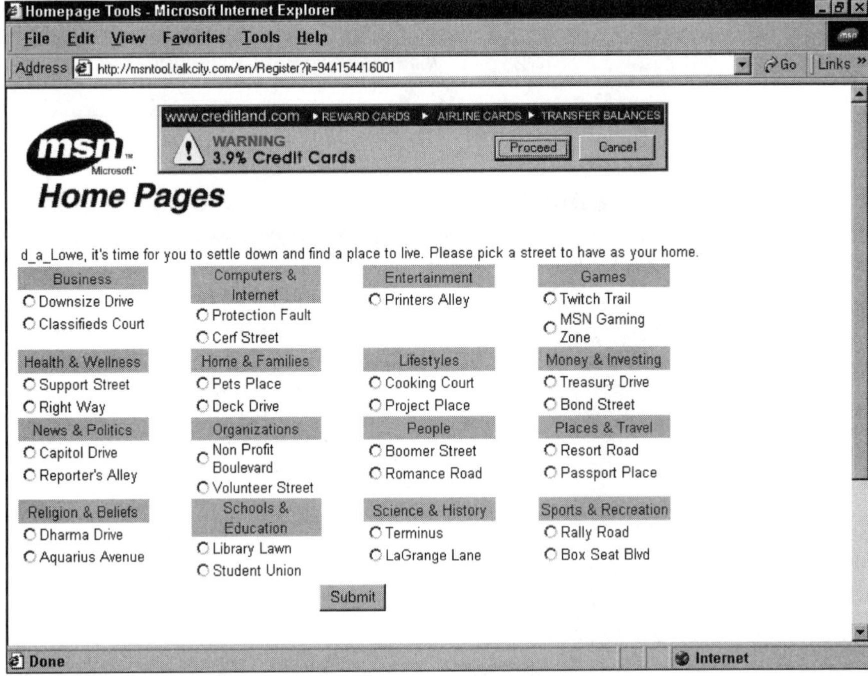

Figure 19-6: Selecting your street.

7. **Check the option button next to the street under the category where you want your page to reside.**
8. **Click the Submit button.**

   The Congratulations page appears, shown in Figure 19-7, confirming that you're officially signed up for a free MSN home page.
9. **Write down your user name and password so you don't forget them.**

   You're done!

Although you have signed up, you haven't yet actually created a home page. To find out how to do that, read on.

Creating Your First Home Page

After you signed up for an MSN home page, it's time to actually create the page. Fortunately, you don't have to be a computer expert to create an MSN home page. In fact, you don't have to know anything at all about the inner workings of the Web, such as HTML or Java. MSN makes creating a home page as easy as creating a simple word processing document.

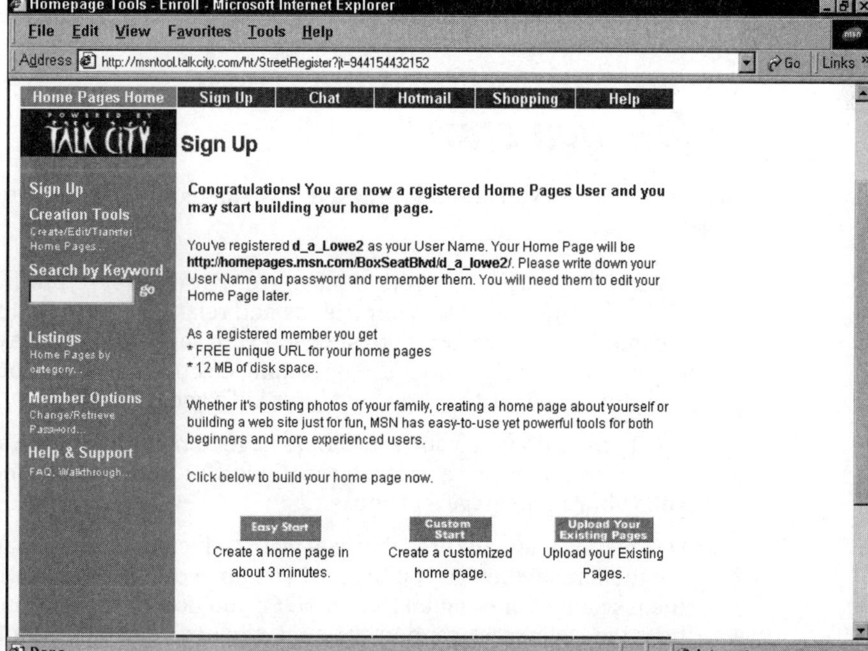

Figure 19-7: Congratulations! You have successfully signed up for an MSN home page.

If you *do* know something about HTML, you may want to skip this section. See Chapter 20 for information about using more advanced tools to create your MSN home page.

MSN provides an easy-to-use template, which you can use to create a basic home page with the following basic elements:

- A page title. The default title is "Welcome to My Home Page," but you can easily change the title.
- Room for two images: one centered beneath the title, the other at the left edge of the page.
- Basic information about yourself, such as your name, e-mail address, and biographical information.
- Your personal interests.
- The latest news about you or your family.
- A favorite quotation.
- Links to your favorite Web pages.

You can choose from almost 100 images to use for the background of your home page, and you can supply information such as keywords and a description that will help others locate your page.

Visualizing your home page before you start

Before you begin, you should make a few basic decisions about your home page:

- What is the purpose of your home page? For example, your home page's purpose might be to let your friends and relatives know about last summer's family vacation, to show off your model railroad layout, to express your views about the upcoming election, to be a tribute to your favorite movie, or to brag about your kid's soccer exploits.
- What street do you want your home page to reside on? Browse through the list of categories and streets in Table 19-1 and pick the one that best suits your home page's purpose.
- Do you have any pictures that you want to include on your page? If so, get them ready before you begin. If you are working from snapshots, have them scanned into digital form first. (If you don't own a scanner, you can have your pictures scanned at a copy shop or a one-hour photo shop.)

- Do you want to include any copyrighted material on your home page? If so, get permission from the copyright holder before you add the material to your page. For example, don't create a Web page with song lyrics or movie stills unless you first get permission.

Molding a simple page into a masterpiece

After you come up with a concept for your home page, you're ready to begin creating your masterpiece. The easiest way to create a home page is by following these simple steps:

1. **From the MSN Home Pages page, click the Creation Tools hyperlink.**

   The Creation Tools page appears, as shown in Figure 19-8.

2. **Click the Create a Simple Home Page hyperlink.**

   The simple home page template appears, which enables you to select various options for your home page, as shown in Figure 19-9.

3. **If you want to change the page style, click the Change Page/Background Style button.**

   This brings up the page shown in Figure 19-10 that lets you select from one of more than 100 different styles for your page. The style you select determines the image that is displayed as the background for your page as well as the colors and fonts used for text on your page.

   To change the page style, click the style category of your choice (such as Business or Entertainment) to view the selection of styles. Then, click one of the styles that appear within that category. Your home page template re-appears with the new style in effect.

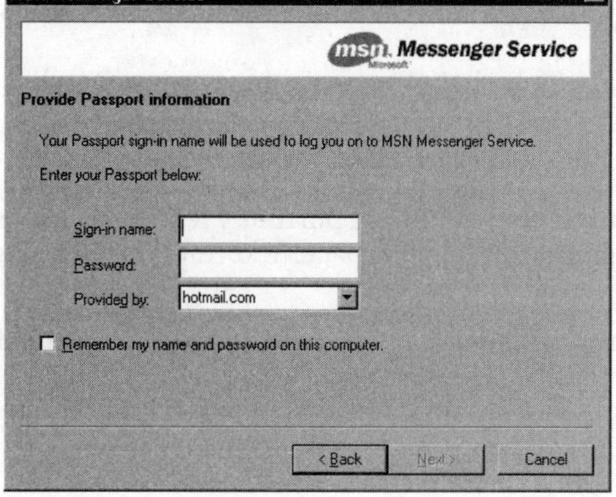

Figure 19-8: The Home Pages Creation Tools page.

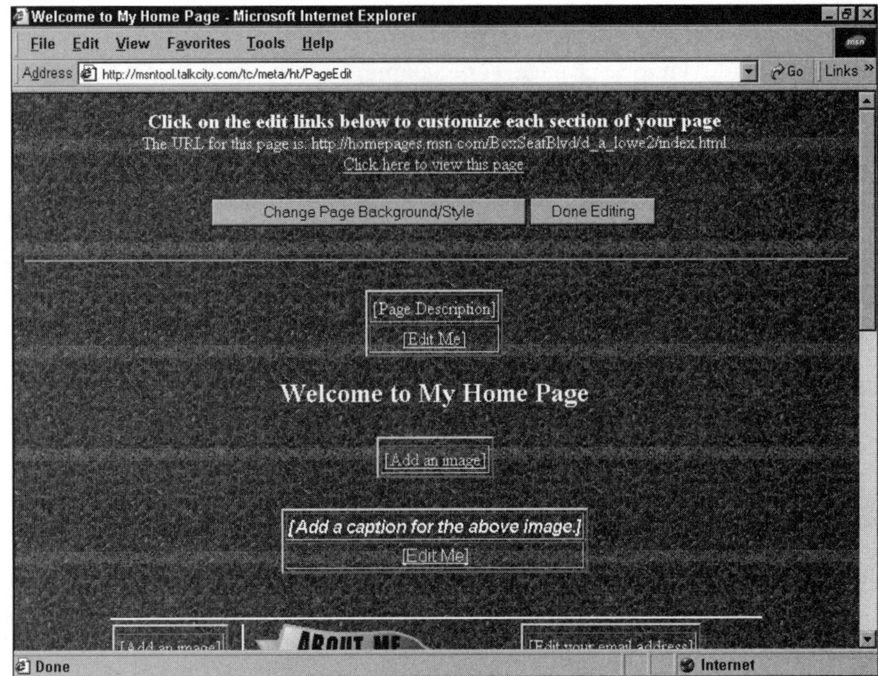

Figure 19-9: Creating a simple home page.

4. **Click the Edit Me hyperlink that appears in the Page Description box.**

   This brings up the Page Description page, as shown in Figure 19-11.

5. **Type the information requested on the Page Properties page, and then click the OK button.**

   The Page Properties page requests the following information:

   - **Title:** The title of your Web page.
   - **Author:** Your name.
   - **Keywords:** Words that others might use when searching for your home page.
   - **Description:** A brief description of your home page.
   - **Classification:** Yet another opportunity for you to supply descriptive information about your page. You can type anything you want here.
   - **Background sound:** If you have a sound file you would like to have played whenever someone visits your page, click the Upload button to copy the sound file to MSN's computer and attach the sound to your page.

Figure 19-10: Changing the page style.

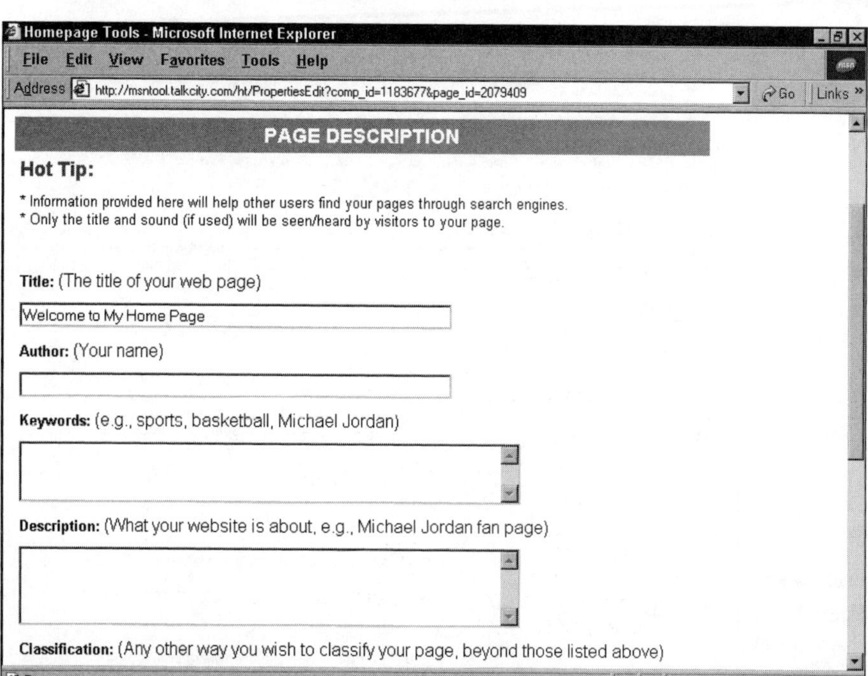

Figure 19-11: Changing the page properties.

After clicking OK, your home page reappears. If you do not want to add an image to your home page, you may skip Steps 6 through 13.

6. **If you have an image that you want to add to the page, click the Add an image hyperlink.**

   The Image page appears, as shown in Figure 19-12.

7. **Click the Upload button.**

   The Upload an Image File page appears.

8. **Click the Browse button.**

   A Choose File dialog box appears.

9. **Select the file that you want to upload from the directory and then click Open.**

   If necessary, use the Look in control to find the file that you want to upload. When you click Open, the Upload an Image File page reappears.

10. **Click the OK button.**

    The file is uploaded to the MSN Home Pages computers. Depending on the size of the file, this could take anywhere from a few seconds to a few minutes, so be patient. When the upload finishes, the Image Component page reappears (refer to Figure 19-12).

Homepage Tools - Microsoft Internet Explorer
File Edit View Favorites Tools Help
Address http://msntool.talkcity.com/ht/ImageEdit?comp_id=2478618&page_id=2079409
Go Links
Image Component
Place a picture on your web site.
Step 1. Optional: Copy an image from your computer to your MSN web site (it will then appear in the list on your Site Manager screen).
Upload
Hot Tip:
* For best results, the image should be a .jpg or .gif file.
* If the image you wish to use already appears in the list on your Site Manager screen, go straight to Step 2.
* If the image you wish to use is on somebody else's web site, and you have permission to use it on your page, go straight to Step 2.
Step 2. Select your image from one of the following two locations.
Select an image already in the list on your Site Manager screen:
None
Or: Enter a URL for an image somewhere on the Internet:
Example:
http://images.talkcity.com/img/v6/logo.gif
Done
Internet

Figure 19-12: Adding an image.

11. **Check the Select an Image Already on Your Site option, and then select the image from the drop-down list if the image isn't already selected.**

    You have to scroll down to see this section of the Image Component page, as shown in Figure 19-13.

12. **Click the OK button located at the bottom of the Image Component page.**

    Your home page reappears with the image inserted, as shown in Figure 19-14.

13. **Click the Edit Me hyperlink in the Add a Caption for the Above Image box.**

    The Text Component page appears, as shown in Figure 19-15.

14. **Type a title and description of the image for your home page and click OK.**

    You may use the Title Font, Title Color, Text Font, and Text Color buttons to change the font and color for the text.

15. **To edit text in other sections of your home page, click the appropriate Edit Me hyperlink, type the text that you want, and then click OK.**

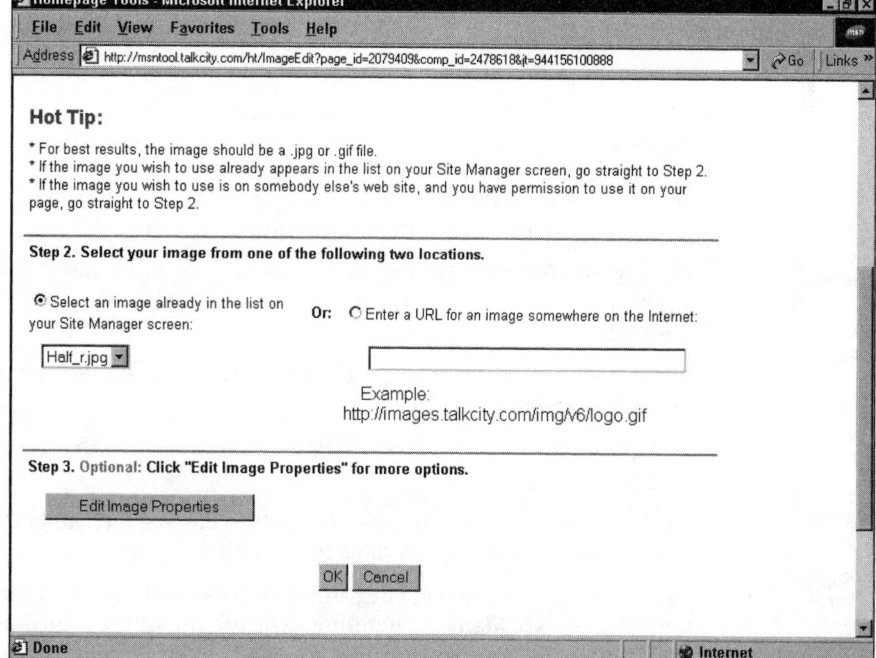

Figure 19-13: Selecting the image you have uploaded on the Image Component page.

Figure 19-14: The home page with an image.

16. **To add hyperlinks to your favorite sites, click Edit Links, add your links, and then click Done.**

    When you click Edit Links, the List of Links page appears, as shown in Figure 19-16. For each link that you want to add, type a name for the link in the Name box, select one of the pages on your Web site from the drop-down list or type the URL of the link in the URL text box, and then type a description of the link in the Description text box.

    The List of Links page has room for up to three links, but you can add additional links by clicking the Add Another Link button that appears at the bottom of the page.

17. **After everything is just right, click the Done Editing button at the top of your home page.**

    A Site Manager page appears, listing the various files that you have created for your page.

    See Chapter 20 to find out how to use the Site Manager to edit your home page or to add new pages to your site.

18. **To view your home page, click the Web page address link that appears beneath the Site Manager heading near the top of the Site Manager page.**

    Your home page displays. (Refer to Figure 19-1 to see how my home page appears.) To return to the Site Manager, click the Back button in your Web browser.

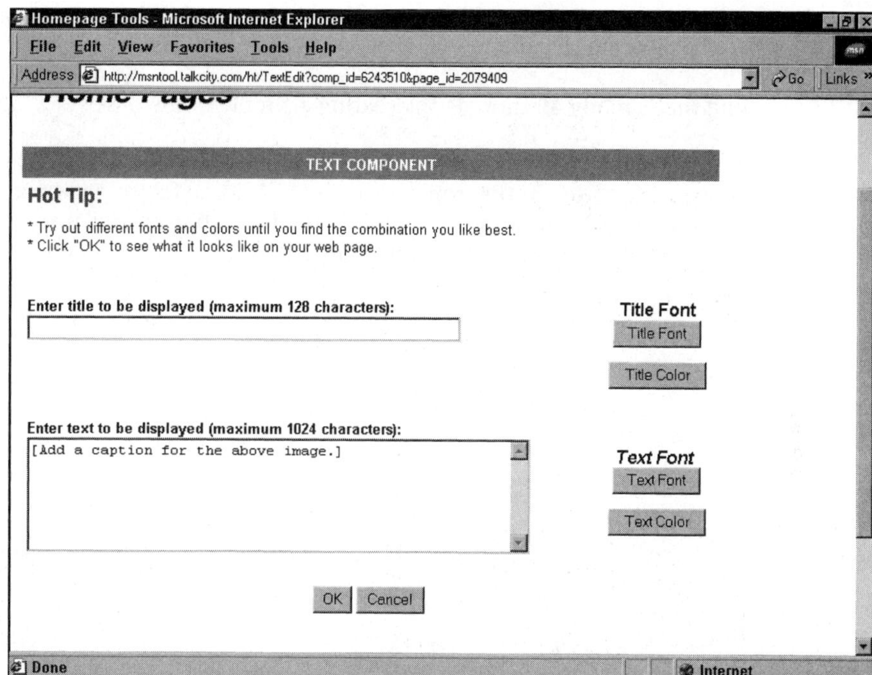

Figure 19-15: The Text Component page.

Homepage Tools - Microsoft Internet Explorer

File Edit View Favorites Tools Help

Address http://msntool.talkcity.com/ht/LinkListEdit?comp_id=927826&page_id=2079409 Go Links

LIST OF LINKS

Hot Tip:

* The list of links can be used to link to other pages on your site or to other web sites.

Link#	Name	URL	Description	Delete
1				
	MSN	Link to Page on your site: / OR, Enter Other URL: (e.g.: http://home.microsoft.com/) http://home.microsoft.com/	MSN.com Home	
2				
		Link to Page on your site: / OR, Enter Other URL: (e.g.: http://home.microsoft.com/)		
3				
		Link to Page on your site: / OR, Enter Other URL: (e.g.: http://home.microsoft.com/)		

Done Internet

Figure 19-16: Adding your favorite links.

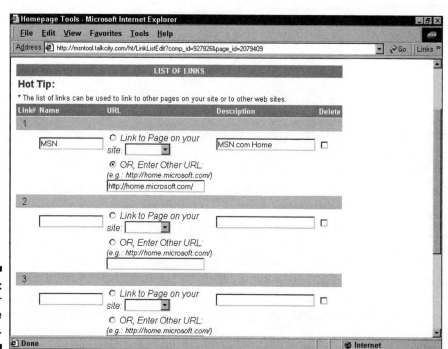

19. **Click the Sign Out button to return to the MSN Home Pages main page.**

And that's really all there is to creating a simple home page.

If you want to change your home page, return to the Site Manager page by choosing Creation Tools from the main MSN Home Pages page and then choosing Edit Your Home Page. Select the page that you want to edit and then click the Edit button. Congratulations!

Chapter 20

Using MSN Site Manager

In This Chapter

- Site Manager basics
- How to edit, copy, delete, and rename files
- Adding a new file to your site

Okay, so you've created a simple home page with a brief description of you and your family and a picture of your vacation to Disney World last year. Now what? Is that all there is to it?

Of course not! MSN Home Pages makes it easy to add on to your home page. For example, you can create an additional Web page and link it to your home page to showcase photos of your prize squash that looks like Richard Nixon. Another page might feature your favorite recipes, such as your world famous Tuna Surprise and your beloved Indestructible Fruitcake. Once you add these pages, surely everyone will want to visit your Web site.

The MSN page you need to master to make such important changes to your home page is called the Site Manager. With the Site Manager, you can add new pages to your site, edit pages that need to be updated, and delete pages you don't want to keep.

Summoning the Site Manager

The MSN Home Pages Site Manager is the key to managing your MSN Web site. Figure 20-1 shows the Site Manager in action.

As you can see, the Site Manager lists all of the files that make up your Web site — HTML files, picture files, and any other files you may have created or uploaded to the MSN Web server. For each file, the Site Manager lists the file name, the time and date you last modified the file, and the size of the file. In addition, Site Manager tells you how much of your 12MB of disk space that your files take up.

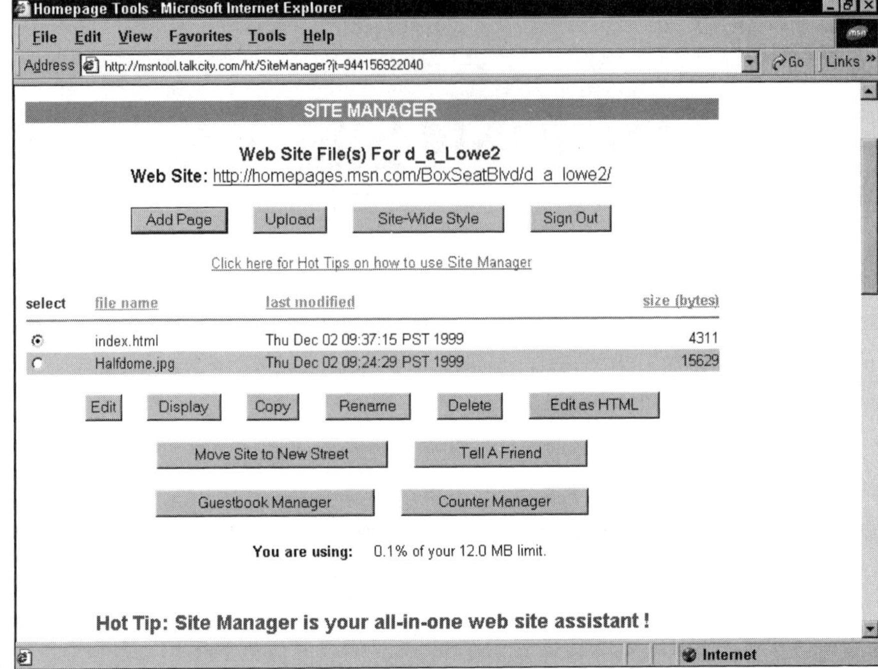

Figure 20-1: The Site Manager lets you manage the pages that make up your MSN Home Pages Web site.

Your main home page file is listed in Site Manager under the name `index.html`.

MSN Home Pages expects to find a file named `index.html` at your Web site. If you change the name of the `index.html` file, Internet users who visit your Web site will see an unattractive list of the files in your Web site rather than your carefully crafted home page. In other words, don't rename your `index.html` file.

Notice that each of the files listed in Site Manager has a Select button next to it. You can click one of these buttons to select one of the files in your Web site. Once you have selected a file, you can then click one of the buttons that appears at the bottom of the Site Manager page to edit, display, copy, rename, delete, or edit the HTML for the file. I describe how each of these buttons works in later sections in this chapter. (The Edit and Edit as HTML buttons work only for HTML files.)

To call up the Site Manager, follow these simple steps:

1. **From the MSN home page, click the Free Home Pages hyperlink to go to the MSN Home Pages page.**

   Or, type `homepages.msn.com` in your Web browser's Address field and press the Enter key. Either way, the MSN Home Pages page appears.

2. **Click Creation Tools.**

   A page listing the MSN Home Pages creation tools appears.

3. **Click Edit Your Home Page.**

   A login page appears, asking you to enter your MSN Home Pages user ID and password.

4. **Type your user ID and password and then click the Log In button.**

   At last, the Site Manager page greets you.

Because you have to go through so many steps to get to Site Manager, I suggest you add Site Manager to your Favorites menu so you can call up Site Manager with a single click of the mouse. To add Site Manager to your Favorites, call up the Favorites➪Add to Favorites command.

Editing Your Home Page

If you create your home page by using the MSN Home Page template, as described in Chapter 19, or by using one of the custom templates described in the "Adding a New Page" section later in this chapter, you can use Site Manager to modify the page.

Site Manager will only let you edit HTML files which you created using one of the MSN templates. You cannot use Site Manager to edit other types of files, such as picture or sound files.

To edit your home page, follow these steps:

1. **Click the Select button that appears next to the page that you want to edit.**

   Your main MSN home page is identified in the list as `index.html`.

2. **Click the Edit button.**

   The editable page appears, as shown in Figure 20-2. (This is the same page that appeared when you first created the page.)

3. **Make the changes that you want to the page.**

   To make changes to the page, click the editing links that appear throughout the page, such as [Edit Me] and [Replace this image].

4. **When you are finished, click the Done Editing button.**

Figure 20-2: Editing an existing page.

That's all there is to it. Clicking the Done Editing button causes Site Manager to save the file with any changes you made. You are then automatically returned to the Site Manager page. If you look at the listing for the page you edited, you'll note that the Last Modified date has been changed to show the time and date when you saved the file.

If you decide that you do not want to save the changes you have made to a page, click your Web browser's Back button rather than the Done Editing button in Step 4. This returns you to the Site Manager page without saving your changes.

Displaying a Page or File

To display a page from your Web site, select the page by clicking its Select button, and then click the Display button at the bottom of the page. The page displays as shown in Figure 20-3.

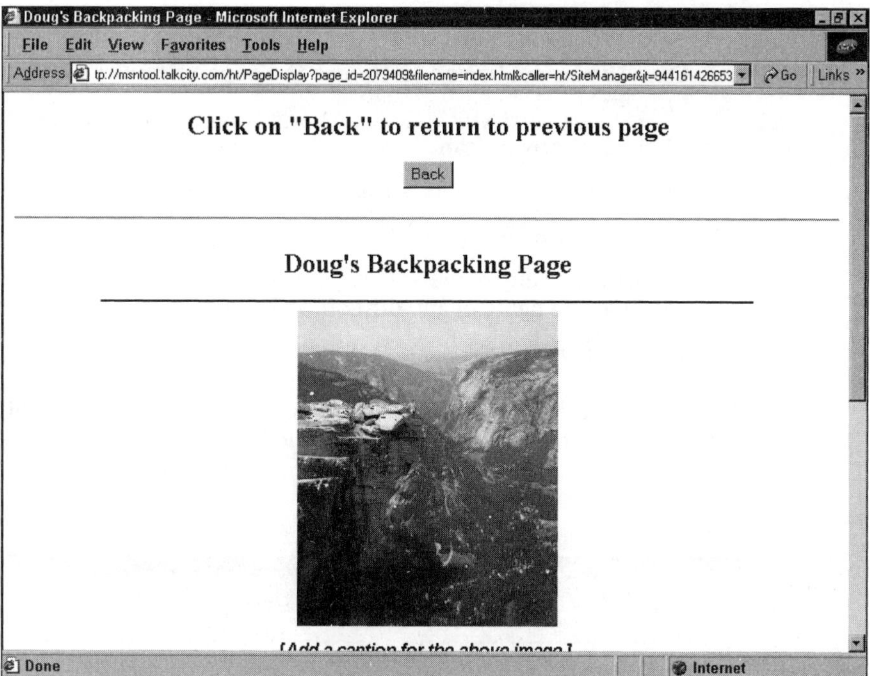

Figure 20-3: Displaying a page.

Notice that the Site Manager adds a Back button to the top of the page. You can click this button to return to Site Manager. When a visitor displays the same page in his or her browser, the Back button is not shown.

You can also use the Display button to view picture files that you have uploaded to your Web site. The picture displays by itself on a separate page, with no caption or information. The Back button doesn't appear when you display a picture, so you'll have to click your browser's Back button to return to Site Manager.

Copying a Page or File

Suppose you've created a great Web page describing last summer's vacation to lovely and scenic Trona, California, and now you want to create a similar page dedicated to this year's exciting trip to Baker, California, home of the world's largest thermometer. Rather than start from scratch, Site Manager lets you make a copy of the Trona page. You can then edit the copy to make whatever changes are necessary to describe Baker.

To create a copy of a page at your Web site, follow these steps:

1. **Click the Select button to choose the page or image file that you want to copy.**
2. **Click the Copy button.**

   The Copy File page appears as shown in Figure 20-4.
3. **Type a new name for the file.**

   You can type any name you wish, provided the name you type is different from the name of any other file that already exists on your site.
4. **Click the OK button.**

A new file is created with the name you typed in Step 3, and the Site Manager reappears, where you can see the new file listed. You can then select the new file, click Edit, and make whatever changes you need to make.

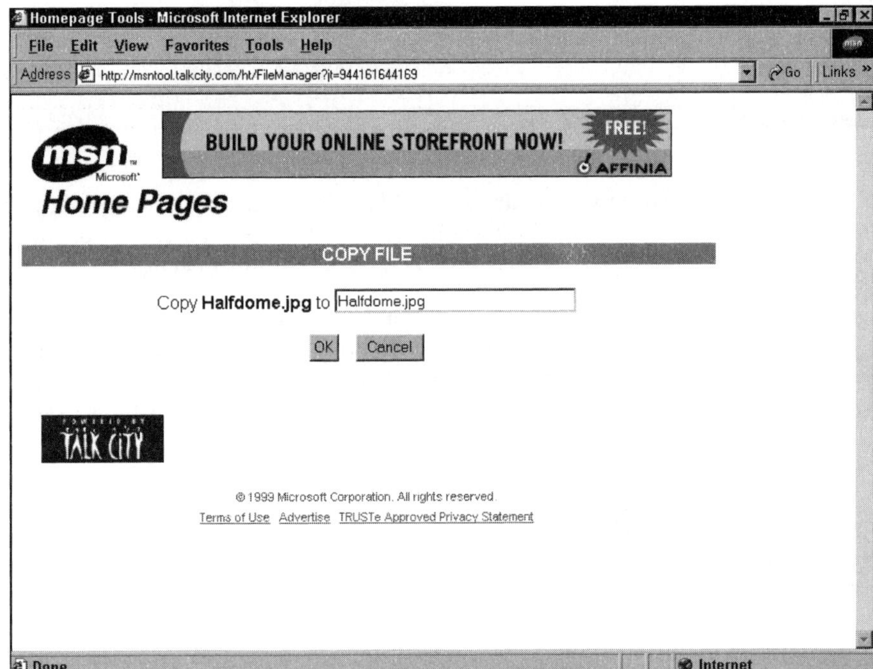

Figure 20-4: Copying a file.

Renaming a Page or Other File

You can change the name of any file in your Web site by following these steps:

1. **Select the file whose name you want to change.**
2. **Click the Rename button.**

   The Rename File page appears, as shown in Figure 20-5.
3. **Type a new name for the file.**

   Use any name you wish, but make sure the name is not the same as the name of any other file on your Web site.
4. **Click the OK button.**

The Site Manager page displays again, showing the new name for the file.

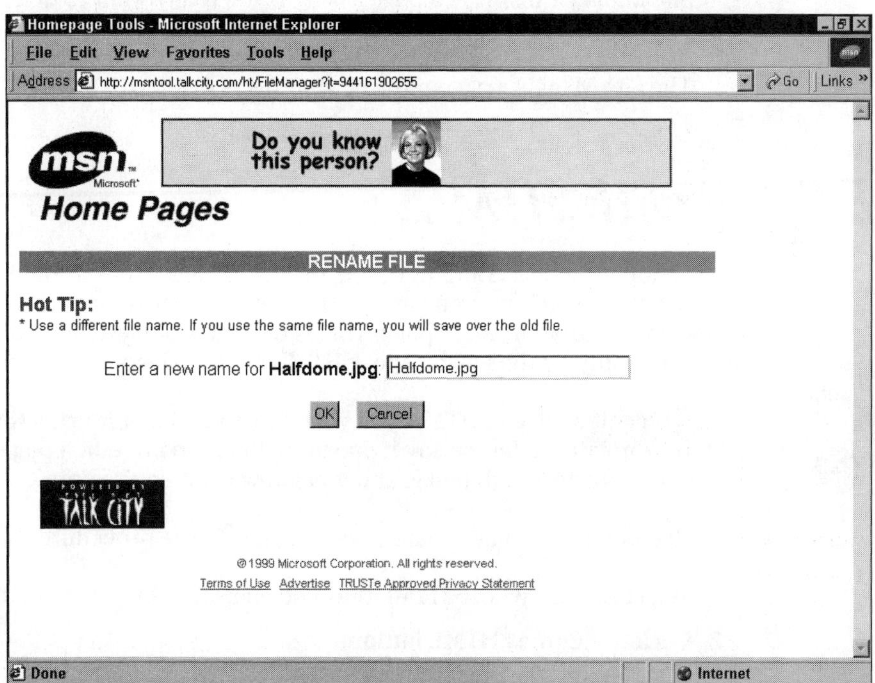

Figure 20-5: Renaming a file.

Also, be aware that Site Manager does not automatically update links to files that you rename. For example, if your main page (`index.html`) contains a hyperlink to a file named `trona.html`, and you then rename `trona.html` to `baker.html`, the hyperlink to `trona.html` is *not* automatically updated to link to `baker.html`.

Deleting a Page or File

As you work with your Web site, you may discover that you have uploaded a file that you no longer need. Since the file is now just taking up precious disk space, you should delete the file if you are certain that you won't be using it again soon. To delete a file, follow these steps:

1. **Select the file that you want to delete.**
2. **Click the Delete button.**

   Site Manager displays a page asking if you really want to delete the file.
3. **Click the Delete button.**

   The Site Manager page returns; your file is deleted.

Editing with HTML

If you happen to be a computer guru, or if you have a 10-year-old in the house that can show you how, you can use the Site Manager to directly edit the HTML codes for your home page. This is definitely something that should be attempted only by those who speak HTML in their sleep.

Once you edit a page in HTML, you won't be able to edit it using the MSN editing template. So let me say it one more time: Do not edit a page in HTML unless you are an HTML junkie and you know what you're doing.

Now that you've been adequately warned, here's the procedure:

1. **Select the file whose HTML that you want to edit.**
2. **Click the Edit as HTML button.**

   The HTML codes for the page displays, as shown in Figure 20-6.

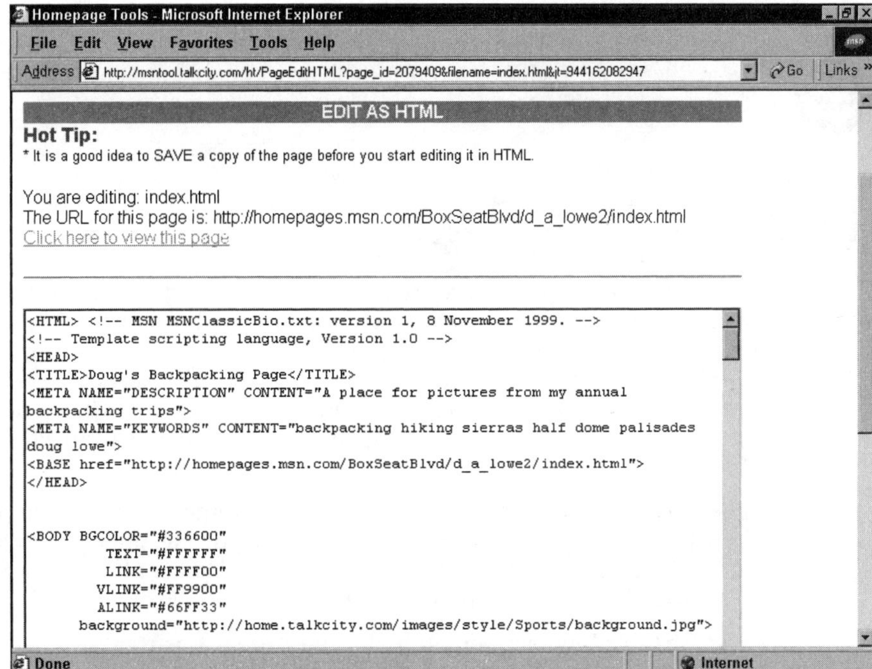

Figure 20-6: Editing a page by using HTML.

3. **Make whatever HTML changes you want in the big HTML text box.**

   Good luck.

4. **To preview the page, click the Click here to view this page hyperlink.**

   This feature allows you to preview your changes without first having to save them.

5. **When you are finished tweaking the HTML, click the Save button at the bottom of the page.**

   The page is saved.

   Once you click the Save button, you can no longer edit the page from Site Manager by clicking the Edit button. Instead, the only way you'll be able to edit the page in the future is with the Edit as HTML button.

   If you are not happy with the HTML changes you've made, you can click Cancel instead of Save. This returns you to the Site Manager without saving your changes.

If you really want to play with your Web pages' HTML code, you should consider using a real HTML editor such as FrontPage 2000 or FrontPage Express from Microsoft. See Chapter 21 for the procedures for using these programs to create free MSN home pages.

Adding a New Page

Site Manager lets you easily create new pages to add to your Web site. You can base the new page on any of the following templates:

- **Classic Bio:** Includes room for two pictures plus sections about yourself, such as your name, e-mail address, interests, and the latest news about yourself. The Classic Bio template is the one that is used when you create a simple home page as described in Chapter 19.
- **Photo Album:** Lets you display up to four photos on a single page. If you have more than four photos to show off, you can create several photo album pages and link them together. (MSN limits photo album pages to four pictures per page so that each page will download quickly.)
- **Birth Announcement:** Actually, there are two variants of this template: one for a boy, the other for a girl. These templates create a simple layout that lets you include a picture of the baby and the basic baby data, such as the time and date of birth and the baby's length and weight.
- **Wedding Announcement:** This is a great template for nerdy tightwads who don't want to pay for real wedding invitations. (Hey, I have three daughters . . . maybe I'll use this template myself someday, hopefully many, many years from now.)

The task of creating a new page is pretty much the same no matter what template you use. The following procedure shows you how to create a photo album page step-by-step:

1. **From the Site Manager page, click Add Page.**

   The Add Page page appears, which contains a single text box asking for the name of the page that you want to create.

2. **Type a filename for your new page in the New Page File Name text box.**

   Choose a file name that isn't used by any of the other files in your Web site. If you want, you can add `html` for the file name extension, like this: `vacation.html`. If you leave the `html` extension off, Site Manager will add it for you automatically.

If you are going to create several photo album pages and link them together, use numbers in the file names, like this: `vacation1`, `vacation2`, `vacation3`, and so on. This makes it easier for you to keep track of them and know which are which.

3. **Click Continue.**

   The page shown in Figure 20-7 appears, listing the layouts you can use for the new page.

4. **Click the Choose This Layout hyperlink that appears beneath the layout that you want to use.**

   The editing page appears with your selected layout. Figure 20-8 shows the editing page for the Photo Album template.

5. **Edit the page however you want.**

   Click the [Edit Me] hyperlink to add text to the page. To add pictures, click the [Add an image] hyperlink and follow the instructions that appear onscreen to upload your image files.

   For information about setting up navigation buttons for photo album pages, see the "Editing Navigation Buttons" section later in this chapter.

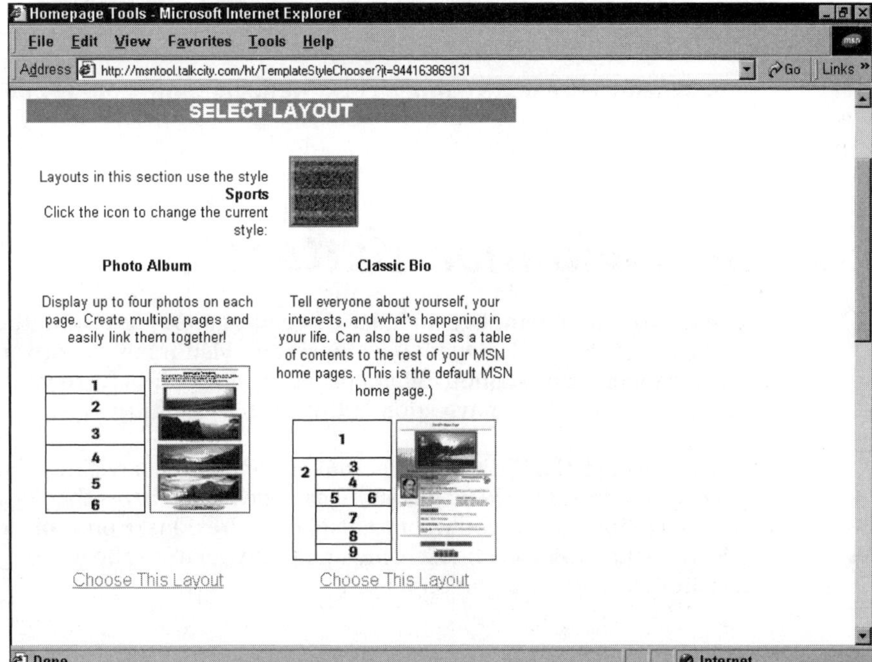

Figure 20-7: Layouts you can use for your new page.

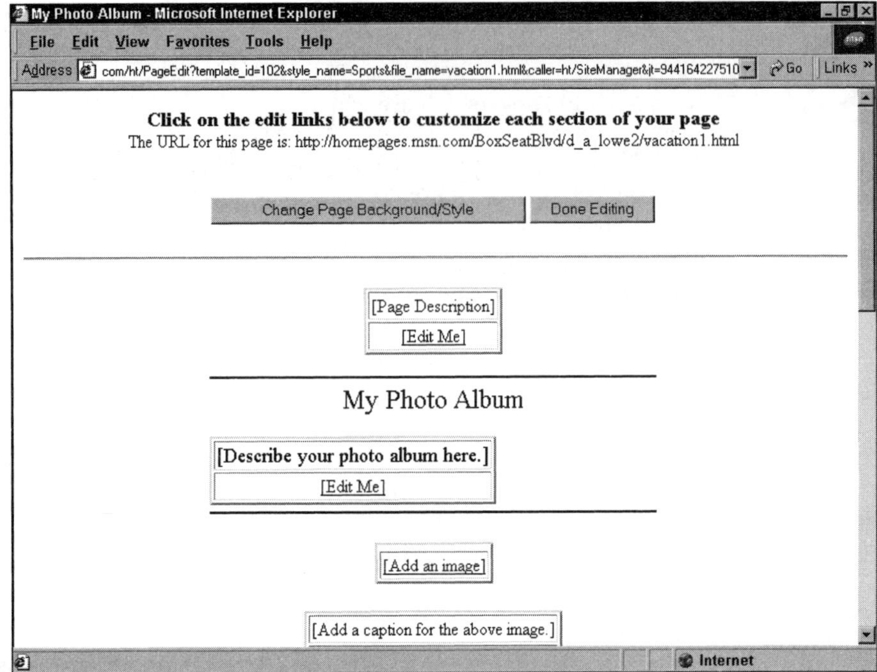

Figure 20-8: Editing a photo album page.

6. **When you're done editing, click, well, the Done Editing button.**

   The Site Manager page appears.

Editing Navigation Buttons

The Photo Album template includes three navigation buttons at the bottom of the page that are designed to let your site's visitors move forward or backward through several photo album pages or return directly to your home page. Setting up these navigation buttons can be a bit tricky.

When you click the [Edit Me] hyperlink for one of the navigation buttons, the page shown in Figure 20-9 appears. This page has controls that let you pick the navigation button you want to display — Previous, Home, or None — and a list box that lets you choose which page in your Web site will display when a visitor clicks the navigation button.

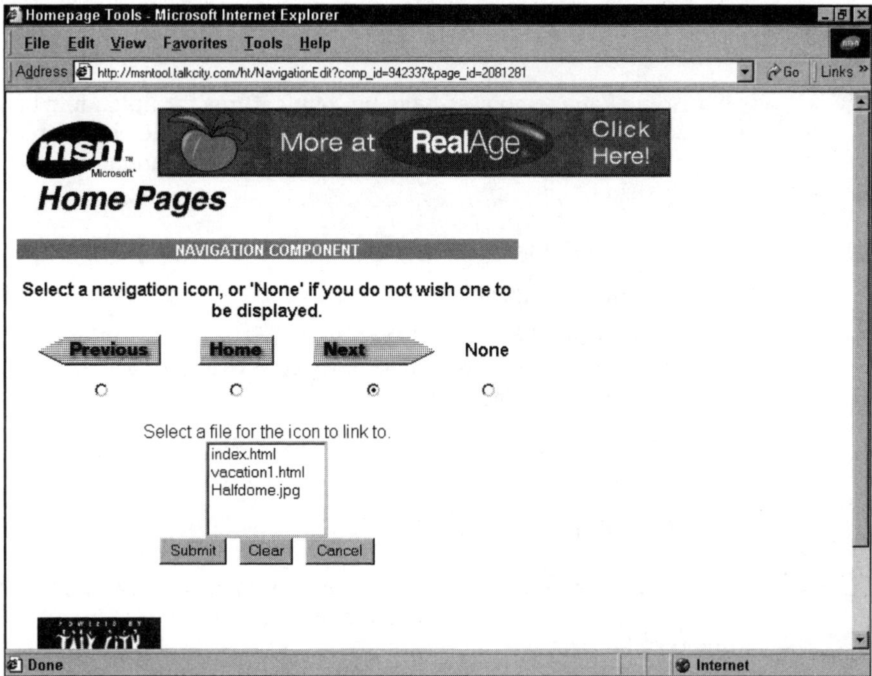

Figure 20-9: Editing a navigation button.

The Photo Album template will only let you assign a navigation button to a page that you have already created. Thus, you cannot set the Next button to link to the next photo album page in sequence if you have not yet created that page. For this reason, the easiest way to set up the navigation buttons is to first create all your photo album pages without worrying about the navigation buttons. Then go back, edit each of the pages, and set up the navigation buttons later.

Here are some thoughts to keep in mind when you set up these navigation buttons:

- For the first page in a series of photo album (or any sequential-type pages of this nature) pages, remove the Previous button. Click the [Edit Me] hyperlink for the Previous button, select None for the button type, and then click the Submit button.
- Similarly, for the last page in a series, remove the Next button.
- For each photo album page, set the Home button to link to your home page (`index.html`).

Uploading a New File

MSN Home Page templates have built-in features for uploading image files to your MSN disk area. However, if you choose instead to work directly with HTML files, you'll need to upload your image files manually. To do so, follow these instructions:

1. **Click the Upload button from the Site Manager page.**

   The upload page appears.

2. **If you know the name of the file, type the name in the text box. Otherwise, click the Browse button to bring up a standard Windows Choose File dialog box.**

3. **After you've located the file, click Open.**

   The upload page reappears.

4. **Click OK to upload the file.**

If you have more than one or two files to upload, you may want to utilize a more efficient method for uploading multiple files. For more information, see Chapter 21.

Changing Your Web Page Style

When you created the first page of your MSN Web site, you selected one of nearly 100 styles to use for the page. MSN uses the same style for additional pages you create. But what if you get bored with the style you chose? No problem! Site Manager lets you easily change the style that is used to display your Web pages. Here's the procedure:

1. **From Site Manager, click the Site Properties button.**

   This summons the Site-Wide Style page, shown in Figure 20-10, which lets you select a new style for your site.

2. **Click the style icon.**

   A page listing the other style options appears. The styles are grouped into categories such as Art/Music, Entertainment, and Sports.

3. **Choose a style category.**

   A collection of styles for your category appears.

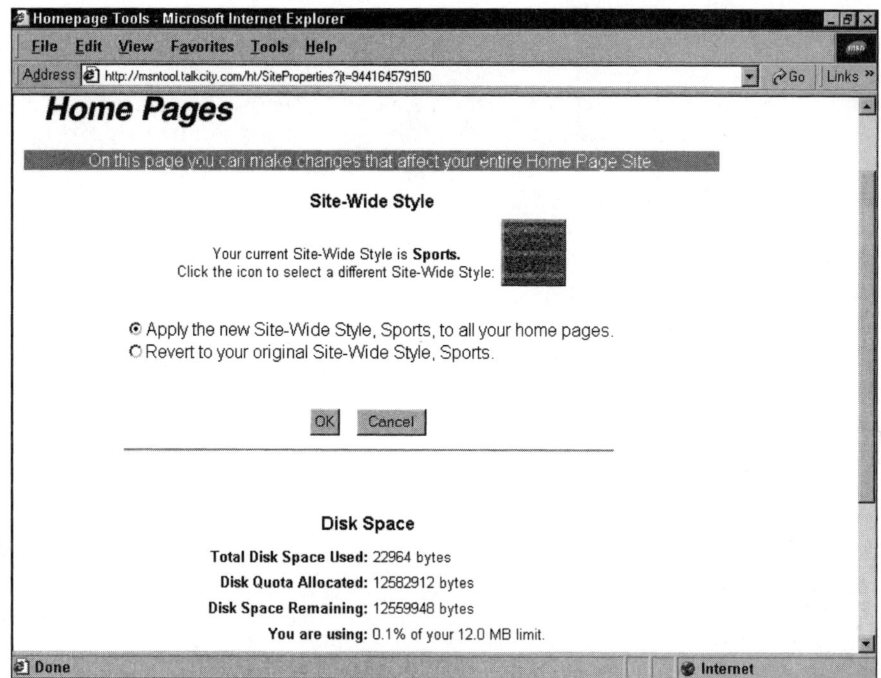

Figure 20-10: Changing styles.

4. **Click the style that you want to use.**

   You are returned to the Site-Wide Style page.

5. **Click the OK button.**

   That's all there is to it! The Site Manager page appears, and your Web pages are now utilizing the style that you have chosen.

The site-wide style applies only to pages you created by using one of the MSN templates (Classic Bio, Photo Album, Birth Announcement, or Wedding Announcement). Pages that you created with another Web publishing program such as FrontPage or pages you created directly in HTML do not use the site-wide style.

Chapter 21

Uploading Files to Your MSN Home Page

In This Chapter

- Uploading files with the Web Publishing Wizard
- Uploading files with Netscape Navigator
- Uploading files with FTP

MSN's Home Page templates are designed to let people who are not experienced Web page designers create their own simple Web pages. As such, they are limited in what they can do. MSN's Home Page templates are great for creating simple home pages that list your interests, hobbies, and opinions, and for showcasing photographs of your latest family vacation. And the site-wide styles you can choose from limit the appearance of your Web pages.

If you want more control over the appearance of your MSN home page, you'll need to use a more sophisticated Web creation program such as FrontPage Express, FrontPage 2000, or even Microsoft Office. Then, once you have created your Web pages, you can upload them from your computer to the MSN server computer.

This chapter is *not* about how to create Web pages using programs such as FrontPage or Office. There are books aplenty on those programs, including my own *Creating Web Pages For Dummies Quick Reference*, which of course I highly recommend you buy in large quantities.

Instead, this chapter shows you three different ways to take the files that you create with one of these programs from your computer to the MSN Web server computers by using the

- Web Publishing Wizard, which comes with Windows 98 and Internet Explorer 5.
- Built-in FTP features of Netscape Navigator.
- FTP command, which comes with Windows 95 and Windows 98.

Note that you can use the Site Manager's Upload button to post your Web files to the MSN Web server. If you have only one or two files to upload, this is the simplest method. For more information, see Chapter 20.

Uploading Files with the Web Publishing Wizard

The Web Publishing Wizard is designed to automate the task of copying your Web files to a Web server without having to deal directly with FTP commands. The Web Publishing Wizard comes with Windows 98, Windows NT, and with Internet Explorer 5, so you may already have it on your computer. If you don't, you can easily download it from the Microsoft Web site, located at `www.microsoft.com`.

The first time you use the Web Publishing Wizard, you have to set it up for the MSN Home Page server as described in the following section. After you set up the Web Publishing Wizard, you can use the procedure I describe in the "Updating your Web files" section to upload your Web files to the MSN Home Pages server whenever necessary.

Using the Web Publishing Wizard the first time

The first time you use the Web Publishing Wizard, you have to supply the wizard with the information it needs to configure itself for the Web server that hosts your Web page. To do so, follow these steps:

1. **Click the Start button in the Windows taskbar, and then choose Programs⇨Accessories⇨Internet Tools⇨Web Publishing Wizard.**

   The Web Publishing Wizard appears, as shown in Figure 21-1.

Figure 21-1: The Web Publishing Wizard springs to life.

2. **Click Next to continue.**

   The Web Publishing Wizard displays a dialog box, shown in Figure 21-2, asking you to provide the location of the files that you want to upload to the Web server.

Figure 21-2: The Web Publishing Wizard wants to know what files you want to upload to the Web server.

3. **Type the name and path of the file or files that you want to upload to the Web server, or select the location by clicking the Browse Files button.**

   To upload a single HTML file, type the name and path of the file (along with the drive and the folder that contains it) in the File or Folder Name field. Or click the Browse Files button, select the file that you want to upload from the dialog box that appears, and click Open.

To upload an entire folder of files, either type the name of the folder in the File or Folder Name field or click the Browse Folders button, select the folder from the dialog box that appears, and click OK.

If you want to include files from any subfolders contained within the folder you specify, check the Include Subfolders check box.

4. **Click the Next button.**

   The Name the Web Server dialog box appears. In it, the Web Publishing Wizard asks you to provide a name for the Web server that you want the files uploaded to.

5. **Type a name for your Web server in the Descriptive Name field.**

6. **Click the Next button.**

   The Specify the URL and Directory dialog box appears. The wizard needs to know the Internet address for your Web page.

7. **Type `ftp://userid@homepages.msn.com` in the URL or Internet Address field.**

   Of course, substitute your actual user ID for `userid`. For example, if your user ID is Agent86, type `ftp://Agent86@homepages.msn.com`.

   Note that the folder you selected in Step 3 is automatically entered into the Local Directory field for you.

8. **Click the Next button.**

   The wizard displays its final dialog box. The Web Publishing Wizard is ready to upload your files to the Web server.

9. **Click the Finish button.**

   The Enter Network Password dialog box appears.

10. **Type your username and password and click the OK button.**

    The Web Publishing Wizard connects to your Web server and begins to copy the files from your computer to the server. A progress dialog box, similar to the one shown in Figure 21-3, displays as the files are copied.

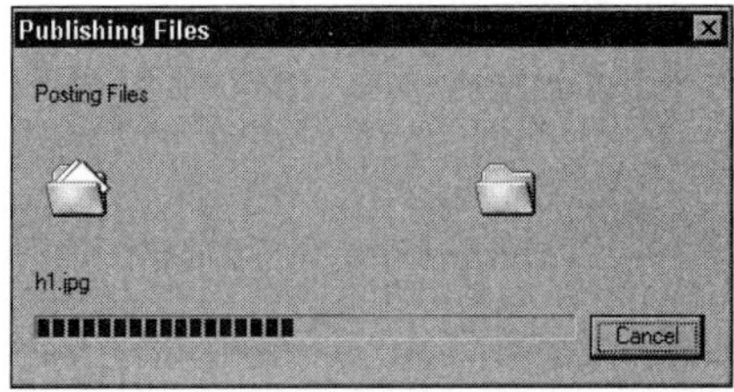

Figure 21-3: Now we're making progress.

After the file copying business concludes, the dialog box shown in Figure 21-4 appears.

Figure 21-4: Finished! Your files are successfully copied from your computer to the Web server.

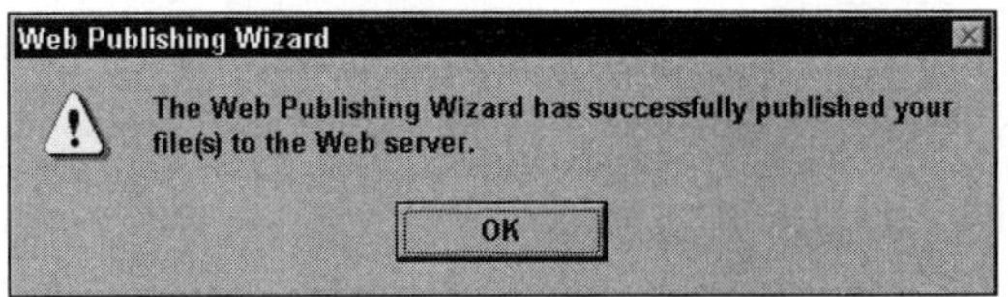

11. **Click the OK button.**

    The wizard vanishes.

Updating your Web files

The Web Publishing Wizard keeps track of almost everything it asks of you when you run it the first time. As a result, after you post your Web pages to your Web server once, you can upload updates quickly, without having to muddle through most of the Web Publishing Wizard screens.

The following procedure shows how easy it is to upload Web pages to your Web server after you've configured the Web Publishing Wizard:

1. **Start the Web Publishing Wizard by choosing Start⇨Programs⇨Accessories⇨Internet Tools⇨Web Publishing Wizard.**

   The Web Publishing Wizard appears (refer to Figure 21-1).

2. **Click the Next button.**

   The Web Publishing Wizard asks which file or folder you want to upload. The wizard defaults to the file or folder you uploaded the last time you ran the wizard, so you don't have to do anything if you want to upload the same files again.

3. **Click the Next button again.**

   The wizard asks which server to use. Again, the default is set for the same server you used the last time you ran the wizard. If you have used the Web Publishing Wizard to post files on more than one Web server, the servers you have used will appear in a drop-down list.

4. **Click the Next button yet one more time.**

   The wizard displays its final screen.

5. **Click the Finish button.**

   The wizard connects to the server, uploads the files, and then displays a confirmation dialog box saying that the upload is a rousing success.

6. **Click the OK button.**

   That's all there is to it!

Uploading Files with Netscape Navigator

If you are a Netscape Navigator user, you can upload files to your MSN home page account by using the Navigator built-in FTP features. Follow these steps:

1. **Type** `ftp://userid@homepages.msn.com` **in the Location box and press Enter.**

   Type your actual user ID in place of `userid`. For example, if your user ID is Agent86, type `ftp://Agent86@homepages.msn.com`.

   A password dialog box will appear.

2. **Type your password and then click the OK button.**

   Navigator will twiddle its electronic thumbs for a moment as MSN's FTP server logs you in. Once the server decides that you are who you say you are, a list of the files in your home page directory displays, as shown in Figure 21-5.

3. **Choose the File⇨Upload File command.**

   The File Upload dialog box appears.

4. **Choose the file you want to upload, and then click Open.**

   You may have to rummage around your hard disk to find the file you want to upload. When you click Open, the file is uploaded to the FTP server.

If you use Netscape Composer to create your Web page, you can also post your Web page files by clicking the Publish button. This brings up the dialog box shown in Figure 21-6. Fill in the requested information, and then click OK to upload your files.

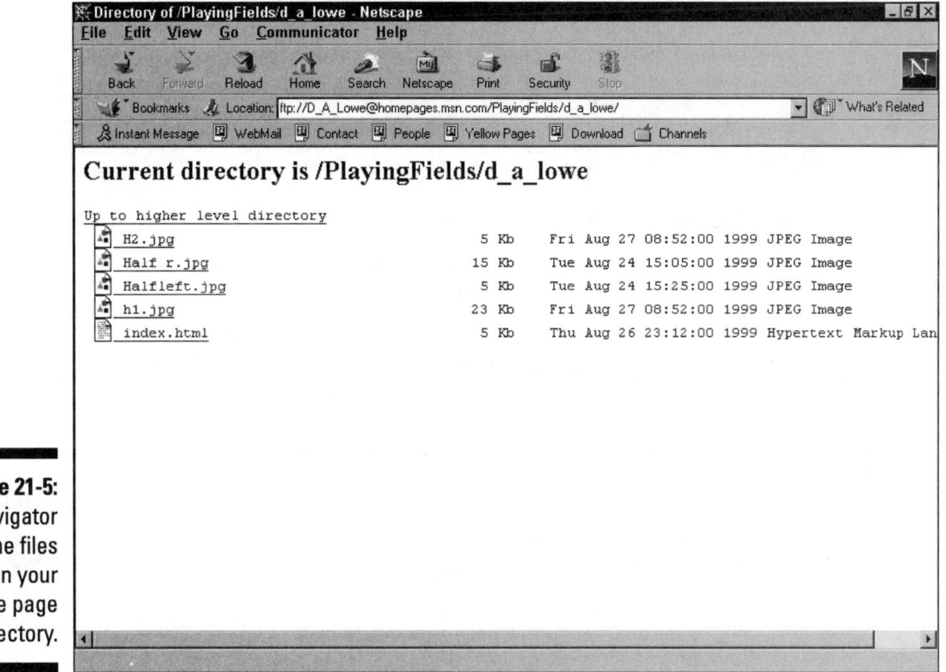

Figure 21-5: Navigator lists the files in your home page directory.

Figure 21-6: Publishing files from Netscape Composer.

Uploading Files with FTP

If you are a Windows 95 or Windows 98 user, you can use the FTP command from an MS-DOS command prompt to upload files to MSN's Home Page server. Although the FTP command requires that you type cryptic commands, it is often the fastest and easiest way to upload your files.

If the thought of typing commands makes you nauseous, use the Web Publishing Wizard instead. See the section "Uploading Files with the Web Publishing Wizard" earlier in this chapter.

The following procedure spells out the steps for uploading files using the MS-DOS FTP command:

1. **Gather all of the files you need to upload into a single folder.**
2. **Open an MS-DOS command window by choosing Start⇨Programs⇨MS-DOS Prompt.**
3. **Use the `CD` (Change Directory) command to change to the folder that contains the Web files that you want to transfer to the Web server.**
4. **Type the following command:** `ftp homepages.msn.com`**.**
5. **When prompted, type your user ID and password.**

   After you have successfully logged into the FTP server, you see an FTP prompt that looks like this:

   ```
   ftp>
   ```

   This prompt indicates that you are connected to the FTP server, and the FTP server processes any commands you type, not by the DOS command prompt on your own computer.
6. **Type this command:**

   ```
   mput *.*
   ```

   This command copies all the files from the current directory on your computer (which you set back in Step 3) to the FTP server computer.

   As each file is copied, a prompt similar to this one appears:

   ```
   mput yourfile.html?
   ```

   Type **Y** and then press Enter to copy the file to the FTP server. Type **N** and then press Enter if you want to skip the file.

   When all the files have been copied, the `FTP>` prompt displays again.
7. **Type bye to disconnect from the FTP server.**

   The MS-DOS prompt returns.
8. **Type Exit to close the MS-DOS command window.**

Transferring an Entire Web Site to MSN

One other MSN Home Page feature you should know about is EZ WebTransfer, which is designed to make it easy for you to move an entire Web site from another Web server to your MSN site. This feature is useful if you have previously created a Web site and want to move that site to MSN.

When you use EZ WebTransfer, you must provide a Web address which EZ WebTransfer uses as a starting point — known as the source page — to copy the Web site to MSN. EZ WebTransfer starts by copying the source page to MSN. Then, EZ WebTransfer works its way through all of the pages that the source page links to, copying them to MSN as well, provided that those pages are stored within the same directory as the source page.

To use EZ WebTransfer, go to the MSN Home Pages site, click Creation Tools, and then click Transfer Your Home Page to MSN. The EZ WebTransfer page will appear, as shown in Figure 21-7.

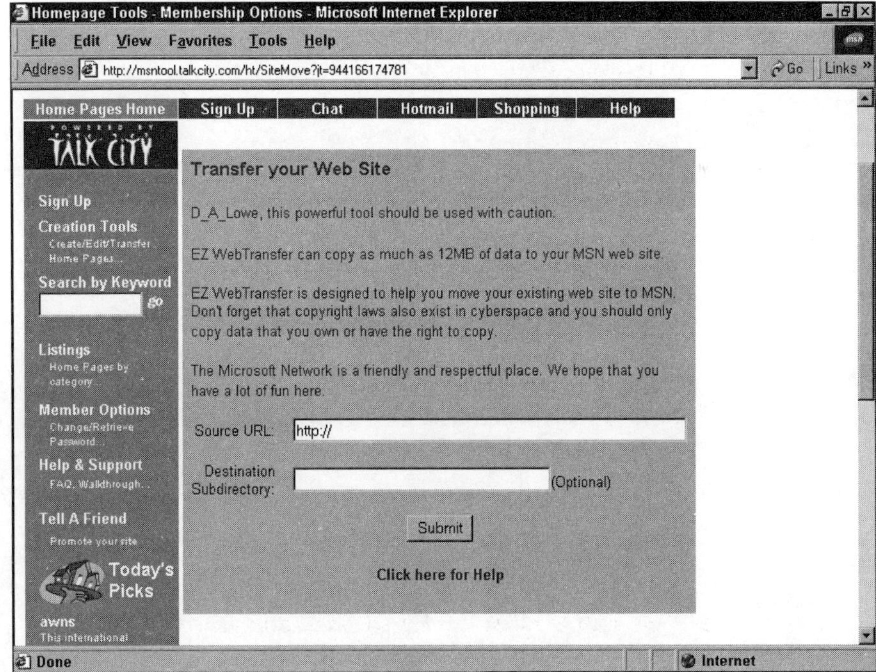

Figure 21-7: EZ WebTransfer simplifies the task of moving your Web site to MSN.

Type the complete address of the source page in the Source URL field. If you want the files to be copied into your main MSN home page directory, leave the Destination Subdirectory field blank. If you want EZ WebTransfer to create a subdirectory to copy the files to, type the name of the subdirectory you want to create in this field. Click Submit to begin the transfer.

Here are some thoughts to ponder before you charge full speed ahead with EZ WebTransfer:

- If you leave the Destination Subdirectory field blank, EZ WebTransfer will replace any files that exist on your MSN Web site with files that have the same name in the Source URL Web site, without asking your permission first. For this reason, I recommend you always use the Destination Subdirectory field to create a subdirectory to copy the files to.
- EZ WebTransfer will copy a maximum of 12MB of files to your MSN site.
- EZ WebTransfer attempts to adjust links to pages within the Web site so that the links point to the MSN copies of the page.

Part VI

The Part of Tens

"Did you click 'HELP' on the MSN.com menu bar recently? It's Mr. Gates. He wants to know if everything's alright."

In this part . . .

If you keep this book in the bathroom (which is probably where it belongs), the chapters in this part are the ones you'll read the most. Each of these chapters consists of ten (more or less) things that are worth knowing about the various aspects of using MSN. Without further ado, here they are, direct from the home office in sunny Fresno, California.

Chapter 22

Ten Tips for Using MSN Efficiently

In This Chapter

- Personalizing your start page
- Storing your favorite Web sites
- Adding Web sites to the Links toolbar
- Creating desktop shortcuts
- Clicking all the right places
- Searching efficiently
- Chatting efficiently

MSN can be a fun place to explore, but because it's so big, losing your way is easy. The tips presented in this chapter are designed to make your MSN browsing more efficient so that you won't get lost in the woods. All of these tips are covered elsewhere in this book; they are gathered together here merely for convenience.

Personalizing Your Start Page

The standard msn.com home page contains links to MSN content pages such as Investor, Expedia, and the Gaming Zone, as well as the top news stories of the day and other useful information. However, by personalizing your msn.com home page, you can bring the information you need most right to your start-up page. By personalizing msn.com, you can get stock quotes, news headlines on the subjects that interest you, sports scores, movie reviews, and other useful information all on one page so you don't have to waste time surfing through page after page to find the information you need.

To personalize your MSN home page, click Change Content near the top of the home page. Then, choose the content items that you want to add to your personalized home page. For more information, see Chapter 5.

Stashing Goodies in Your Favorites Menu

Internet Explorer's Favorites menu lets you gather up your favorite Web pages into a single location so you can get to them easily. When you find yourself visiting an MSN page frequently, add it to the Favorites menu so you can go to that page directly from any other Web page, without having to navigate your way through MSN to get to the page. For example, if you play Hearts at the Gaming Zone, you can add the Hearts page to your Favorites menu. Then, you can go directly to the Hearts page at any time simply by choosing Hearts from the Favorites menu.

To add an item to your Favorites menu, follow these steps:

1. **Go to the page that you want to add to your Favorites menu.**
2. **Choose Favorites➪Add to favorites.**

   This brings up the Add Favorite dialog box.
3. **If you don't like the description of the page listed in the Name text box, type a new description.**
4. **Click the OK button.**

In Netscape Navigator, Favorites are referred to as Bookmarks. To bookmark an MSN page in Navigator, follow these steps:

1. **Go to the page that you want to bookmark.**
2. **Click the Bookmarks button.**
3. **Choose Add Bookmark from the menu that appears.**

Customizing Your Links Toolbar

An even faster way to access the pages that you use most is to add them to your Links toolbar. The Links toolbar, located at the top of the Internet Explorer window, contains buttons that let you go to frequently used Web pages with a single click of the mouse.

When you first install Internet Explorer, the Links toolbar includes links to Web sites that Microsoft thinks you should visit often, such as the Microsoft corporate Web site, the Microsoft Windows Web site, and other Microsoft sites. But you can easily add your own sites to the Links toolbar. Just follow these steps:

1. **Go to the page that you want to add to your Links toolbar.**
2. **Drag the page icon from the Address bar to the Links toolbar.**

This step is a little tricky. The page icon appears right next to the Web page address in the Address toolbar. Point the mouse at this icon, and then press and hold the left mouse button. Next, move the mouse to the position on the Links toolbar where you want the link to appear. When you release the mouse button, a button for the page appears.

To remove a link from the Links toolbar, right-click the link and then choose the Delete command.

Netscape Navigator has a similar feature known as the Personal Toolbar. To add a page to the Personal Toolbar, follow these steps:

1. **Go to the page that you want to add to your Personal Toolbar.**
2. **Click the Bookmarks button.**
3. **Choose File Bookmark⇨Personal Toolbar Folder⇨Personal Toolbar Folder.**

Creating Desktop Shortcuts

Yet another way to go quickly to an MSN page that you use frequently is to create a desktop shortcut for the page. Then, you can call up the page at any time by double-clicking the shortcut on your desktop.

To create a desktop shortcut, follow these steps:

1. **Go to the page that you want to create a shortcut for.**
2. **Right-click in an empty portion of the page and choose the Create Shortcut command.**

   This brings up the dialog box.

   If the Create Shortcut command doesn't appear in the menu, right-click somewhere else on the page. The Create Shortcut command won't appear if you right-click a link, picture, or other object on the page.

3. **Click the OK button.**

   The shortcut is created on your desktop.

Windows uses the Web page address as the name of the shortcut. In some cases, this may be acceptable. But often, the name turns out to be gibberish. For example, if you create a shortcut to the Gaming Zone Hearts page, the shortcut name appears as `sidebar.aspgame=hrtz`.

To change the name to something more meaningful, close all open windows by clicking the Show Desktop button in the Windows toolbar. Then, right-click the shortcut and choose the Rename command. Type a new name for the shortcut and press the Enter key.

Be careful about creating too many desktop shortcuts. If you create too many shortcuts, your desktop will become cluttered.

Discovering Weird Places to Click

MSN is a very mousy place, but more places to click exist than you are probably aware of. Here are some offbeat ways to get your clicks:

- Sometimes there are links on the page that aren't obvious. Move the mouse pointer over different areas of the page to find out. If the mouse pointer changes to a hand, you've found a link.
- You can right-click many objects on MSN pages to get a pop-up menu of commands that apply to the object. For example, right-click a picture on an MSN page to get a menu of commands that lets you save the picture to a file, print the picture, or use the picture as your Windows desktop wallpaper.
- If you are an MSN Internet Access user, you can double-click the MSN icon that appears in the corner of the Windows taskbar to bring up a menu that lists MSN's major areas and gives you access to MSN Internet Access services, such as checking your bill or changing your password.

Using MSN Search Features

The best way to find information on MSN and the Internet is to use MSN's powerful searching tools. Unfortunately, if you don't use MSN's search tools wisely, you can spend hours looking for something without ever finding it. For more information about using MSN's search features, see Chapter 4.

Here are some tips for using MSN's search features efficiently:

- Choose your search keywords carefully. If you search for broad terms like "Animals" or "History," you'll get thousands of results to sift through. If your search words are too narrow, you won't get any results. It's usually best to start with search words that you think may be too narrow, then move to more general words if you don't get the results you want. The Internet is a huge place, and you'll be surprised how many results you get from searches you might at first think are too specific. (For example, I recently searched for "Bald starship captain" and got 283 results, most of them correctly identifying Patrick Stewart from *Star Trek: The Next Generation*.)

- Search from the MSN Search Page rather than from the search text box that appears on the msn.com home page. The MSN Search Page lets you use advanced search features that can lead to more efficient searches.
- Use the Save Results feature to save the most promising search results so you can visit those sites later. To save a search result, click the floppy disk icon that appears next to the result on any Search Results page. To view your saved results, click Saved Results at the top of the MSN Search page.

Chatting Tips

If you enjoy online chatting, here are some tips that can streamline your time online:

- Don't waste your time with MSN's Web-based chat. Microsoft Chat, which is a free part of Internet Explorer 5, is much more efficient and powerful.
- In Microsoft Chat, turn off comics view. Text view allows you to see many more messages at once.
- Ignore obnoxious chatters by right-clicking the offending person's icon in the member list and choosing Ignore from the menu that appears.
- Turn off the annoying arrival and departure messages. In Microsoft Chat, call up the View⇨Options command, click the Settings tab, and then uncheck the Show Arrivals/Departures option.

For more information about chatting, see Chapter 9.

Chapter 23

Ten Things That Often Go Wrong

In This Chapter

- Getting the latest version of Internet Explorer
- Troubleshooting your modem connection
- Accessing your forgotten password
- Interpreting strange messages about cryptic and unexpected errors
- Recovering the Internet Explorer window
- Searching for a downloaded file
- Experiencing a disconnect in the middle of a large Internet download
- Locating your favorite MSN or Web page
- Starting a nuclear war

Actually, probably more like 10,000 things can go wrong, but this chapter describes some of the things that go wrong most often.

I Don't Have the Latest Version of Internet Explorer!

No problem. The latest and greatest version, Internet Explorer 5, is available from many sources, and it's free. If you have any type of access to the Internet, you can find Internet Explorer 5 at the Microsoft Web site, located at the following address:

```
www.microsoft.com/windows/ie
```

If you don't have access to the Internet or you don't want to contend with a horrendously long download (it can take hours if you download all of Internet Explorer's bells and whistles), you can order the entire Internet Explorer 5 package on a CD from the Microsoft Web site for a mere $6.95.

Yes, you certainly can use Netscape Navigator to access MSN. However, since MSN is the Microsoft Web site and Internet Explorer is the Microsoft Web browser, you'll find that MSN works best when you access it using the latest version of Internet Explorer.

I Can't Get Connected!

You double-click the Internet Explorer or Netscape Navigator icon, the Connect To dialog box appears and you type in your name and password, but that's as far as you get. For some reason, you are unable to connect to the Internet. Arghhhhh!

Many, *many* things could be wrong here. Here are a few general troubleshooting procedures that should help you solve the problem, or at least to narrow it down:

- Make sure that the modem is securely connected to the telephone wall jack and the correct jack on the back of the modem. Phone cables are finicky things. Sometimes they jar loose. They go bad sometimes, too, so replacing the cable may solve the problem. If you're not sure which jack is the correct one, you'll have to consult the manual that came with the modem.
- Make sure that the modem is not in use by another program, such as a fax program or the Windows HyperTerminal program.
- Make sure that your teenager isn't talking on a phone that shares the same phone line as the modem. (This happens to me all the time.)
- Try calling your Internet access number on a regular phone and see if it answers. If you get a busy signal or it just rings on and on and on, something may be wrong with the local access number. Try again later, and call your service provider's customer service if the problem persists.
- Double check the phone number in the Connect To dialog box. If your Internet service provider has an alternate phone number, try that one instead.
- Windows has some built-in troubleshooters that may help you find and correct your problem. Click the Start button, and then click Help to bring up the Windows help. Click Troubleshooting, next click Windows Troubleshooters to reveal a list of the built-in troubleshooters, and then click Modem to start the Modem troubleshooter.

If you just installed the modem or if the modem has never worked right, you should make sure that the modem is configured to use the proper Communications Port within your computer. To change the port setting in Windows 98, follow these steps:

1. **Click the Start button and choose Settings⇨Control Panel.**
2. **Double-click the Modems icon.**
3. **Click the Properties button.**
4. **Change the Port setting for the modem.**
5. **Click the OK button twice.**
6. **Try dialing in again.**

Sometimes, removing and reinstalling the modem within Windows saves the day. If all else fails, you can try by following these steps:

1. **Click the Start button and choose Settings⇨Control Panel.**
2. **Double-click the Modems icon.**
3. **Click the modem to select it, and then click the Remove button.**
4. **Click the Add button.**
5. **Follow the Install a New Modem wizard to reinstall the modem.**

I Forgot My Password!

Didn't I tell you to write it down and keep it in a safe place? Sigh. If you really did forget your password, and you didn't write it down anywhere, you have to call your Internet Service Provider for assistance. If you can convince them that you really are who you say you are, they'll allow you to reset your password.

Now, to avoid this kind of time-consuming mess, write down your password and store it in a secure location. Here's a list of several not-so-secure places to hide your password:

- In a desk drawer, in a file folder labeled *Not My Internet Password.*
- On a magnet stuck to the refrigerator. (No one, including you, will ever be able to pick it out from all the other junk stuck up there.)
- On a sticky note attached to your computer monitor, where anyone who comes across your computer can see it.
- On the inside cover of this book, in Pig Latin so that no one will be able to understand it.
- Carved on the back of a park bench.
- On the wall in a public restroom.
- Tattooed on your left buttock, backward so that you can read it in a mirror.

I Got a Weird Error Message

This happens sometimes when you try to follow a link to a cool Web page, or you type in a URL of your own and press Enter. Instead of being greeted with the expected page, you get a cryptic message similar to this one:

```
Internet Explorer cannot open the Internet site
        http://www.whatever.com
A connection with the server could not be established.
```

Sometimes no dialog box appears, but instead of the page you're looking for, you just get a page with some bland text that says something like:

```
HTTP/1.0 404 Object Not Found
```

These error messages and others like them mean that your Web browser can't find the page you tried to access. There are several possible explanations for this:

- You typed the URL incorrectly. Maybe it should have been `www.whoever.com` instead of `www.whatever.com`.
- The page you are trying to display may no longer exist. The person who created the page may have removed it.
- The page may have been moved to a new address. Sometimes you'll get a message telling you about the new address, sometimes not.
- The Web site that hosts the page may be having technical trouble. Try again later.
- The page may be just too darn popular, causing the server to be busy. Try again later.

My Web Browser Disappeared!

You know you are signed in to the Internet, but you can't seem to see Internet Explorer or Navigator. The window has mysteriously vanished!

Here are a few things to check before giving up in despair:

- Find the Taskbar, that Windows thingy that usually lurks down at the bottom of your screen. The Taskbar has a button for every window that's open. Find the browser window in the Taskbar and click on it. That should bring the window to the front. (If the Taskbar isn't visible, you have to move the mouse all the way to the bottom edge of the screen to make it appear. Also, if you've moved the Taskbar, it may be on the top, left, or right edge of the screen rather than the bottom.)

- If no browser window appears in the Taskbar, you may have closed Internet Explorer but remained connected to the Internet. To make your browser come alive again, just click the Internet Explorer or Navigator button in the Taskbar's quick-launch toolbar. Since you are already online, you don't have to go through the Connect To dialog box again.
- You may have been disconnected from the Internet for one reason or another. Normally when that happens, a dialog box will appear, informing you that you have been disconnected and offering to reconnect. If not, you can reconnect by choosing the Start➪Programs➪Accessories➪Dial Up Networking command and then double-clicking the icon for your Internet connection.

You can tell if you're connected to the Internet by looking for the little modem icon in the corner of the Taskbar, next to the clock. If the icon is present, you are connected. If the icon is missing, you're not.

I Can't Find a File I Downloaded!

Don't worry. The file is probably around, you're just not looking in the right place. Internet Explorer and other browsers display a Save As dialog box which you must complete before downloading a file, so presumably you know where the file has been saved. However, it's all too easy to simply click OK when this dialog box appears without really looking at where it's being saved.

Fortunately, all you have to do is right-click a graphic object or a text link, and then choose the Save As command from the menu that appears. This will summon the Save As dialog box, which will by default open the same folder the dialog box was opened to last. Just check the Save In field at the top of the dialog box to find out what folder you saved your file in, and then click Cancel to dismiss the Save As dialog box without actually saving anything.

If you cannot remember the name of the file you downloaded, here's a trick that may help you find it:

1. **Open a My Computer window for the folder in which you saved the file.**

   Click My Computer, and then navigate your way through your drives and folders until you come to the one you saved the file in.

2. **Choose View➪Details.**
3. **Choose View➪Arrange Icons➪By Date.**

   The file list is sorted into date sequence, with the newest files appearing at the bottom of the list.

4. **Look at the files at the bottom of the list.**

   Hopefully, one of these files rings a bell.

Another way to find your file is to click the Start button and choose Find⇨Files or Folders. Type the name of the file in the Named text box, choose Local Hard Drives in the Look in list box, and then click the Find Now button.

Disconnected in the Middle of a Two-Hour Download with Only Ten Minutes to Go!

Wow. Tough break. Unfortunately, MSN doesn't have any way to restart a big download, picking up where you left off. The only solution is to download the entire file again.

Don't blame me, I'm just the messenger.

I Can't Find My Favorite Page!

I've faced this problem myself. The Internet is such a large place that it's easy to stumble into a page you really like, and then not be able to find it again later.

The best way to avoid such frustration is to add any cool page you stumble across to your Favorites (Internet Explorer) or Bookmarks (Navigator) the moment you stumble across the page. That way, you can always find the page again by choosing it from the Favorites or Bookmarks menu. If you later decide that it's not such a great page after all, you can always delete it from Favorites or Bookmarks.

I've Started a Nuclear War!!!

If you're minding your own business, enjoying a nice game of "Global Thermonuclear War" at `http://www.wargames.com` (there really is no such site), and you suddenly hear air raid sirens and see mushroom clouds on the horizon, don't panic. See if you can interest the computer in a nice game of chess instead.

Really, this isn't your fault. Nothing you do can start a nuclear war from the Internet. Experienced computer users have been trying to start nuclear wars on the Internet for years, and no one has succeeded, at least not yet.

Chapter 24

Ten Safety Tips for Kids on the Net

In This Chapter

- Safety tips for kids and their parents
- Ways to help keep the Internet a safe place for everyone

MSN and the Internet are inherently risky places for kids (and adults too). Along with pictures of Neil Armstrong on the moon, your kids can just as easily find pictures you probably don't want them to see. And while chatting online can be fun and enlightening, it can also be unhealthy and possibly even dangerous.

This chapter lists ten or so important safety tips that parents should drill into their kids' heads before they allow them to go online.

Note: I really don't want to be an alarmist here. Overall, the online world is a pretty wholesome place. Don't be afraid to let your kids venture out online, but don't let them go it alone, either. Make sure that they understand the ground rules.

Do Not Believe People Really Are Who They Say They Are

When you sign up for a Hotmail account or log in to a chat room, you can type anything you want for your member ID. And no one makes you tell the truth in e-mail, newsletter, or chats. Just because someone claims to be a 16-year-old female is not reason enough to believe it. That person can be a 12-year old boy, a 19-year old girl, or a 35-year old pervert.

Never Give Out Your Address, Phone Number, Real Last Name, or Credit Card Number

If you're not sure why rule #2 exists, see rule #1.

It's okay to provide this type of information over a secure connection when you are shopping online, but you should never give out personal information via e-mail or an online chat.

Never Pretend to Be Someone You're Not

The flip side of not believing who someone says he or she is, is that other people may believe that you are who you say you are. If you are 13 years old and claim to be 17, you're inviting trouble.

We all like to gloss over our weaknesses. When I'm online, I don't generally draw attention to the fact that a substantial portion of my hair is gone, and I'm a bit pudgy around the waistline (well, okay, I'm a *lot* pudgy around the waistline). But I don't represent myself as a super athlete or a rock star, either. Just be yourself.

Watch Your Language

The Internet isn't censored. In fact, it can be a pretty rough place. Crude language abounds, especially on Usenet and in chat rooms. But that doesn't mean you have to contribute to the endless flow of colorful metaphors. Watch your language while chatting online or posting messages.

Don't Obsess

Going online can be fun, but there's more to life than surfing the Net. The best friendships are the ones where you actually spend time in the presence of other people. If you find yourself spending hour upon hour online, maybe you should cut back a bit.

Report Inappropriate Behavior

If something seems really amiss in your online experience — for example, if you think someone is harassing you beyond what you consider normal, or if someone asks you questions of a questionable nature — tell someone.

The best person to complain to is the perpetrator's service provider. If the perp is clever, you may not be able to figure out his or her true e-mail address. But you often can.

Most service providers have a user named *postmaster* to whom you can send such complaints. If you receive harassing mail from idiot@jerk.com, try sending a complaint to postmaster@jerk.com.

If You Feel Uncomfortable, Leave

Don't stick around in a chat session if you feel uncomfortable. Just leave.

Similarly, don't reply to inappropriate e-mail messages or newsgroup articles.

Parents: Be Involved with Your Kids' Online Activities

Parents: Don't let your kids run loose online! Get involved with what they are doing. You don't have to monitor them every moment they are online. Just be interested in what they are doing, what friends they have made over the network, what they like, and what they don't like. Ask them to show you around their favorite Web pages.

Glossary

ActiveX: Microsoft's Web-based object technology, which allows intelligent objects to be embedded in Web documents to create interactive pages. See *object linking and embedding.*

Adam's Ribs: A Rib House in Chicago, near the Dearborn station, from which Hawkeye had an order of Ribs delivered all the way to Korea in a popular episode of M*A*S*H.

address book: A file that stores the e-mail addresses of the people with whom you correspond regularly.

afk: *Away from keyboard,* an abbreviation commonly used when chatting.

AIM: AOL Instant Messenger, America Online's program for exchanging instant messages with other Internet users. Similar to MSN Messenger.

America Online: A popular online information service that also provides Internet access. America Online is often referred to as AOL. To send e-mail to an AOL user, address the message to the user's America Online name followed by the domain name (`@aol.com`). For example, if the user's AOL name is `Barney`, send an e-mail message to `Barney@aol.com`.

anonymous FTP: An FTP site that allows access to anyone, without requiring an account.

AOL: See *America Online.*

applet: A program written in the Java programming language and embedded in a Web page. Applets run automatically whenever a user views the Web page that contains the applet.

article: A message posted to an Internet newsgroup.

ASCII: The standard character set for most computers. Internet newsgroups are *ASCII-only,* meaning that they can support only text-based messages.

attach: Sending a file along with an e-mail message or newsgroup article.

attachment: A file attached to an e-mail message or newsgroup article.

AVI: Microsoft's standard for video files that can be viewed in Windows. AVI is one of the most popular video formats on the Web, but other formats such as QuickTime and MPEG are also widely used. (*AVI* stands for *Audio Video Interleaved*, but that won't be on the test.)

bandwidth: The amount of information that can flow through a network connection. Bandwidth is to computer networks what pipe diameter is to plumbing: the bigger the pipe, the more water can flow.

baud: See *bits per second*. (Actually, a technical difference does exist between *baud* and *bits per second*, but only people with pocket protectors and taped glasses care.)

binary file: A non-ASCII file, such as a picture, sound, video, or a computer program.

BITNET: A large network connected to the Internet. BITNET stands for "Because It's Time Network," and connects colleges and universities in North America and Europe. BITNET mailing lists are presented as Usenet newsgroups under the `bit` hierarchy.

bits per second (bps): A measure of how fast your modem can transmit or receive information between your computer and a remote computer, such as your Internet service provider. You won't be happy browsing the Internet using anything less than a 28,800 bps modem (commonly referred to as a *28.8 modem*). Note that the term *kbps* is often used to designate thousands of bits per second. Thus, 28,800 bps and 28.8 kbps are equivalent.

bookmarks: In Netscape Navigator, a list of Web pages that you visit frequently. See *Favorites*.

brb: *Be right back,* an abbreviation commonly used in chat rooms.

browser: A program that you can use to access and view the World Wide Web. The two most popular browsers are Microsoft Internet Explorer and Netscape Navigator. You can use either browser to access MSN, but MSN is designed to work better with Internet Explorer.

cable modem: One of the fastest ways to connect your computer to the Internet; using your cable TV connection rather than a phone connection.

cache: An area of your computer's hard disk used to store data recently downloaded from the network so the data can be redisplayed quickly.

Cappuccino: An Italian coffee drink.

CarPoint: MSN's Web site featuring information about cars, including reviews and complete purchasing information. Found at `carpoint.msn.com`.

chat: The Internet's equivalent to a conference call: an online conversation between two or more users who are on the Internet at the same time. When you send a message to a chat, everyone in the chat can immediately see your message and respond to it.

chat history: Microsoft Chat keeps a copy of all messages that have been sent during a chat. The chat history begins the moment you join the chat and continues until you exit. You can scroll back through the chat history to review sent messages, and you can save a chat history to a file if you want to keep a permanent record of a chat.

chat room: A virtual "place" (generally a window) where chats on a particular topic can take place. Most MSN Web communities have at least one chat room dedicated to the community topic. Some communities have several rooms.

Chaucer: A dead English dude who didn't spell very well.

clips: Sections of the customizable MSN home page which include information such as the latest headlines, sports scores, stock quotes, and so on.

community manager: The person who oversees a Web community. The manager decides which newsgroups, chat areas, and other services will be available on the forum and tries to keep discussions in the newsgroups and chats on topic.

compressed file: A file that has been processed by a special *compression program* that reduces the amount of disk space required to store the file. If you download the file to your computer, you must decompress the file before you can use it using a program such as WinZip or PKUNZIP (for Windows and DOS, respectively).

CompuServe: A popular online service that also provides Internet access. To send Internet mail to a CompuServe member, address the mail to the user's CompuServe user ID (two groups of numbers separated by a comma) followed by `@compuserve.com`. However, use a period instead of a comma in the user ID. For example, if the user's ID is 55555,1234, send mail to `55555.1234@compuserve.com`. You have to use the period because Internet e-mail standard don't allow for commas in e-mail addresses.

connect time: The amount of time you are connected to the Internet. A few years ago, Internet Service Providers charged you by the hour for connect time. Nowadays, most ISP's (including MSN Internet Access) allow you unlimited Internet connection time for a fixed monthly rate.

cookie: A file that a Web server stores on your computer. The most common use for cookies is to customize the way a Web page appears when you view it. MSN leaves cookies all over your computer. Don't worry; they don't bite.

Cyberspace: An avant-garde term used to refer to the Internet. Originates from William Gibson's novel *Neuromancer.*

decode: The process of reconstructing a binary file that was encoded using the uuencode scheme, used in e-mail and newsgroups. Internet Mail and Internet News can automatically decode encoded files.

decompression: The process of restoring compressed files to their original state. This decompression is usually accomplished with a program such as WinZip or PKUNZIP. (You can download the shareware version of Winzip at `www.winzip.com` and PKUNZIP at `www.pkware.com`.)

decryption: See *Tales from Decrypt* (just kidding). Decryption is the process of unscrambling a message that has been encrypted (scrambled up so that only the intended recipient can read it). See *encryption.*

dial-up script: A special file that contains the instructions used to log you in to your ISP so you can connect to the Internet.

"Dixie": A happy little tune that you can whistle while you are waiting for a Web page to finish downloading.

DNS: *Domain Name Server.* The system that allows us to use almost intelligible names such as `www.microsoft.com` rather than completely incomprehensible addresses such as `283.939.12.74`.

domain: The last portion of an Internet address (also known as the *top-level domain*), which indicates whether the address belongs to a company (`com`), an educational institution (`edu`), a government agency (`gov`), a military organization (`mil`), or another organization (`org`).

domain name: The address of an Internet site, which generally includes the organization domain name followed by the top-level domain, as in `www.idgbooks.com`.

download: Copying a file from another computer to your computer, often via a modem.

e-mail: *Electronic mail,* an Internet service that allows you to send and receive messages to and from other Internet users like virtual letters.

e-mail address: A complete address used to send e-mail to someone over the Internet.

emoticon: Another word for a *smiley* face you create with keystrokes you find around the house.

Encarta: Microsoft's online encyclopedia, found at `encarta.msn.com`.

encode: A method of converting a *binary file* to ASCII text, which can be sent by e-mail or posted to a newsgroup or bulletin board service. When displayed, encoded information looks like a stream of random characters. But when you run the encoded message through a decoder program, the original binary file is reconstructed. E-mail programs such as Outlook Express automatically encodes and decodes messages, so you don't have to worry about using a separate program for this purpose.

encryption: Scrambling a message so that no one can read it, except of course the intended recipient, who must *decrypt* the message before reading it.

ETLA: *Extended Three Letter Acronym.* A four-letter acronym. Computer nerds think that's funny. See *TLA*.

Expedia: MSN's travel site, where you can purchase airline tickets, rent cars and hotel rooms, and plan your next vacation. Found at `expedia.msn.com`.

Explorer bar: In Internet Explorer, the left one-third or so of the main window, which Internet Explorer periodically uses to display a special toolbar when you click the Search, History, Favorites, or Channels buttons.

EZ Web Transfer: An MSN feature that allows you to copy up to 12MB of an entire Web site to your MSN personal home page.

FAQ: A *frequently asked questions* file. Contains answers to the most commonly asked questions. Always check to see if a FAQ file exists for a Web site, Web community or Internet newsgroup before asking basic questions. (If you post a question on an Internet newsgroup and the answer is in the FAQ, you'll get flamed for sure.)

Favorites: In Internet Explorer, a collection of Web page addresses that you visit frequently. See *Bookmarks*.

File Transfer Protocol (FTP): A system that allows the transfer of program and data files over the Internet.

filter: A Hotmail feature that lets you screen out e-mail messages that have certain words in their subject lines or come from certain people.

flame: Hostile postings on a newsgroup, often in response to a dumb posting. (On some newsgroups, just having `aol.com` in your Internet address is cause enough to get flamed.)

freeware: Software that you can download and use without paying a fee.

FTP: See *File Transfer Protocol*.

FTP site: An Internet server that has a library of files available for downloading with FTP.

Gaming Zone: A site within MSN which allows you to play online games against other Internet users.

GIF: *Graphic Interchange Format.* A popular format for small image files that are displayed on the Web, such as icons, buttons, bullets, logos, and so on.

history bar: No, this is not a place where you can sip a martini while discussing the Civil War. Rather, it is a variant of the Explorer bar which lists pages you have visited recently so you can conveniently return to them.

home page: (1) The introductory page at a Web site; sometimes refers to the entire Web site. (2) The first page displayed by your Web browser when you start it, sometimes also called the *start page*.

host computer: A computer to which you can connect via the Internet.

Hotmail: A free e-mail service from MSN.

HTML: *HyperText Markup Language.* A system of special tags used to create pages for the World Wide Web.

HTTP: *HyperText Transfer Protocol* The protocol used to transmit HTML documents over the Internet.

hyperlink: A bit of text or a graphic in a Web page that you can click to retrieve another Web page. The new Web page may be on the same Web server as the original page, or it may be on an entirely different Web server halfway around the globe. Sometimes just called a *link*.

hypermedia: A variation of hypertext in which hyperlinks can be graphics, sounds, or videos, as well as text. The World Wide Web is based on hypermedia, but the term *hypertext* is often loosely used instead.

hypertext: A system in which documents are linked to one another by text links. When the user clicks on a text link, the document referred to by the link is displayed. See *hypermedia*.

IBM: A big computer company.

Instant Messaging: An Internet feature similar to chatting that lets you exchange messages with one or more Internet users. Both America Online's AIM and Microsoft's MSN Messenger Service are Instant Messaging programs.

Internet: A vast worldwide collection of networked computers, the largest computer network in the world. Not invented by Al Gore.

Internet Explorer: Microsoft's Web *browser.*

Internet Relay Chat: Also known as *IRC.* A system that allows you to carry on live text-based conversations (known as *chats*) with other Internet users.

Internet service provider: Also known as *ISP.* A company that provides access to the Internet. MSN Internet Access is an ISP, as is *AOL.*

IP: *Internet Protocol.* The data transmission protocol that allows networks to exchange messages; serves as the foundation for communications over the Internet.

IRC: See *Internet Relay Chat.*

ISDN: A digital telephone line which can transmit data at 128Kbps. ISDNs still costs a bit too much for the average home user. Watch, though — the price will come down.

ISP: See *Internet service provider.*

Java: An object-oriented programming language designed to be used on the World Wide Web; created by Sun Microsystems. Java can be used to add interactivity to Web pages. Java's best quality is that it can run on different Web browsers and even on different types of computers, such as PCs, Macintoshes, and others.

JPEG: *Joint Photographic Experts Group.* A popular format for picture files. JPEG uses a compression technique that greatly reduces a graphic's file size, but also results in some loss of resolution. For photographic images, this loss is usually not noticeable. Because of its small file sizes, JPEG is a popular graphics format for the Internet.

KB: An abbreviation for *kilobyte* (roughly 1,024 bytes).

Kbps: A measure of a modem's speed in thousands of bits per second. The two most common modem speeds are 28.8kbps and 56kbps.

LAN: See *Local Area Network.*

lawyer joke: The original lawyer joke was told by Shakespeare, in King Henry IV, Part II: "The first thing we do, let's kill all the lawyers."

link: See *hyperlink.*

Local area network: Also referred to as a *LAN.* Two or more computers that are connected to one another to form a network. A LAN allows the computers to share resources such as disk drives and printers. A LAN is usually located within a relatively small area such as a building or on a campus.

LOL: *Laughing out loud.* A common abbreviation used to express mirth or joy when chatting online, in e-mail messages, or in newsgroup articles.

lurk: To read articles in a newsgroup without contributing your own postings. Lurking is one of the few approved forms of eavesdropping. Out of politeness, it's always a good idea to lurk for awhile in a newsgroup before posting your own articles.

macro: In Microsoft Chat, a feature that enables you to store an entire response or message and recall it with a simple keyboard shortcut.

mailing list: An e-mail version of a newsgroup. Any messages sent to the mailing list server are automatically sent to each person who has subscribed to the list.

MB: *Megabyte.* Roughly a million bytes.

Microsoft: The largest software company in the world. Among other things, Microsoft is the maker of the many flavors of the Windows operating system, as well as the Microsoft Office suite. Oh, and I almost forgot: Microsoft is the company that brings us MSN.

Microsoft Chat: The Internet chatting program that comes with Internet Explorer. Microsoft Chat has the unique ability to display chats in the form of a comic strip, but most people wisely disable this feature when they discover that the comic strips are cute but annoying.

MIME: *Multipurpose Internet mail extensions.* One of the standard methods for attaching binary files to e-mail messages and newsgroup articles. See *uuencode.*

modem: A device that enables your computer to connect with other computers over a phone line. Most modems are *internal* — that is, they are housed within the computer's casing. *External* modems are contained in their own boxes and must be connected to the back of the computer via a serial cable.

moderated newsgroup: A newsgroup whose postings are controlled by a moderator, which helps to ensure that articles in the newsgroup follow the guidelines established by the moderator.

MPEG: *Motion Picture Experts Group.* A standard for compressing video images based on the popular JPEG standard used for still images.

MSN: The Microsoft Network, a popular Web portal.

MSN Internet Access: Microsoft's dial-up Internet access system, which you can use as your Internet Service Provider if you wish. You do not have to be an MSN Internet Access subscriber to use the MSN Web portal.

MSN Messenger Service: Microsoft's program for *instant messaging.*

MSNBC: A combined production of Microsoft and NBC which presents news and information both online and on cable TV.

Netiquette: Electronic etiquette, the standards of politeness that are observed by civilized network users.

NetMeeting: A free program from Microsoft that enables you to have online meetings with other Internet users. With NetMeeting, you can speak with other Internet users if you have a microphone attached to your computer's sound card, and you can have a video conference if you have a video camera attached to your computer.

Netscape: Netscape Communications was the company that made the popular *Netscape Navigator* browser software for the Internet. Netscape is now a part of the AOL kingdom. Internet Explorer and Navigator are currently duking it out for the title, "Most Popular Web Browser."

newsgroup: An Internet bulletin board area where you can post messages, called *articles,* about a particular topic and read articles posted by other Internet users. There are thousands of different newsgroups on just about every conceivable subject.

news server: A host computer that stores newsgroup articles. You must connect to a news server to access newsgroups. Your Internet Service Provider will supply you with a news server you can use.

nickname: The name used to refer to a person in your Hotmail address book.

object linking and embedding (OLE): A set of standards that enables users to create dynamic, automatically updated links between documents and to embed a document created by one application into a document created by another application.

OIC: *Oh, I see.* A commonly-used abbreviation in chats or e-mail messages.

OLE: See *object linking and embedding.*

online: Connecting your computer to the network.

Outlook Express: A scaled-back version of Microsoft's premier e-mail program, Microsoft Outlook. Outlook Express is free with Internet Explorer.

participant: Someone who can participate in a chat. See also *spectator* and *host computer.*

Passport: An MSN feature that lets you access several services using a single user ID and password.

password: A secret word or phrase you use to access a computer system. Your Internet Service Provider requires you to use a password to access the Internet, as do some MSN features such as Hotmail.

PMJI: *Pardon me for jumping in.* A commonly-used abbreviation in newsgroup articles.

portal: An Internet site that is designed to be your entryway into the Internet, providing links to services such as shopping, news, and entertainment sites, as well as comprehensive search features. MSN is Microsoft's Web portal.

posting: Adding an article to a newsgroup.

PPP: *Point to Point Protocol.* The protocol that allows you to access Internet services.

protocol: A set of conventions that govern communications between computers in a network.

public domain: Computer software or other information that is available free of charge. See *shareware*.

Quick Links: A collection of twenty links to MSN pages that appears near the top of the MSN home page.

QuickTime: One of the most popular formats for videos on the Internet.

ROFL: *Rolling on the floor laughing.* A common abbreviation used in chats, newsgroup articles, and e-mail messages. You'll see frequent variations, such as ROFLPP and ROFLMAO. You can figure those out yourself.

RSAC: Recreational Software Advisory Council, the group that provides a framework for rating online content.

server: A computer that provides services to other computers on the Internet or on a local area network. Specific types of Internet servers include news servers, mail servers, FTP servers, and Web servers.

service provider: See *Internet service provider.*

shareware: A software program that you can download and try — free of charge. The program is not free, however. If you like the program and continue to use it, you are obligated to send in a modest registration fee. See *public domain*.

signature: A fancy block of text that some users routinely place at the end of their e-mail messages and newsgroup articles.

Site Manager: An MSN feature that lets you manage the files that make up your personal home page.

smiley: A smiley face or other *emoticon* created from keyboard characters; used to convey *emotions* in otherwise emotionless e-mail messages or newsgroup posting. Some examples include:

:-)	Feelin' happy
:-D	Super-duper happy
8^)	Glasses-wearing happiness, or perhaps a smiling Orphan Annie (Leapin' Lizards!)
;-)	Conspiratorial wink
:-o	You surprise me
:-(	So sad
:-l	Apathetic

spam: Unsolicited *e-mail* or *newsgroup* postings that do not relate to the topic of the newsgroup. Spam is the electronic equivalent of junk mail.

spectator: In Microsoft Chat, someone who is allowed into a chat room to listen but not allowed to speak. In most chat rooms, this classification is a kind of penalty box for participants who have been unruly.

stationery: An *e-mail* feature that lets you add a background graphic, a *signature*, and a font style to your e-mail messages and newsgroup postings.

taskbar: A Windows feature that displays icons for all open windows, a clock, and the Start button, which you use to run programs. Normally, the taskbar appears at the bottom of the screen, but it can be repositioned at any edge of the screen you prefer. If the taskbar is not visible, try moving the mouse to the very bottom of the screen, or to the left, right, or top edge of the screen.

TCP/IP: *Transmission Control Protocol/Internet Protocol.* The basic set of conventions that the Internet uses to enable different types of computers to communicate with one another.

telnet: A protocol that allows you to log in to a remote computer as if you were actually a terminal attached to that remote computer.

templates: Pre-defined Web pages which you can use to create your own MSN home page.

TIFF: *Tagged Image File Format.* A format for picture files. TIFF files are large compared with other formats such as JPEG and GIF, but preserve all of the original image's quality. Because of their large file size, TIFF files aren't all that popular on the Internet.

thread: An exchange of articles in a newsgroup. Specifically, an original article, all of its replies, all of the replies to replies, and so on.

TLA: *Three letter acronym.* Ever notice how just about all computer terms can be reduced to a three letter acronym? It all started with *IBM.* Now you've got *MSN, URL, AOL,* and who knows what else. So of course there's a TLA for Three Letter Acronym. I guess I should complain; this book is being published by IDG Books.

Uniform Resource Locator: Also known as a *URL.* A method of specifying the address of any resource available on the Internet, used when browsing the Internet. For example, the URL of IDG Books Worldwide, for example, is `www.idgbooks.com`.

upload: Copying a file from your computer to the Internet.

URL: See *Uniform Resource Locator.*

Usenet: A network of Internet newsgroups that contains many of the most popular newsgroups.

uuencode: A method of attaching binary files such as programs or documents to mail messages and newsgroup articles. The other method is called MIME.

Vidcam: A video camera attached to a Web server so that you can view the camera's image over the Net. This setup is kind of a crazy thing to do, but seems to be the rage.

virus: An evil computer program that slips into your computer undetected, tries to spread itself to other computers, and may eventually do something bad like trash your hard disk. Because the Internet does not include built-in virus detection, I suggest you consider using one of the many virus-protection programs available if you are worried about catching a virus.

Yellow Pages: An MSN directory of businesses.

Web: See *World Wide Web.*

Web browser: See *browser.*

Web community: An MSN feature that combines Web pages, chat rooms, and newsgroups to create a place where people with common interests can gather.

Web page: A document available for display on the Word Wide Web. The document may contain links to other documents located on the same server or on other Web servers.

Web Publishing Wizard: A Microsoft program that tries to simplify the task of uploading files to a Web server.

Web server: A server computer where Web documents are stored so they can be accessed on the World Wide Web.

White Pages: An MSN directory of residential phone and address listings.

Wide Area Network: WAN. A computer network which spans a large area, such as an entire campus, or perhaps a network that links branches of a company in several cities.

Windows: The most popular operating system for personal computers. Several incarnations of Windows are in use today, Windows 98 being the most popular.

WinZip: A Windows version of the popular PKZIP compression program, which with its graphics-based interface is much easier to use than PKZIP. Can be found at `www.winzip.com`.

World Wide Web: Also referred to as the *Web* or the *www*. This relatively new part of the Internet displays information using fancy graphics. The Web is based on *links,* which enable the user to travel quickly from one Web server to another.

Yahoo!: One of the oldest and largest Internet search sites.

zipped file: A file that has been compressed using the *PKZIP* or *WinZip* programs.

Index

• A •

• B •

• C •

• Q •

• R •

• U •

• V •

• W •

• Z •

Notes

Discover Dummies Online!

The Dummies Web Site is your fun and friendly online resource for the latest information about *...For Dummies*® books and your favorite topics. The Web site is the place to communicate with us, exchange ideas with other *...For Dummies* readers, chat with authors, and have fun!

Ten Fun and Useful Things You Can Do at www.dummies.com

1. Win free *...For Dummies* books and more!
2. Register your book and be entered in a prize drawing.
3. Meet your favorite authors through the IDG Books Author Chat Series.
4. Exchange helpful information with other *...For Dummies* readers.
5. Discover other great *...For Dummies* books you must have!
6. Purchase Dummieswear™ exclusively from our Web site.
7. Buy *...For Dummies* books online.
8. Talk to us. Make comments, ask questions, get answers!
9. Download free software.
10. Find additional useful resources from authors.

Link directly to these ten fun and useful things at **http://www.dummies.com/10useful**

For other technology titles from IDG Books Worldwide, go to **www.idgbooks.com**

Not on the Web yet? It's easy to get started with *Dummies 101*®: *The Internet For Windows*® *98* or *The Internet For Dummies*®, 6th Edition, at local retailers everywhere.

Find other *...For Dummies* books on these topics:
Business • Career • Databases • Food & Beverage • Games • Gardening • Graphics • Hardware
Health & Fitness • Internet and the World Wide Web • Networking • Office Suites
Operating Systems • Personal Finance • Pets • Programming • Recreation • Sports
Spreadsheets • Teacher Resources • Test Prep • Word Processing

IDG BOOKS WORLDWIDE BOOK REGISTRATION

We want to hear from you!

Visit **http://my2cents.dummies.com** to register this book and tell us how you liked it!

- Get entered in our monthly prize giveaway.
- Give us feedback about this book — tell us what you like best, what you like least, or maybe what you'd like to ask the author and us to change!
- Let us know any other *...For Dummies*® topics that interest you.

Your feedback helps us determine what books to publish, tells us what coverage to add as we revise our books, and lets us know whether we're meeting your needs as a *...For Dummies* reader. You're our most valuable resource, and what you have to say is important to us!

Not on the Web yet? It's easy to get started with *Dummies 101*®*: The Internet For Windows*® *98* or *The Internet For Dummies*®, 6th Edition, at local retailers everywhere.

Or let us know what you think by sending us a letter at the following address:

...For Dummies Book Registration
Dummies Press
10475 Crosspoint Blvd.
Indianapolis, IN 46256